AF348612

TIM ETCHELLS

LET'S PRETEND NONE OF THIS EVER HAPPENED

NEON AND OTHER WORKS

EDITED BY JULE HILLGÄRTNER & TIM ETCHELLS

TIM ETCHELLS
LET'S PRETEND NONE OF THIS EVER HAPPENED
NEON AND OTHER WORKS

Editors: Tim Etchells, Jule Hillgärtner for Kunstverein Braunschweig

Design: David Caines

Texts: Ben Borthwick, Tim Etchells, Jule Hillgärtner

Copy editing and proofreading: Vlatka Horvat

Print and binding: Gutenberg Beuys Feindruckerei GmbH, Langenhangen, Germany

Published by:
Spector Books OHG
Markus Dreßen, Anne König, Jan Wenzel
Harkortstraße 10
D-04107 Leipzig
www.spectorbooks.com

The publisher would like to thank all those who have kindly given their permission for the reproduction of material for this book. Every effort has been made to obtain permission to reproduce the images and texts in this catalogue. However, as is standard editorial policy, the publisher is at the disposal of copyright holders and undertakes to correct any omissions or errors in future editions.

Research and development of the publication was generously supported by PACT Zollverein, Germany and Artichoke, UK.

A catalogue record for this book is available from the National Library of Germany and the Saxony State and University Library.

Distribution:
Germany, Austria: GVA, Gemeinsame Verlagsauslieferung Göttingen GmbH&Co. KG, www.gva-verlage.de
Switzerland: AVA Verlagsauslieferung AG, www.ava.ch
France, Belgium: Interart Paris, www.interart.fr
UK: Central Books Ltd, www.centralbooks.com
USA, Canada, Central and South America, Africa: ARTBOOK/ D.A.P., www.artbook.com
South Korea: The Book Society, www.thebooksociety.org
Japan: twelvebooks, www.twelve-books.com
Australia, New Zealand: Perimeter Distribution, www.perimeterdistribution.com

First edition 2023

Printed in the EU

ISBN 978-3-95905-767-7

Kunstverein Braunschweig e.V.

Director: Jule Hillgärtner
Curator: Benedikt Johannes Seerieder
Assistant Curator: Gesa Vorpahl
Public Relations: Larissa Lammers
Accounting: Christine Gröning
Reception: Iris Schneider, Elisabeth Schuchardt
Technical Manager: Gerald Knöchel
Board: Jens Nowak (Chairman), Andreas Janßen (Vice Chairman), Timo Antons (Treasurer), Annette Schütze, Johannes Waitz, Maresa Wischenbart-Backhaus, David Zink-Yi
www.kunstvereinbraunschweig.de

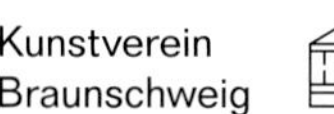

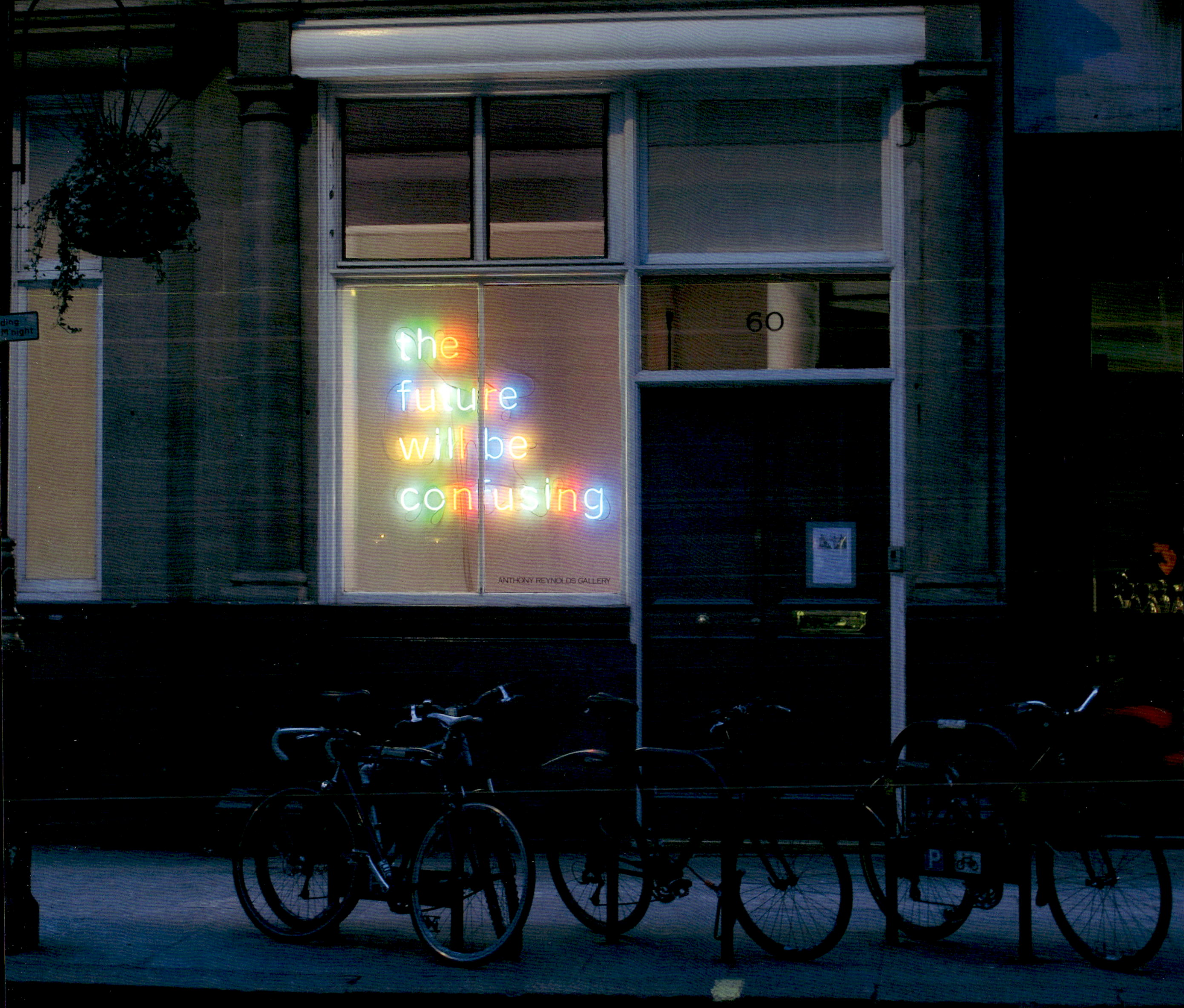
the
future
will be
confusing
60
ANTHONY REYNOLDS GALLERY

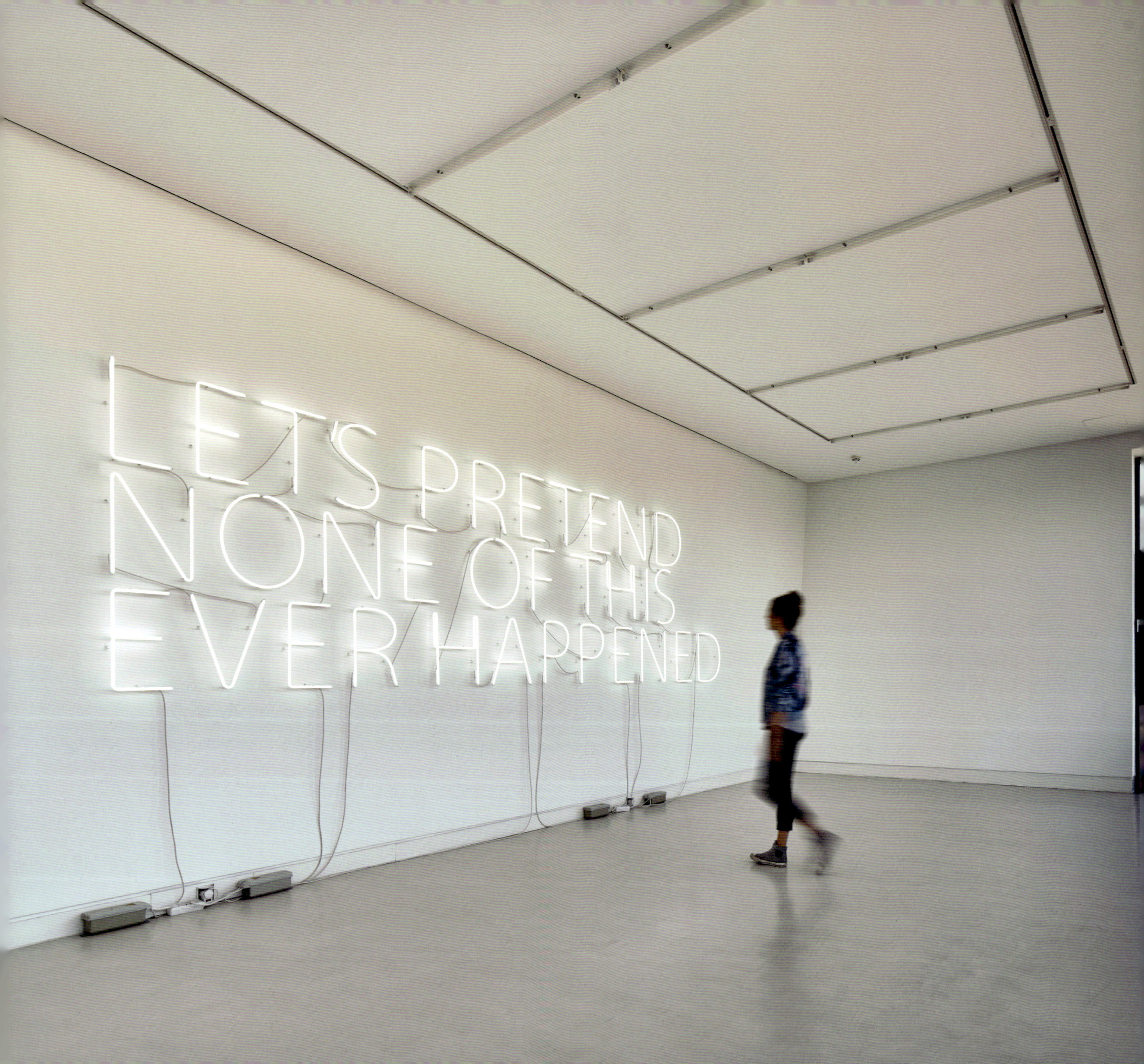
LET'S PRETEND
NONE OF THIS
EVER HAPPENED

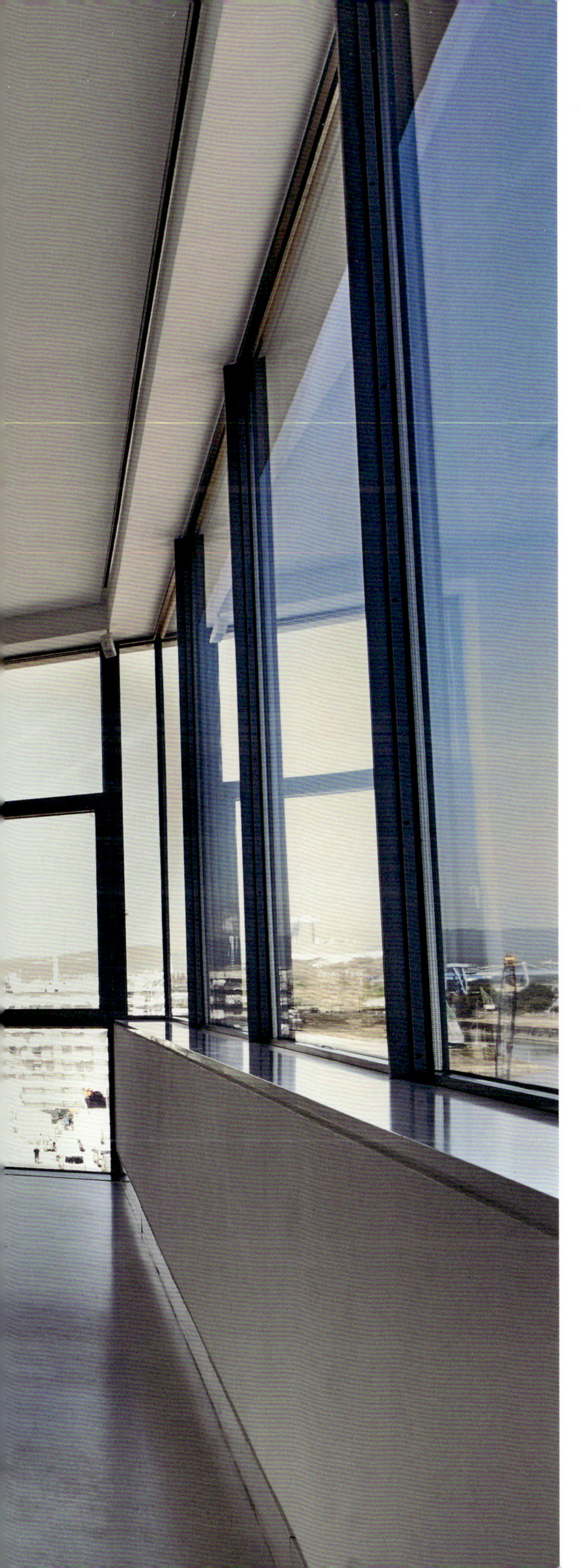

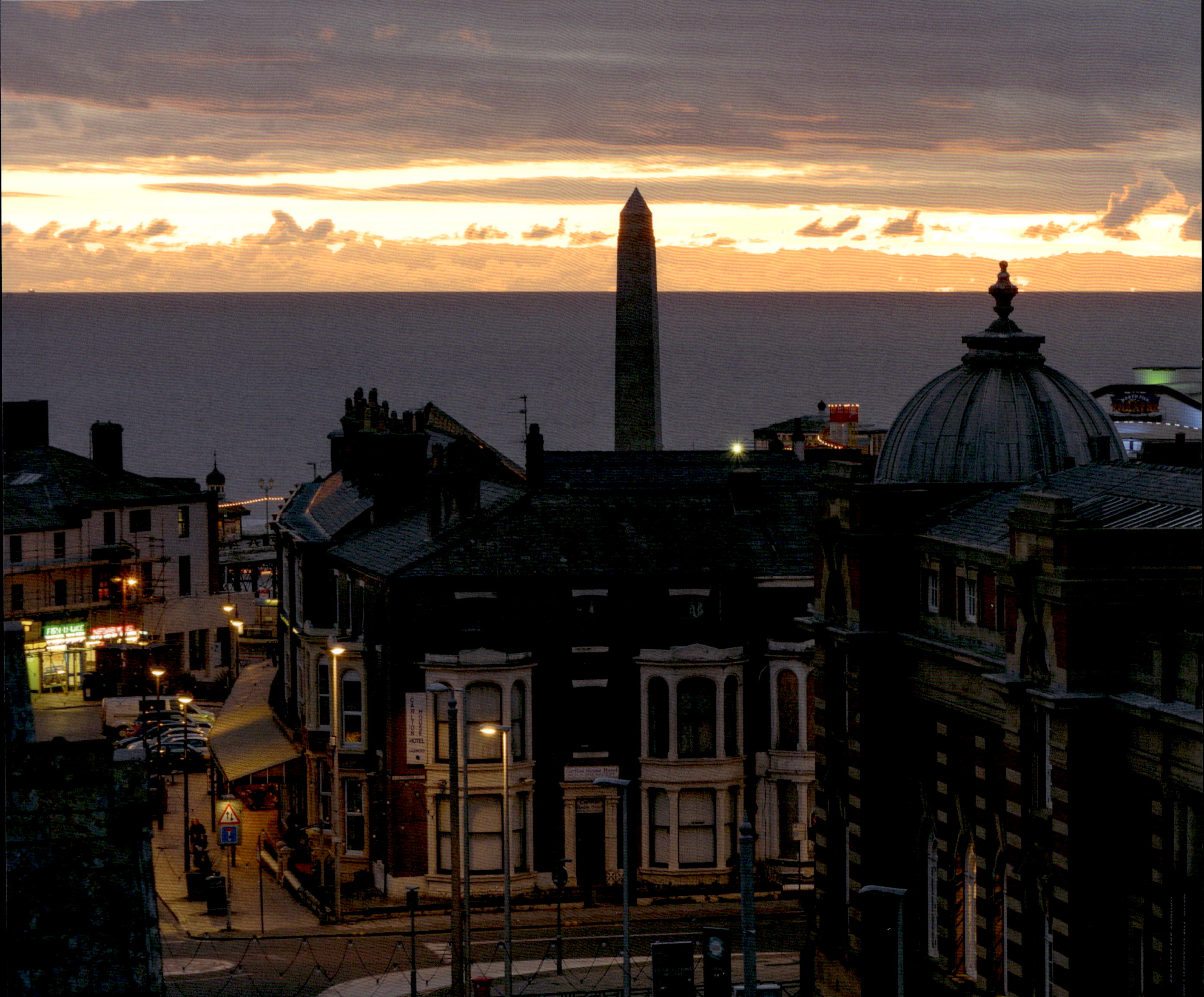

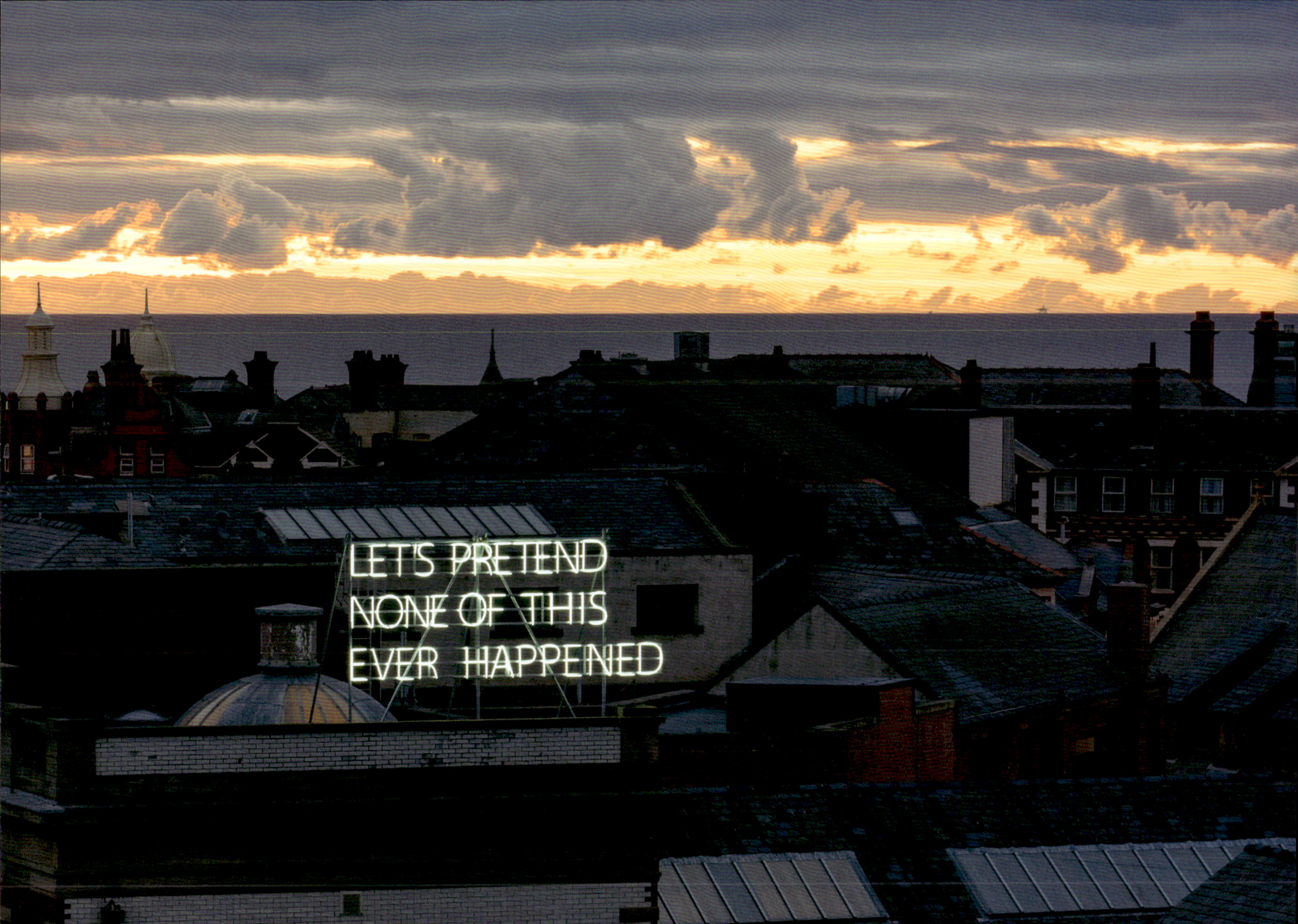
LET'S PRETEND
NONE OF THIS
EVER HAPPENED

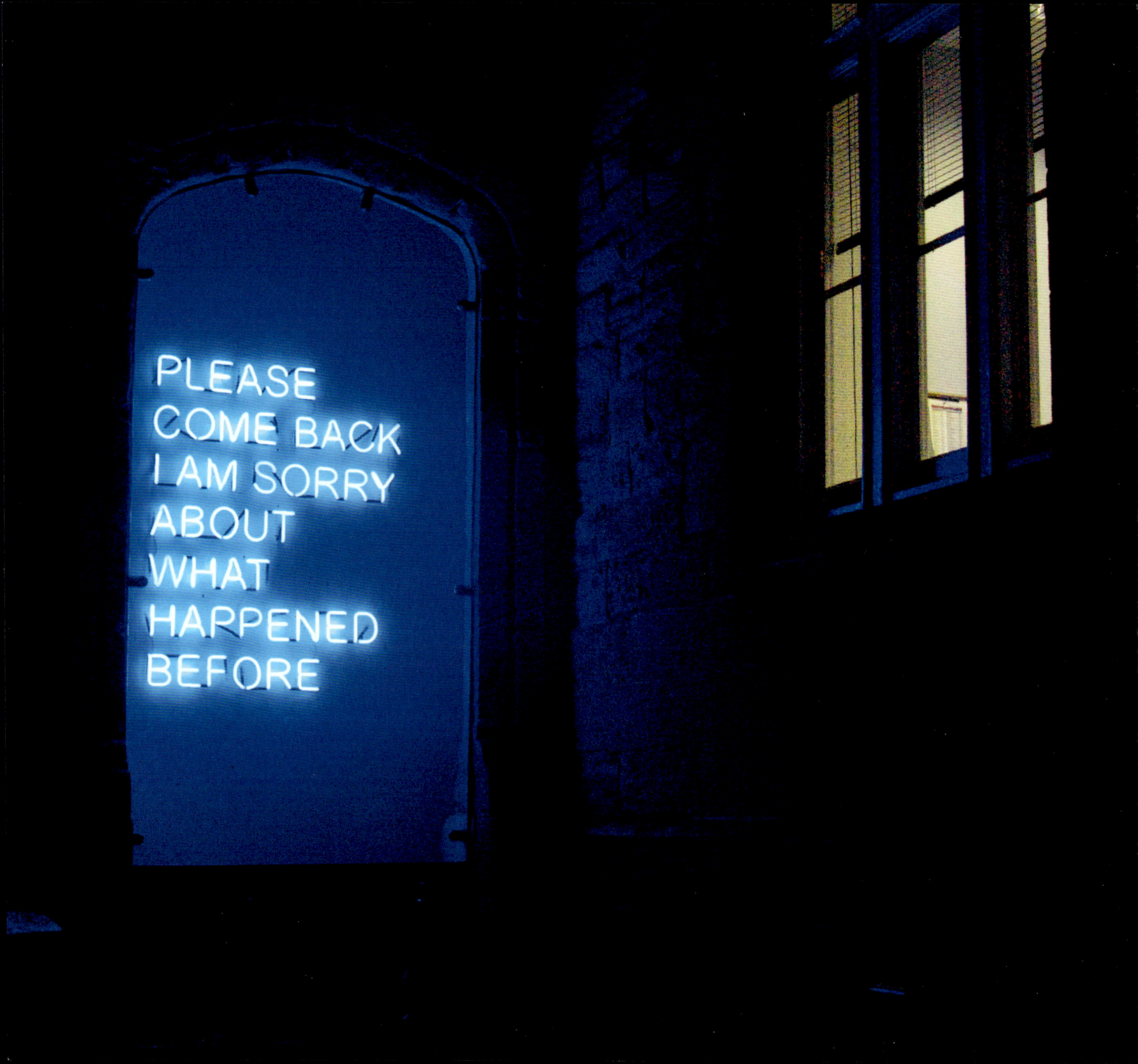

PLEASE
COME BACK
I AM SORRY
ABOUT
WHAT
HAPPENED
BEFORE

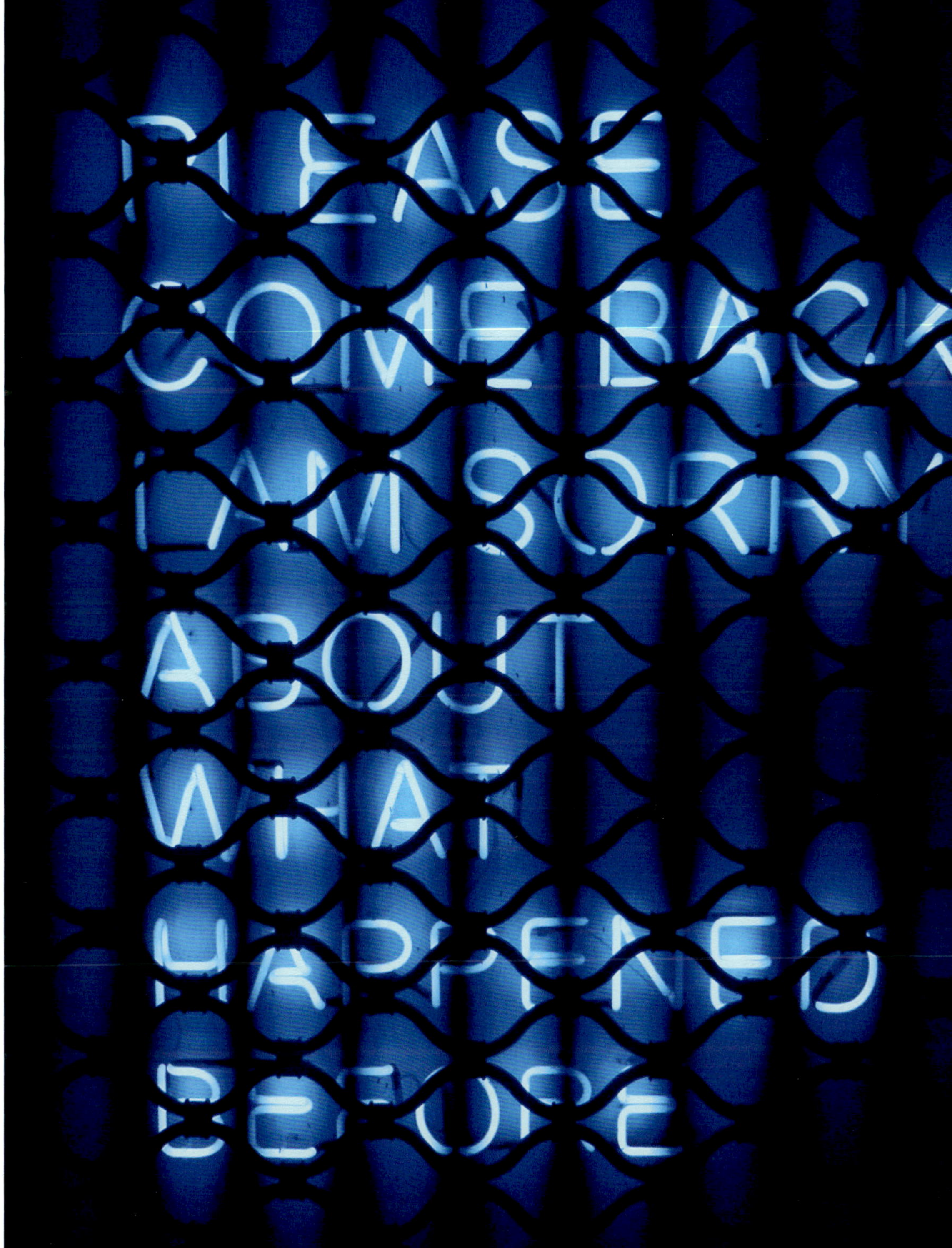
PLEASE
COME BACK
I AM SORRY
ABOUT
WHAT
HAPPENED
BEFORE

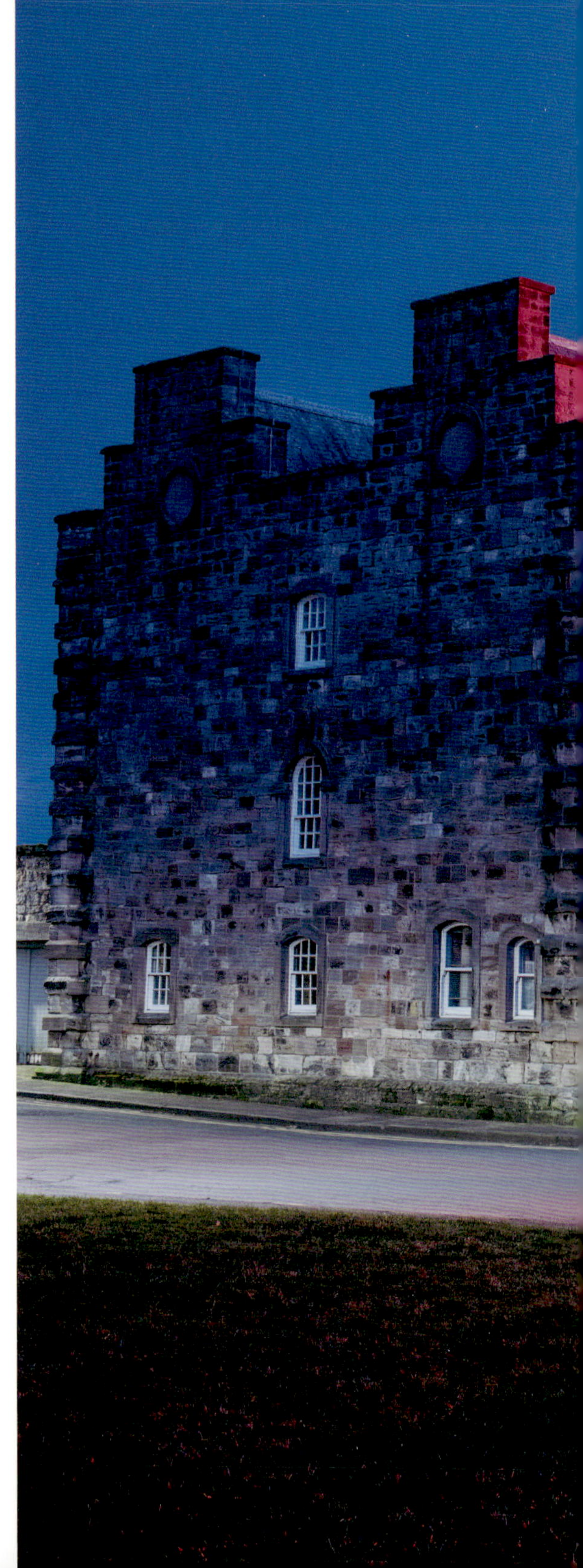

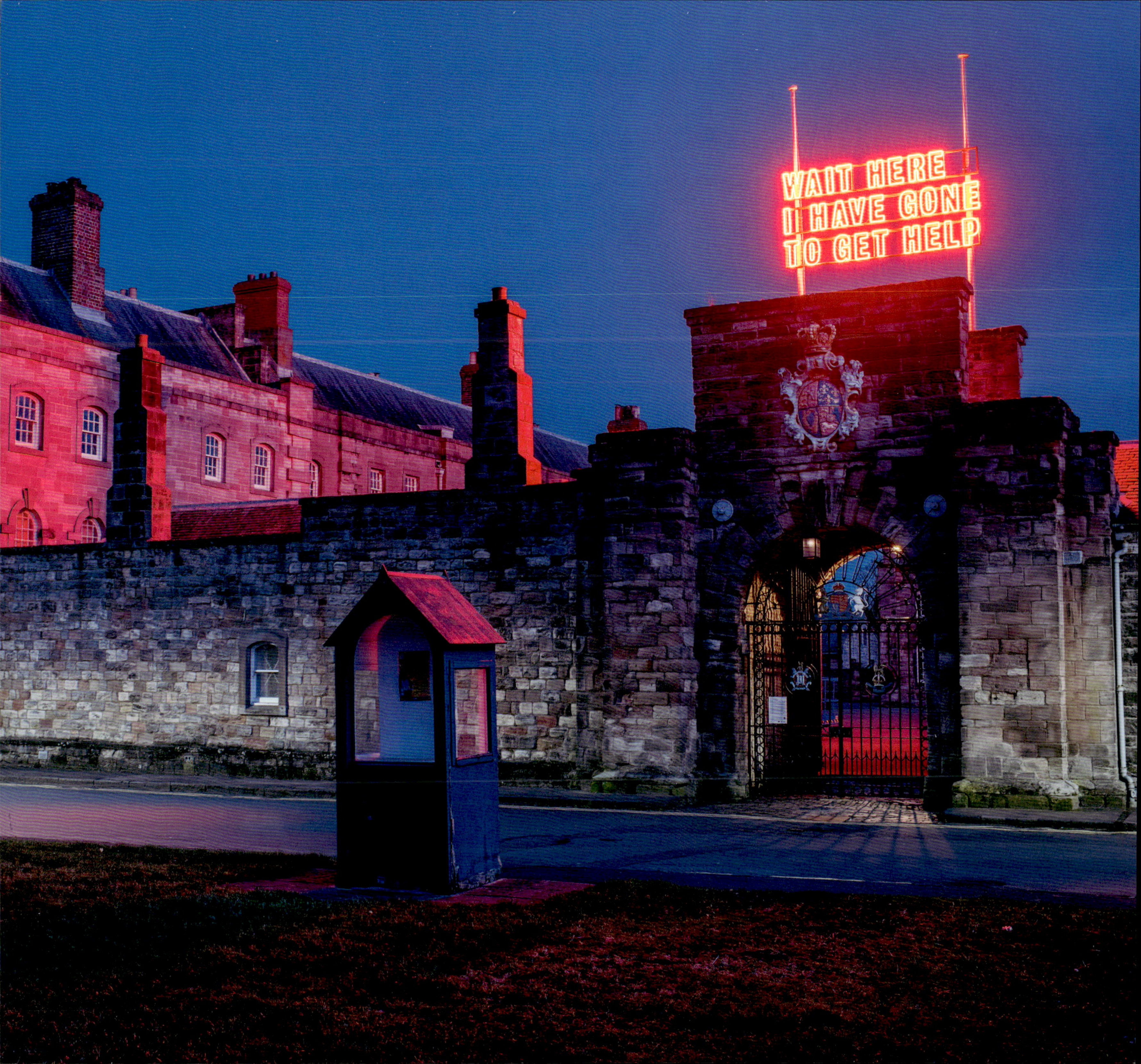
WAIT HERE
I HAVE GONE
TO GET HELP

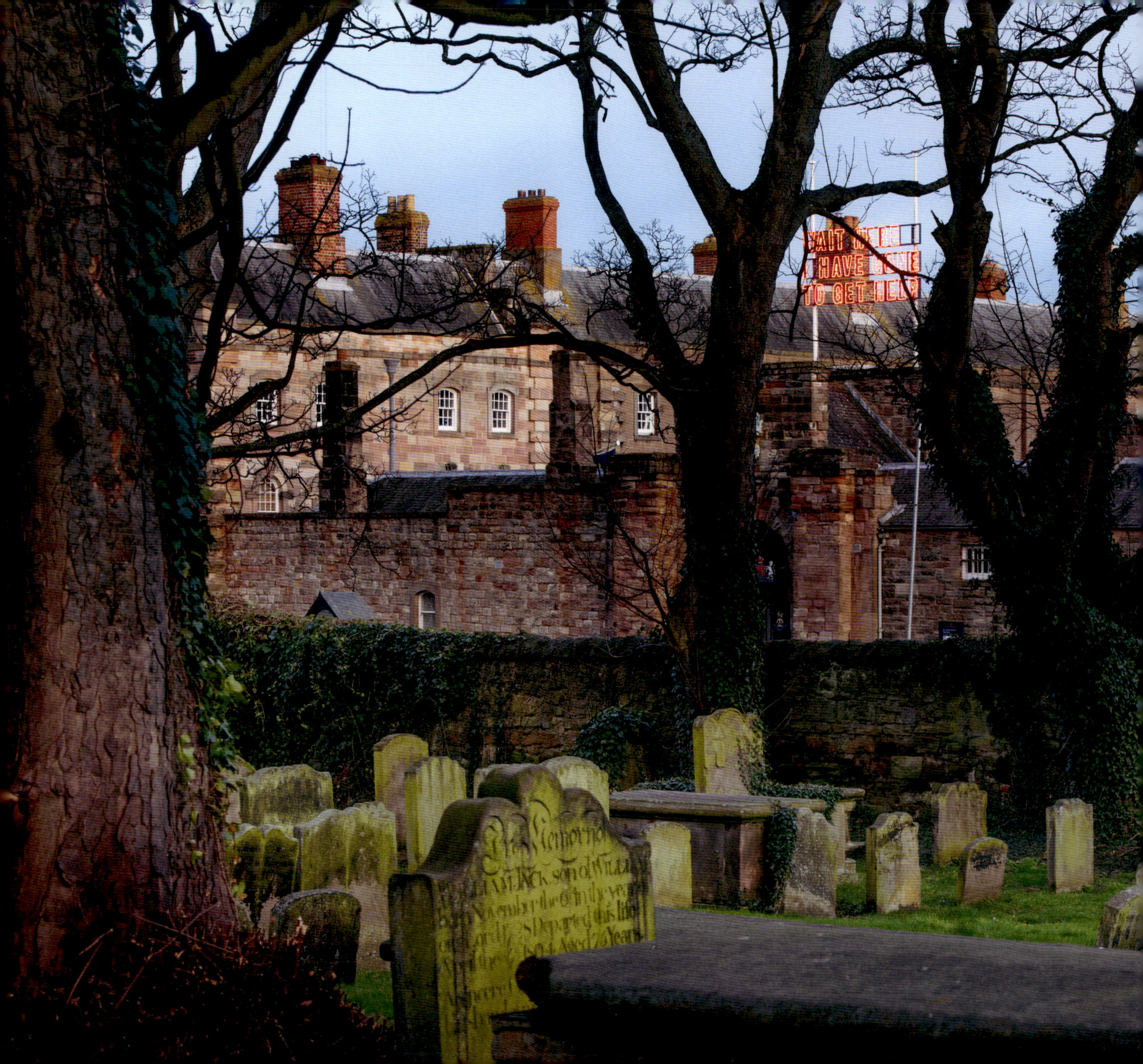
WAIT HERE
I HAVE GONE
TO GET HELP

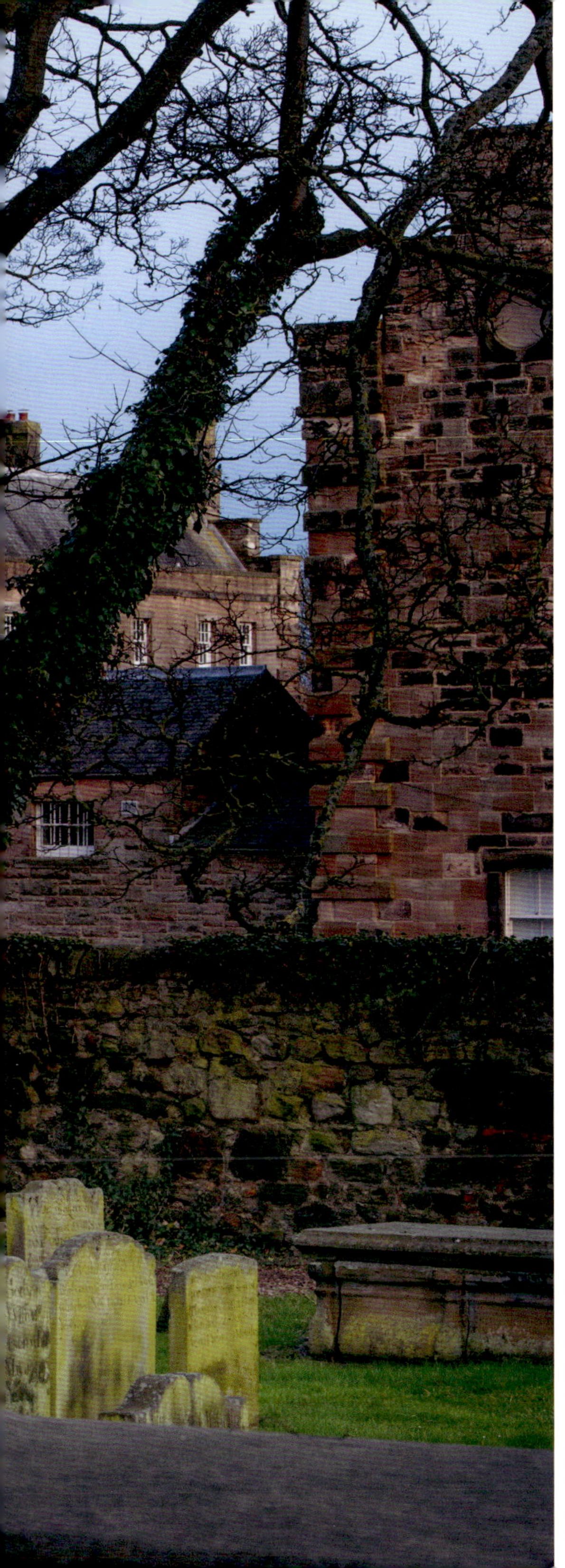

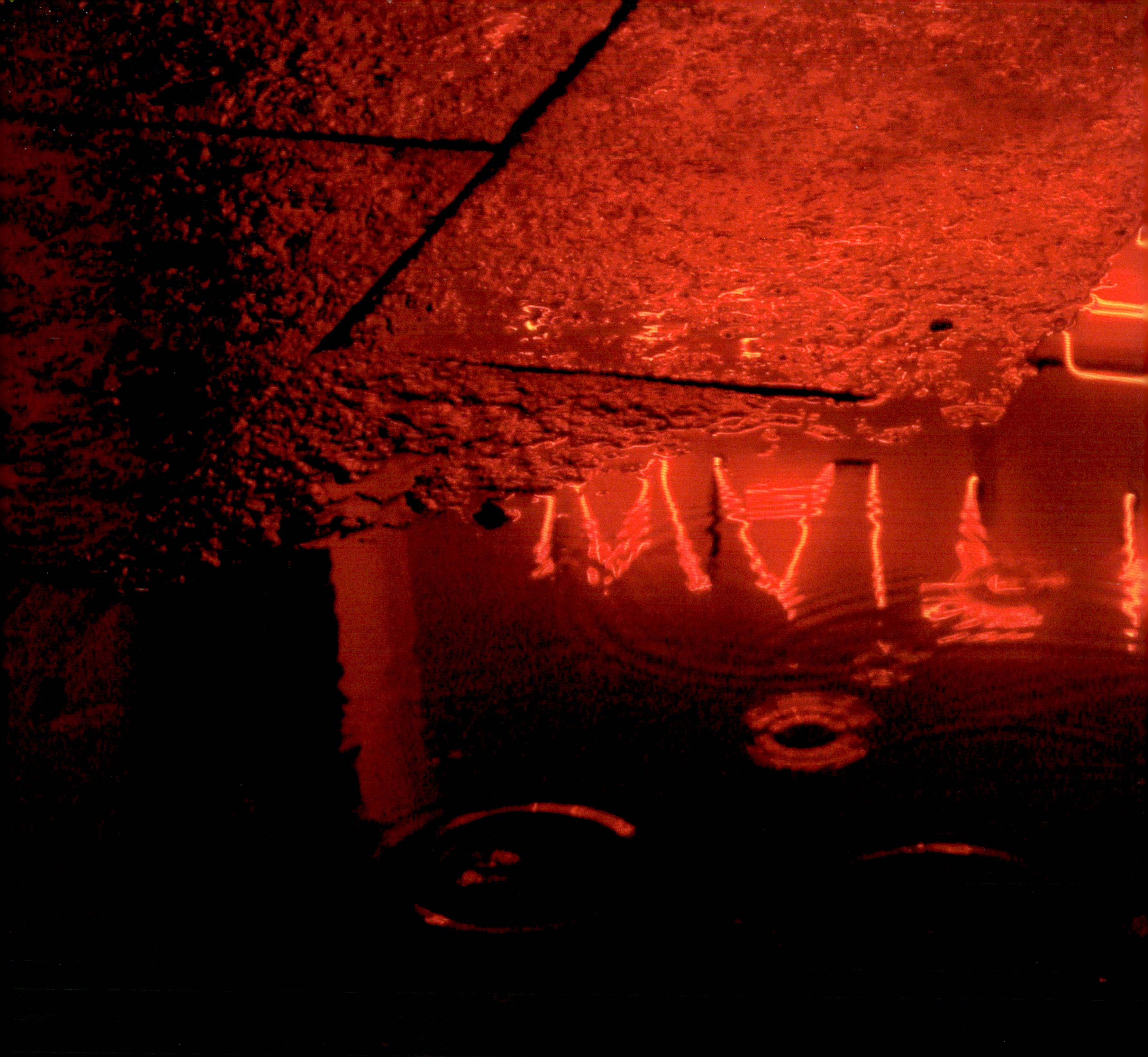

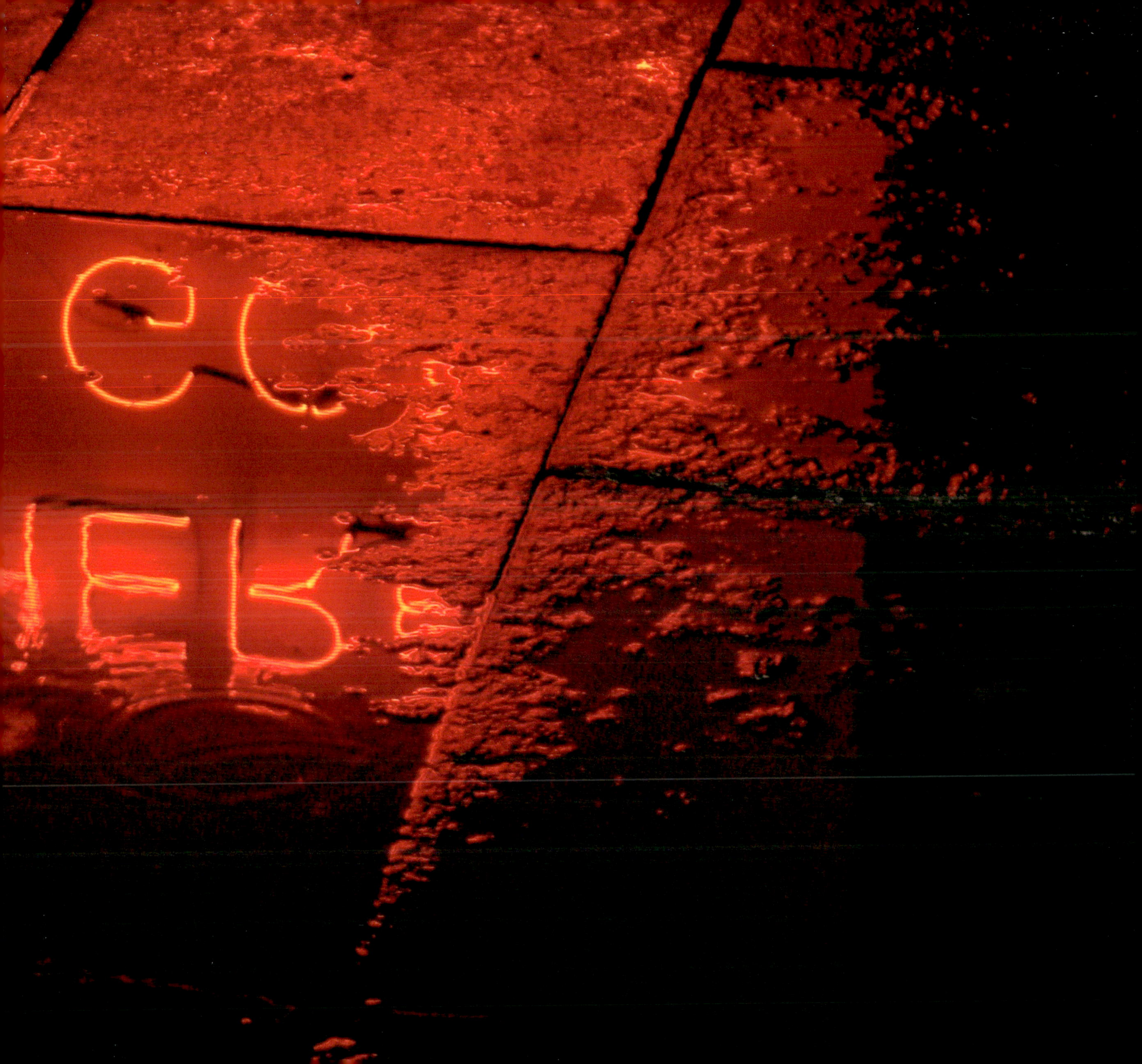

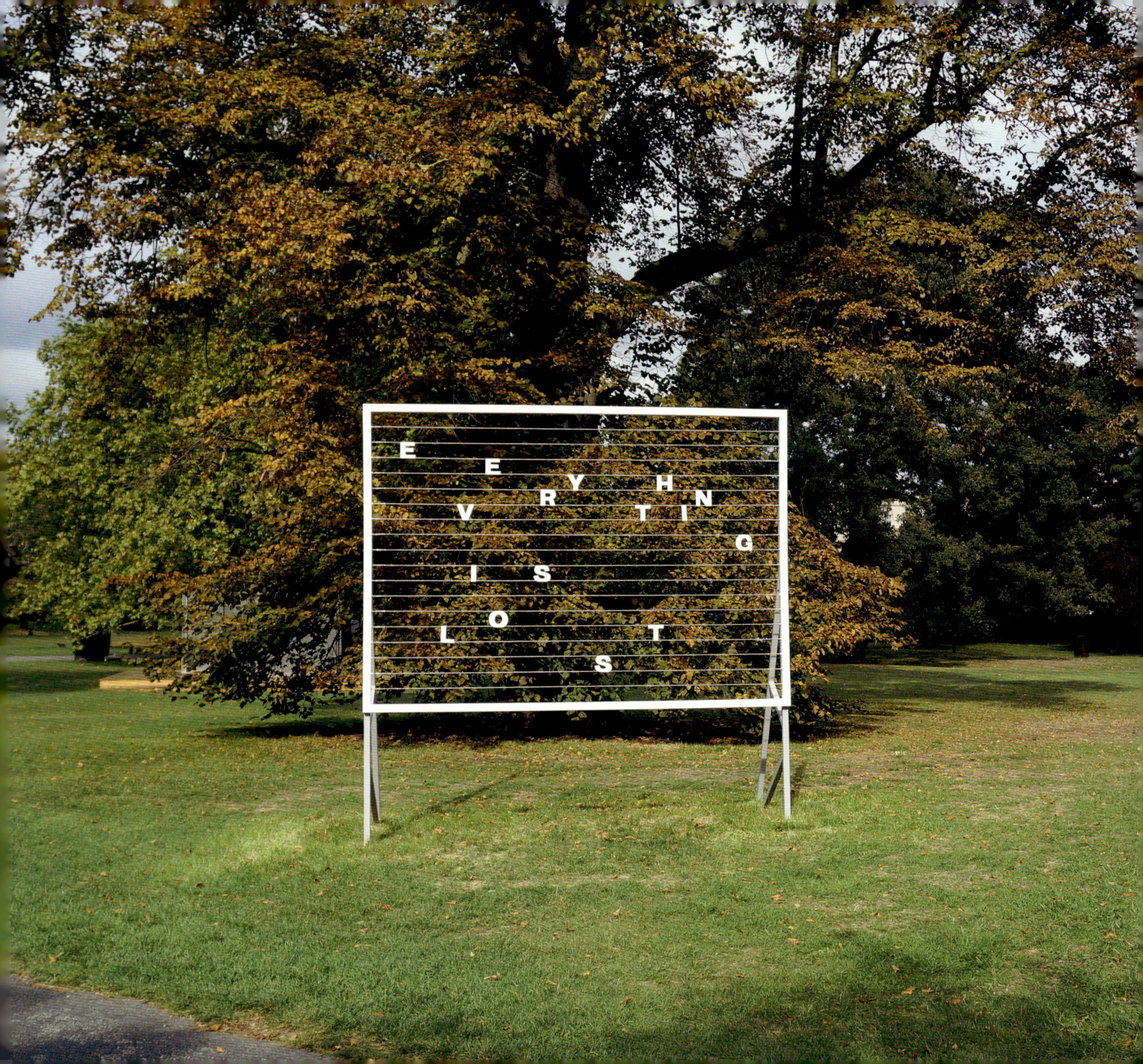

E
E R Y H
V R T I N
G
I S
L O T
S

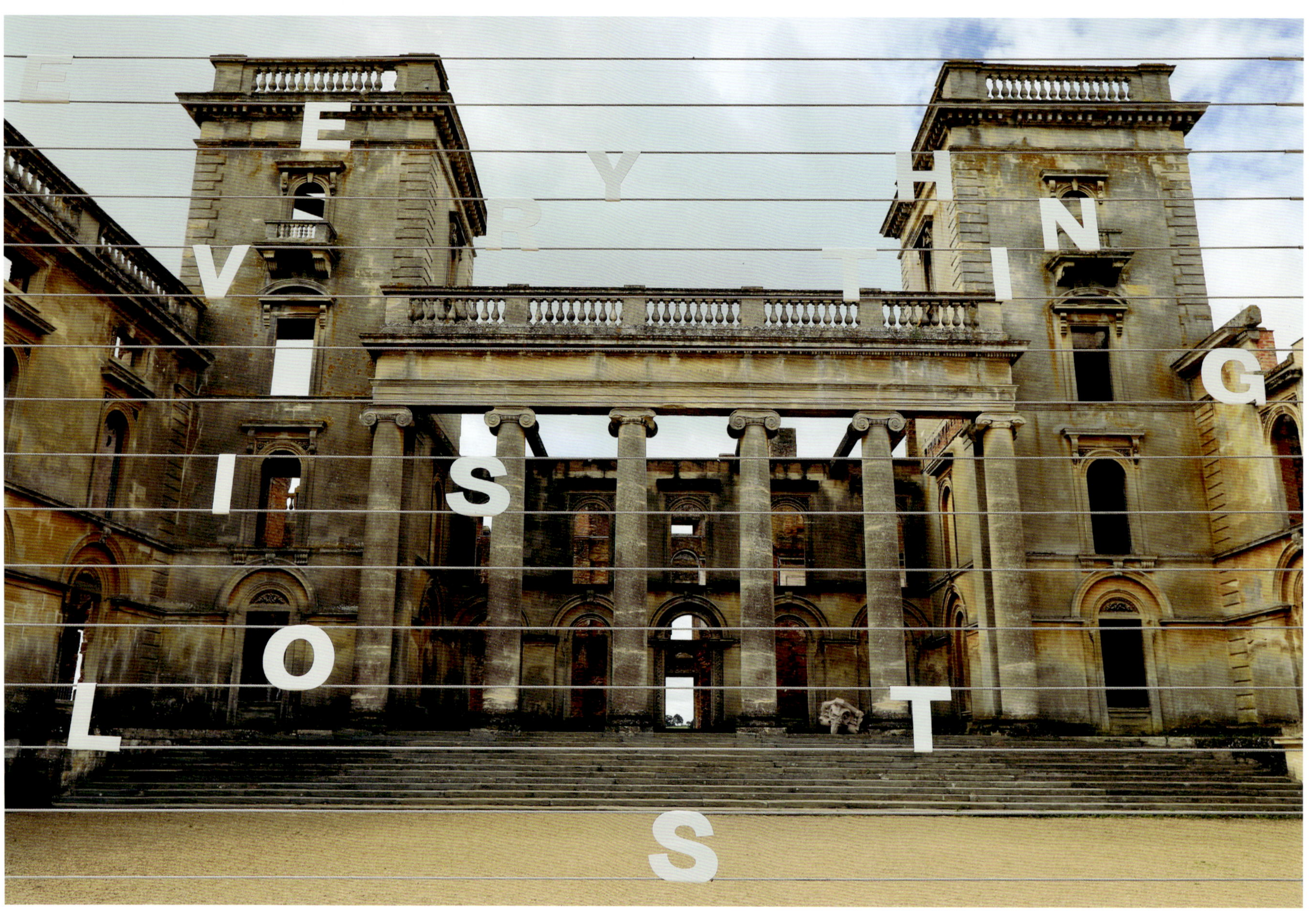
EVERYTHING
VISIT
IS
LOST
S

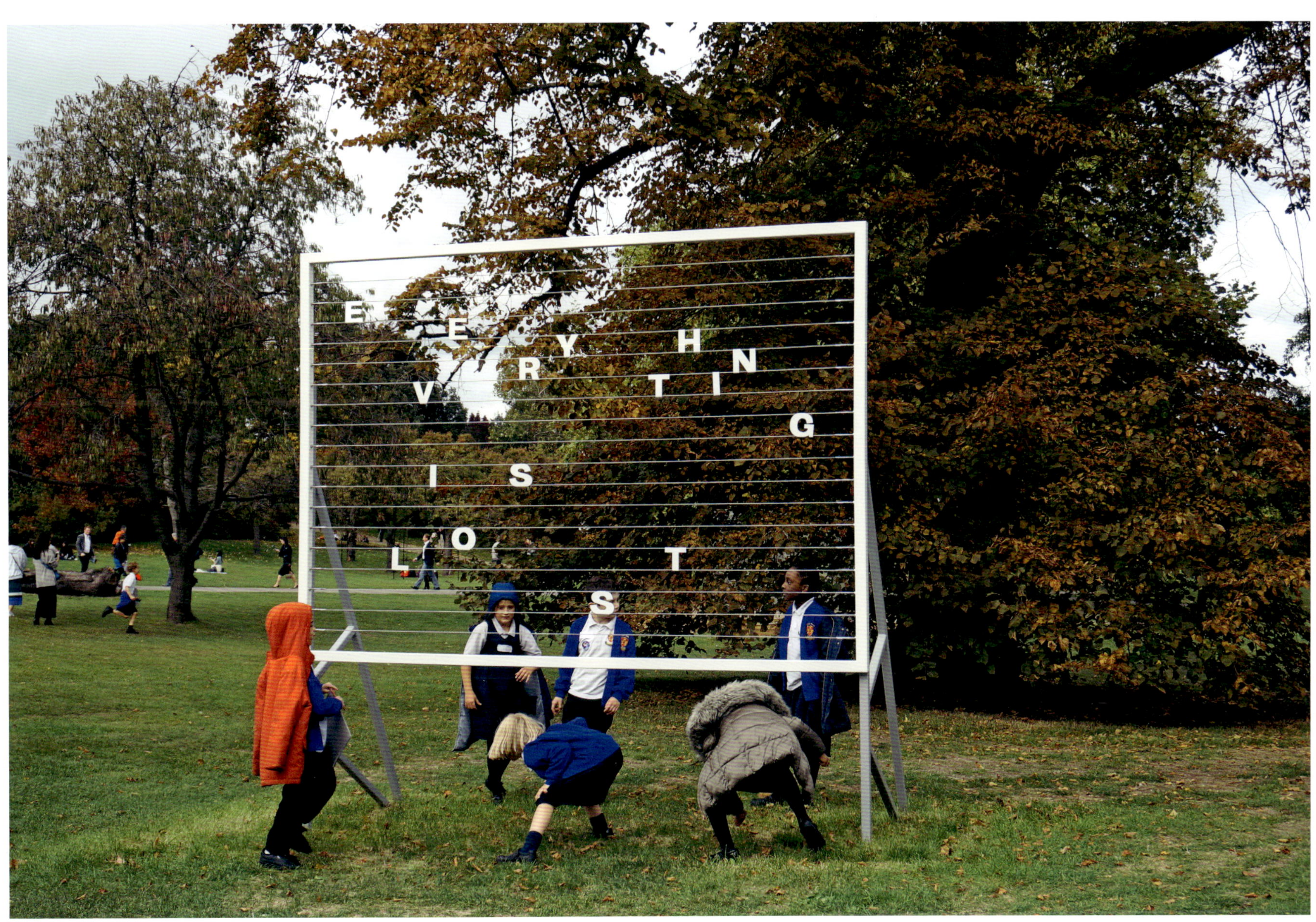

EVERYTHING
IS
LOST

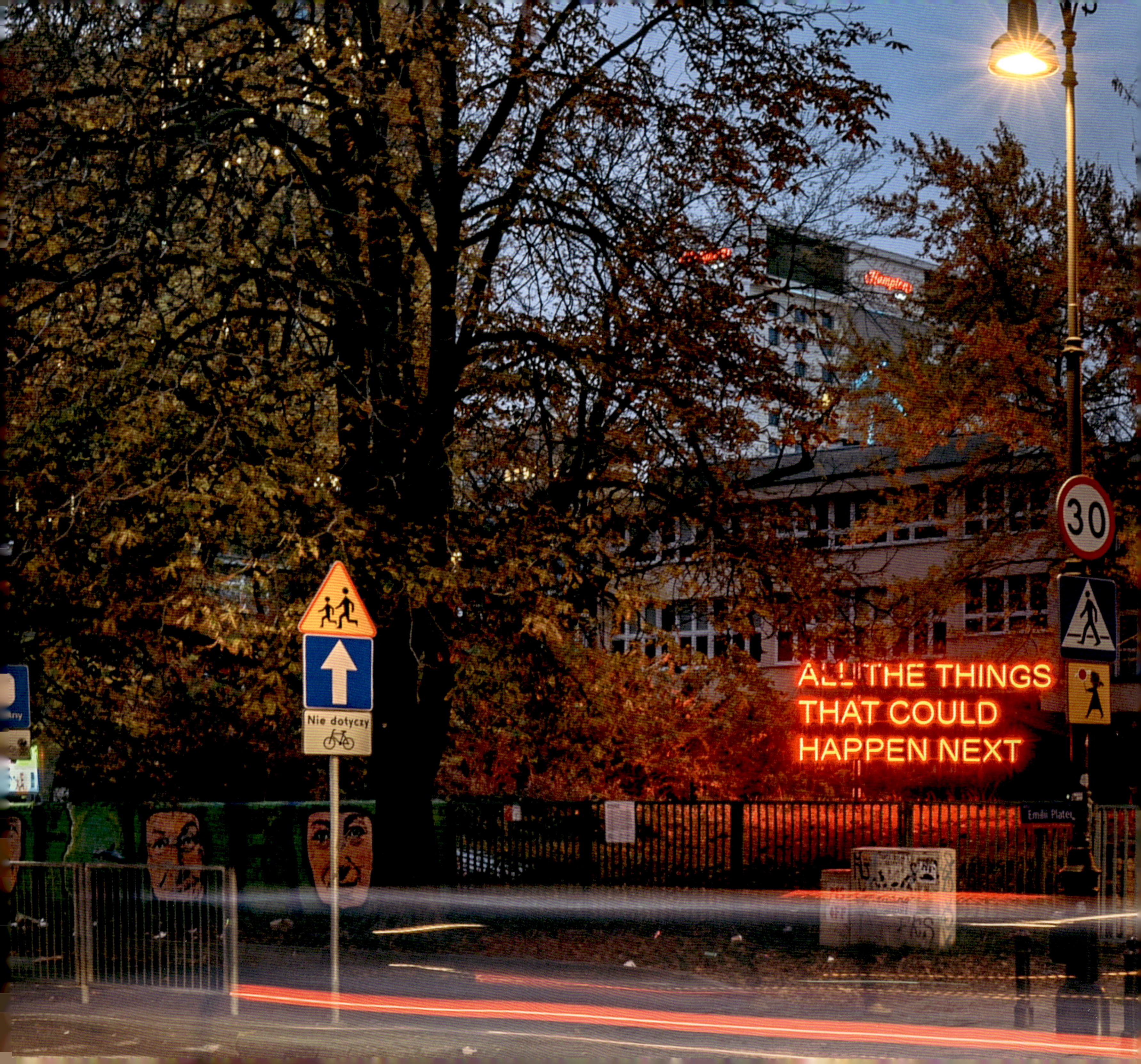

Nie dotyczy
ALL THE THINGS
THAT COULD
HAPPEN NEXT
30
Hampton

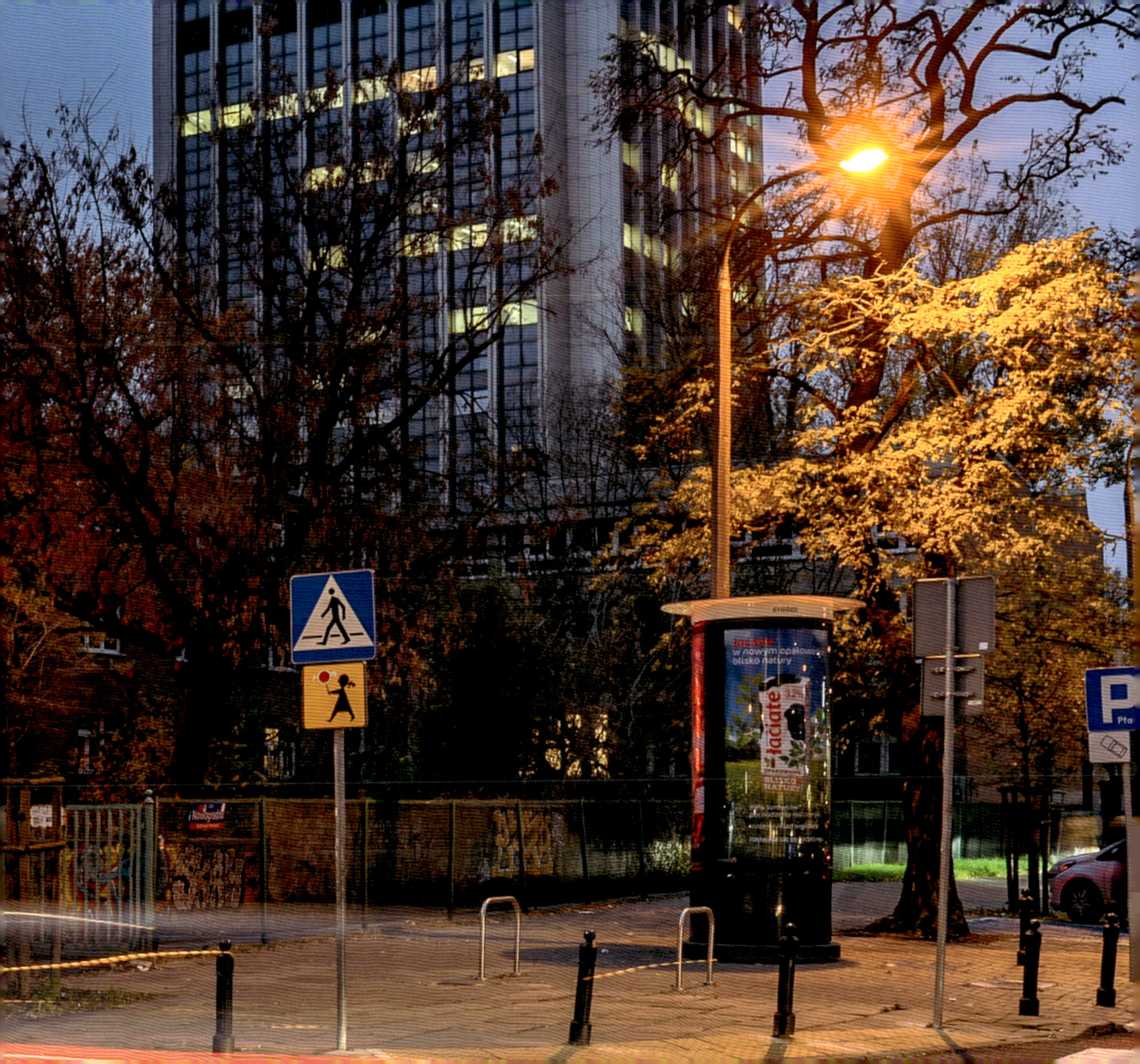
łaciate
w nowym opakowaniu
blisko natury
łaciate
3,29
BLISKO
NATURY
P
Płat

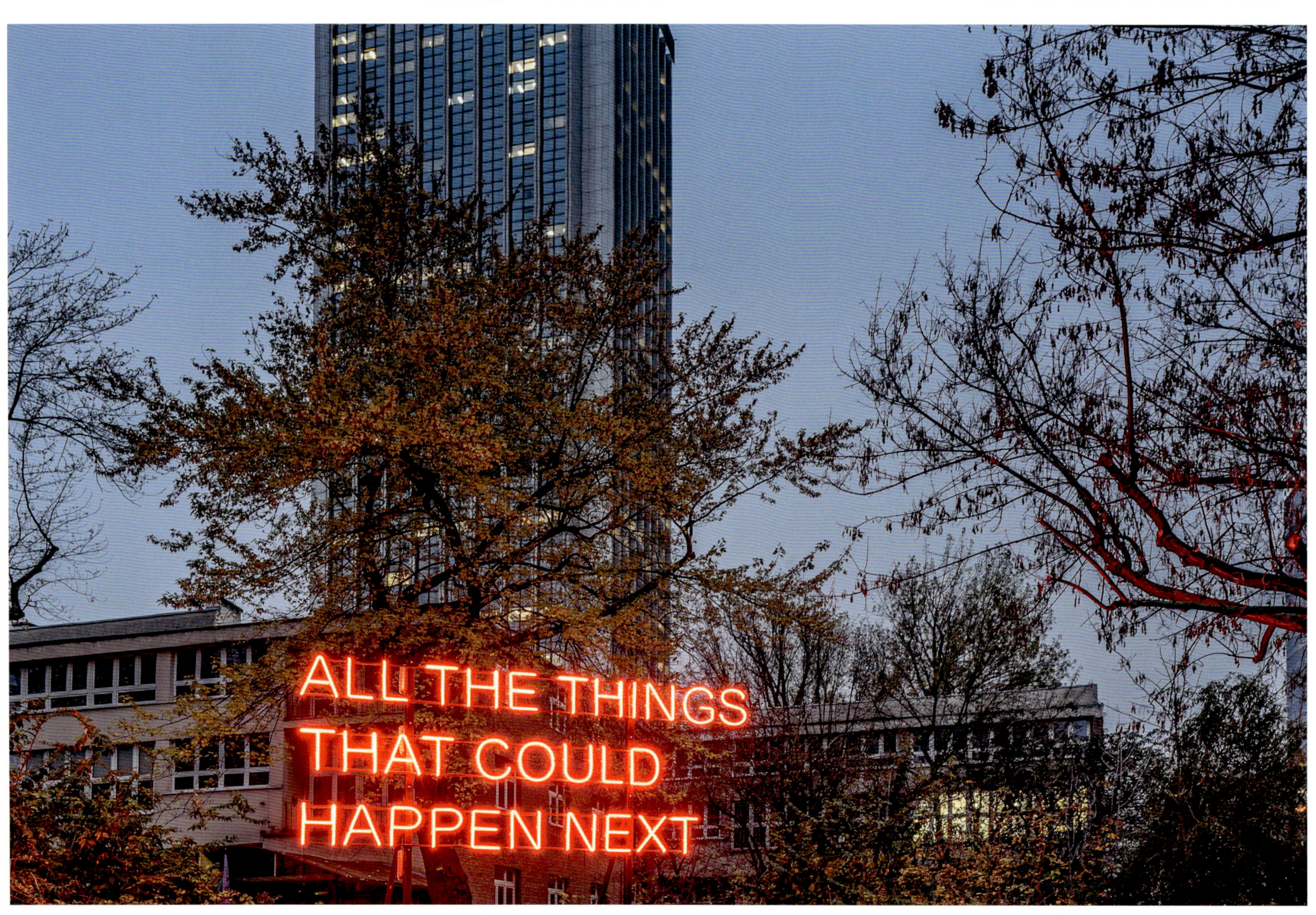
ALL THE THINGS
THAT COULD
HAPPEN NEXT

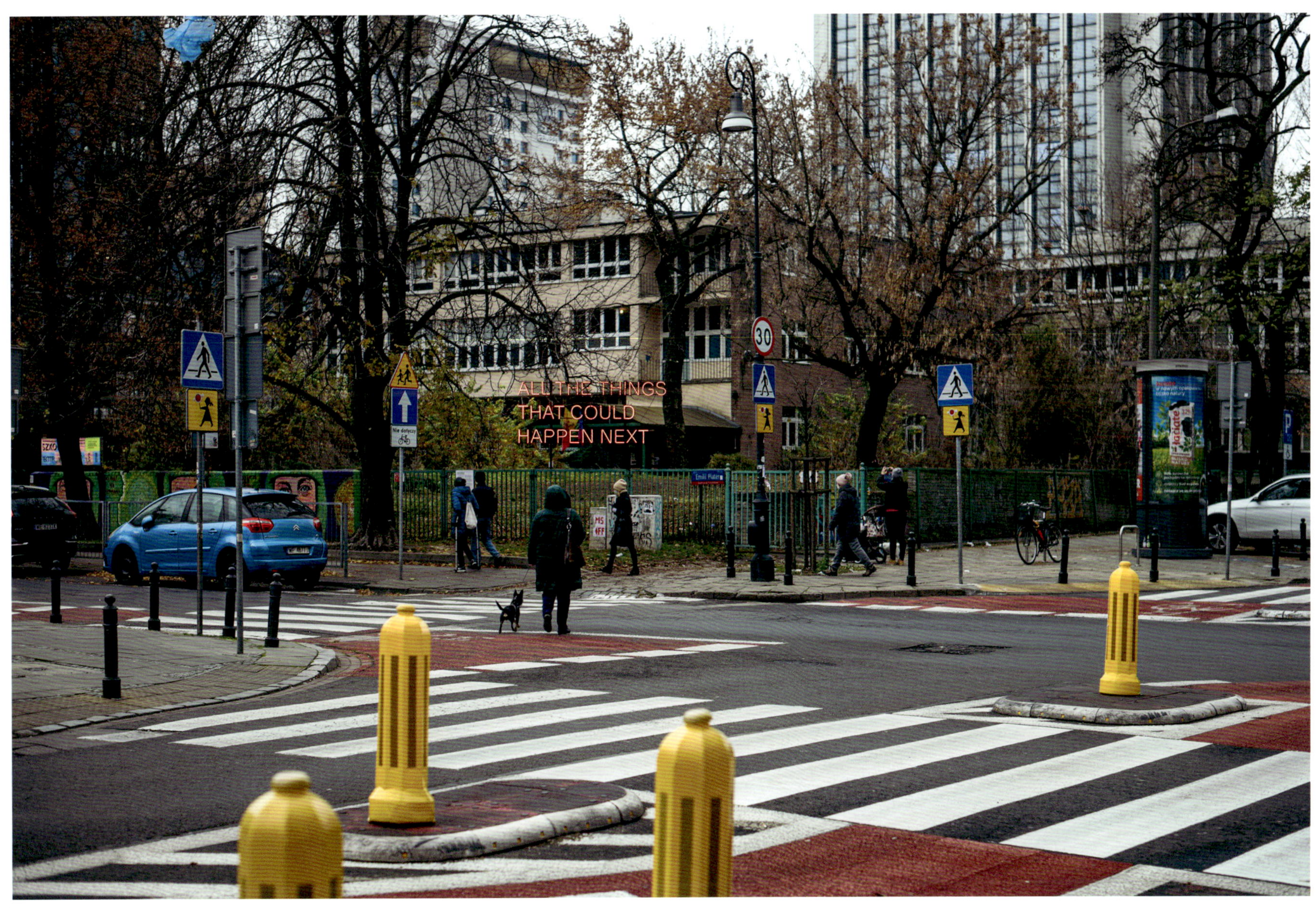
ALL THE THINGS
THAT COULD
HAPPEN NEXT

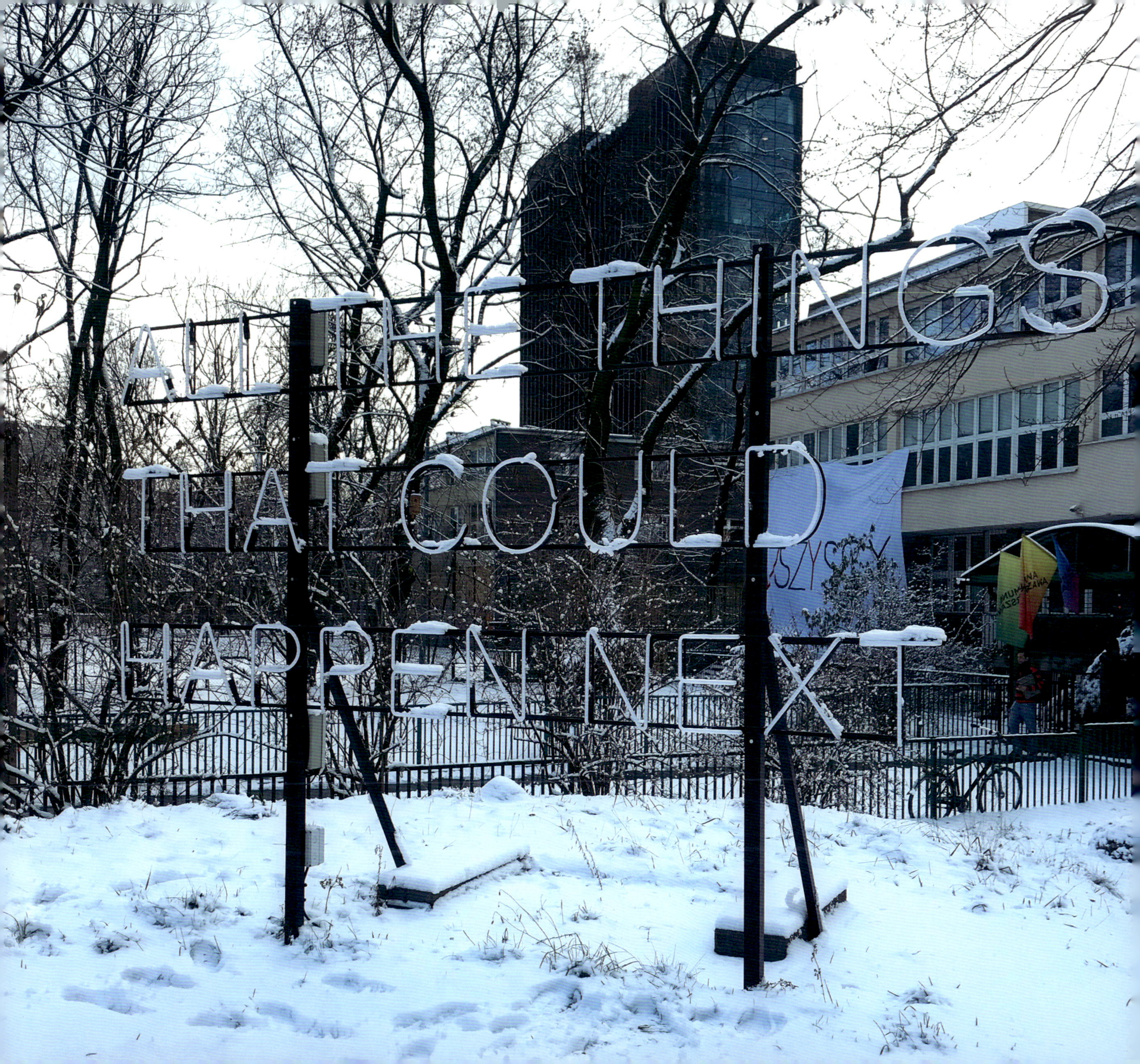
ALL THE THINGS
THAT COULD
HAPPEN NEXT

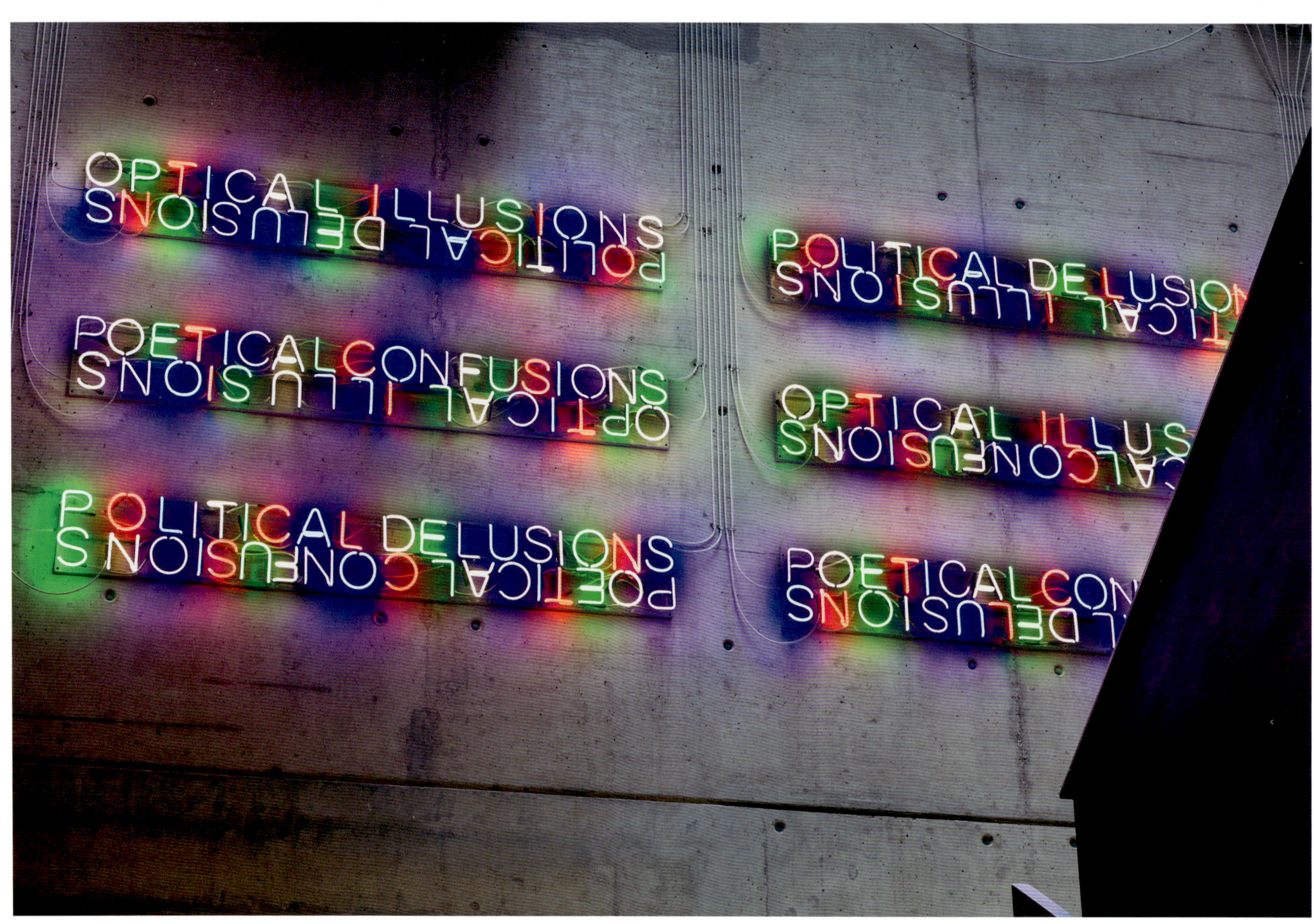

OPTICAL ILLUSIONS
POLITICAL DELUSIONS
POETICAL CONFUSIONS
OPTICAL ILLUSIONS
POLITICAL DELUSIONS
POETICAL CONFUSIONS
POLITICAL DELUSIONS
OPTICAL ILLUSIONS
POETICAL CONFUSIONS

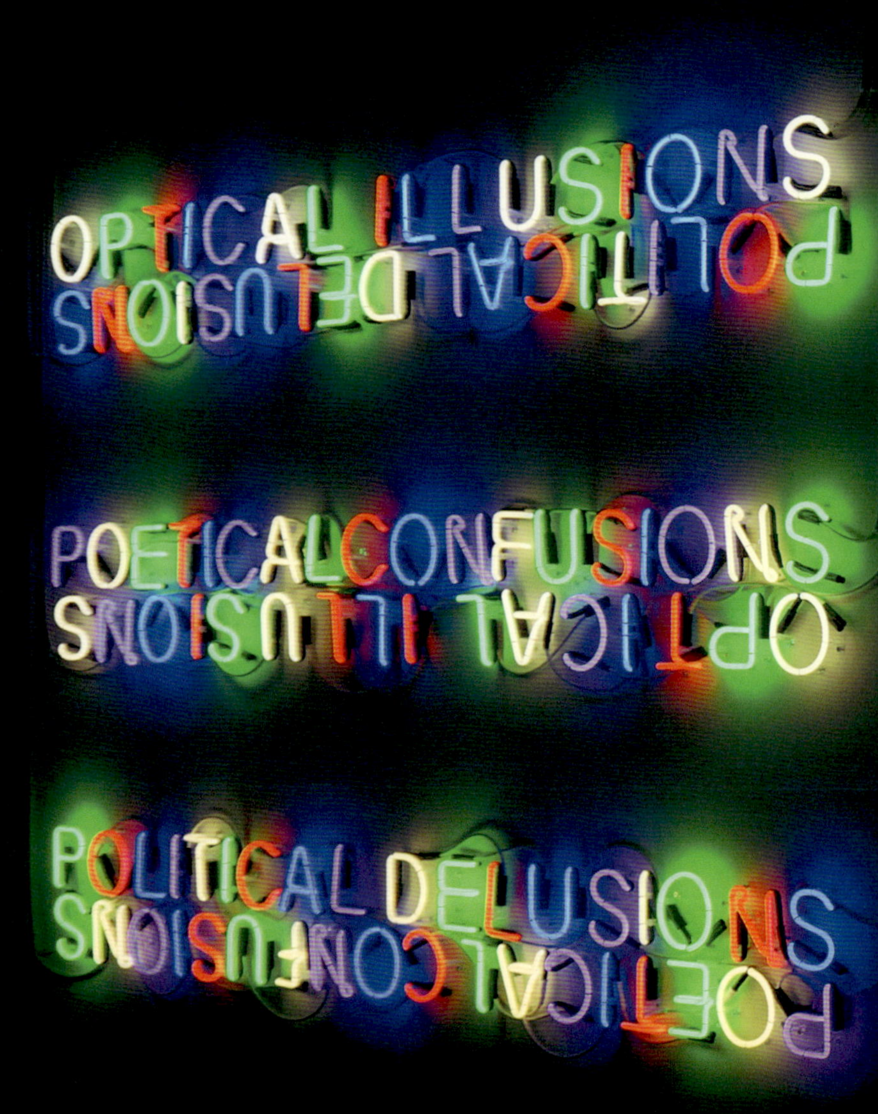
OPTICAL ILLUSIONS
POLITICAL DELUSIONS
POETICAL CONFUSIONS
OPTICAL ILLUSIONS
POLITICAL DELUSIONS
POETICAL CONFUSIONS

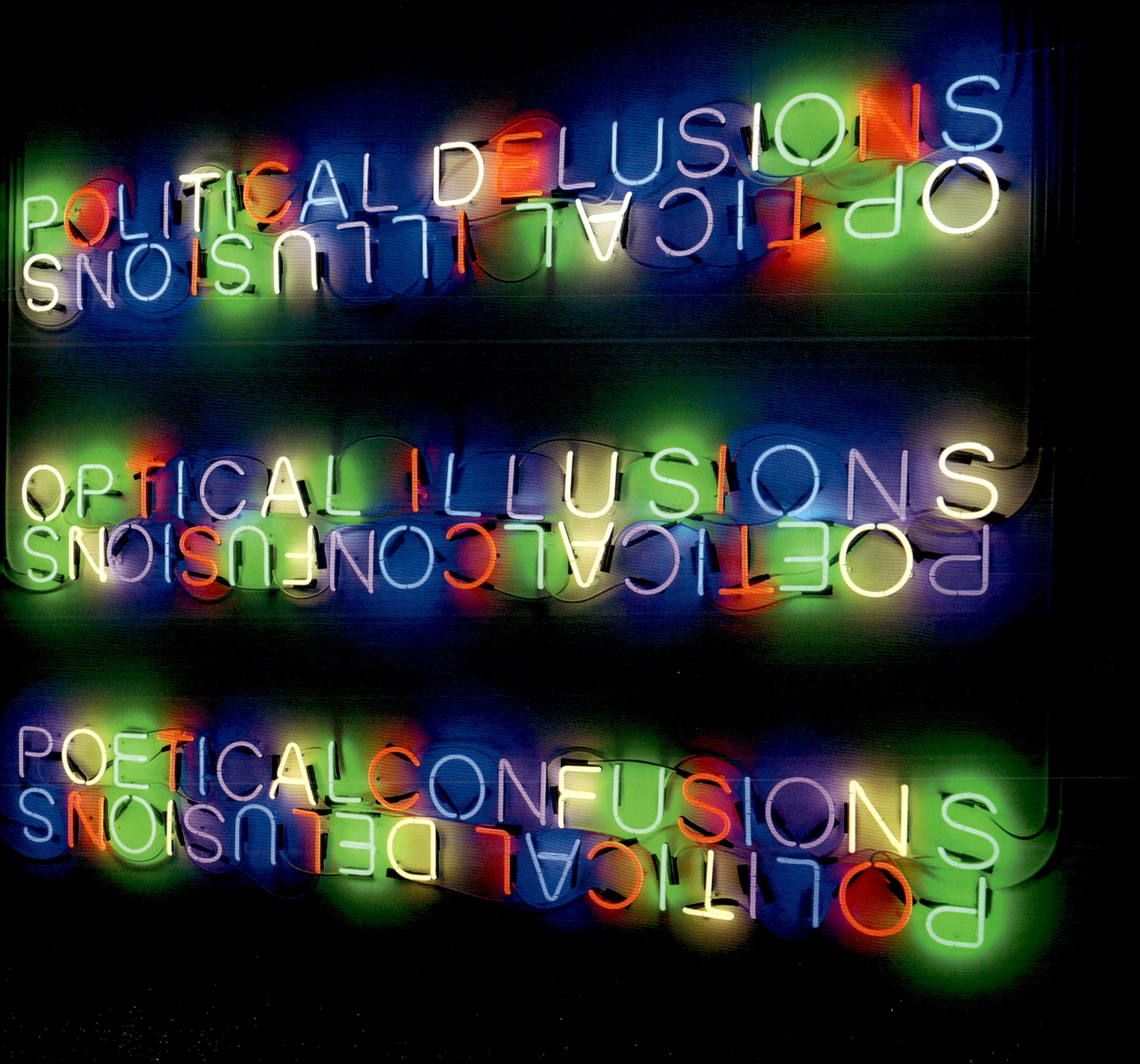

POLITICAL DELUSIONS

OPTICAL ILLUSIONS

POETICAL CONFUSIONS

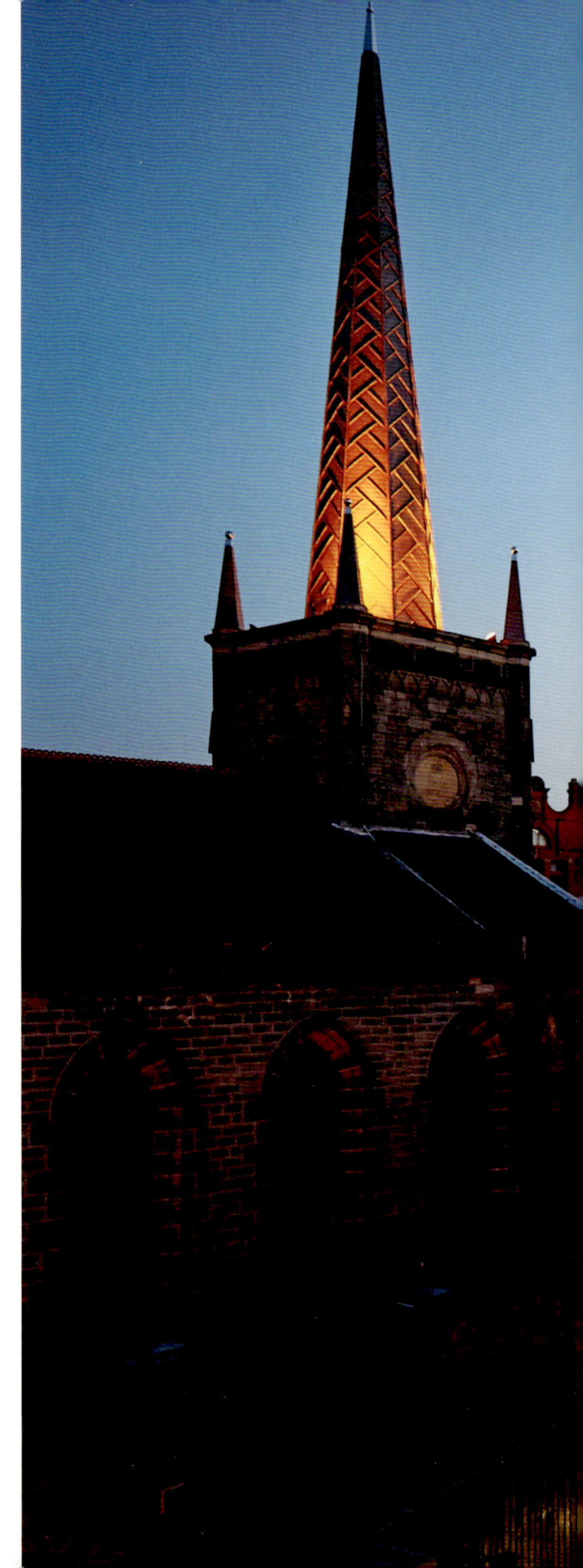

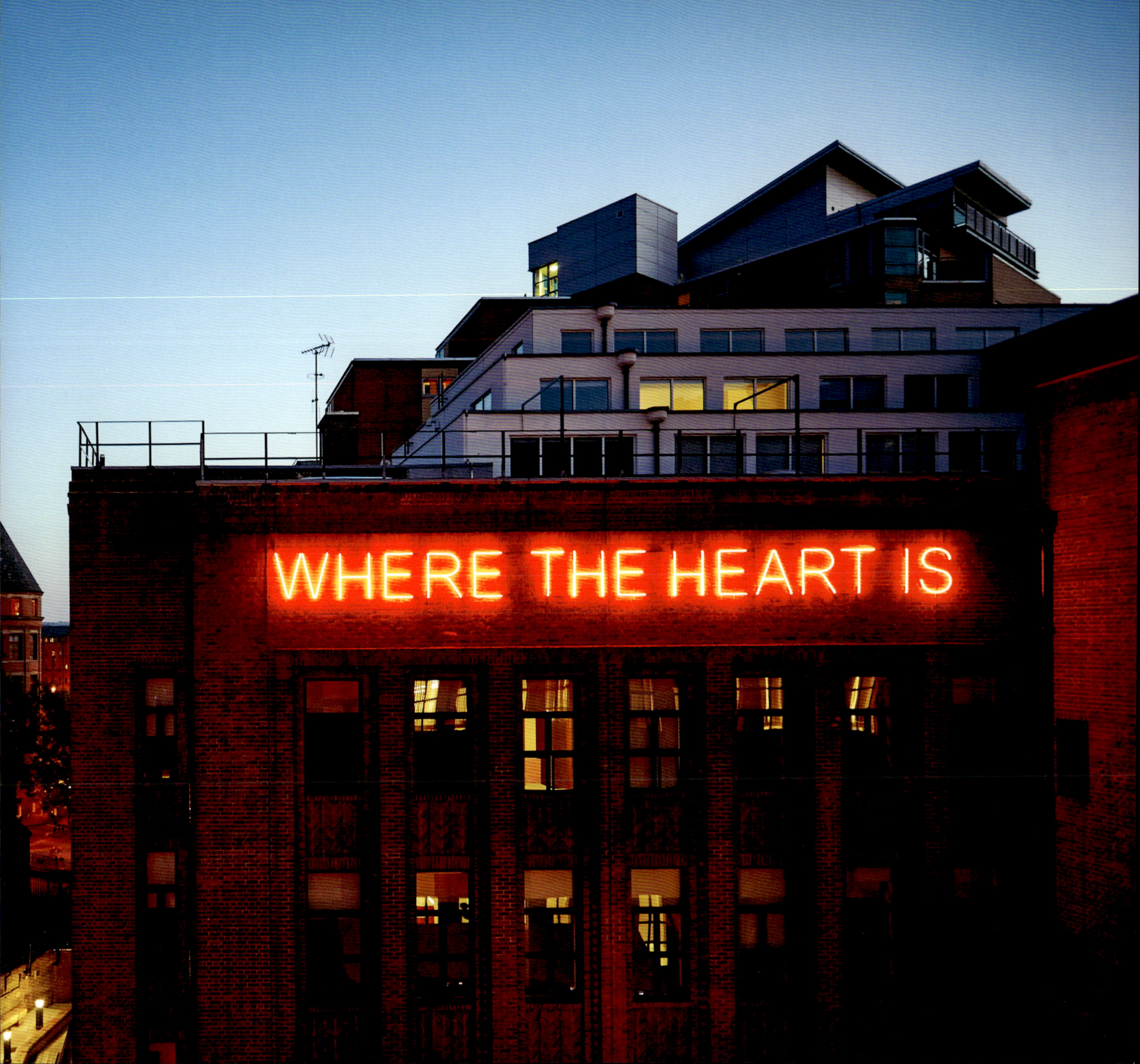

WHERE THE HEART IS

SHOUTING YOUR DEMANDS
FROM THE ROOFTOP
SHOULD BE CONSIDERED
A LAST RESORT

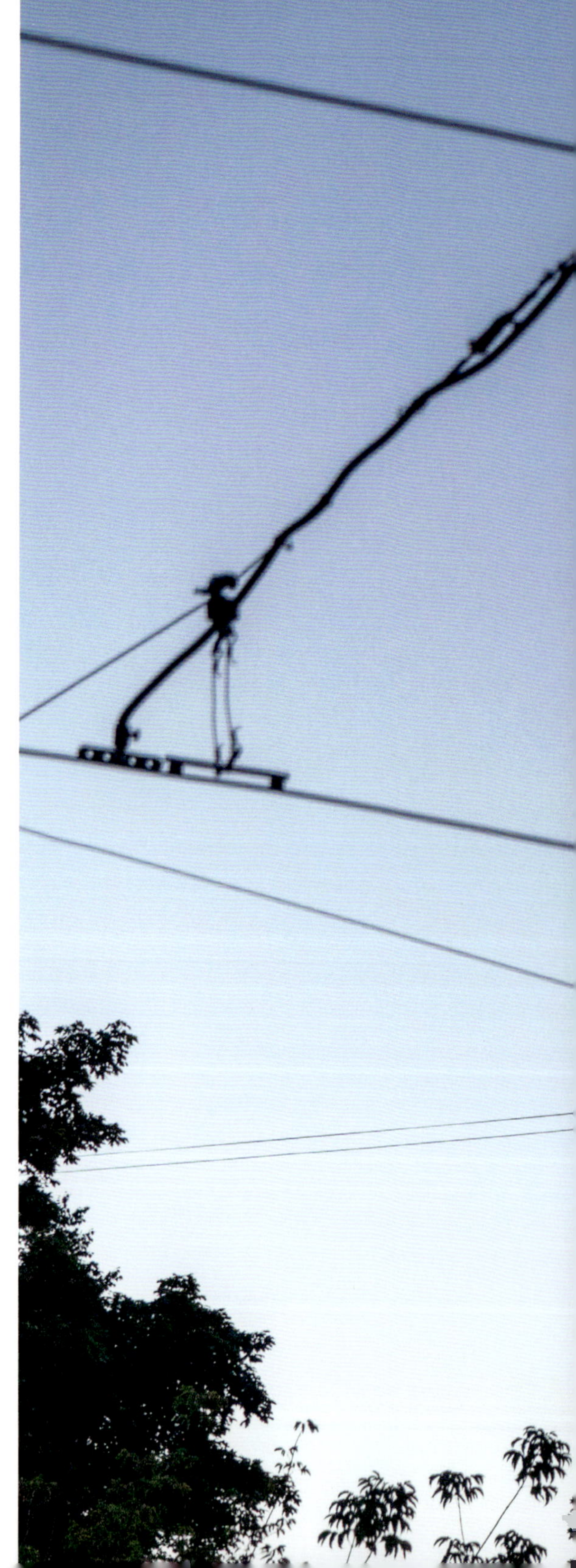

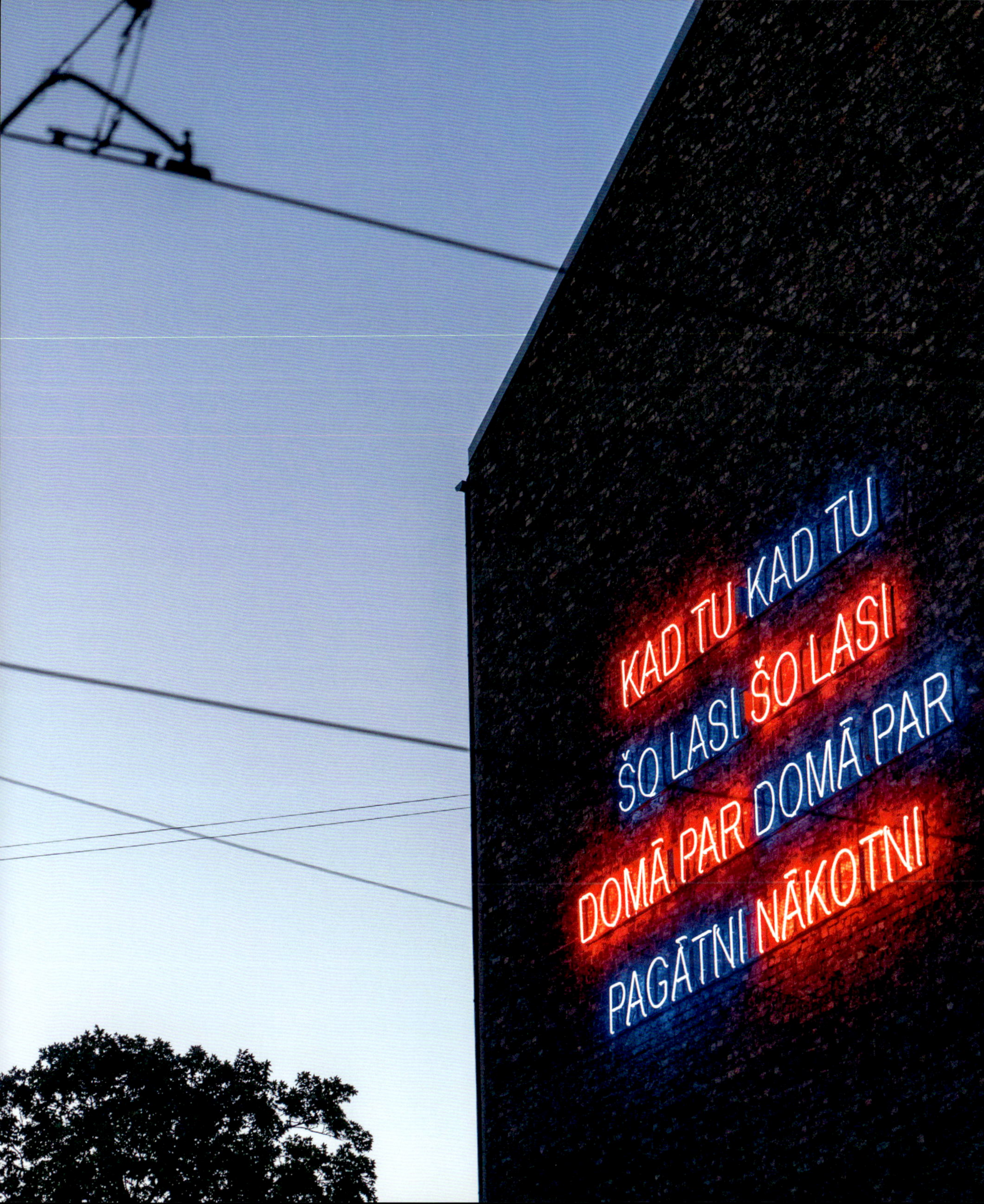

KAD TU KAD TU
ŠO LASI ŠO LASI
DOMĀ PAR DOMĀ PAR
PAGĀTNI NĀKOTNI

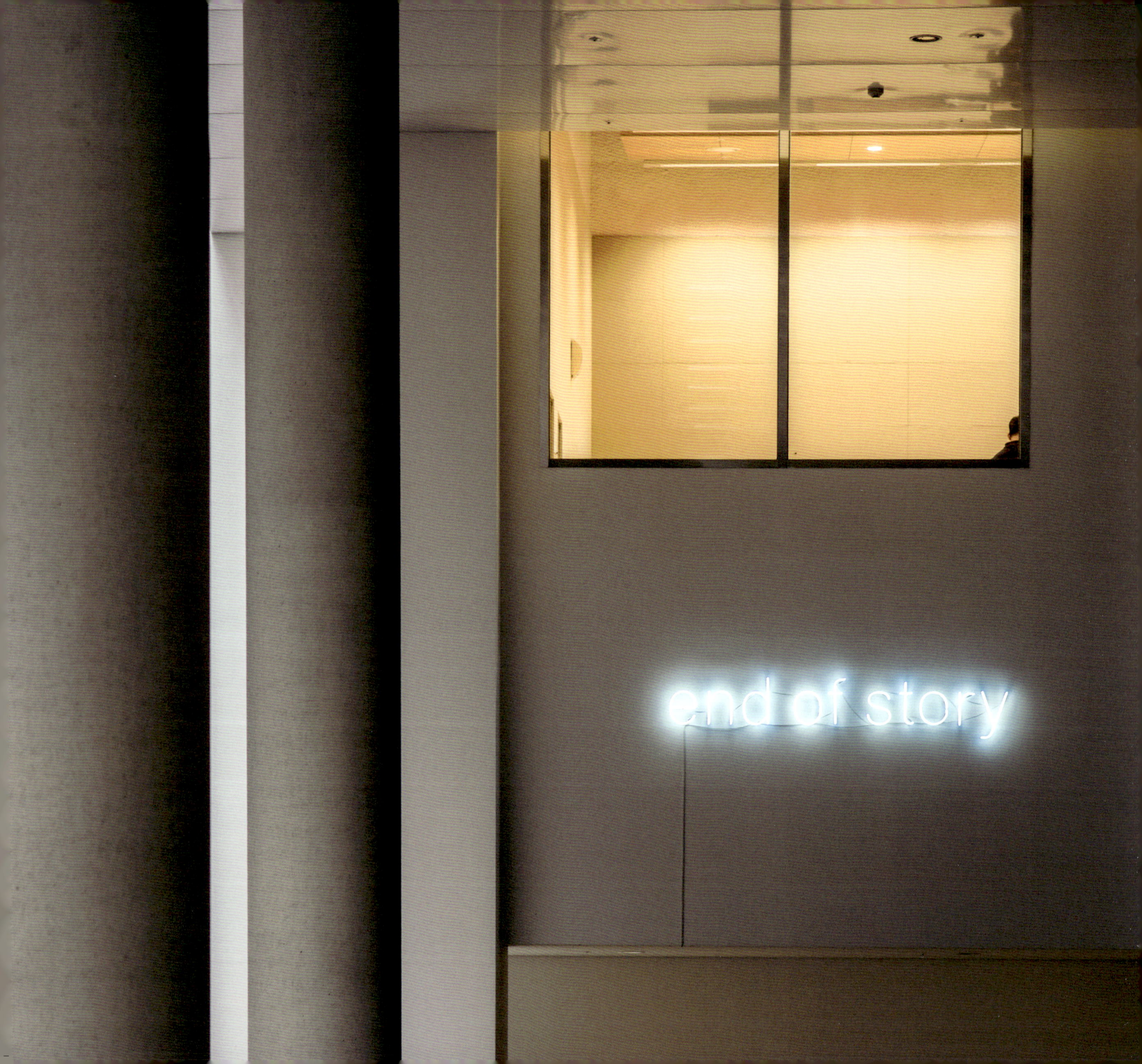

end of story

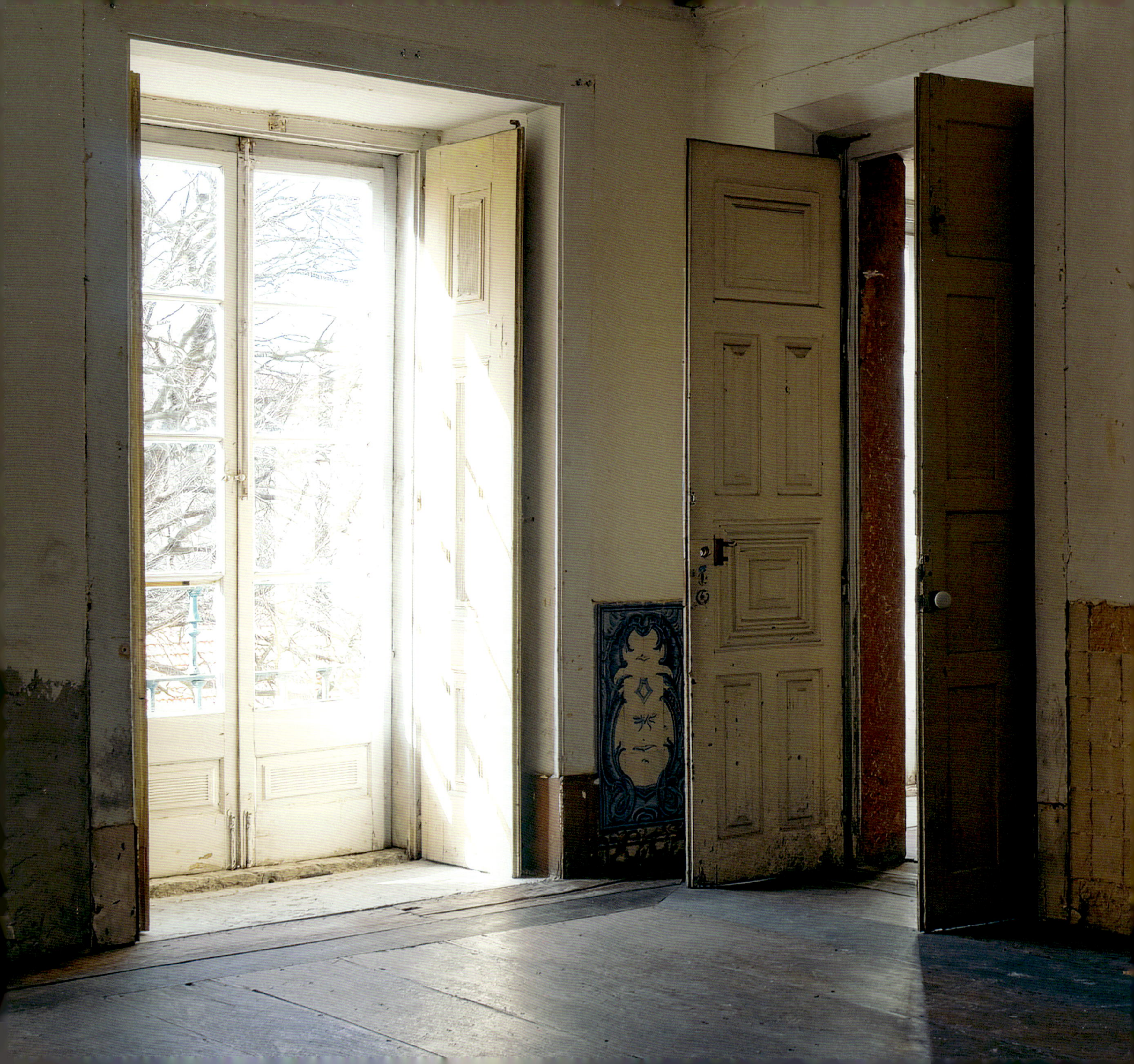

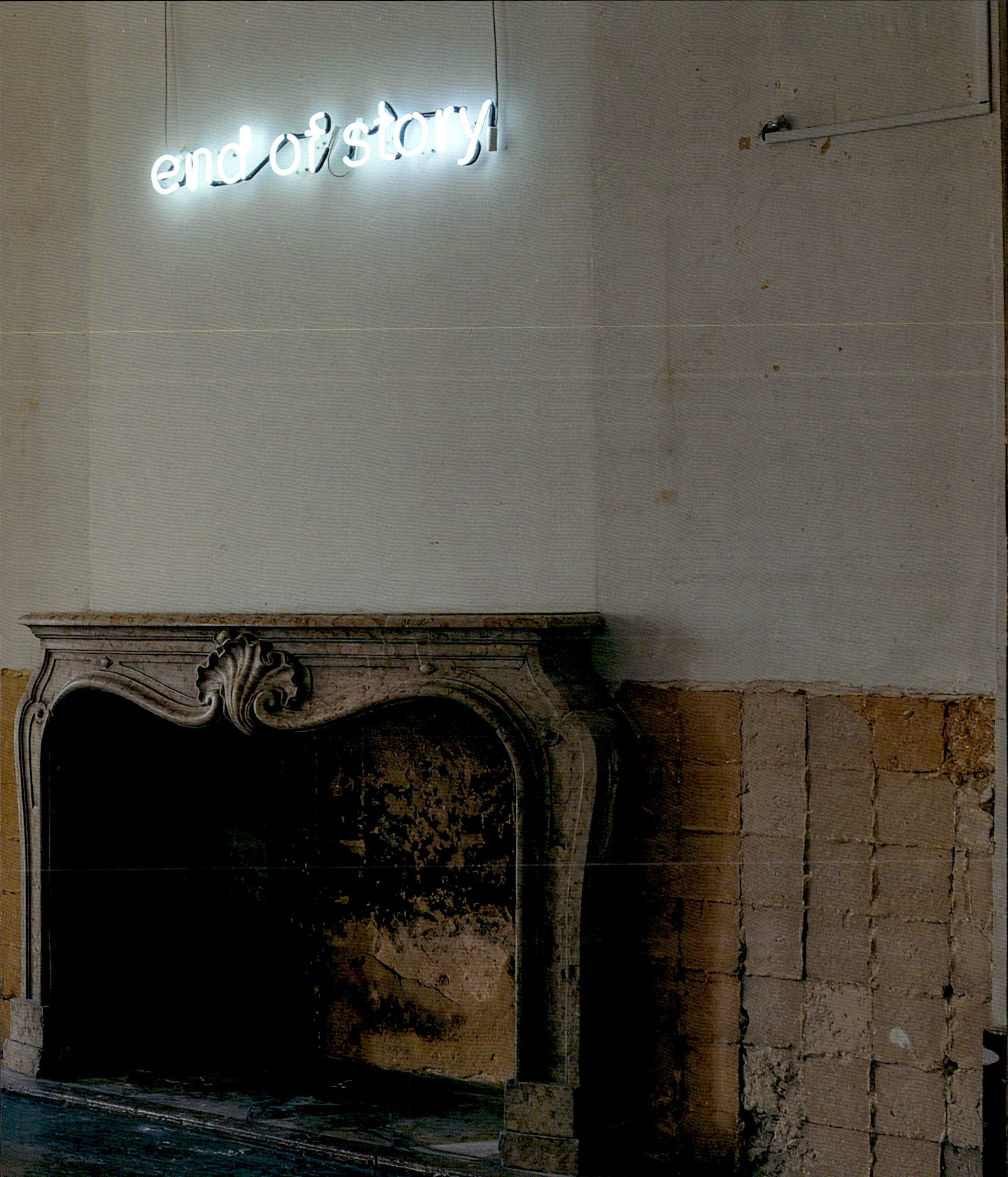
end of story

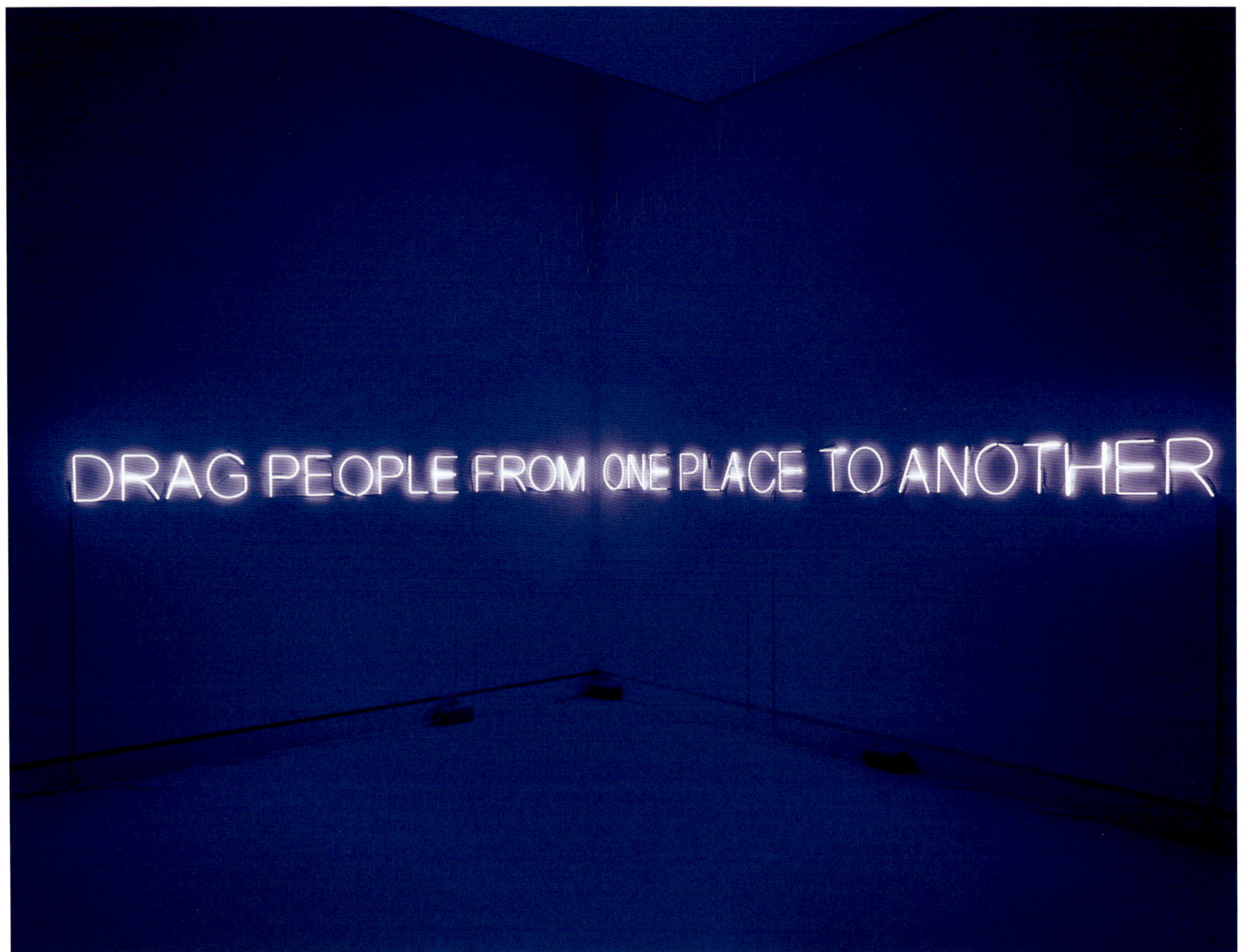

DRAG PEOPLE FROM ONE PLACE TO ANOTHER

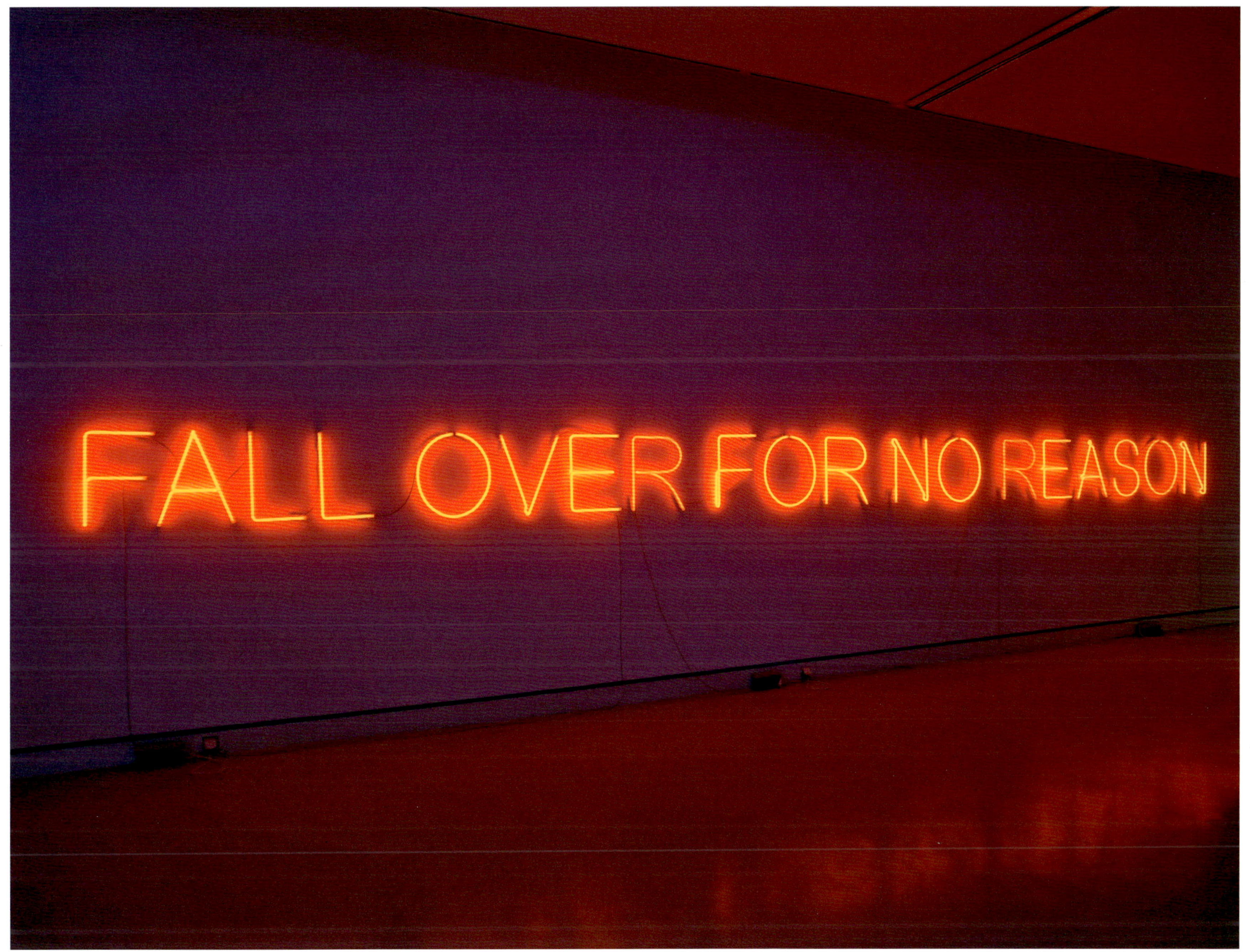

FALL OVER FOR NO REASON

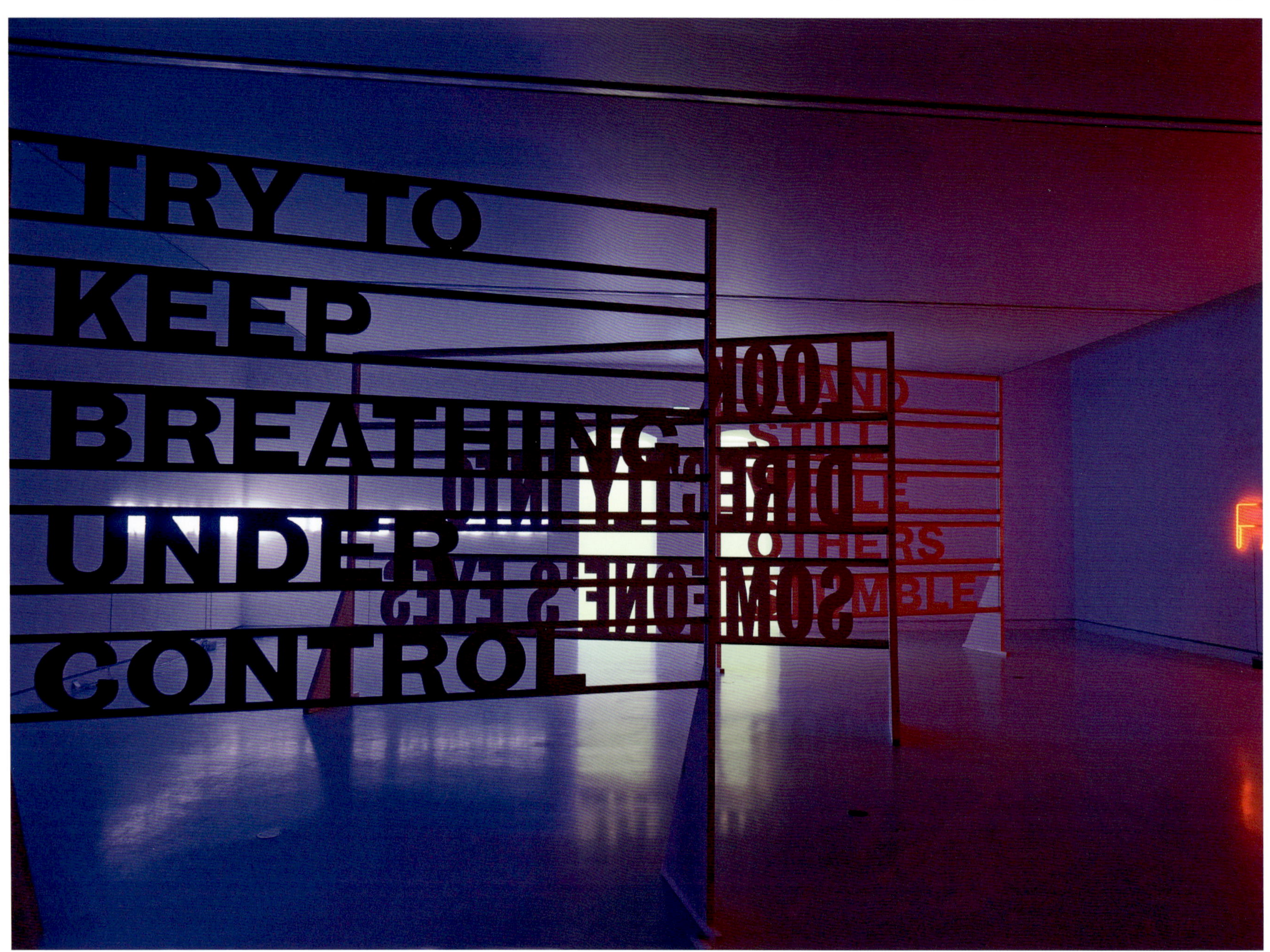

TRY TO
KEEP
BREATHING
UNDER
CONTROL

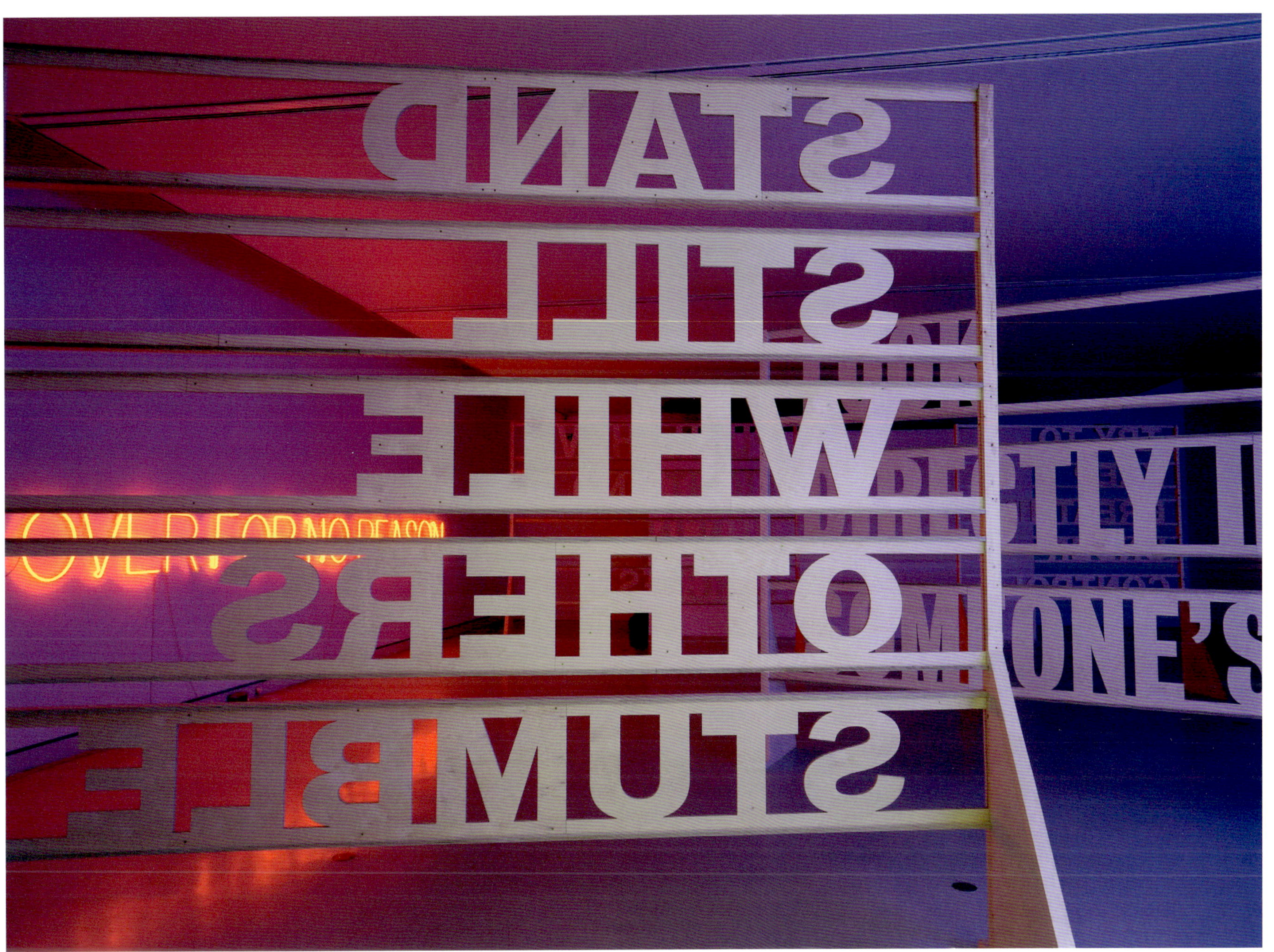
STAND
STILL
WHILE
OTHERS
STUMBLE
OVER FOR NO REASON

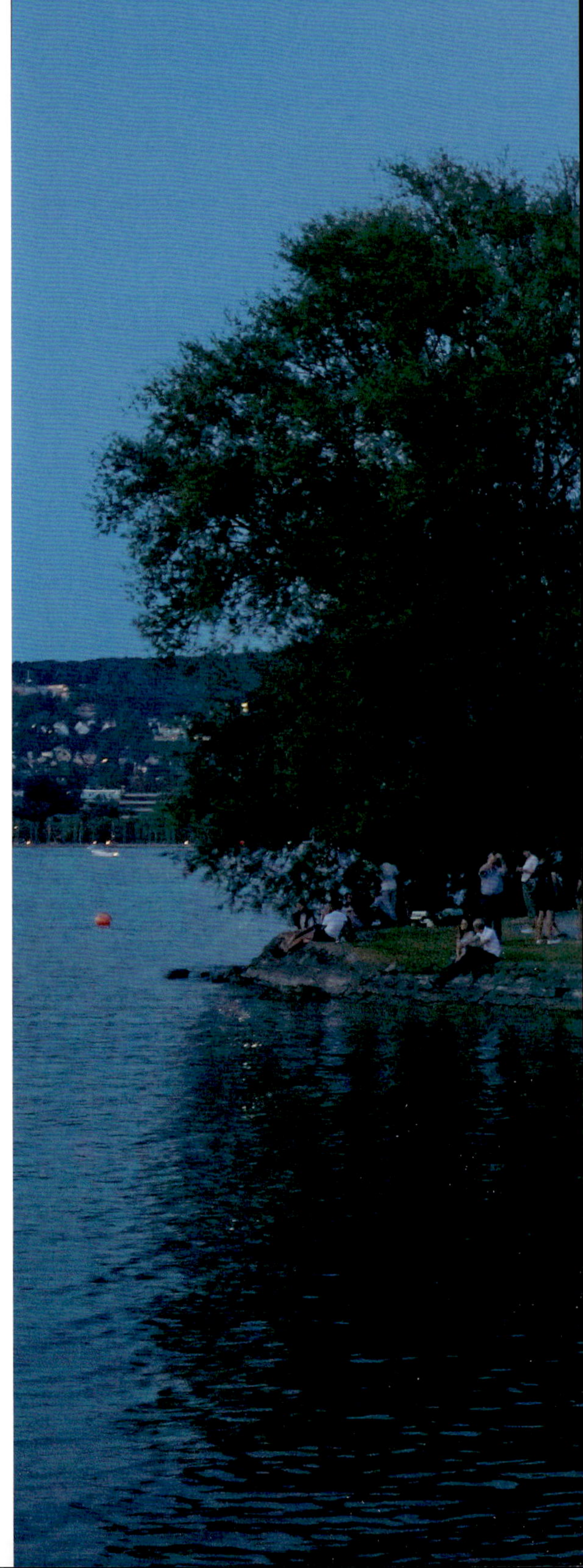

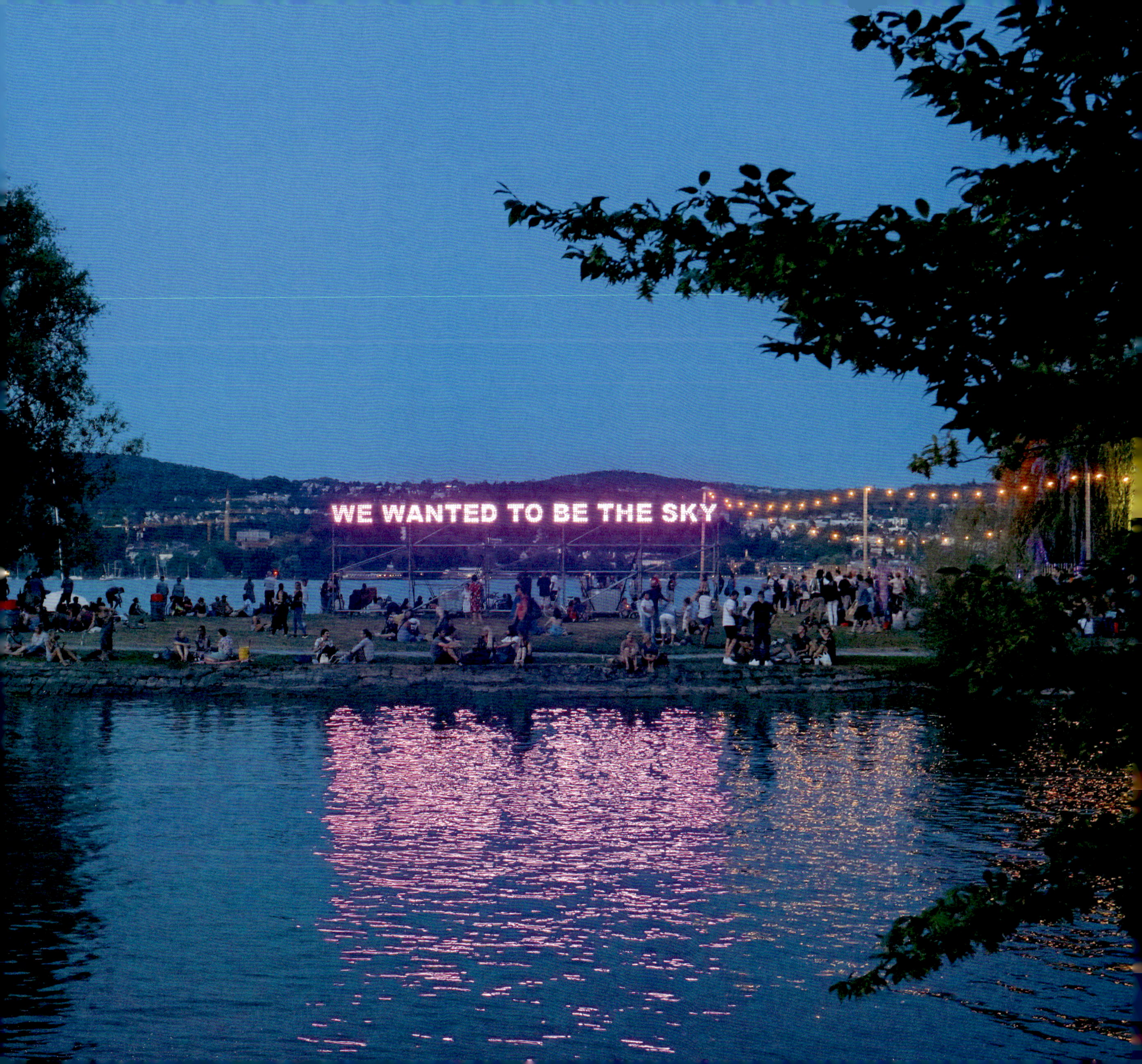
WE WANTED TO BE THE SKY

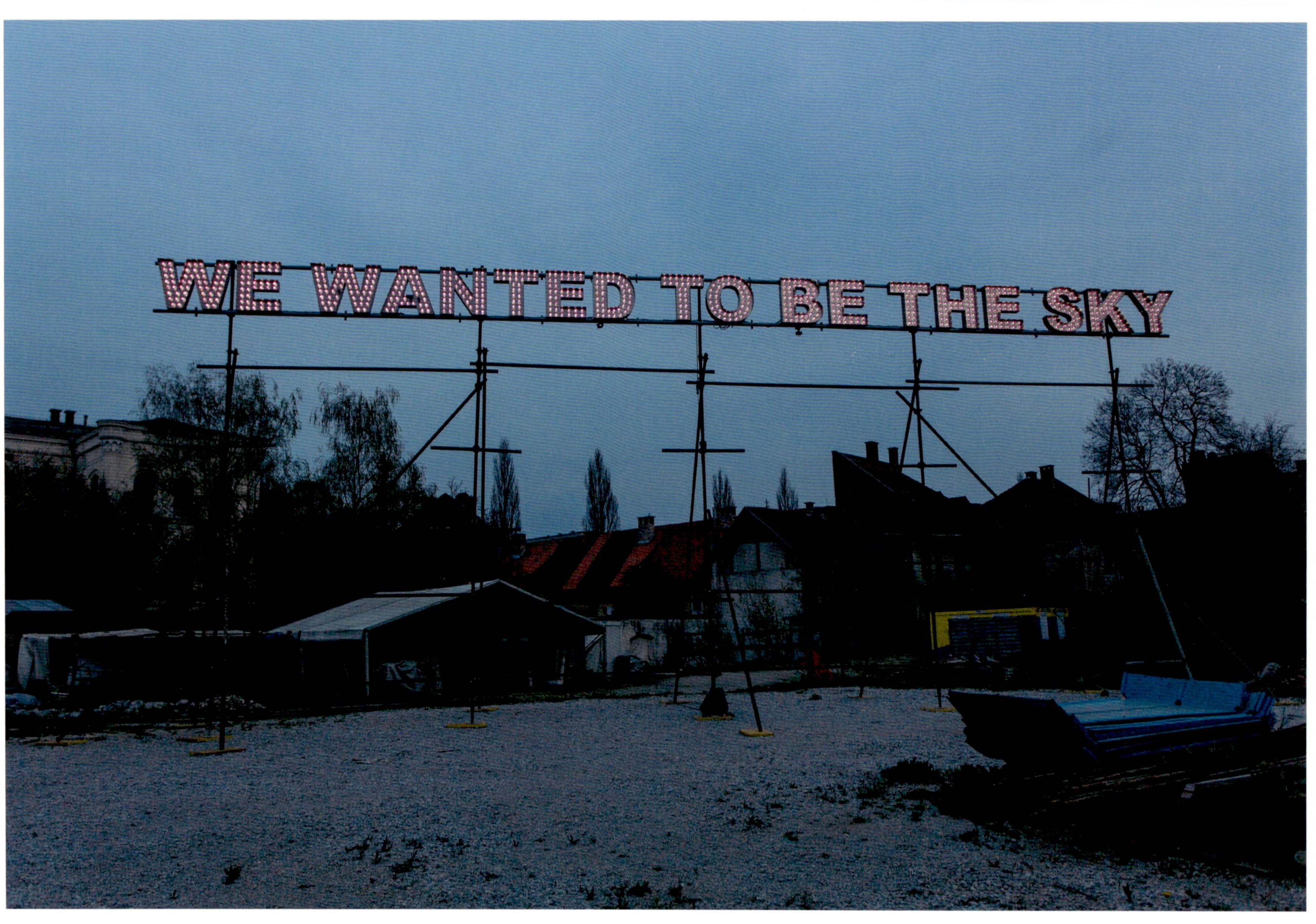
WE WANTED TO BE THE SKY

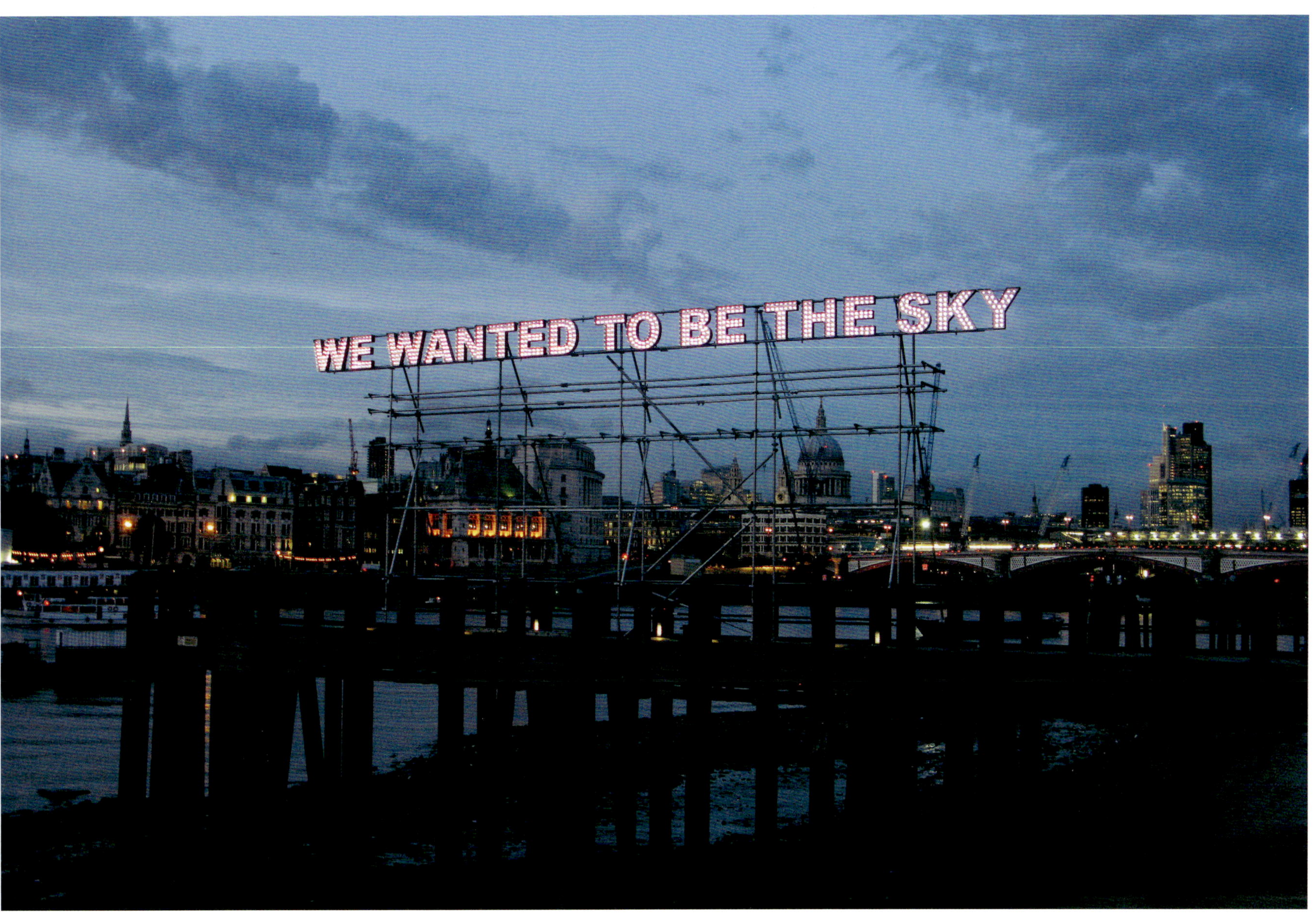
WE WANTED TO BE THE SKY

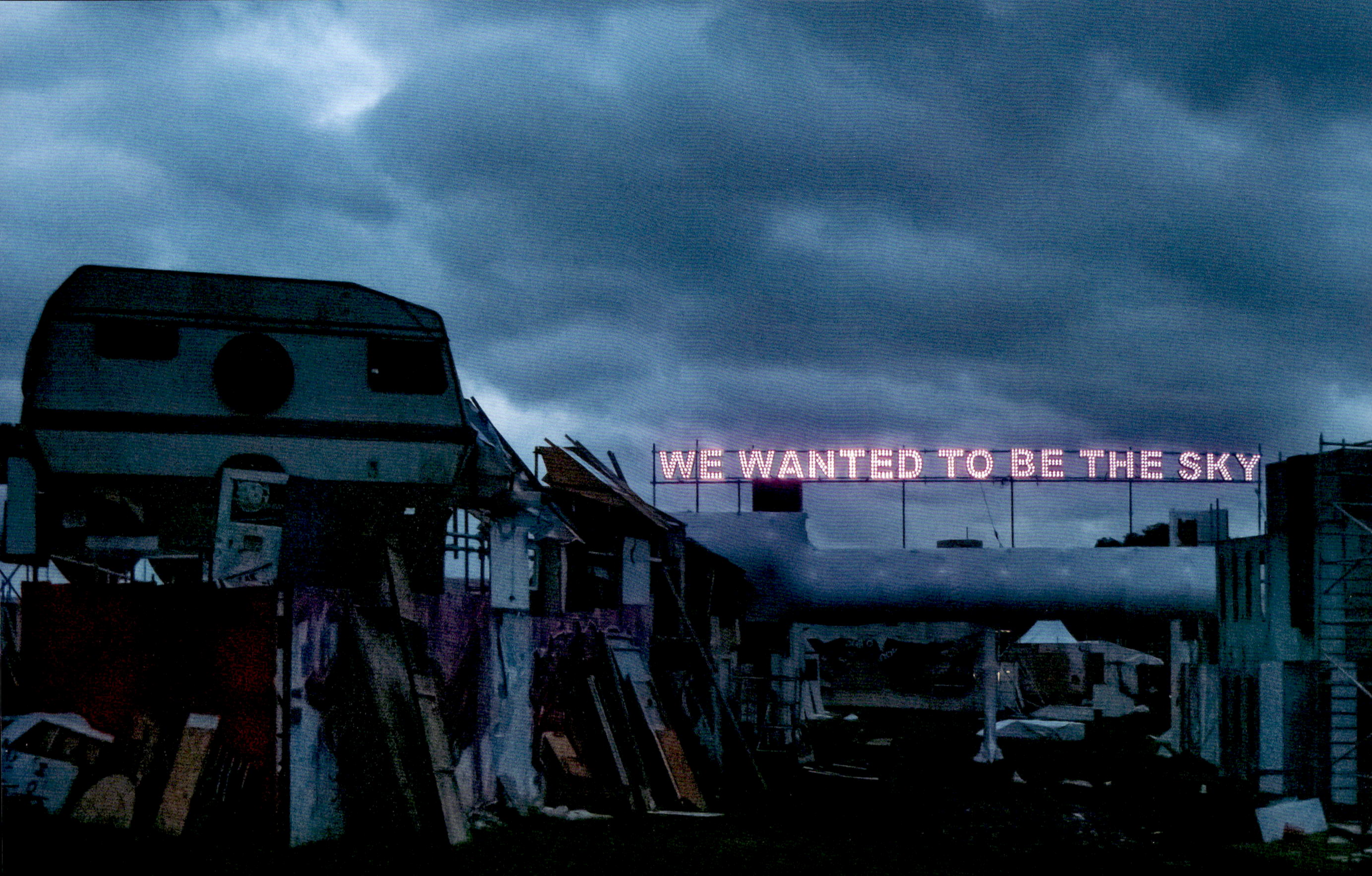
WE WANTED TO BE THE SKY

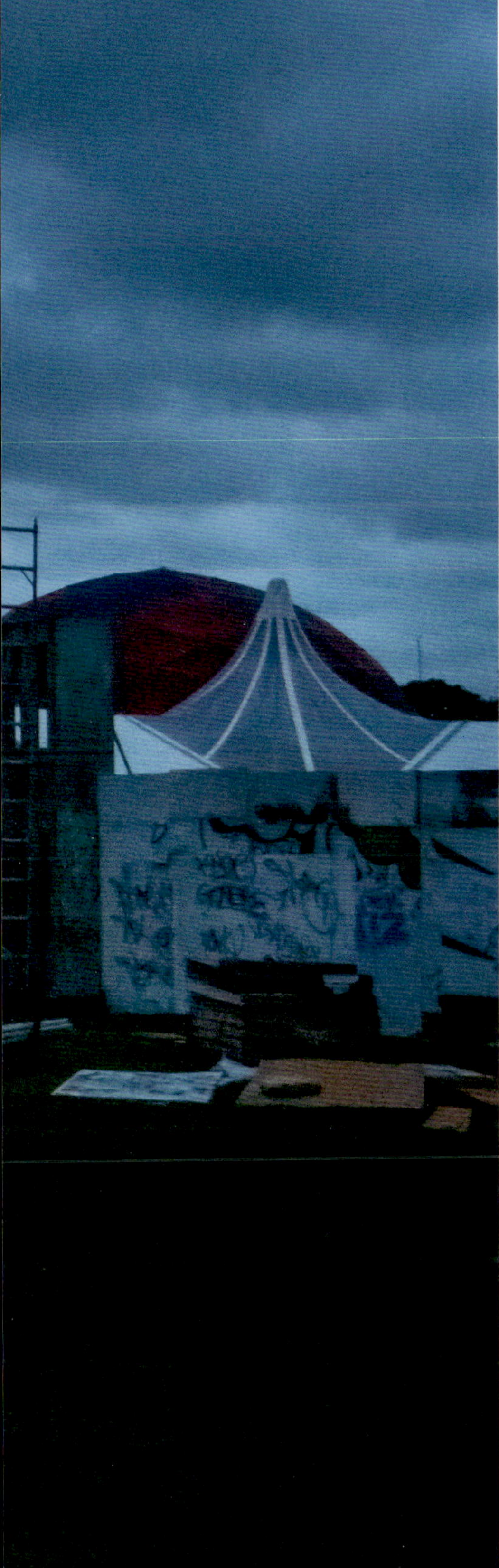

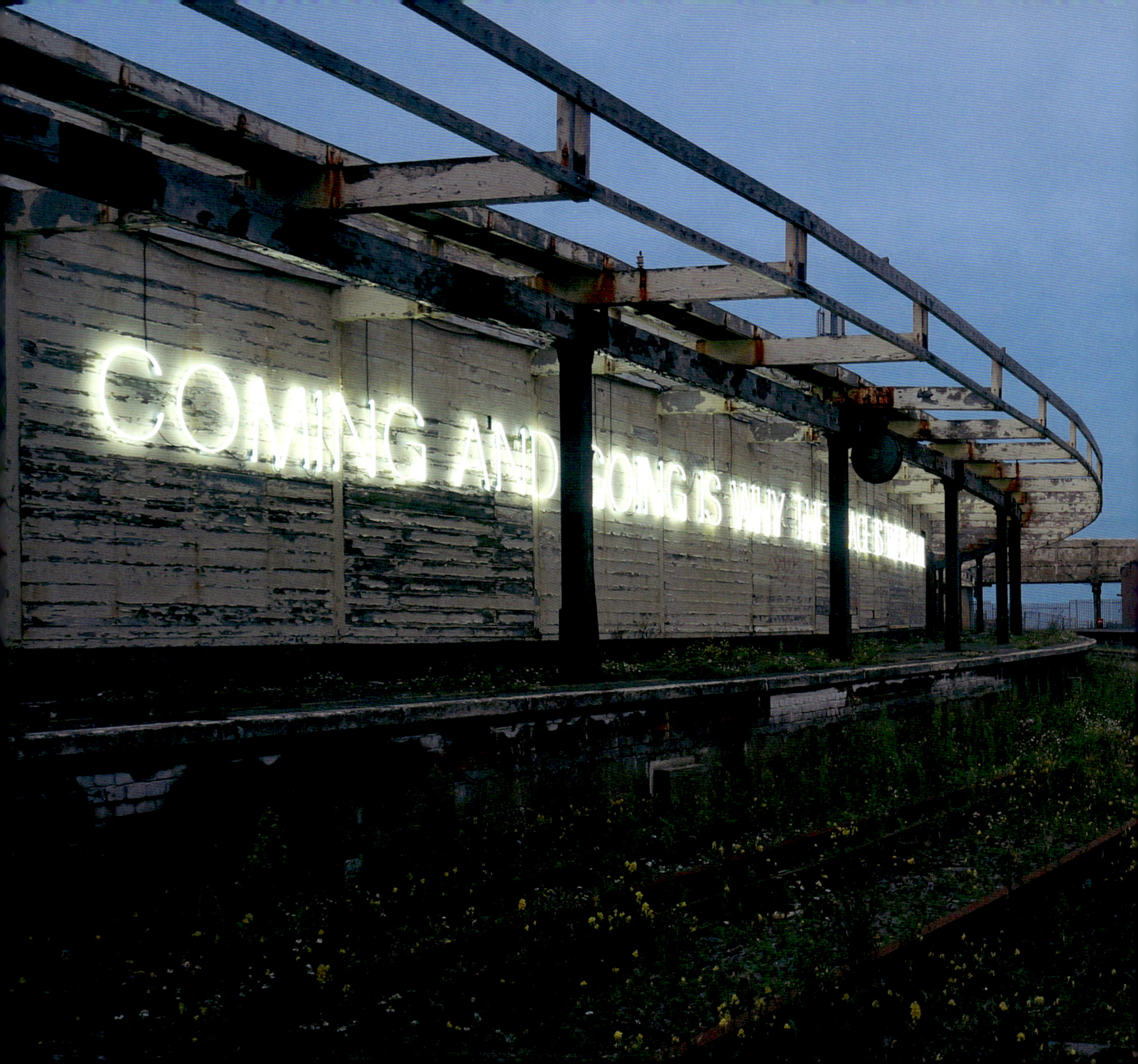

COMING AND GOING IS WHY THE   ACE IS

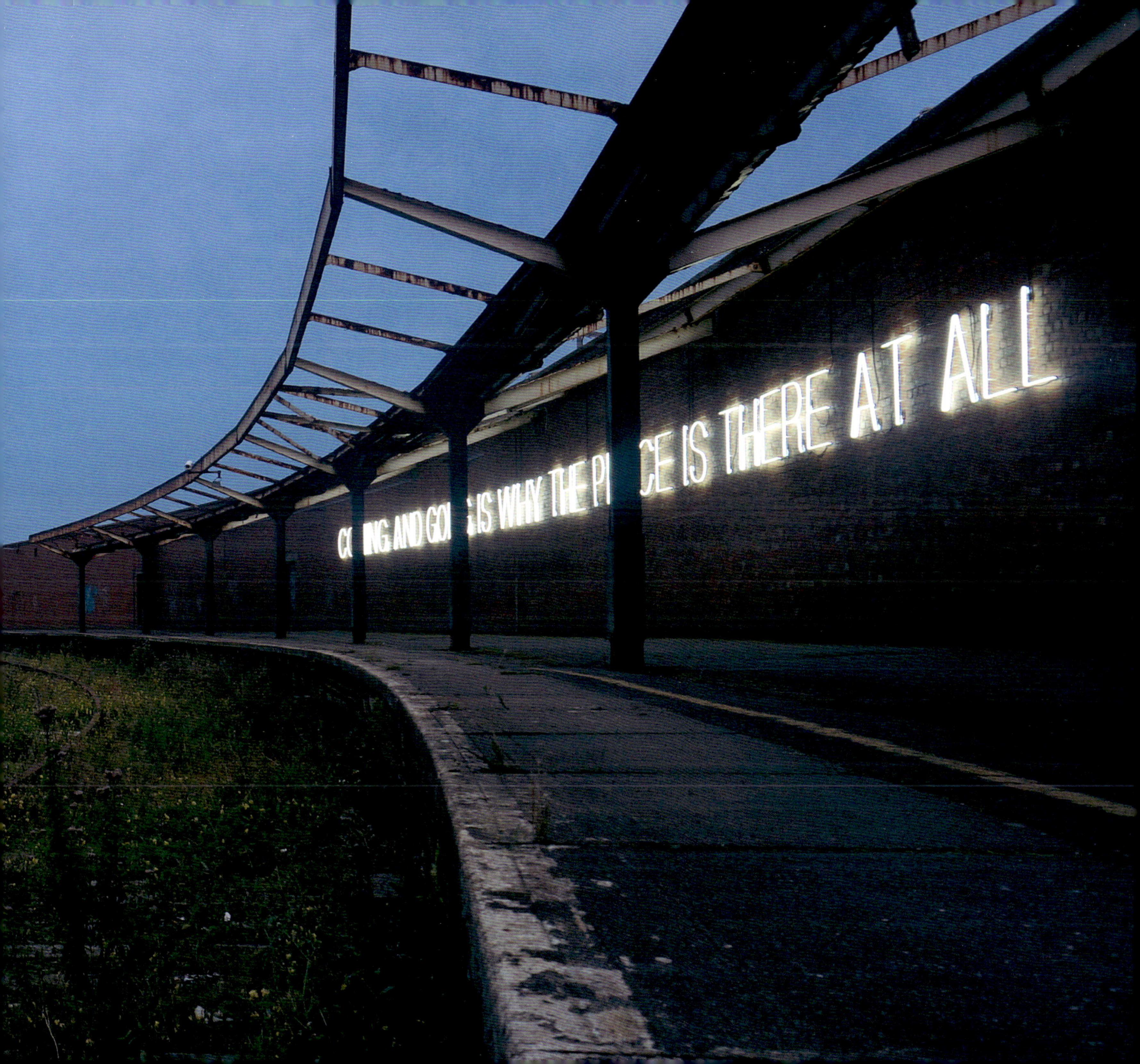
COMING AND GOING IS WHY THE PLACE IS THERE AT ALL

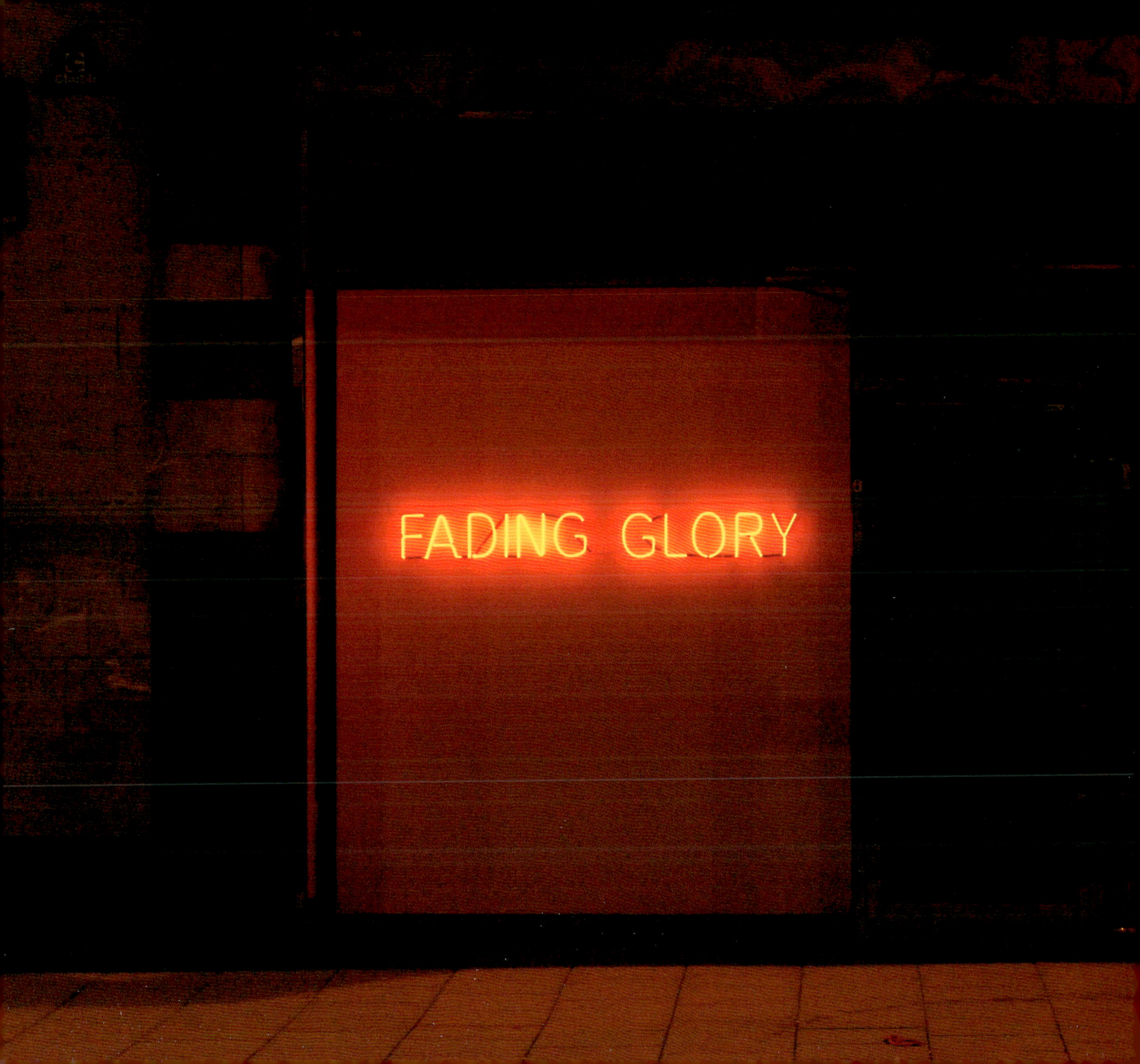
FADING GLORY

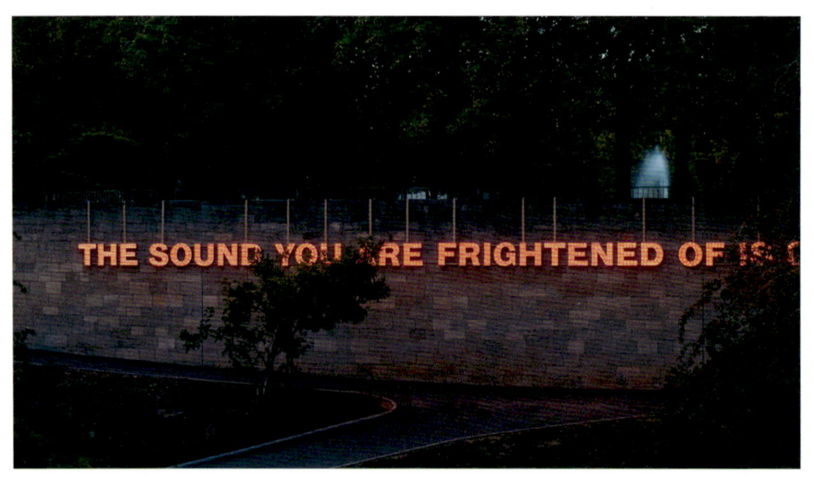

THE SOUND YOU ARE FRIGHTENED OF IS

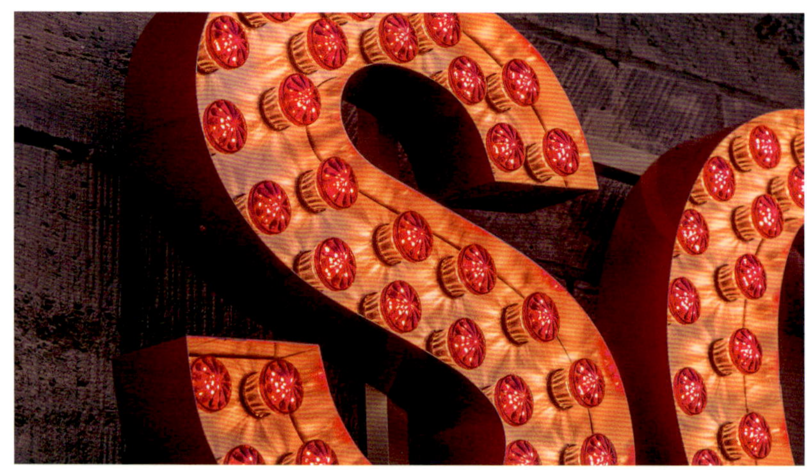

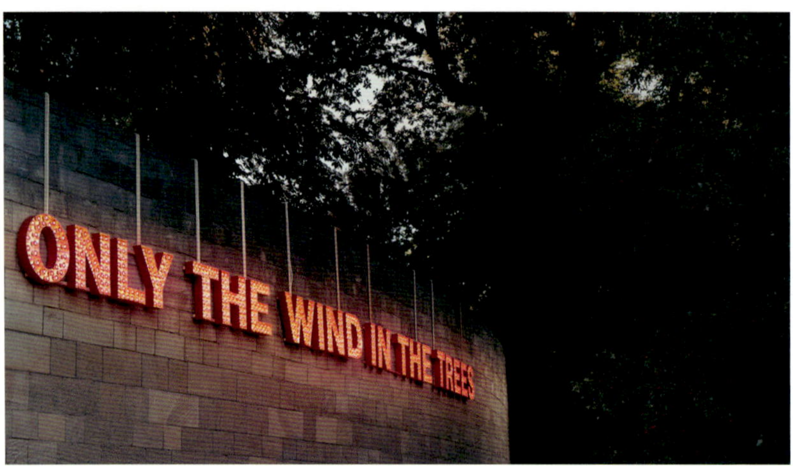

ONLY THE WIND IN THE TREES

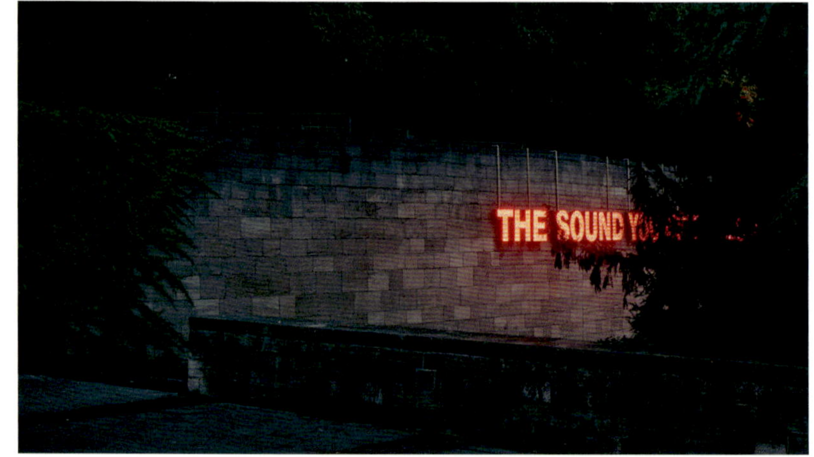

THE SOUND YOU

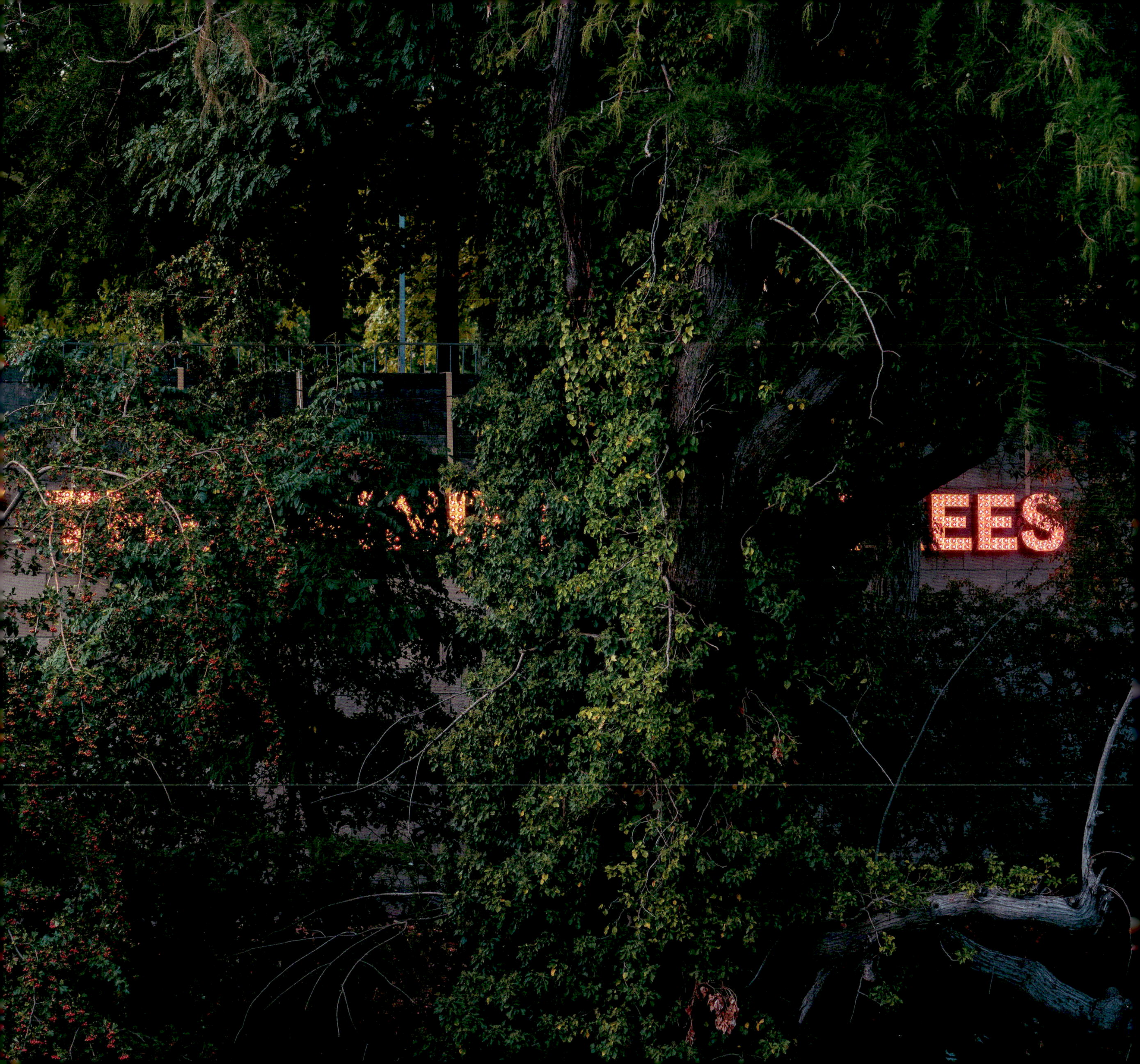

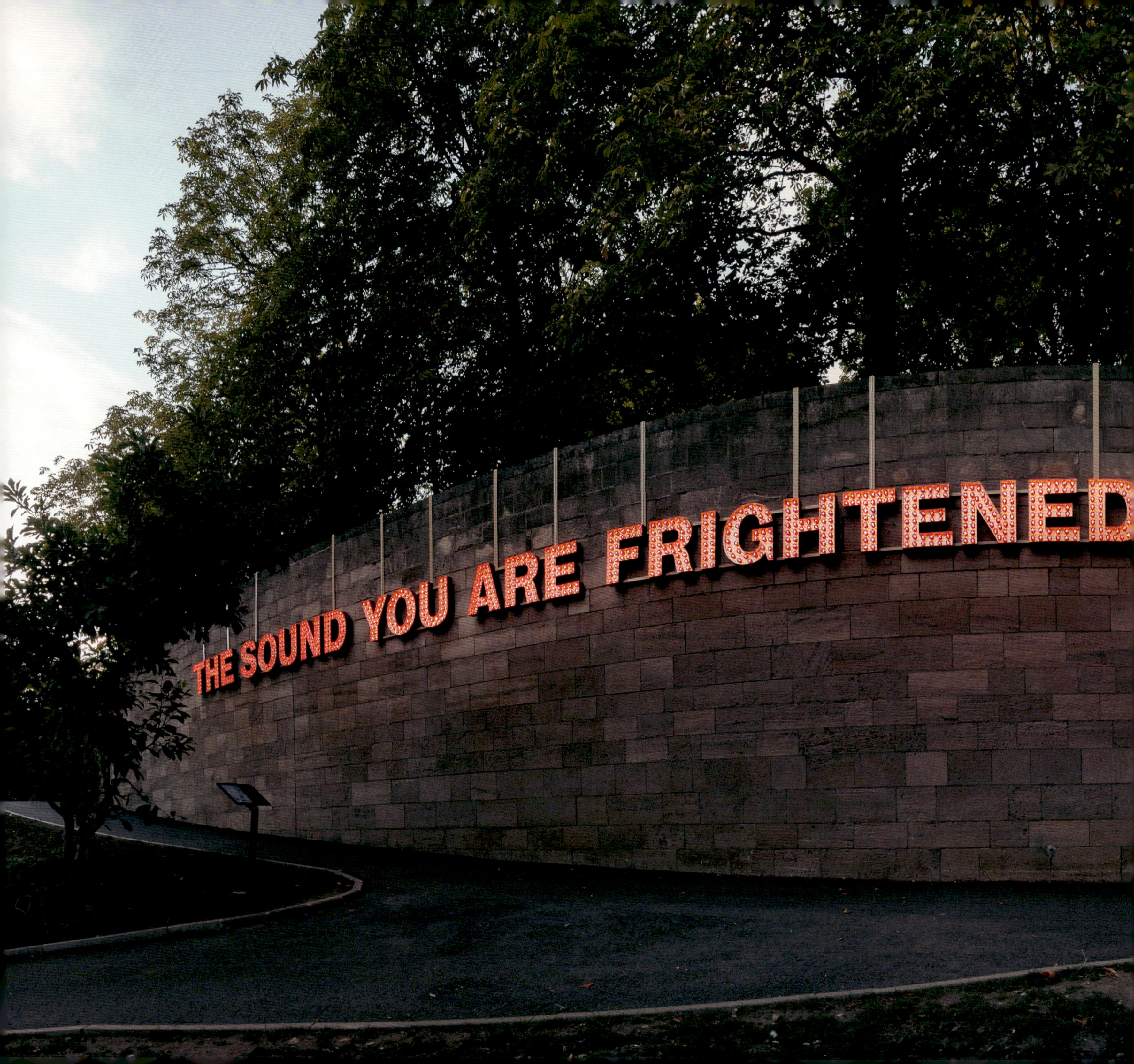
THE SOUND YOU ARE FRIGHTENED

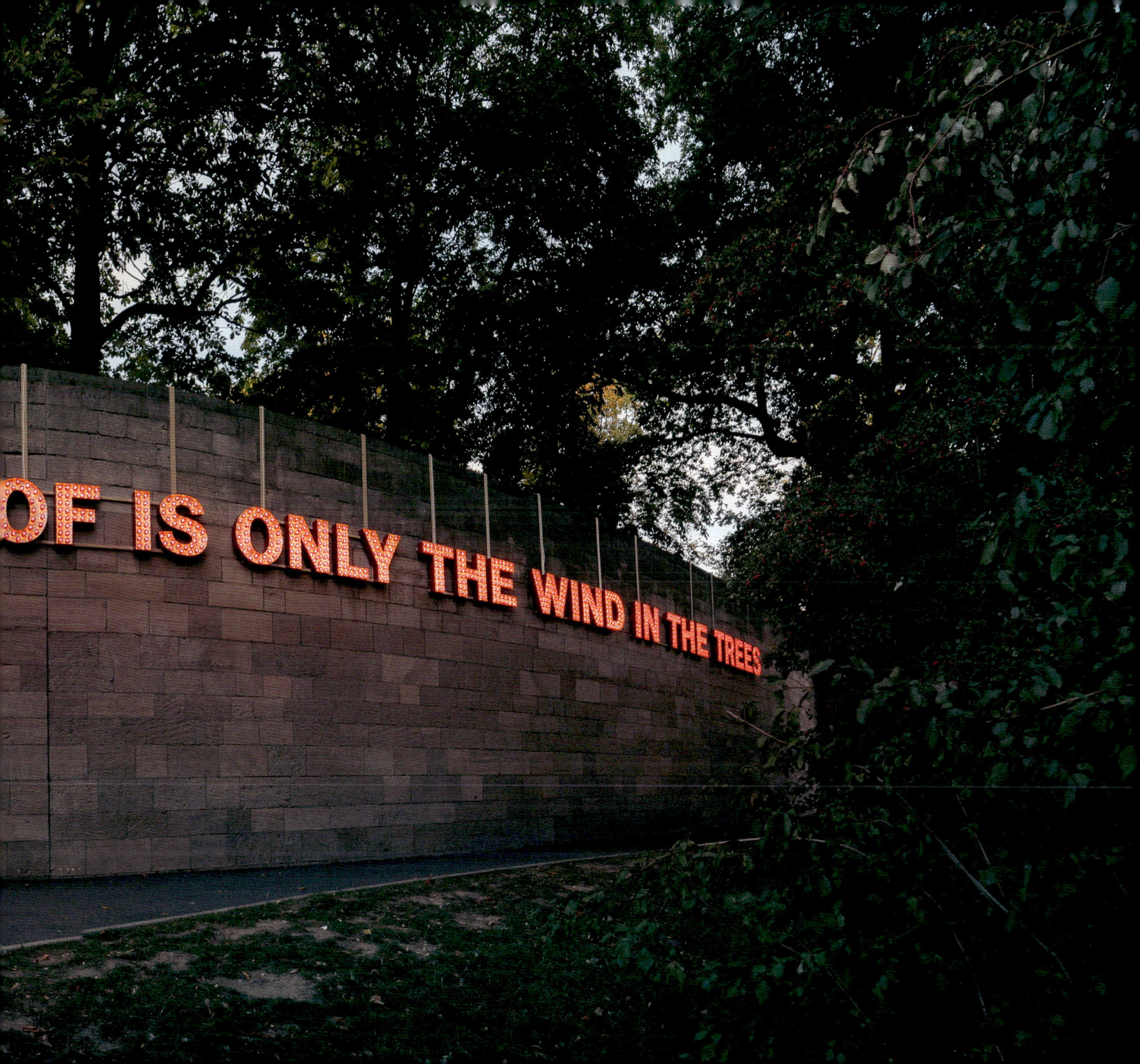
OF IS ONLY THE WIND IN THE TREES

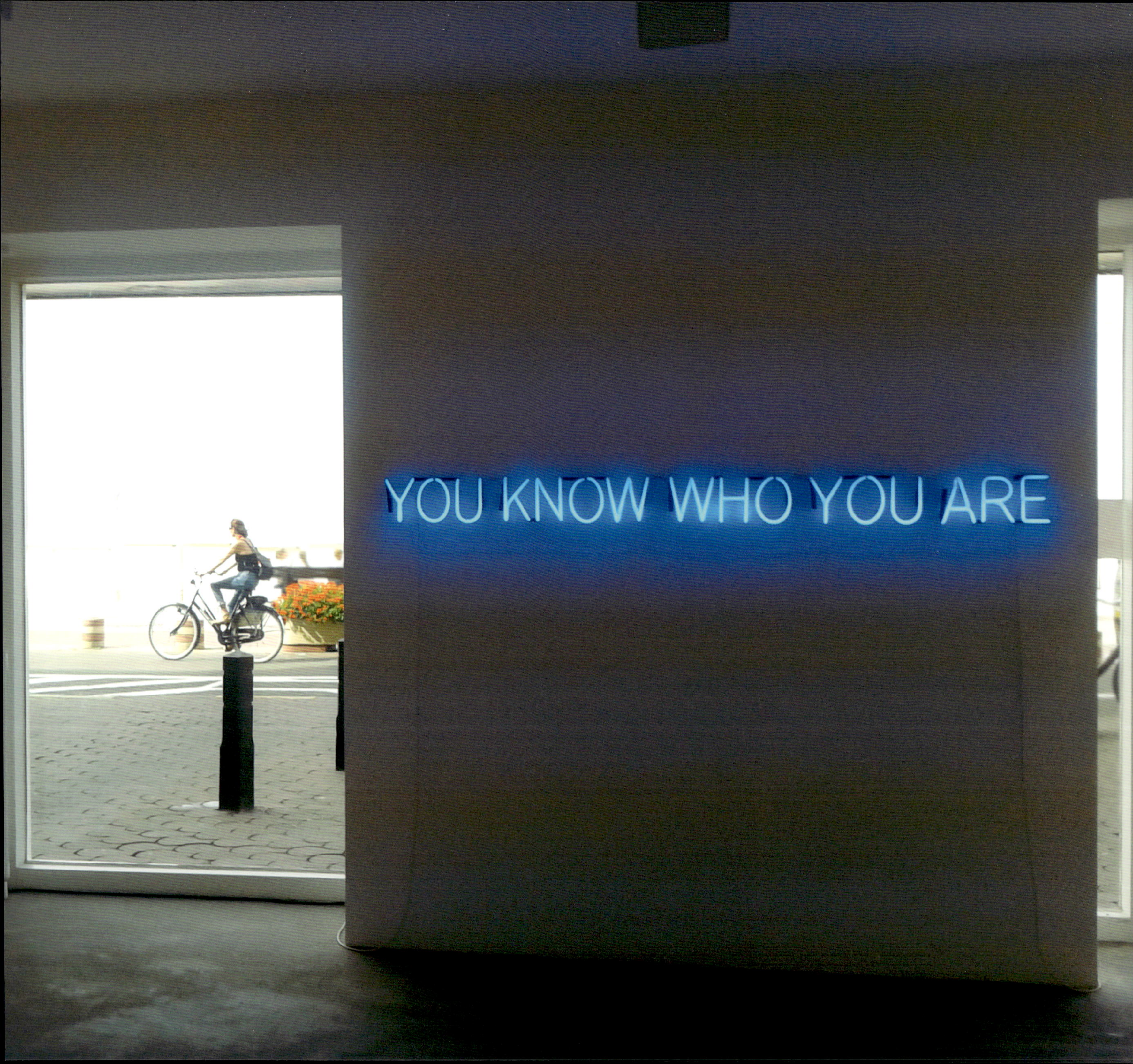

YOU KNOW WHO YOU ARE

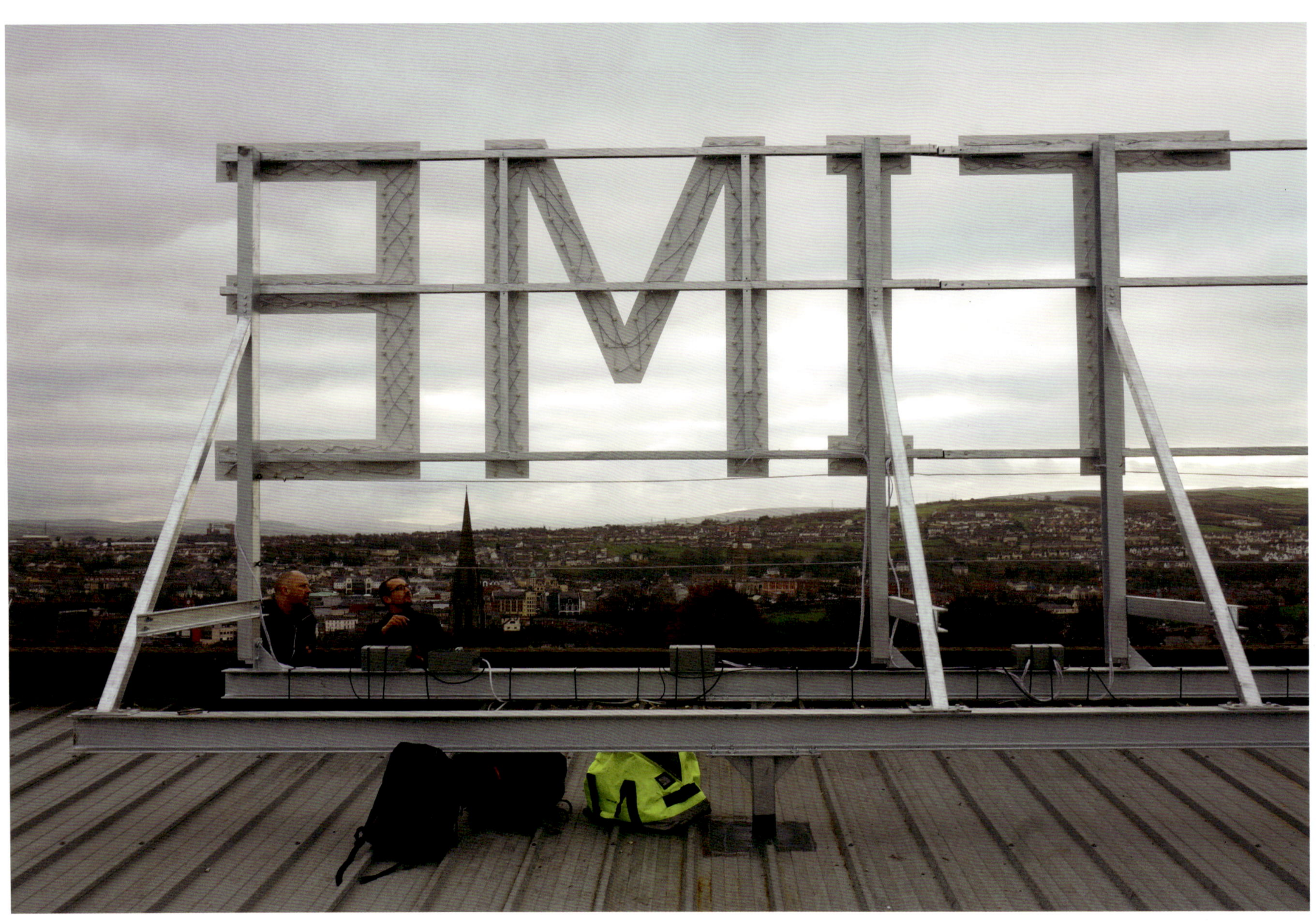

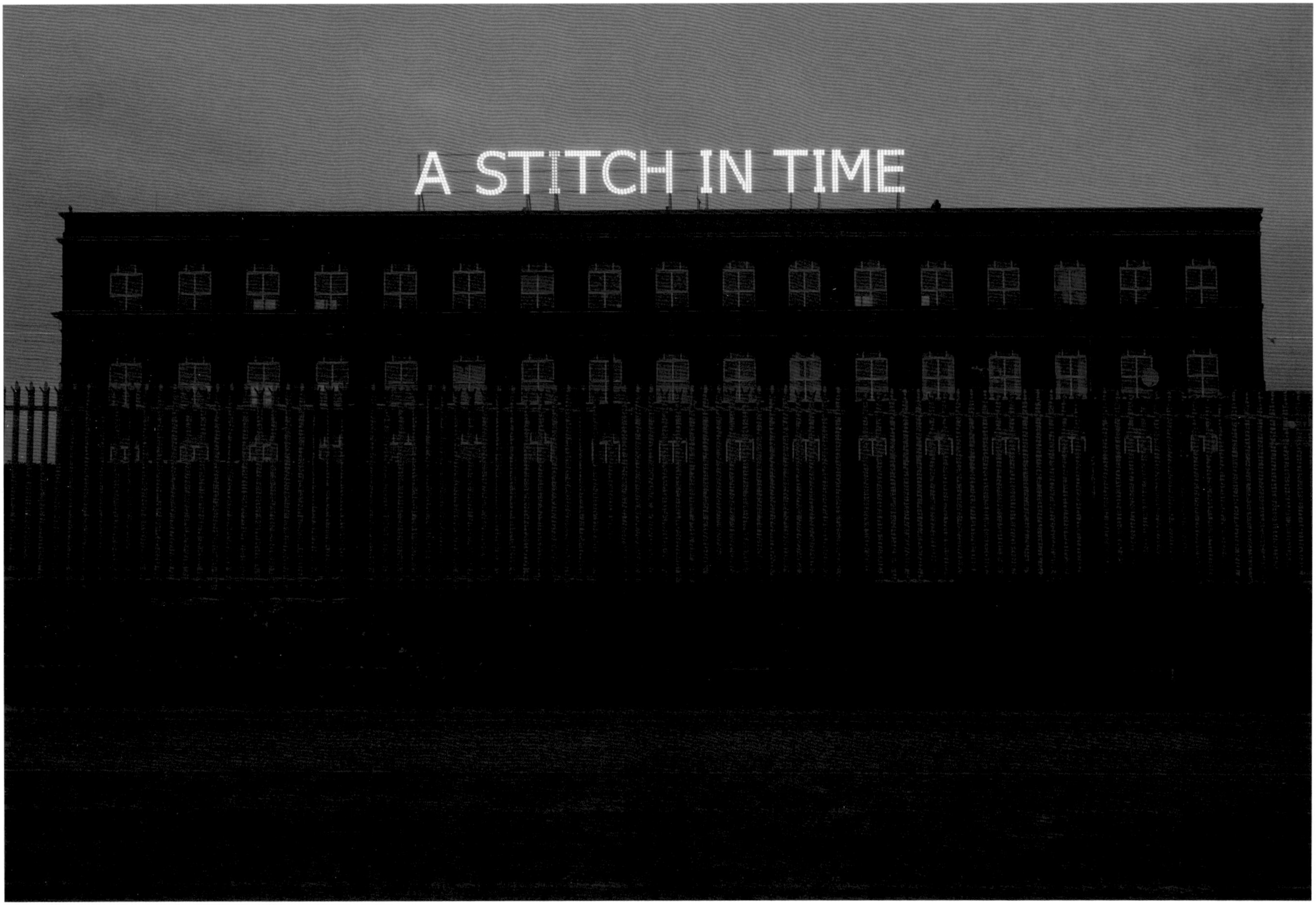

A STITCH IN TIME

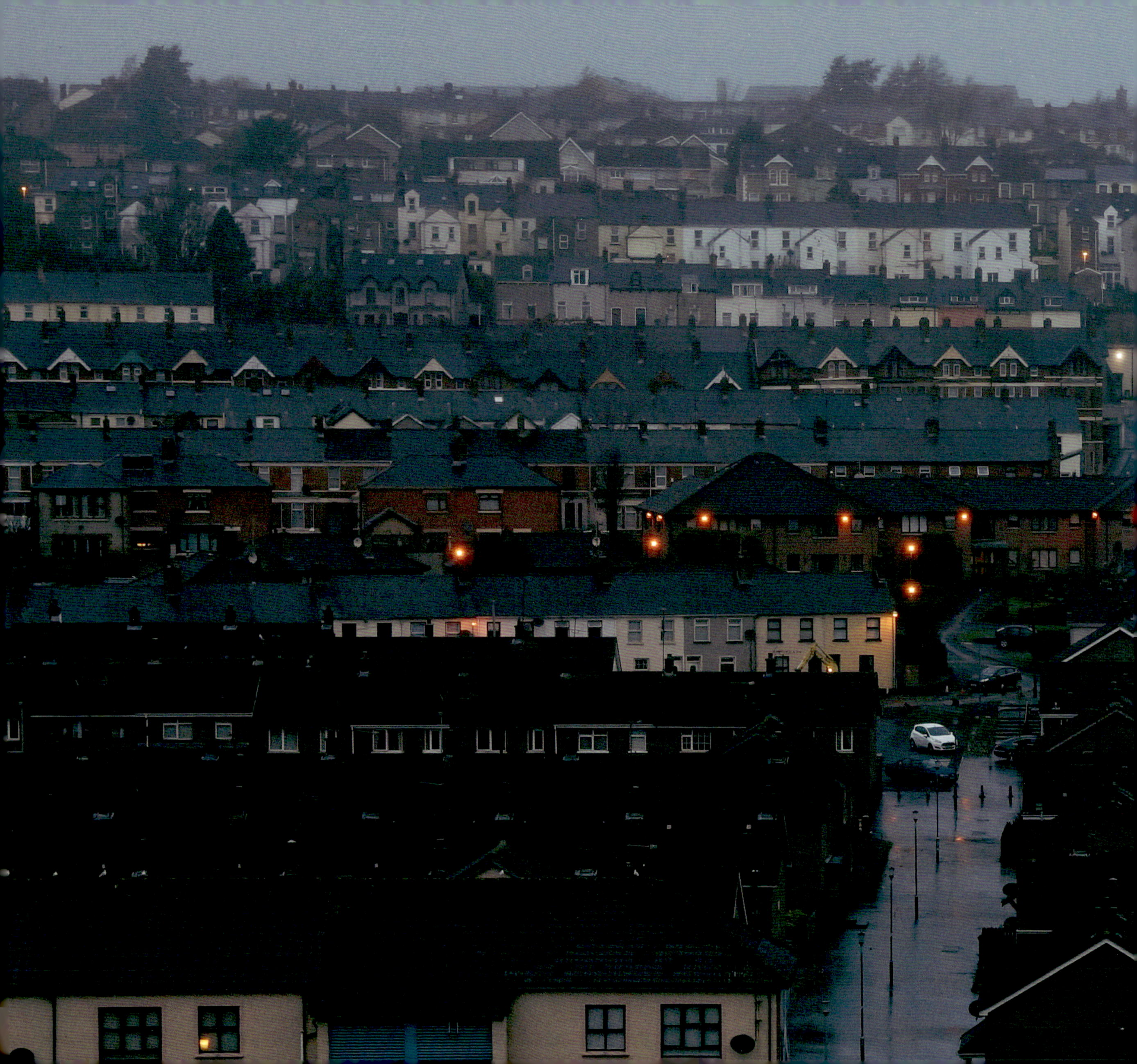

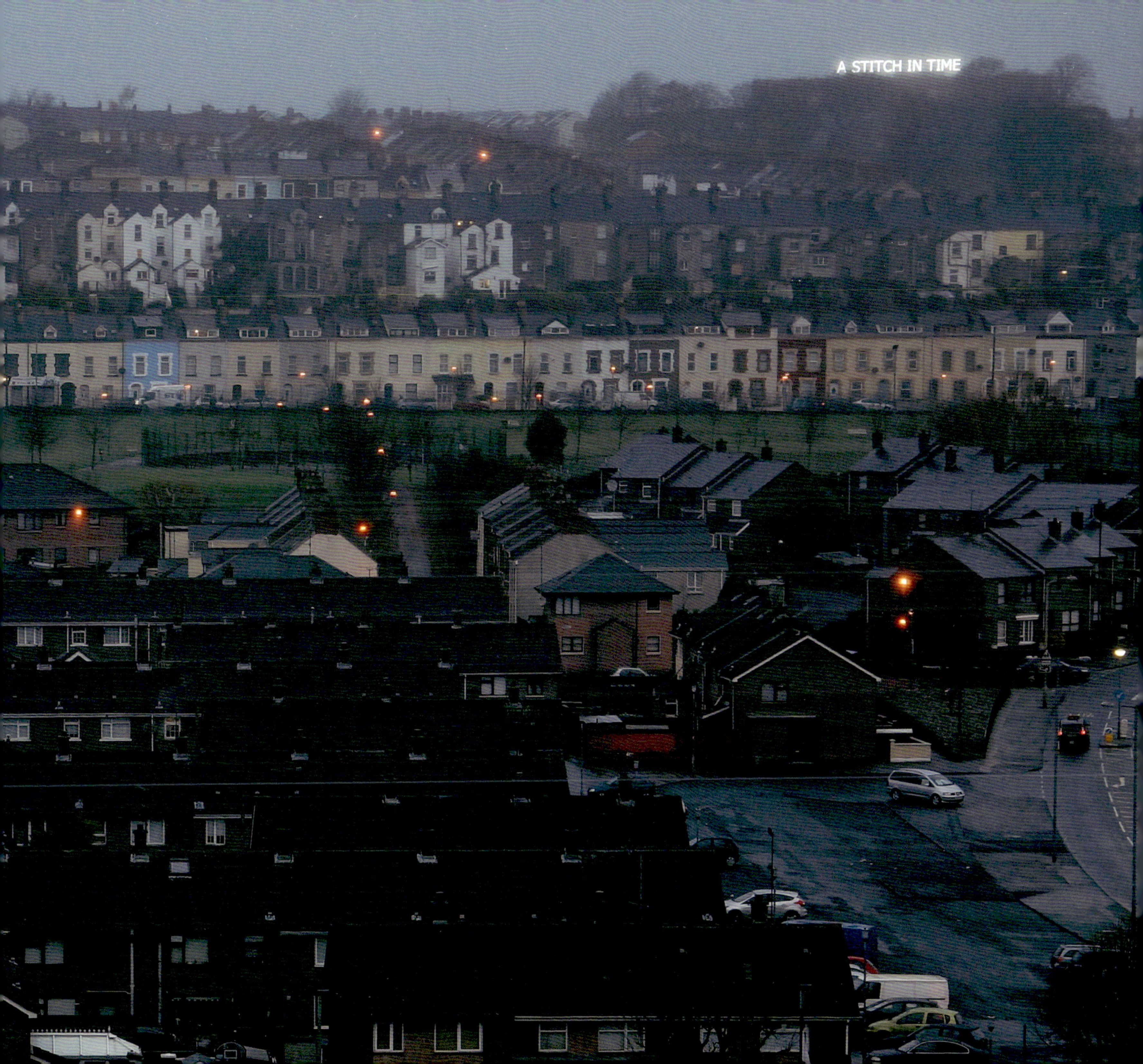
A STITCH IN TIME

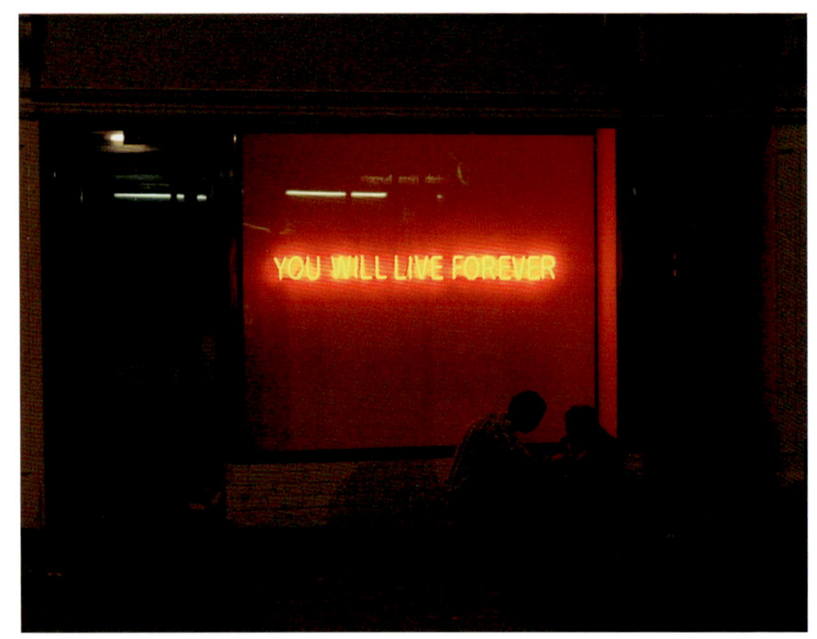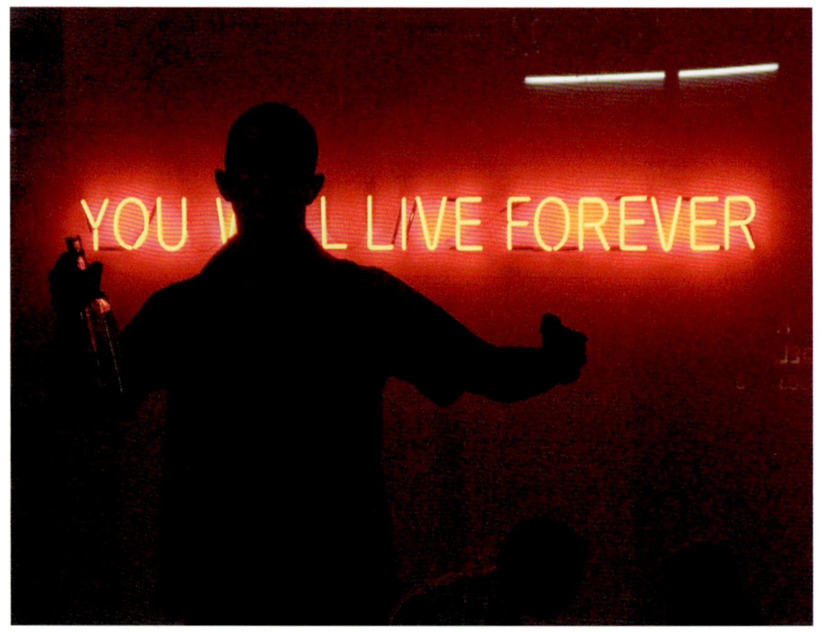
YOU WILL LIVE FOREVER
YOU WILL LIVE FOREVER

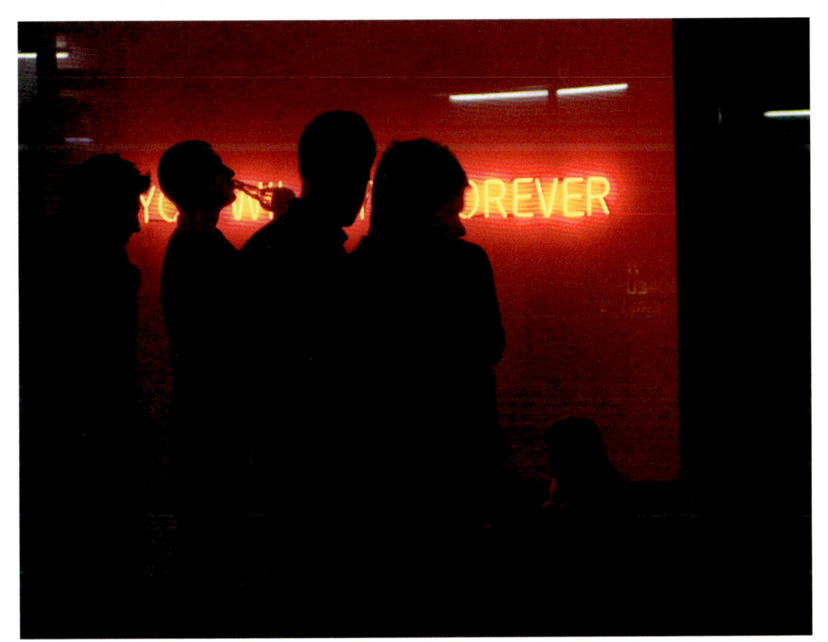

YOU WILL LIVE FOREVER

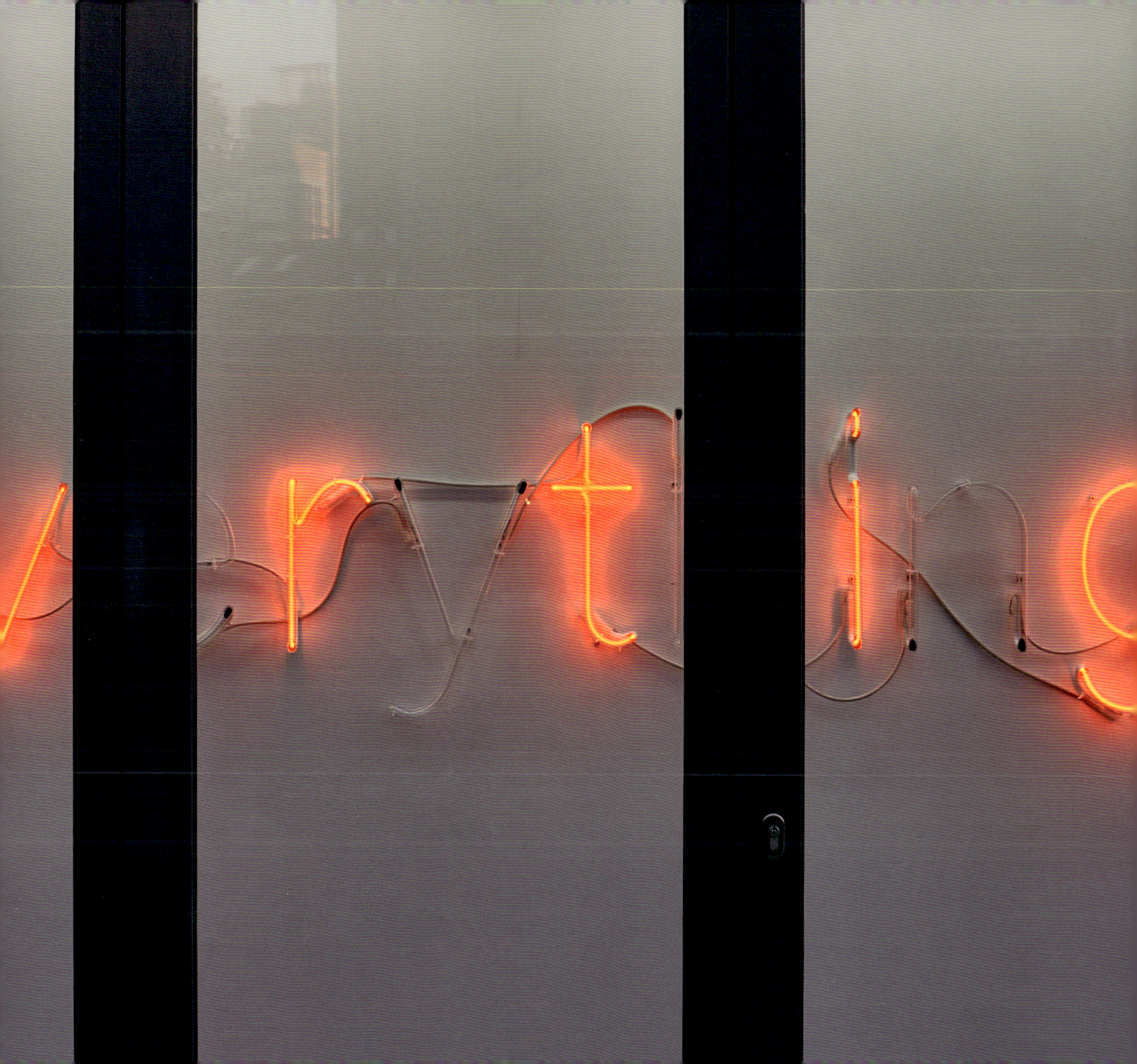

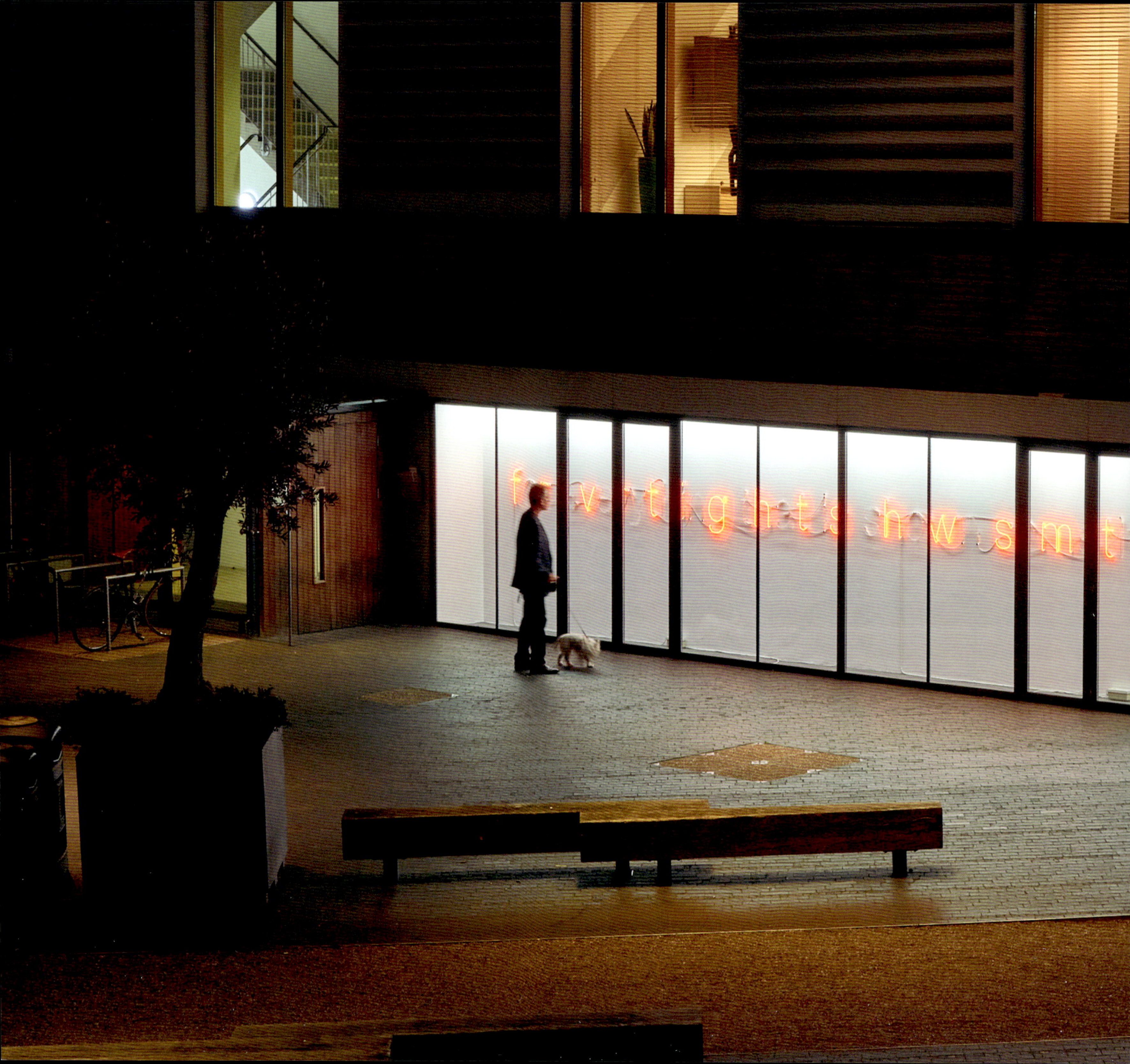

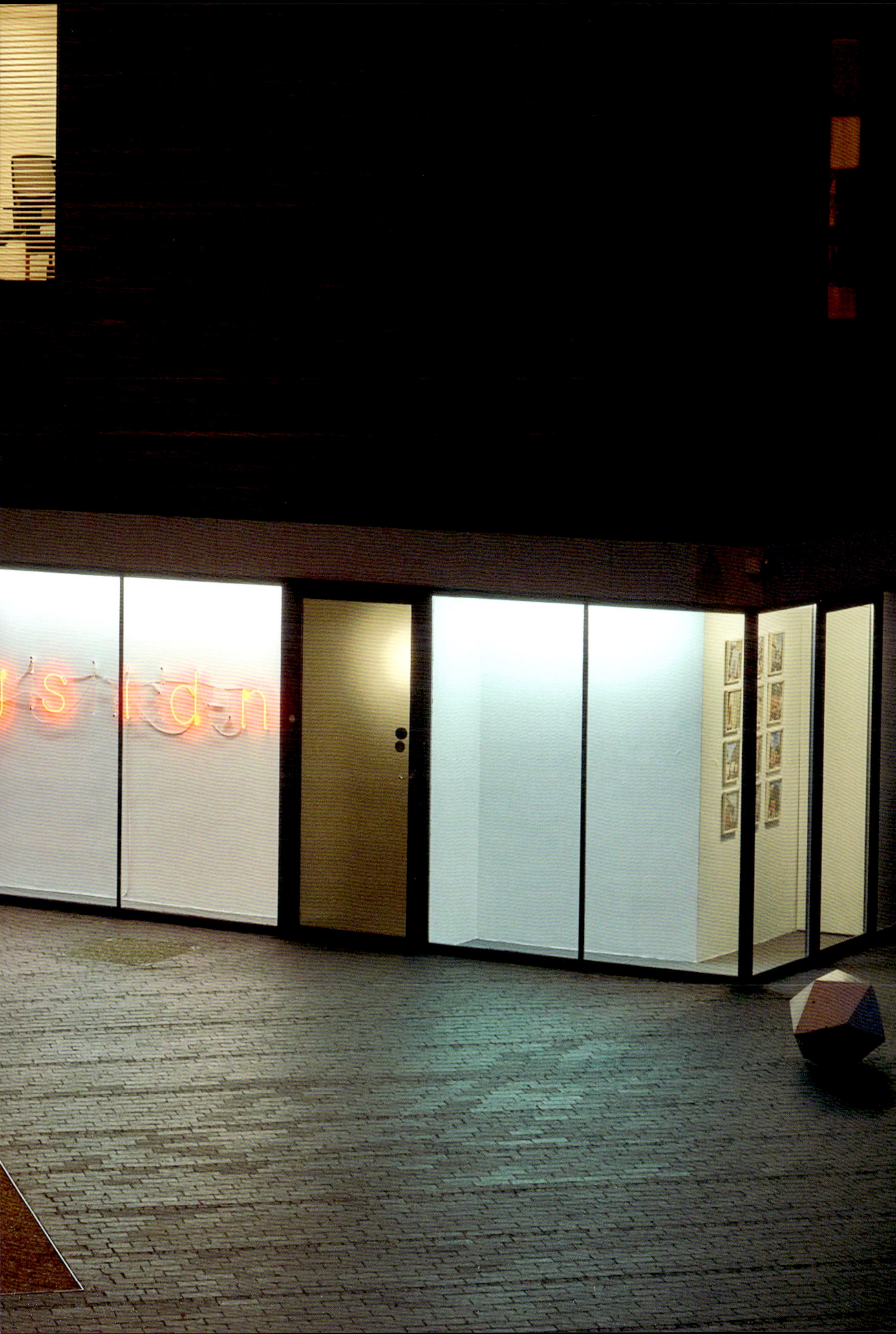

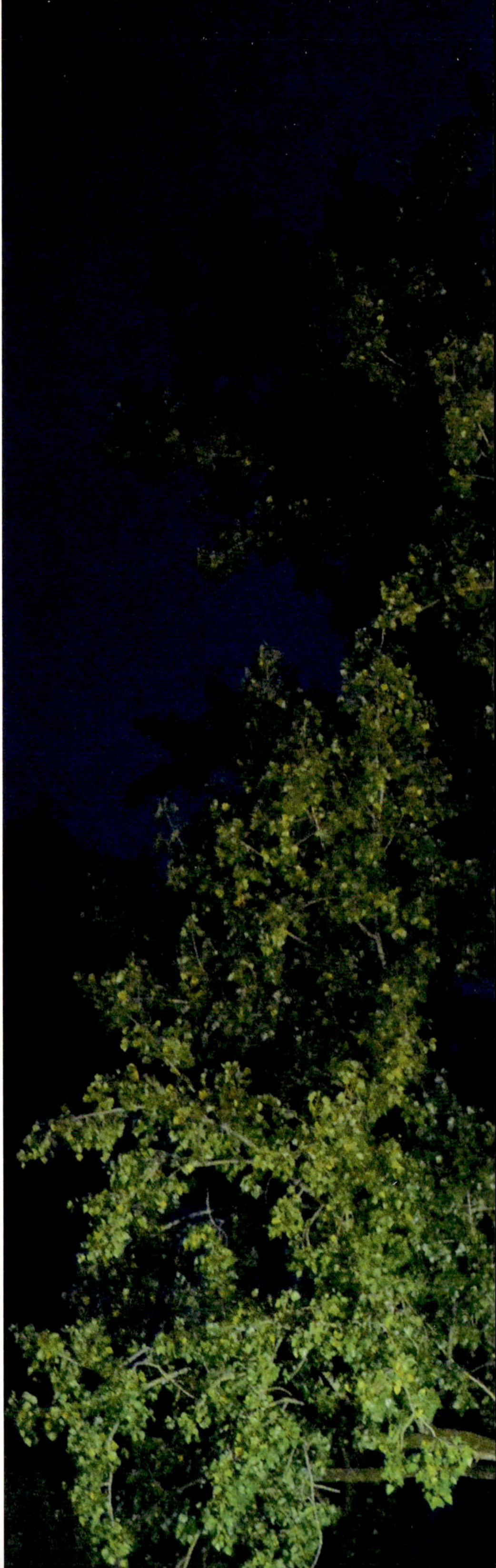

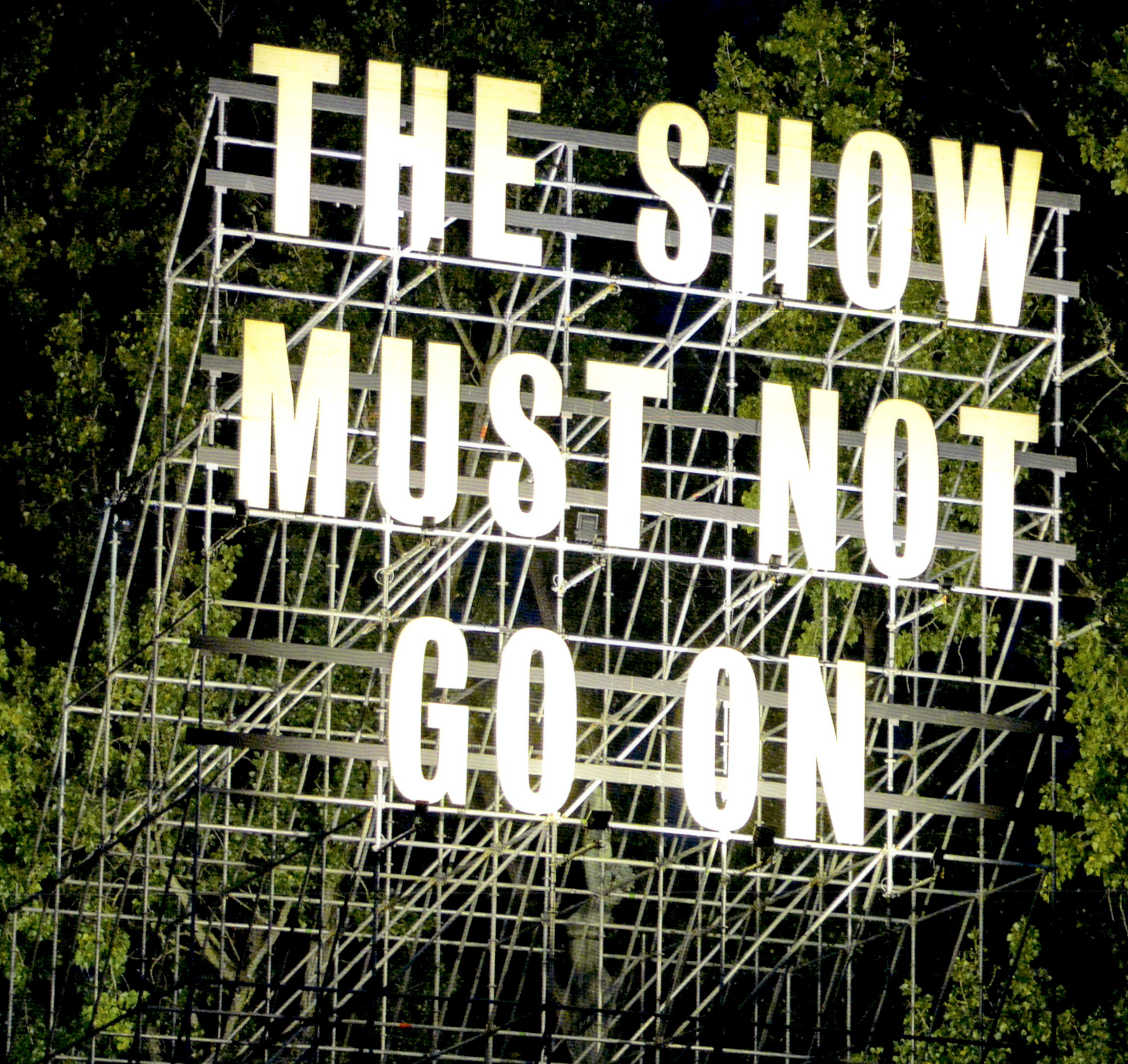
THE SHOW
MUST NOT
GO ON

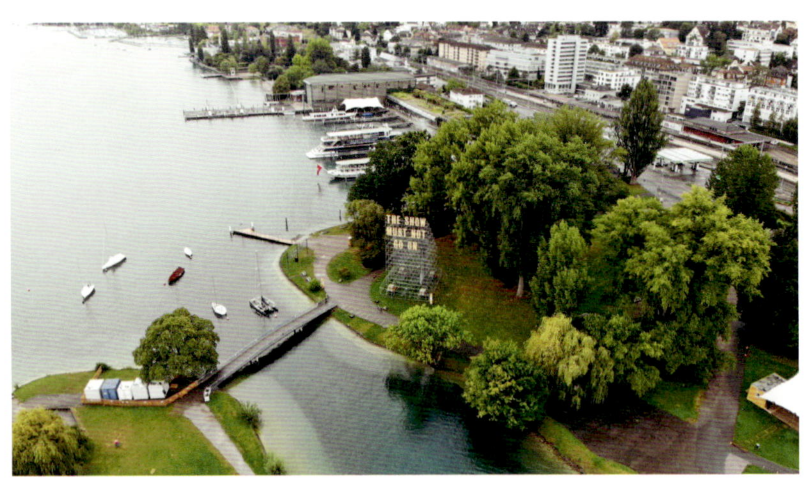

THE SHOW
MUST NOT
GO ON

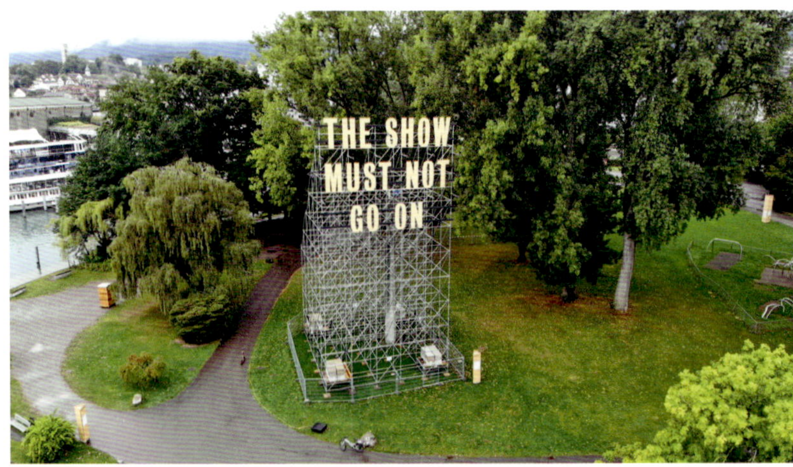

THE SHOW
MUST NOT
GO ON

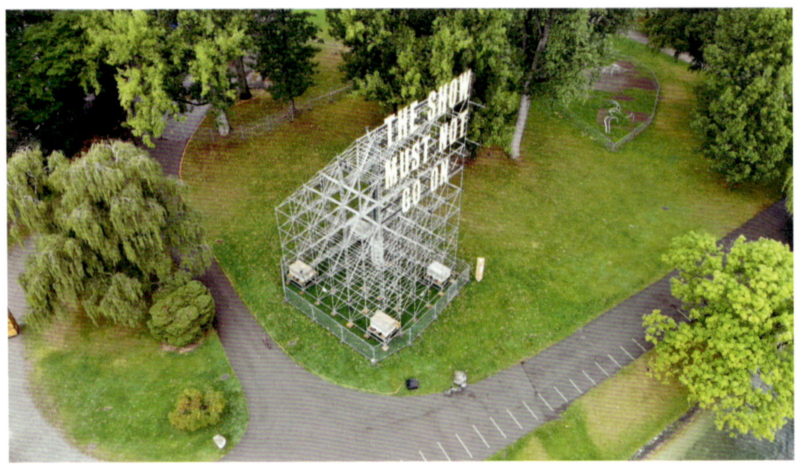

THE SHOW
MUST NOT
GO ON

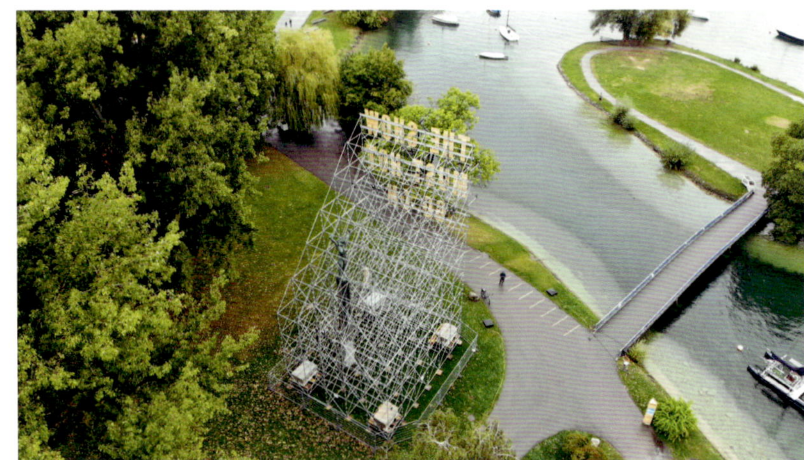

THE SHOW
MUST NOT
GO ON

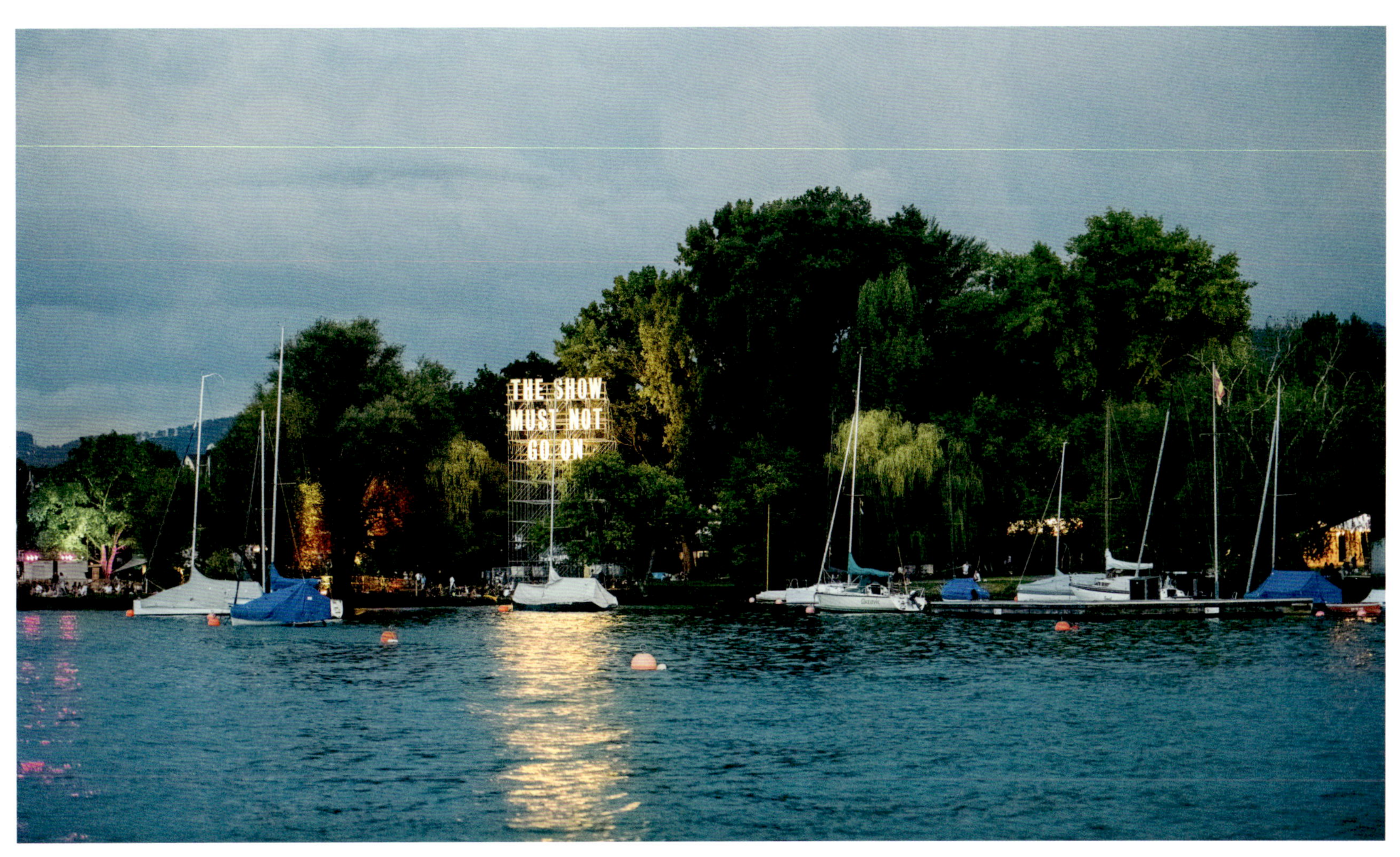
THE SHOW
MUST NOT
GO ON

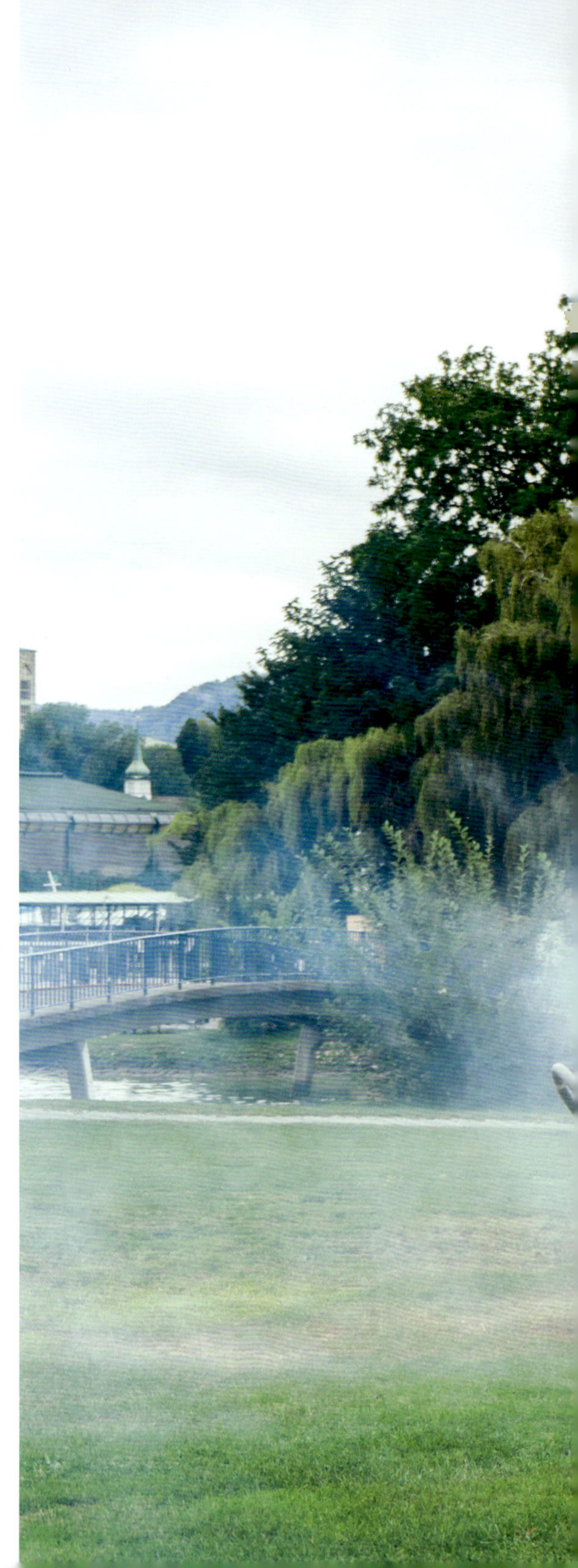

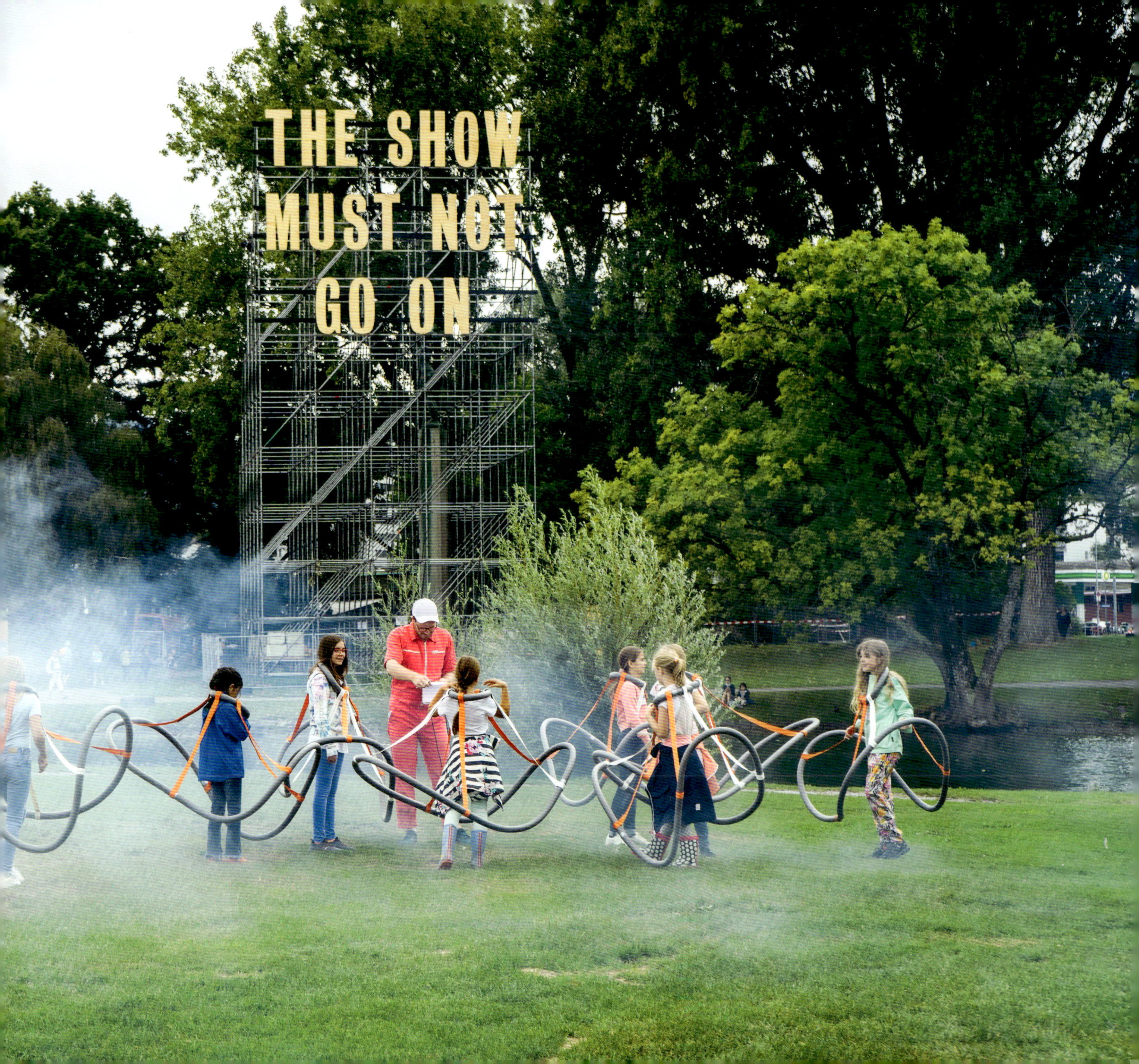

THE SHOW
MUST NOT
GO ON

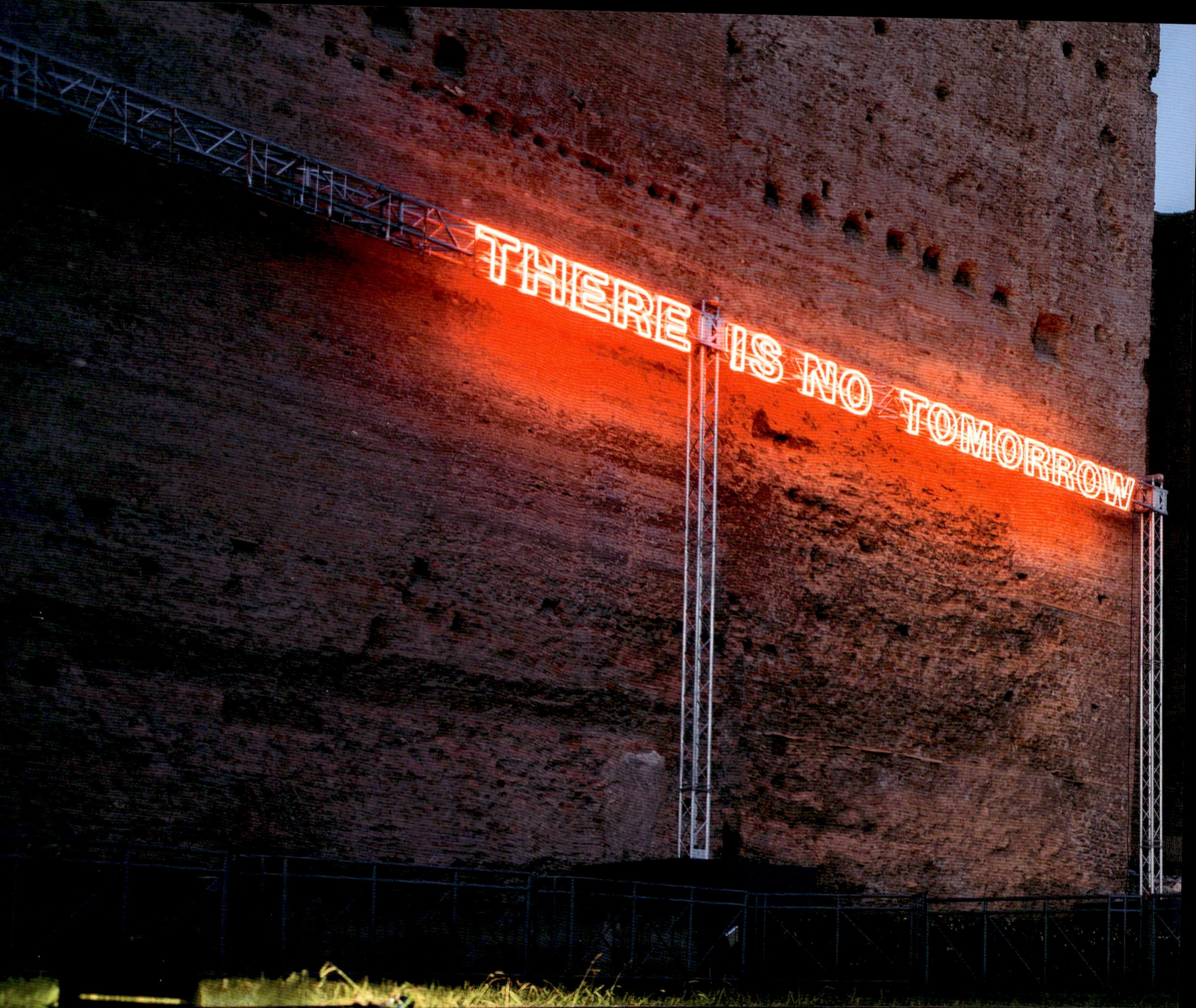
THERE IS NO TOMORROW

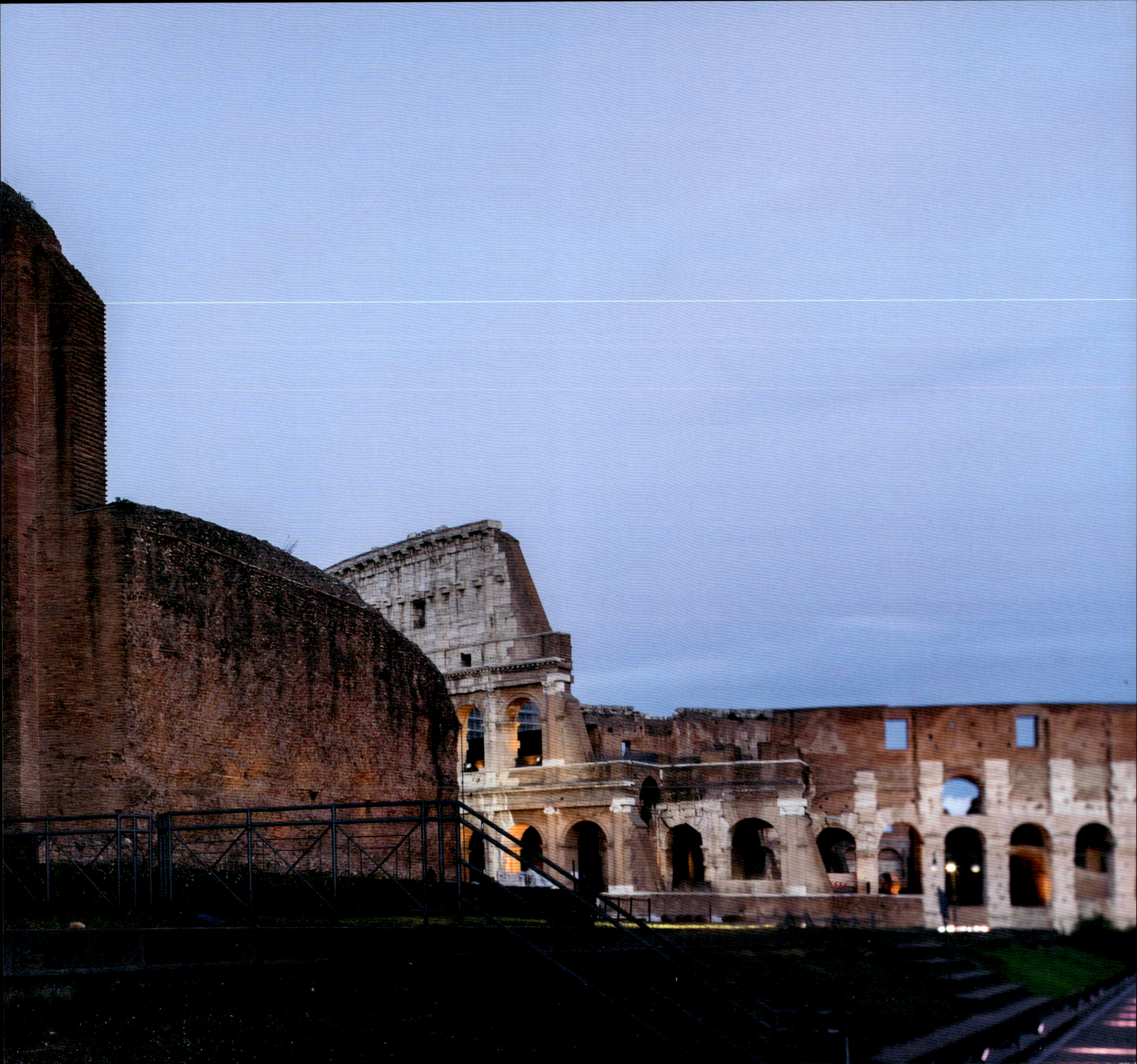

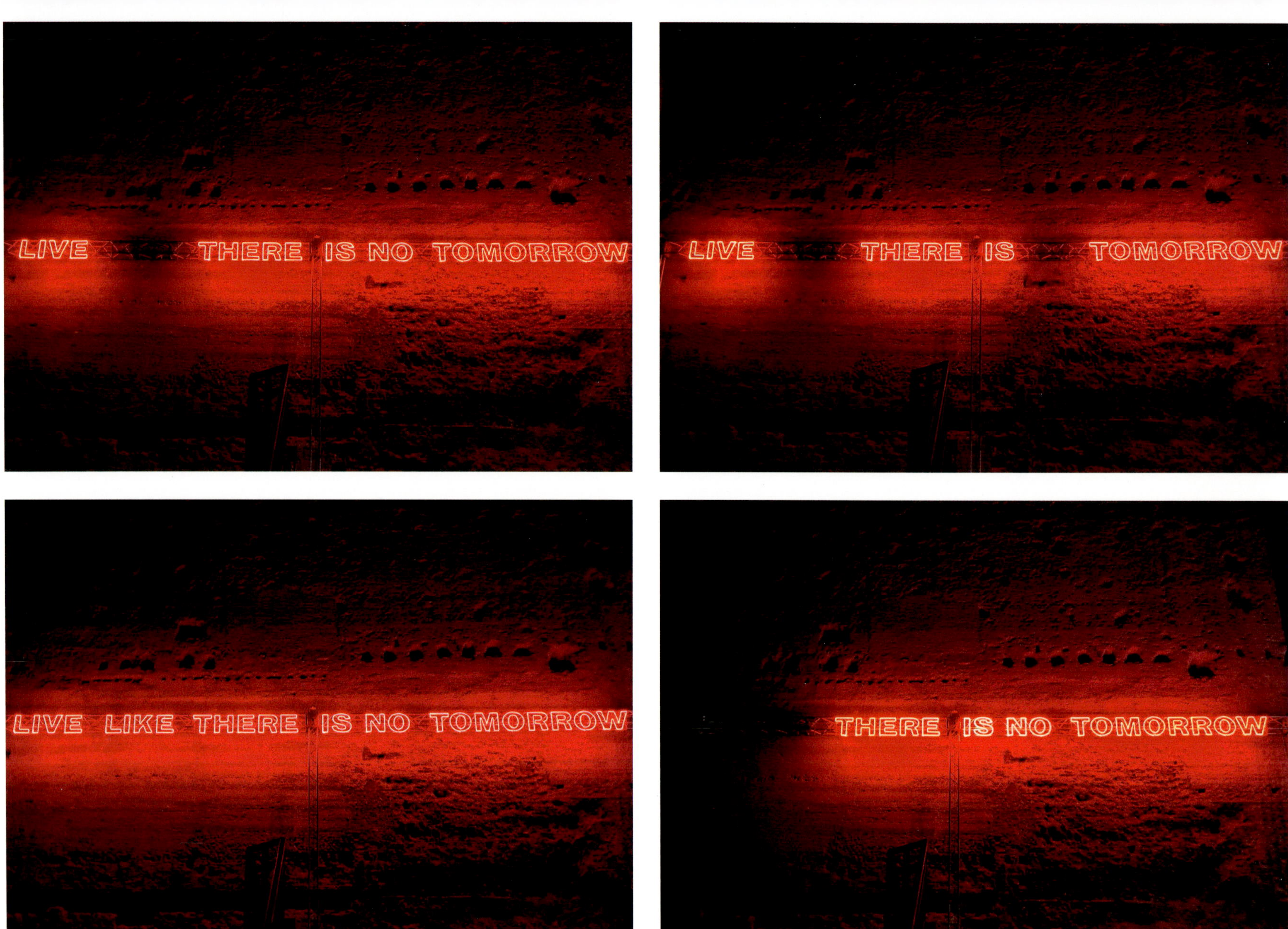
LIVE   THERE   IS NO TOMORROW
LIVE   THERE   IS   TOMORROW
LIVE LIKE THERE   IS NO TOMORROW
THERE   IS NO TOMORROW

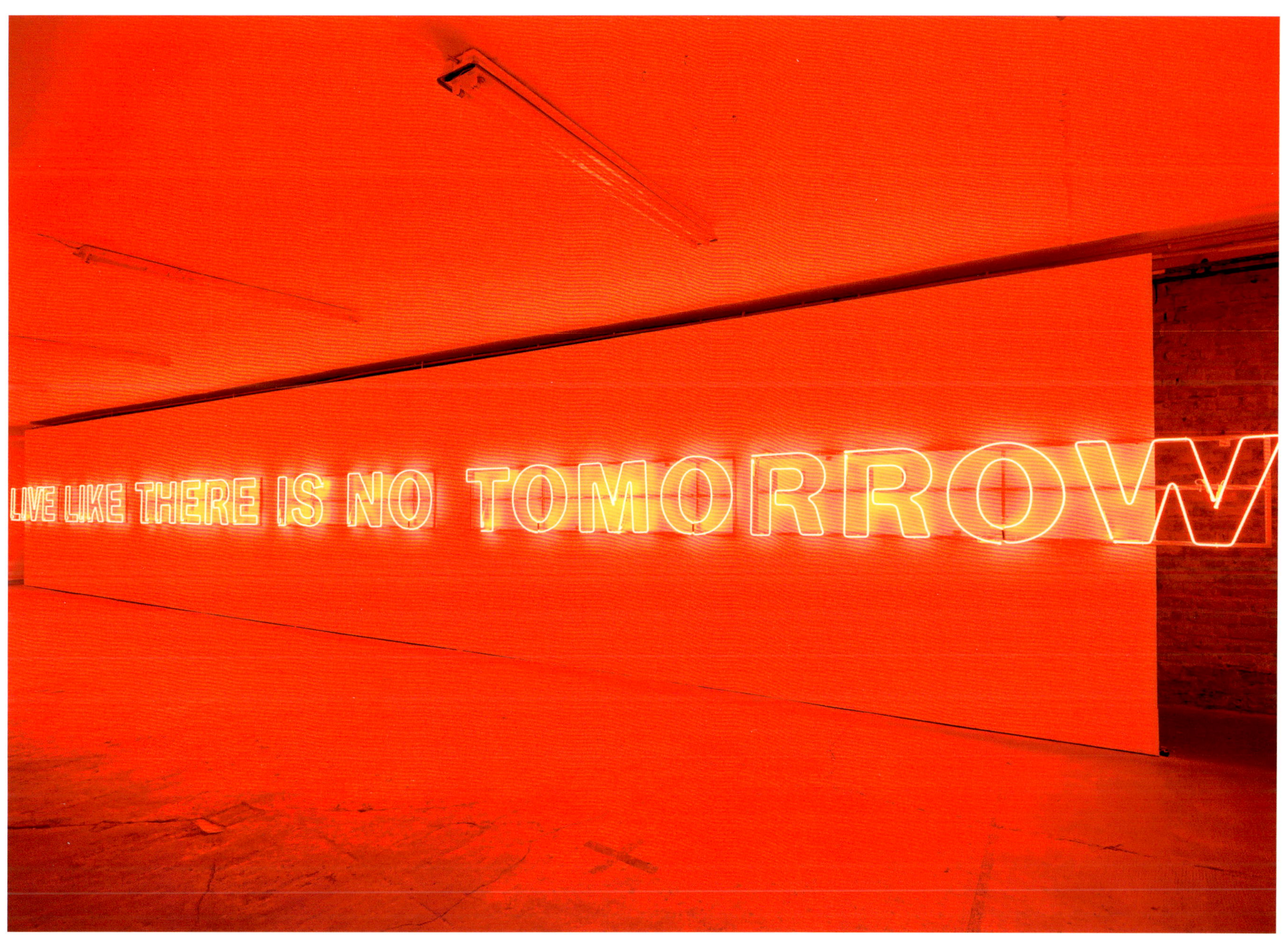

LIVE LIKE THERE IS NO TOMORROW

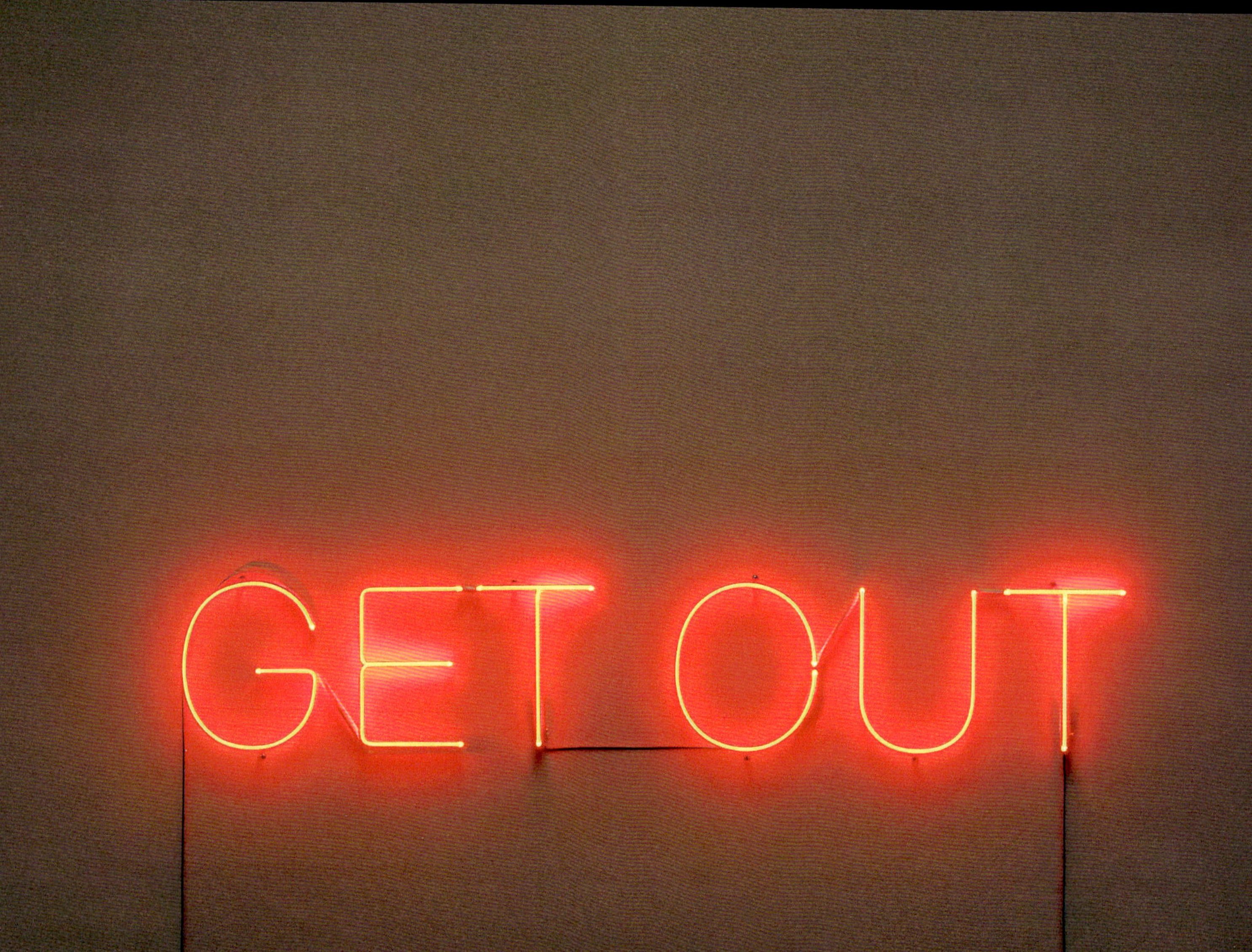

GET OUT

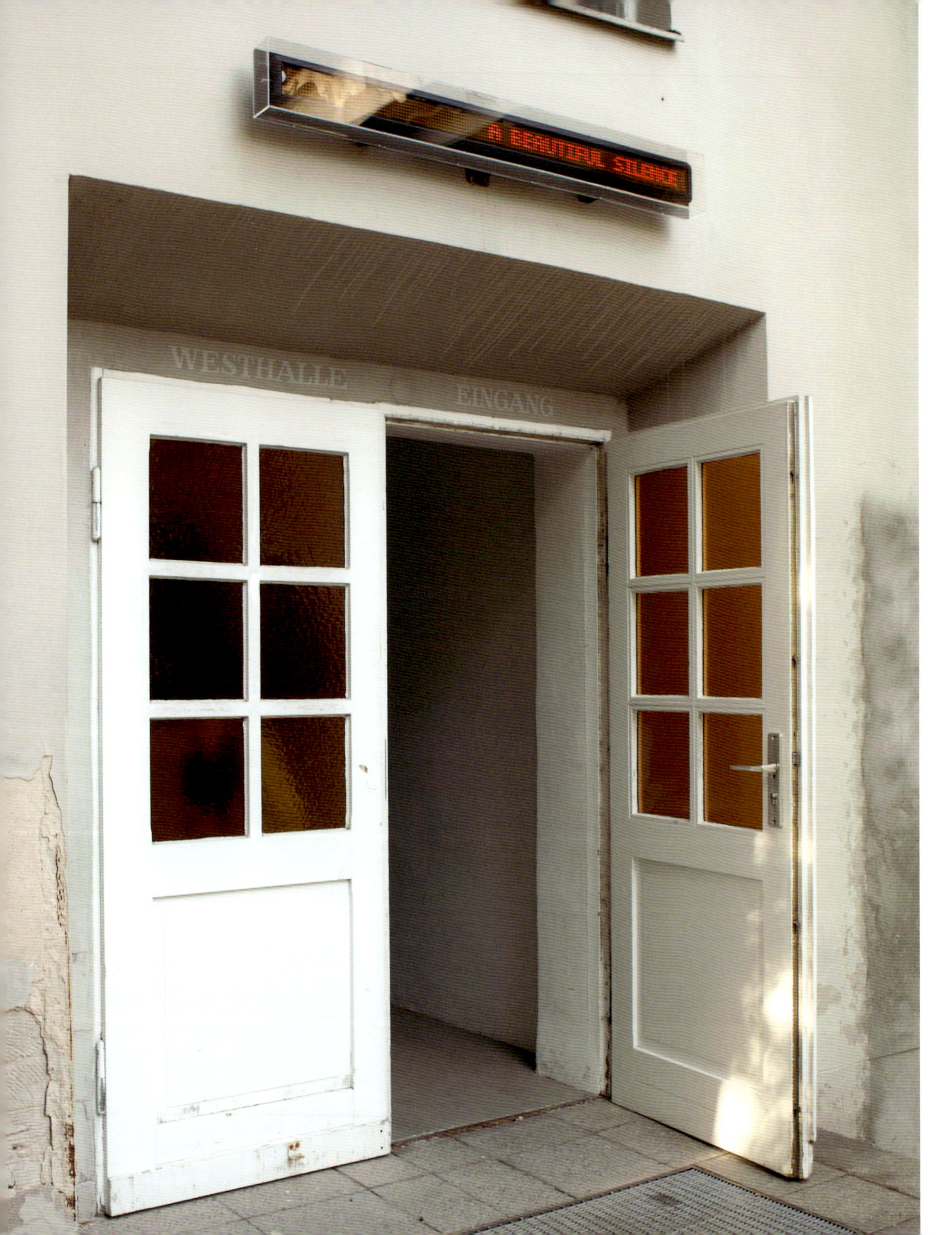

A BEAUTIFUL SILENCE
WESTHALLE
EINGANG

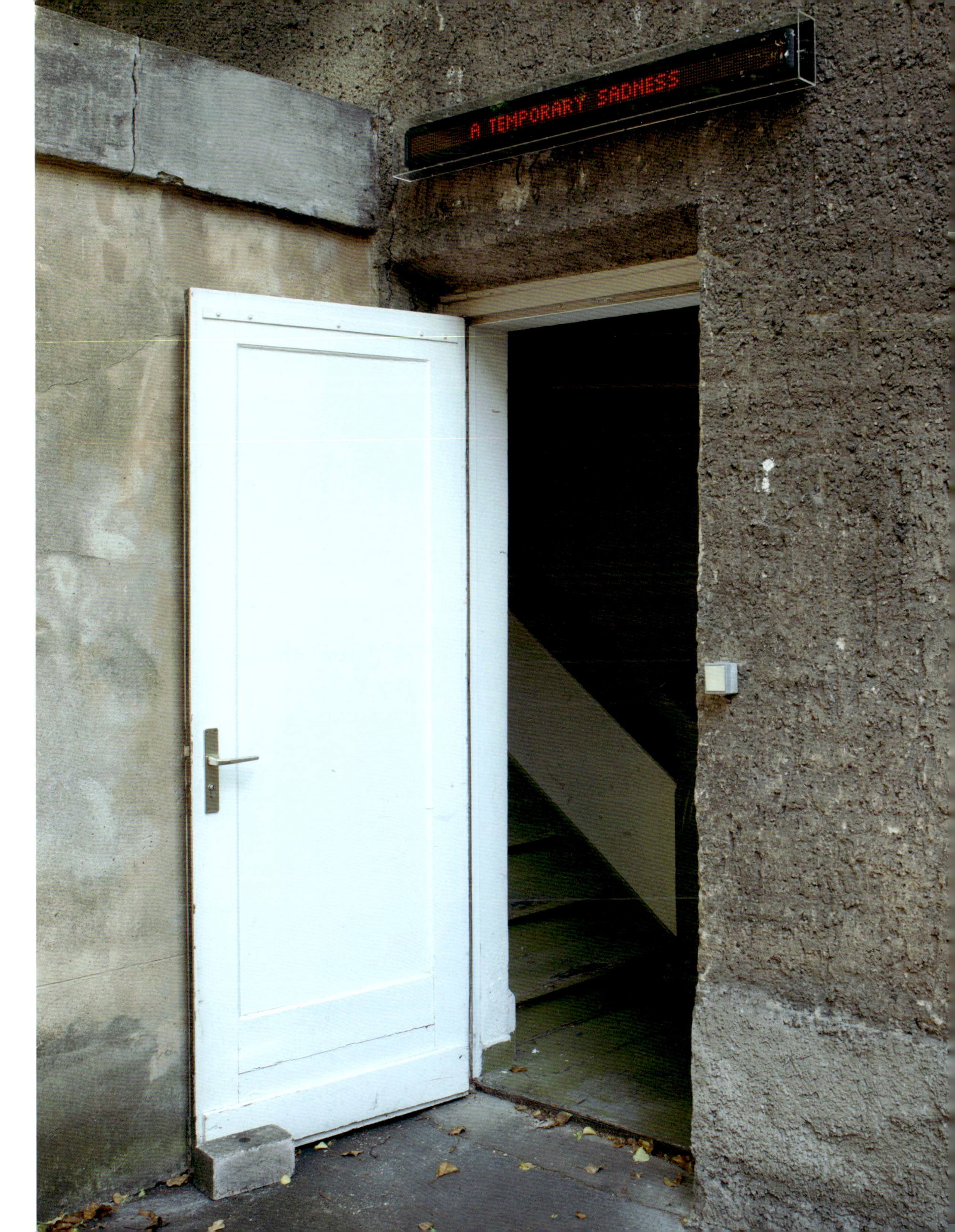
A TEMPORARY SADNESS

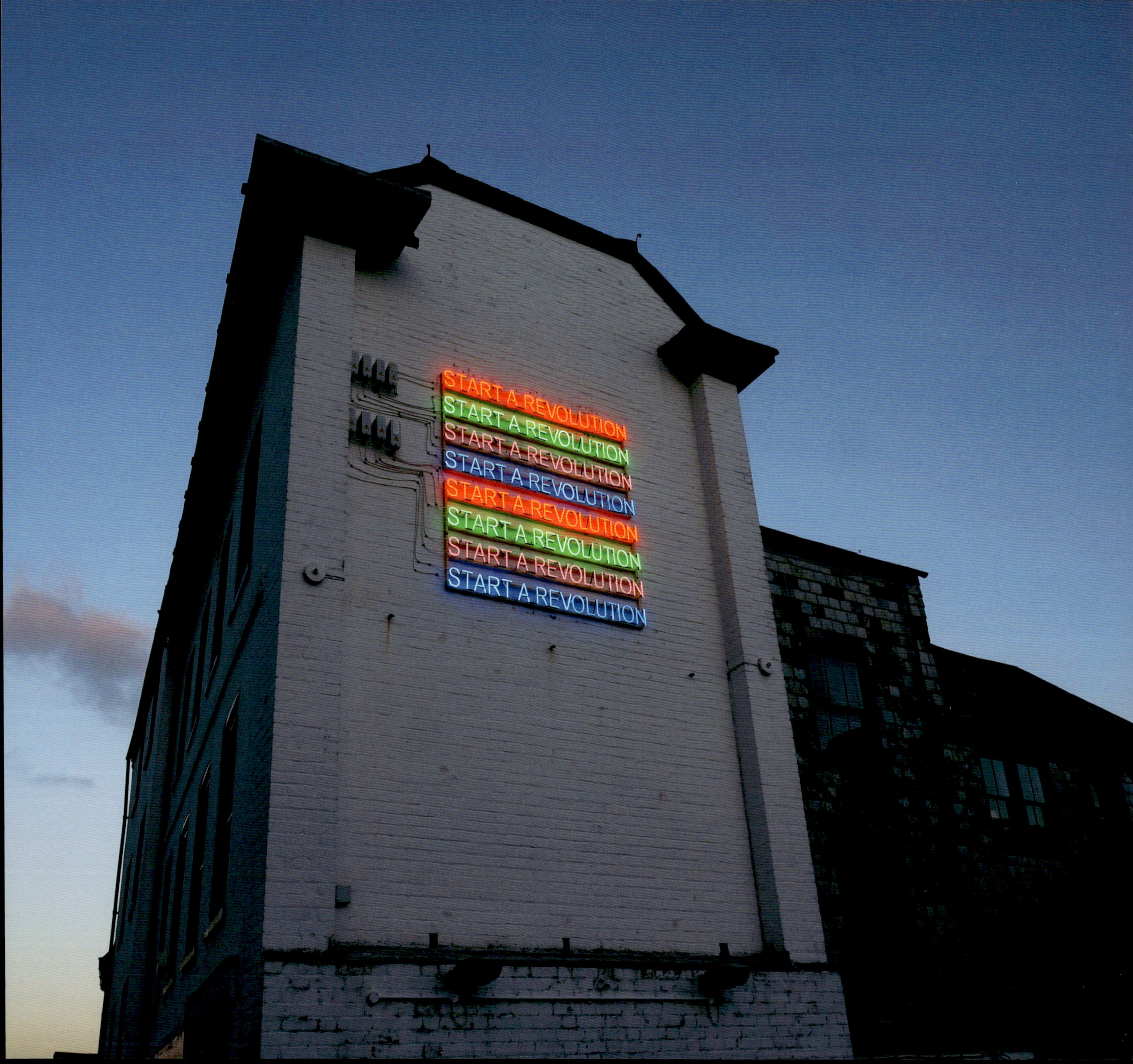
START A REVOLUTION
START A REVOLUTION
START A REVOLUTION
START A REVOLUTION
START A REVOLUTION
START A REVOLUTION
START A REVOLUTION
START A REVOLUTION

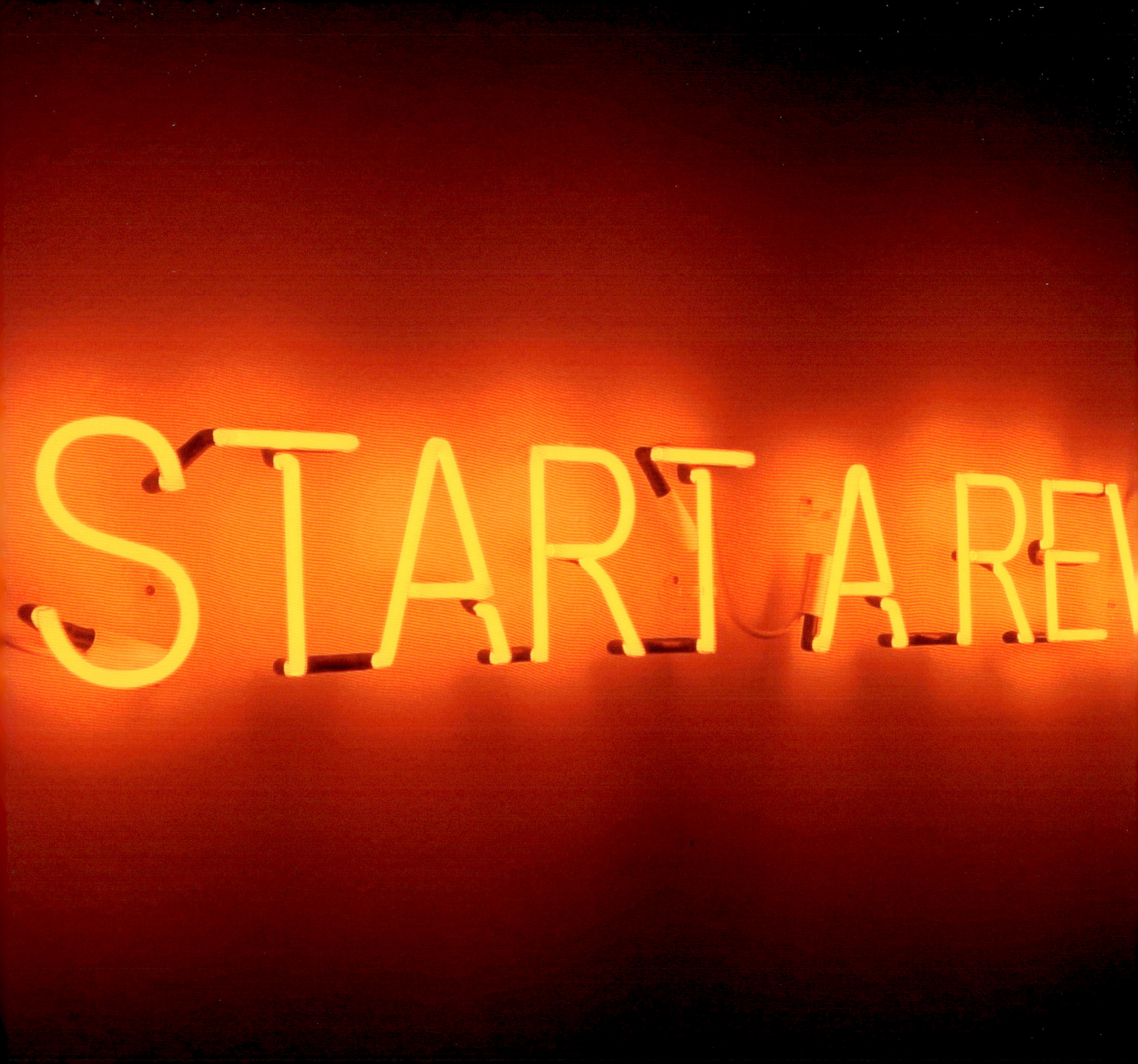

START A RE

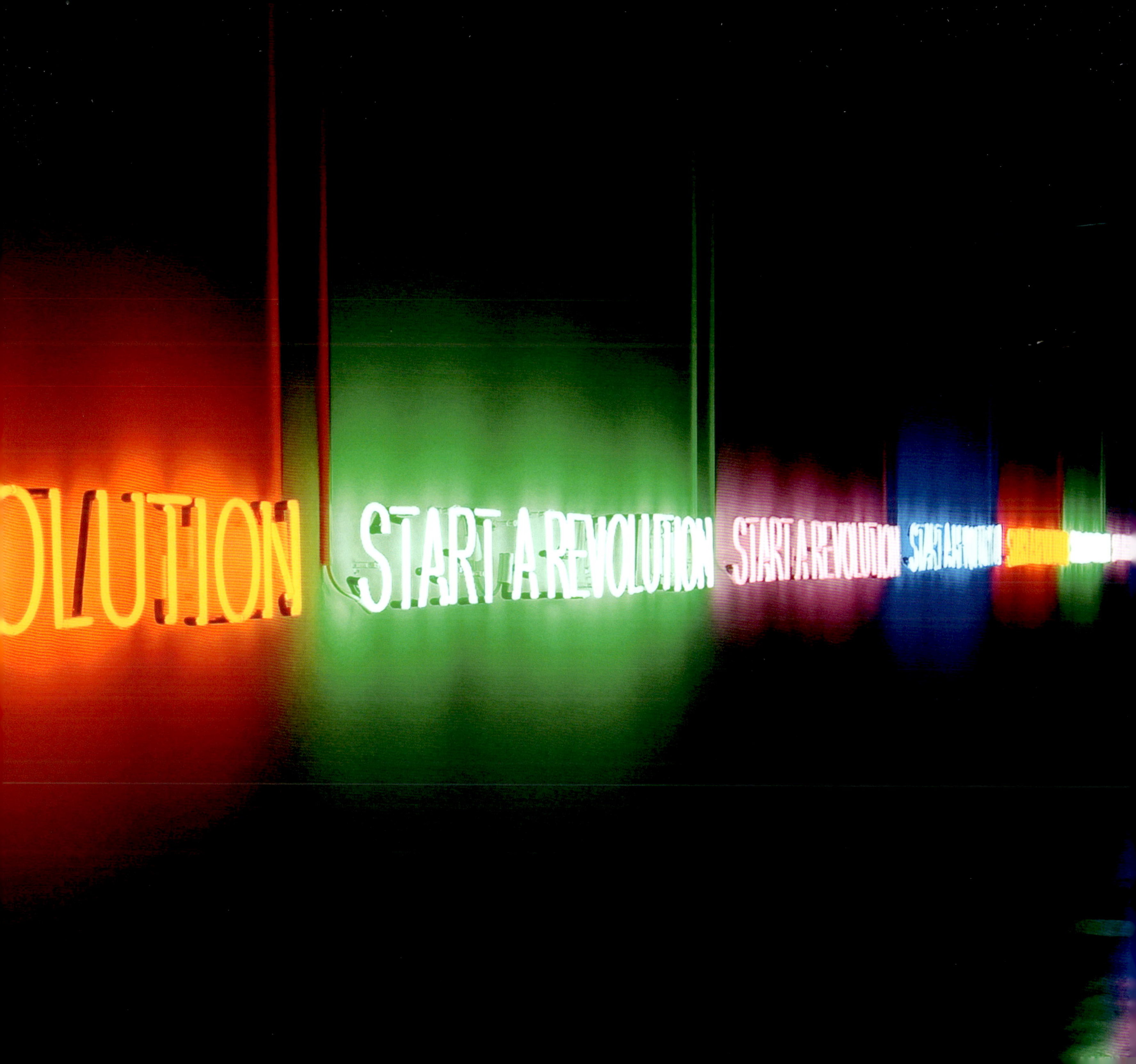

OLUTION
START A REVOLUTION
START A REVOLUTION
START A REVOLUTION

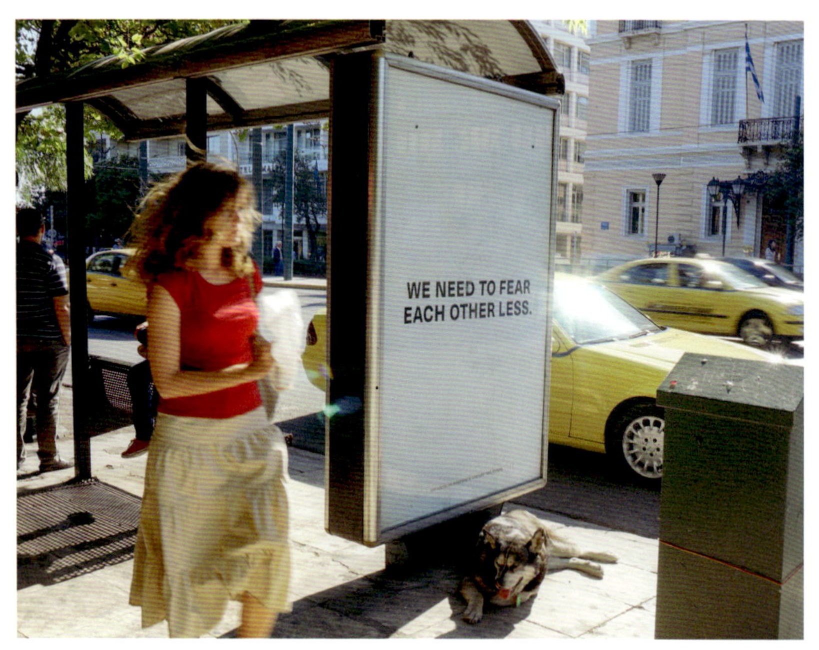
WE NEED TO FEAR
EACH OTHER LESS.

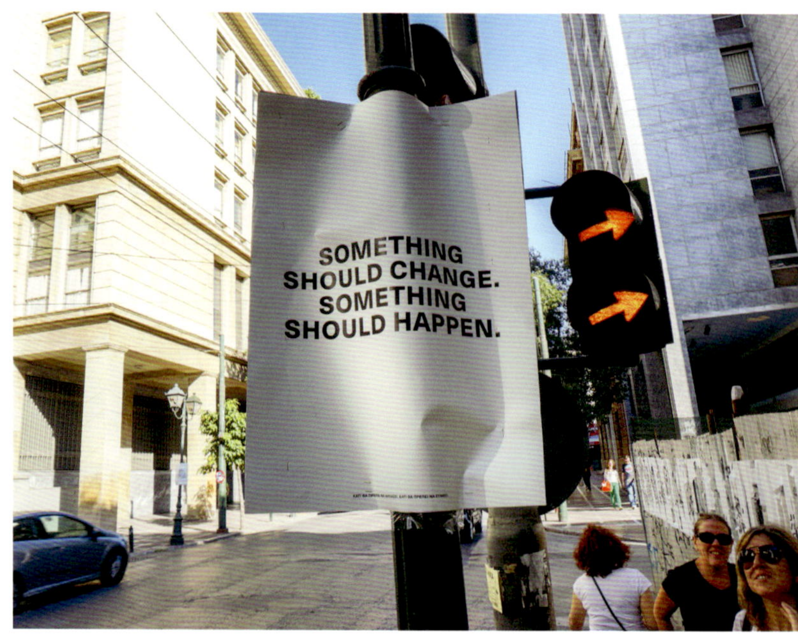
SOMETHING
SHOULD CHANGE.
SOMETHING
SHOULD HAPPEN.

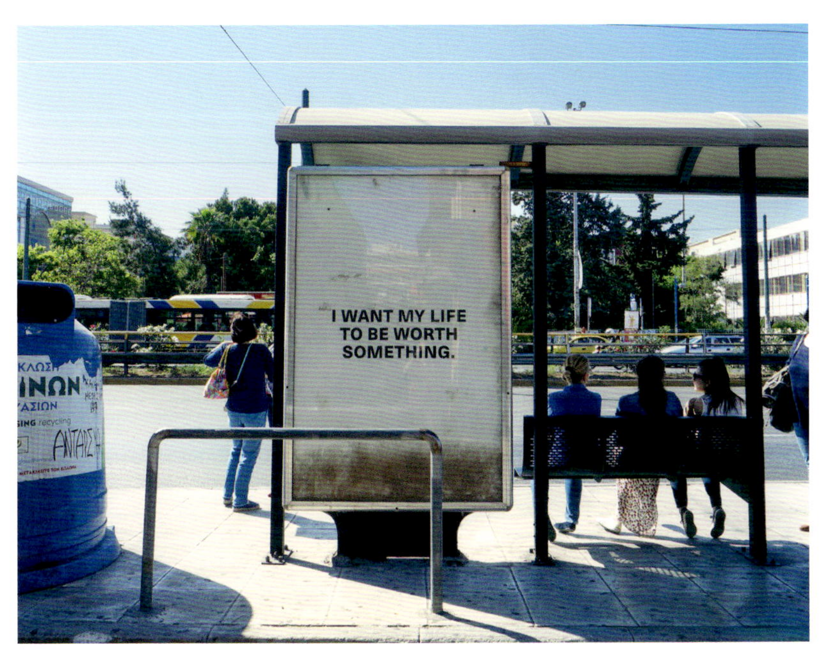
I WANT MY LIFE
TO BE WORTH
SOMETHING.

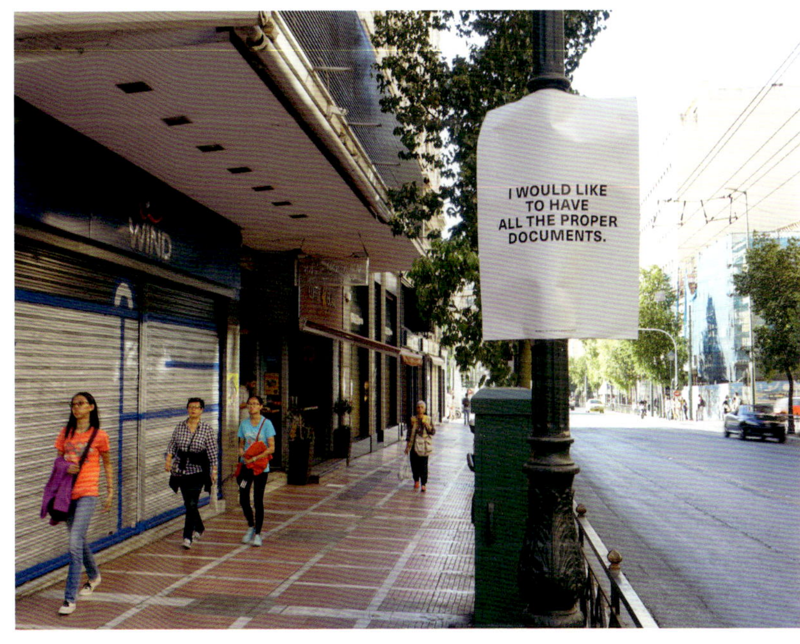
I WOULD LIKE
TO HAVE
ALL THE PROPER
DOCUMENTS.

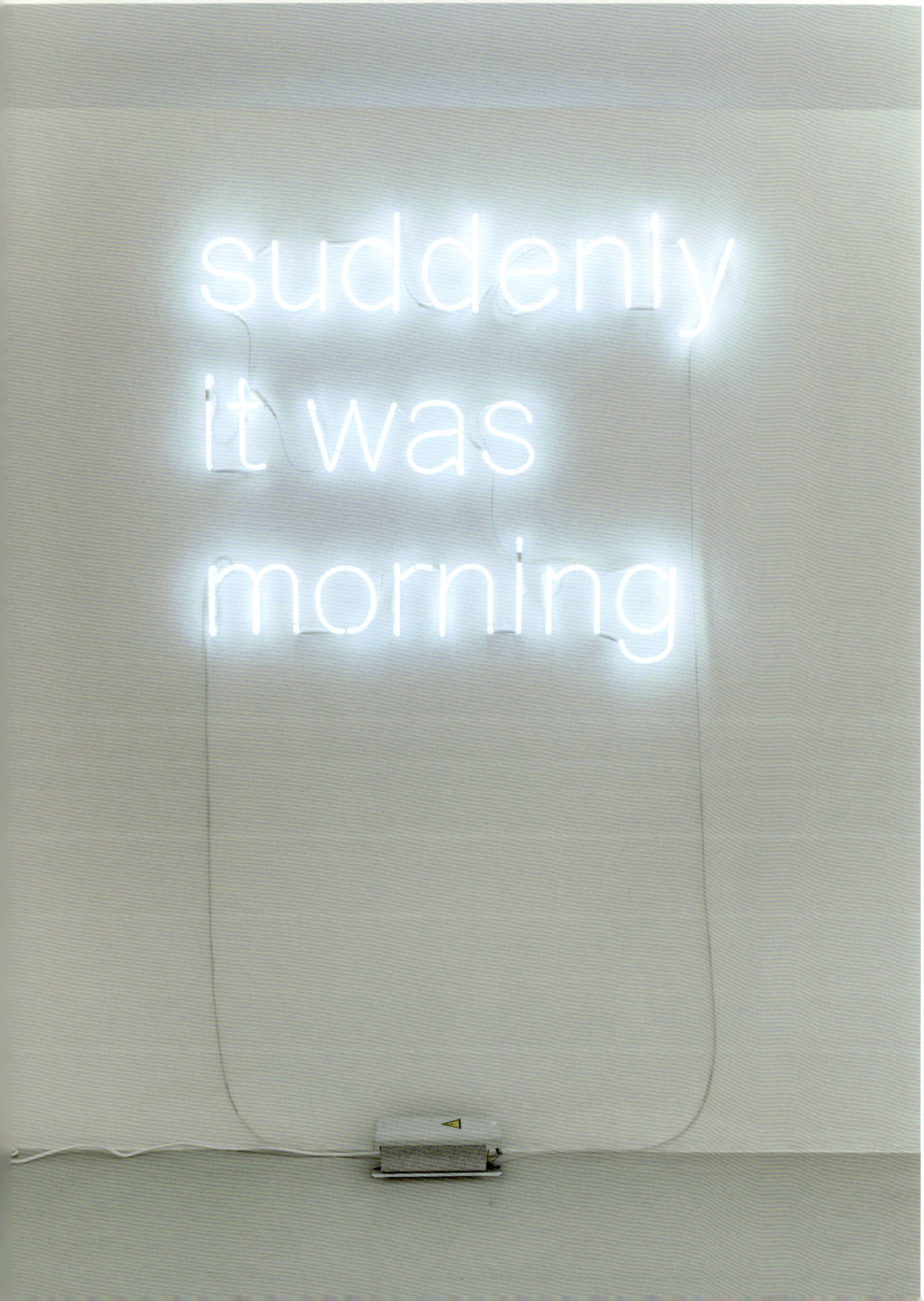

suddenly
it was
morning

suddenly
it was
night

NOTHING FOR YOU

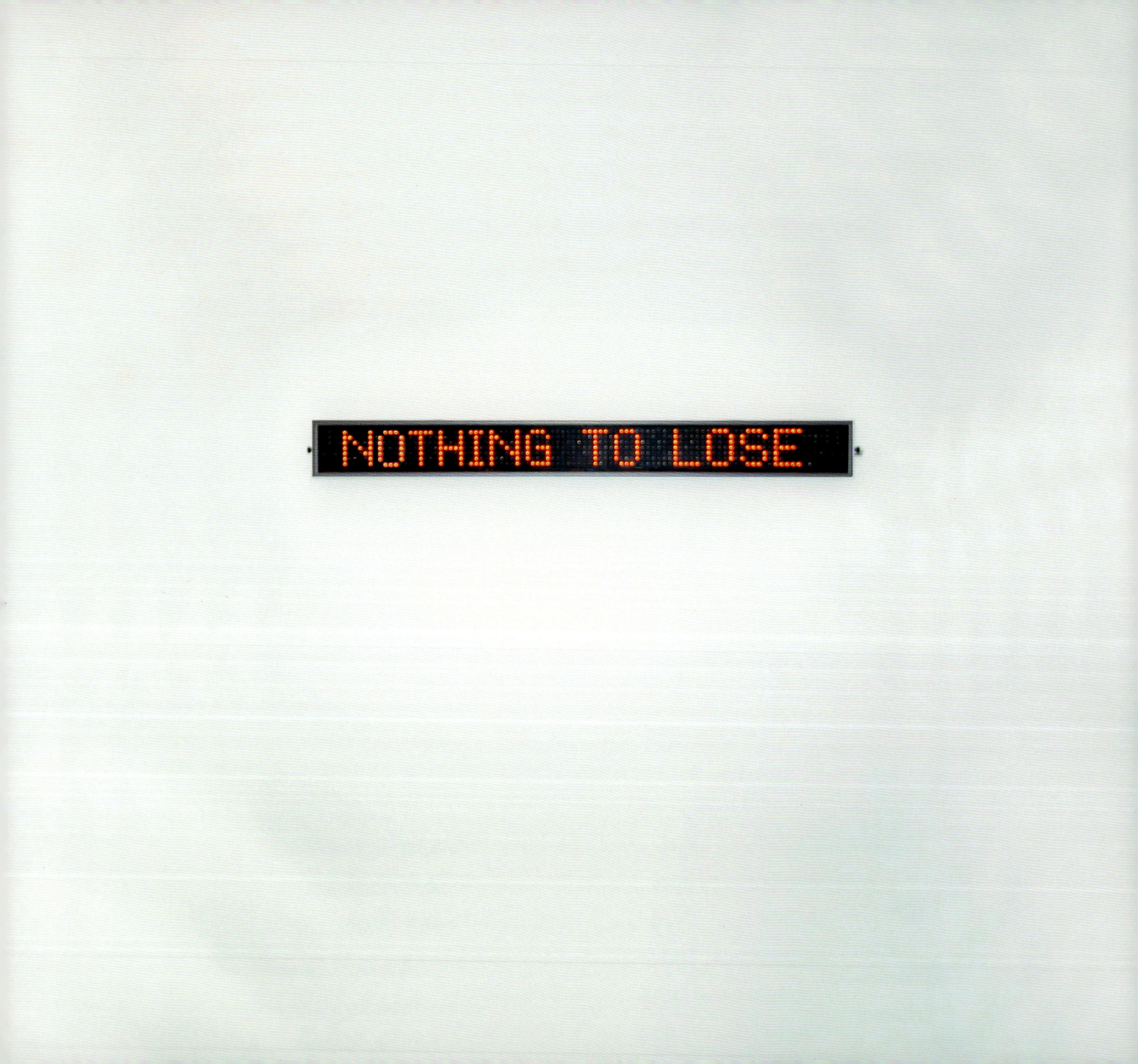

NOTHING TO LOSE

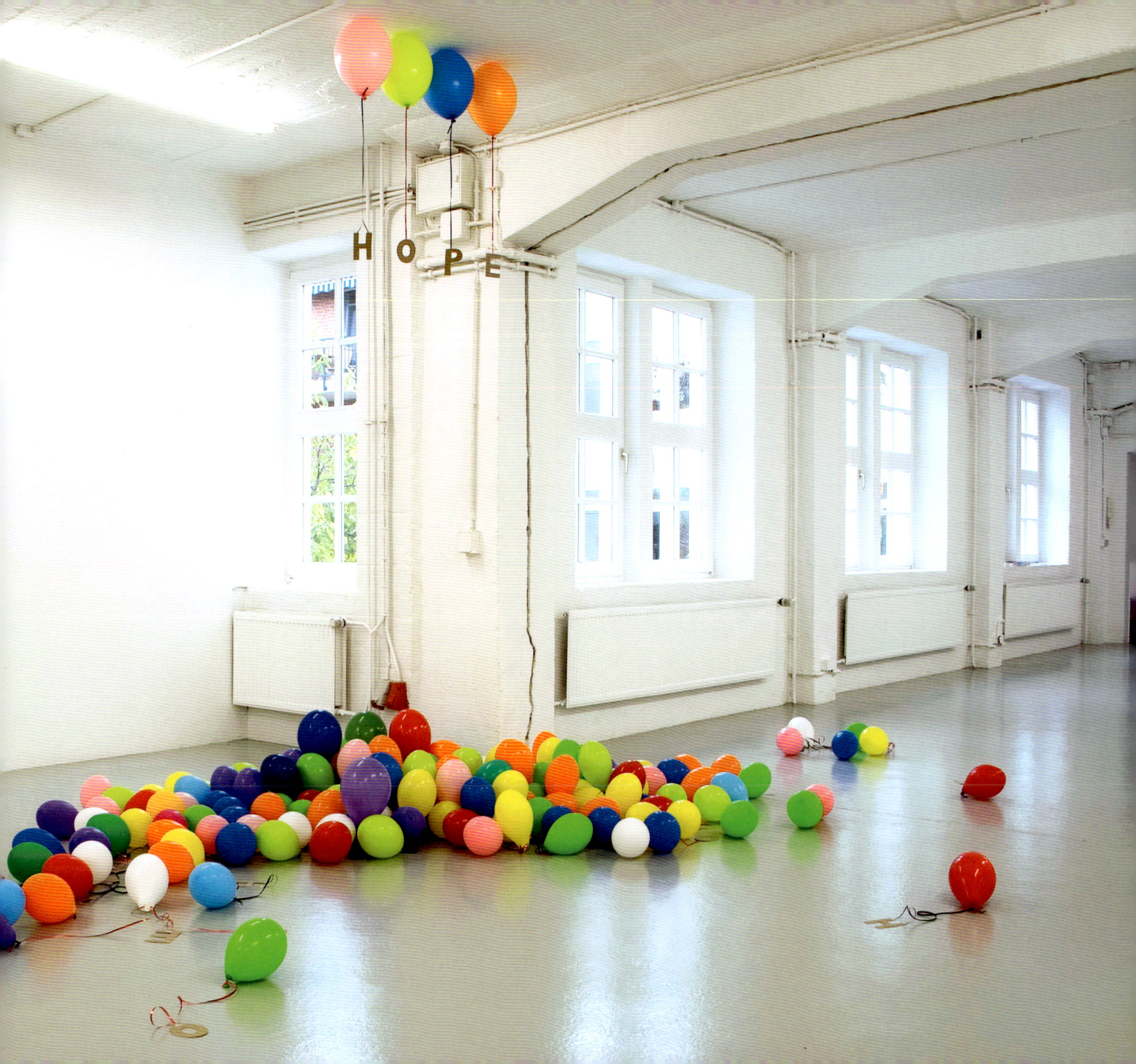
HOPE

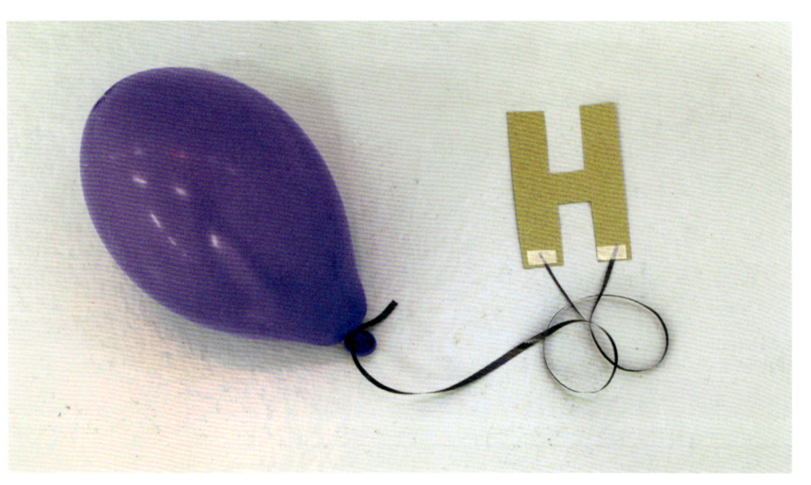
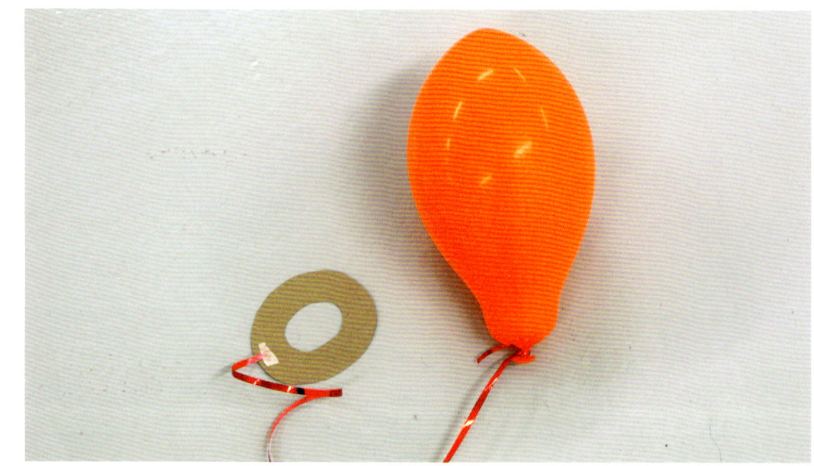

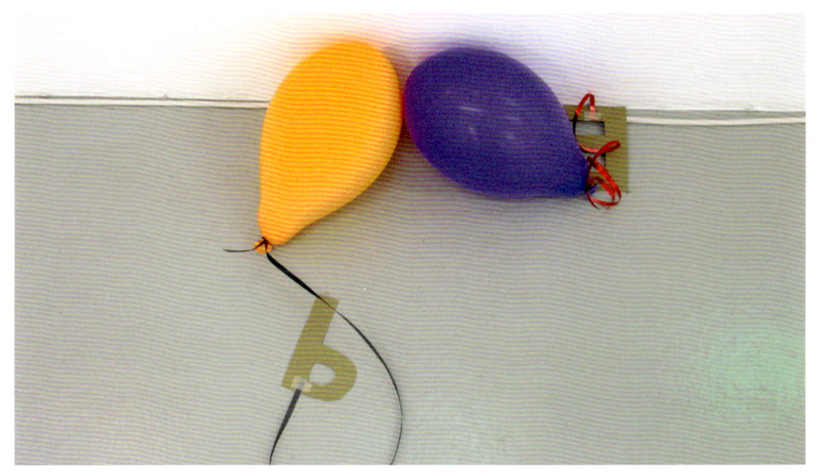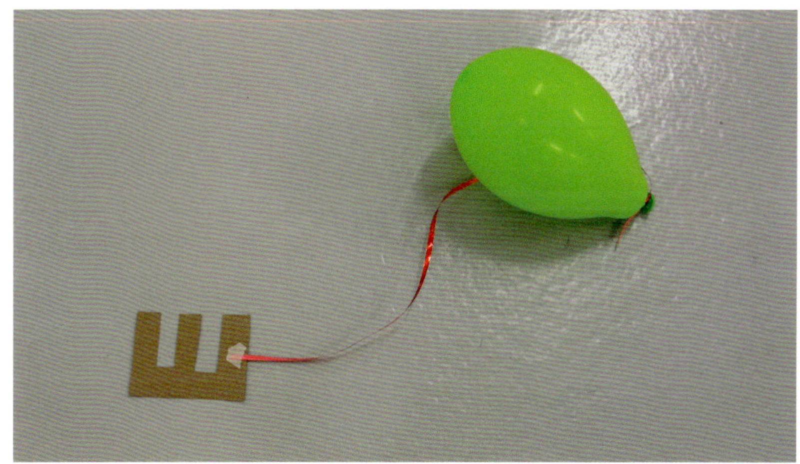

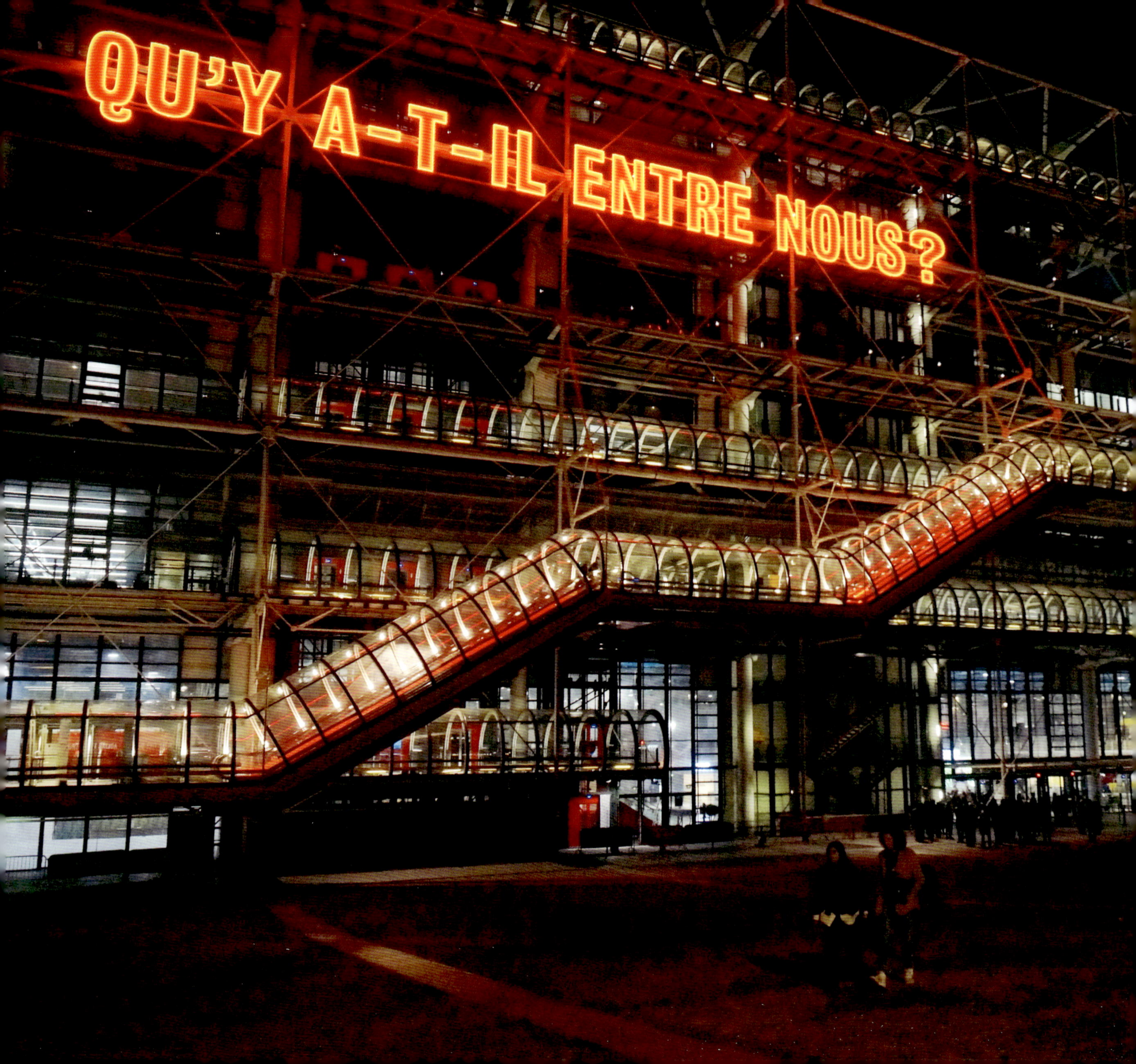
QU'Y A-T-IL ENTRE NOUS ?

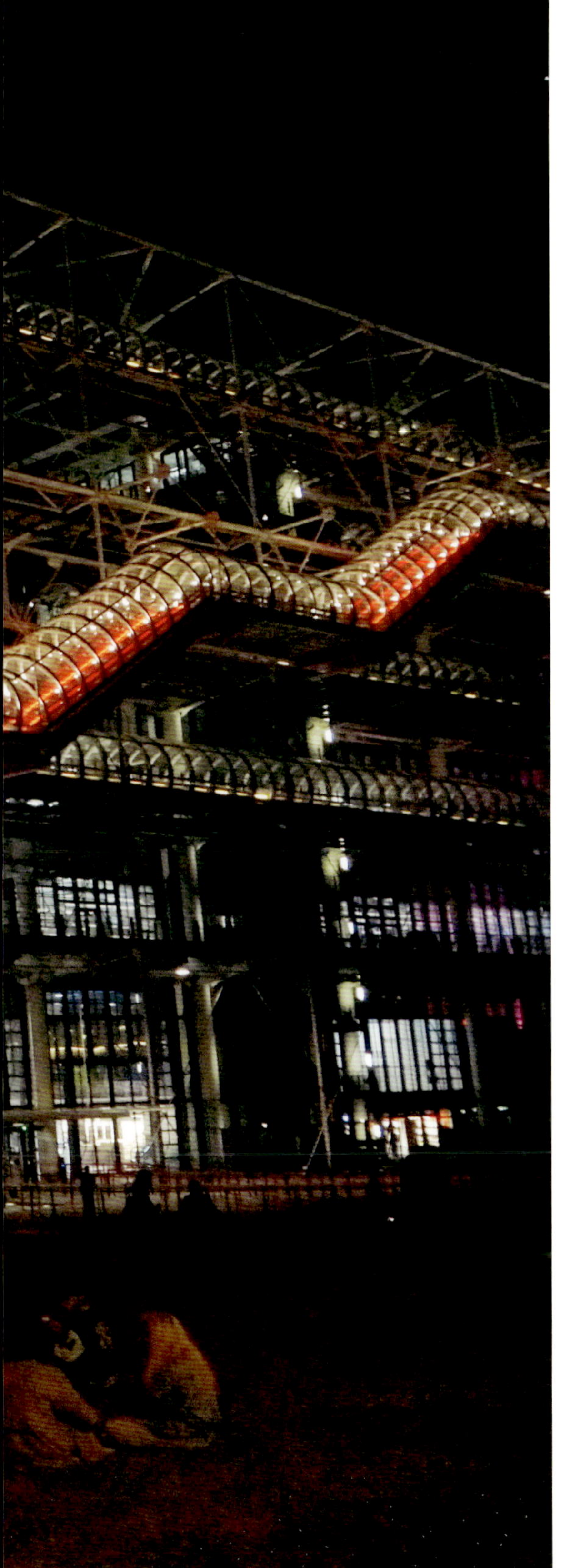

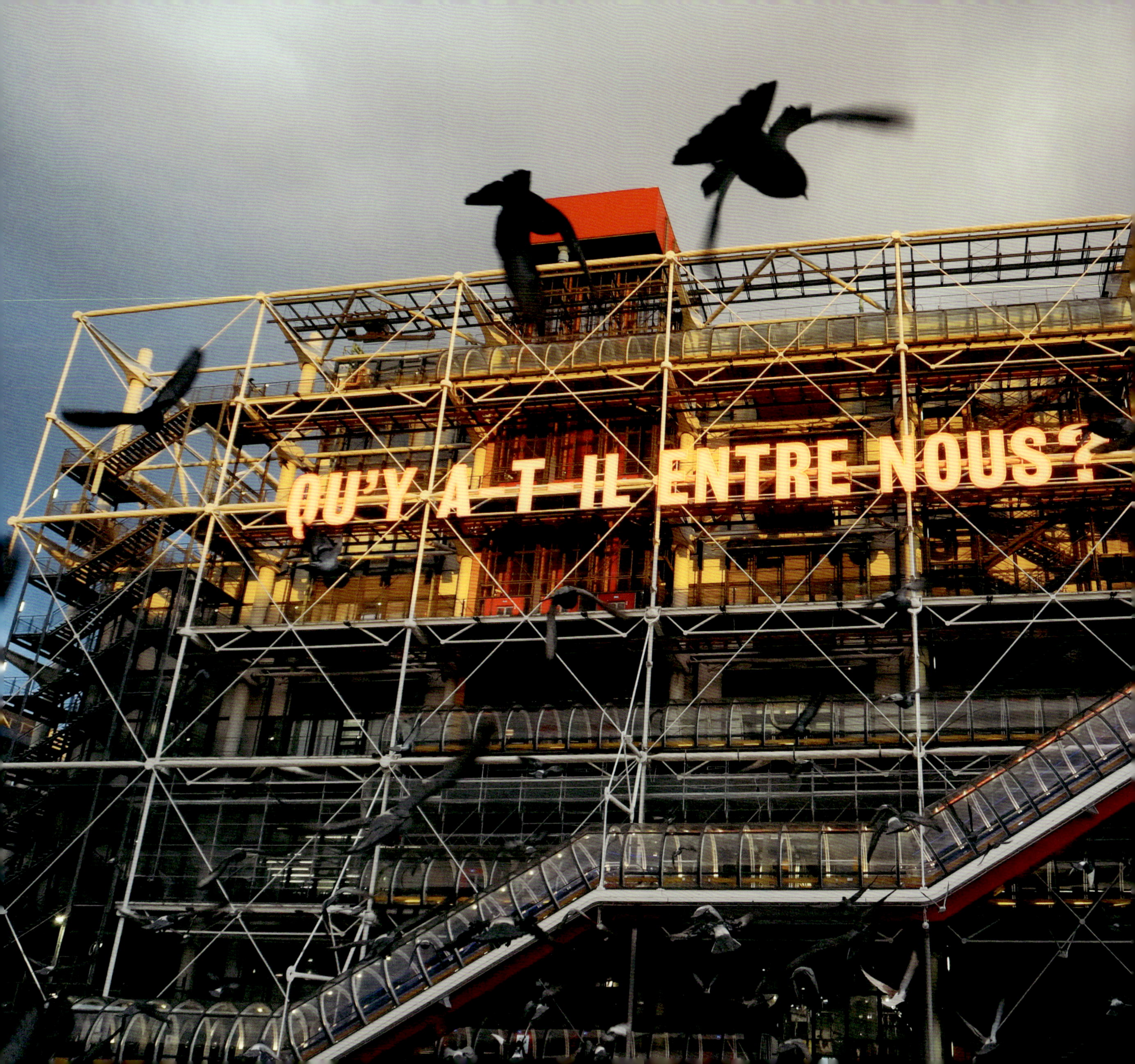
QU'Y A-T-IL ENTRE NOUS?

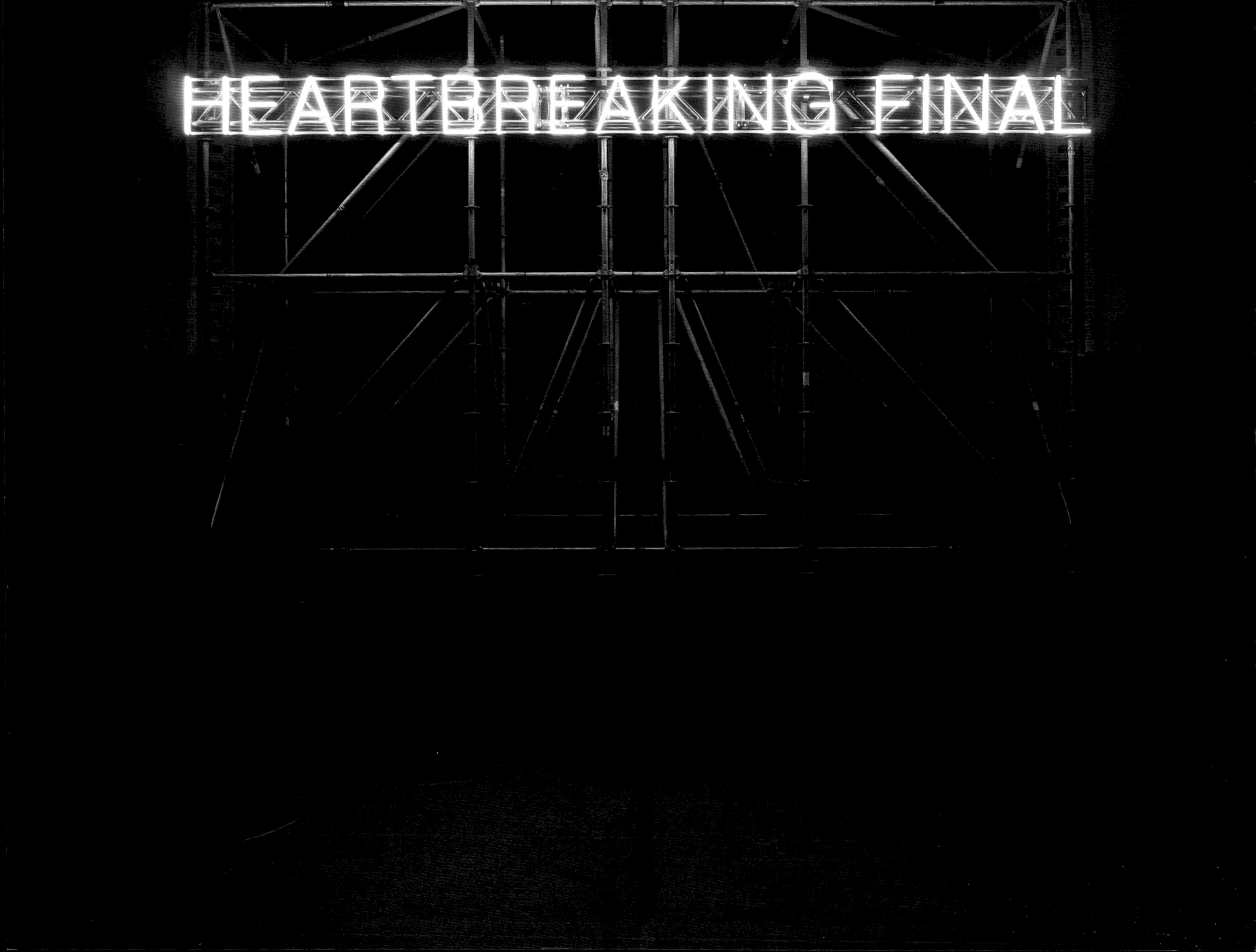

HEARTBREAKING FINAL

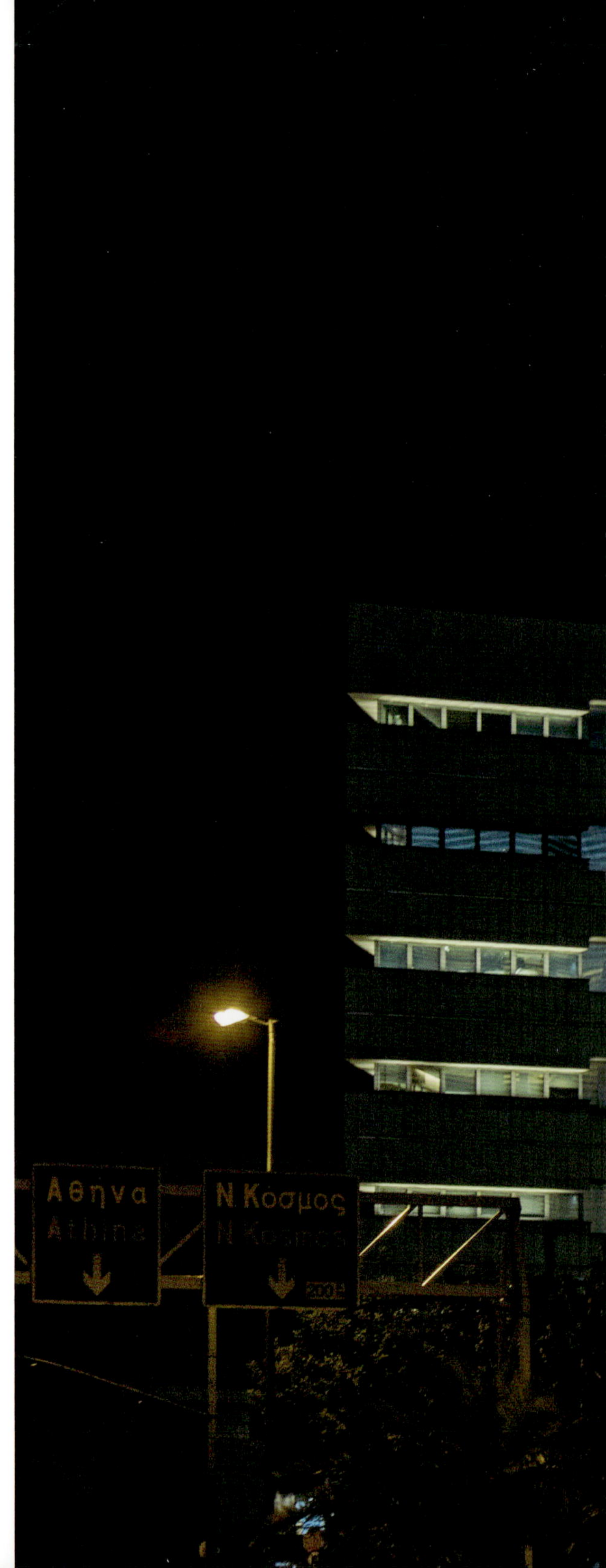

Αθηνα
Athina
Ν Κοσμος
N Kosmos
200 m

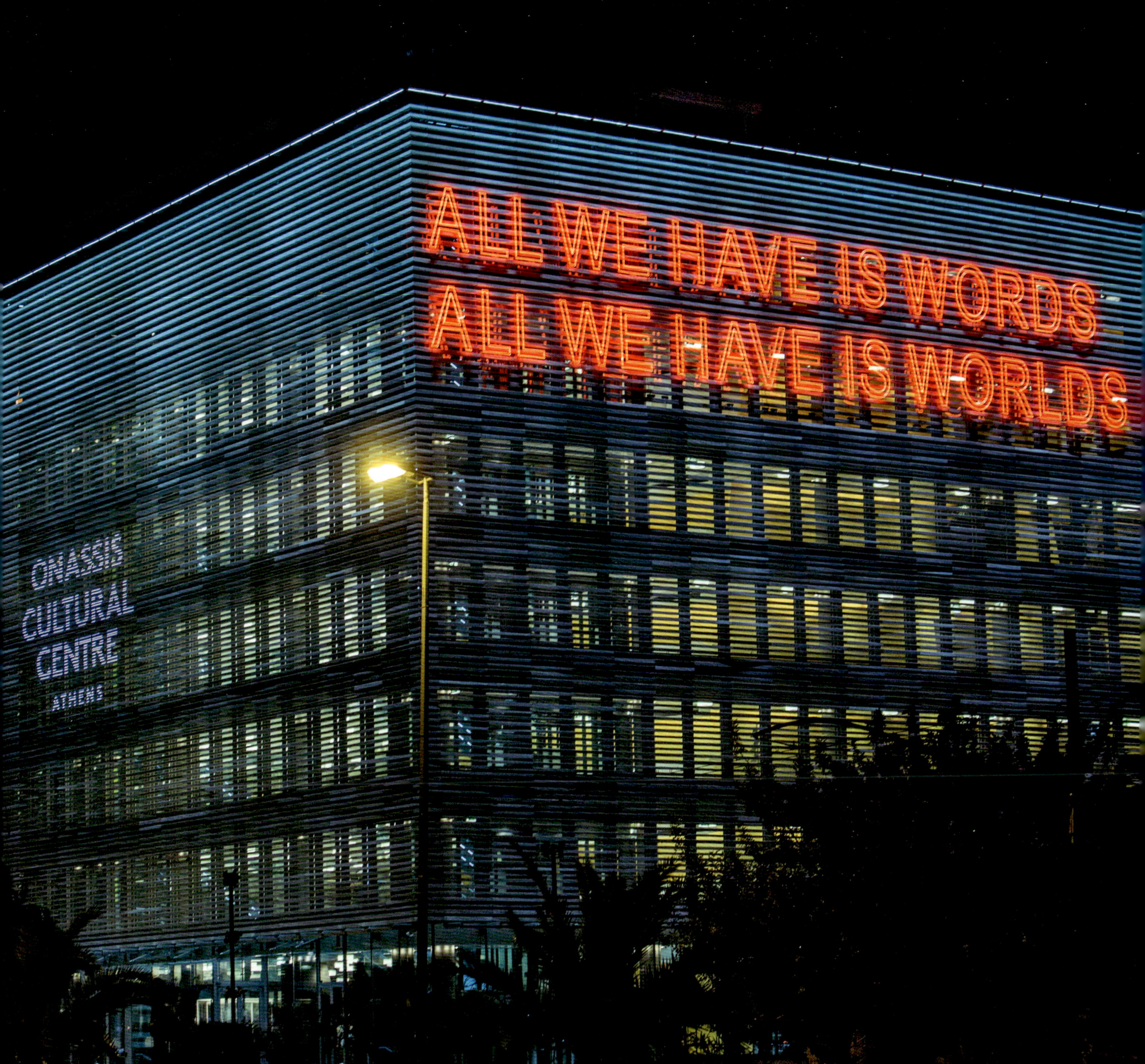

ALL WE HAVE IS WORDS
ALL WE HAVE IS WORLDS
ONASSIS
CULTURAL
CENTRE
ATHENS

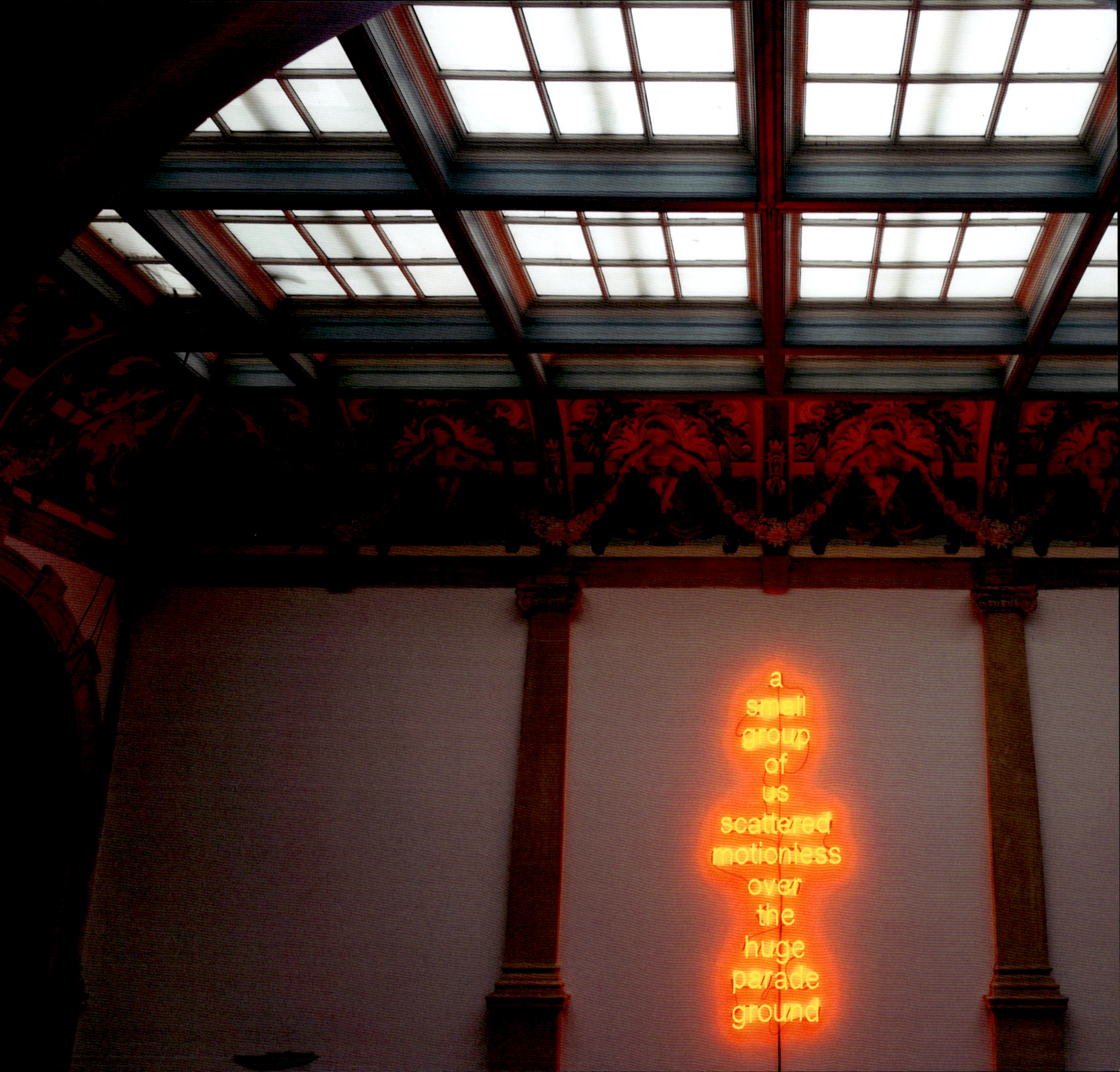

a
small
group
of
us
scattered
motionless
over
the
huge
parade
ground

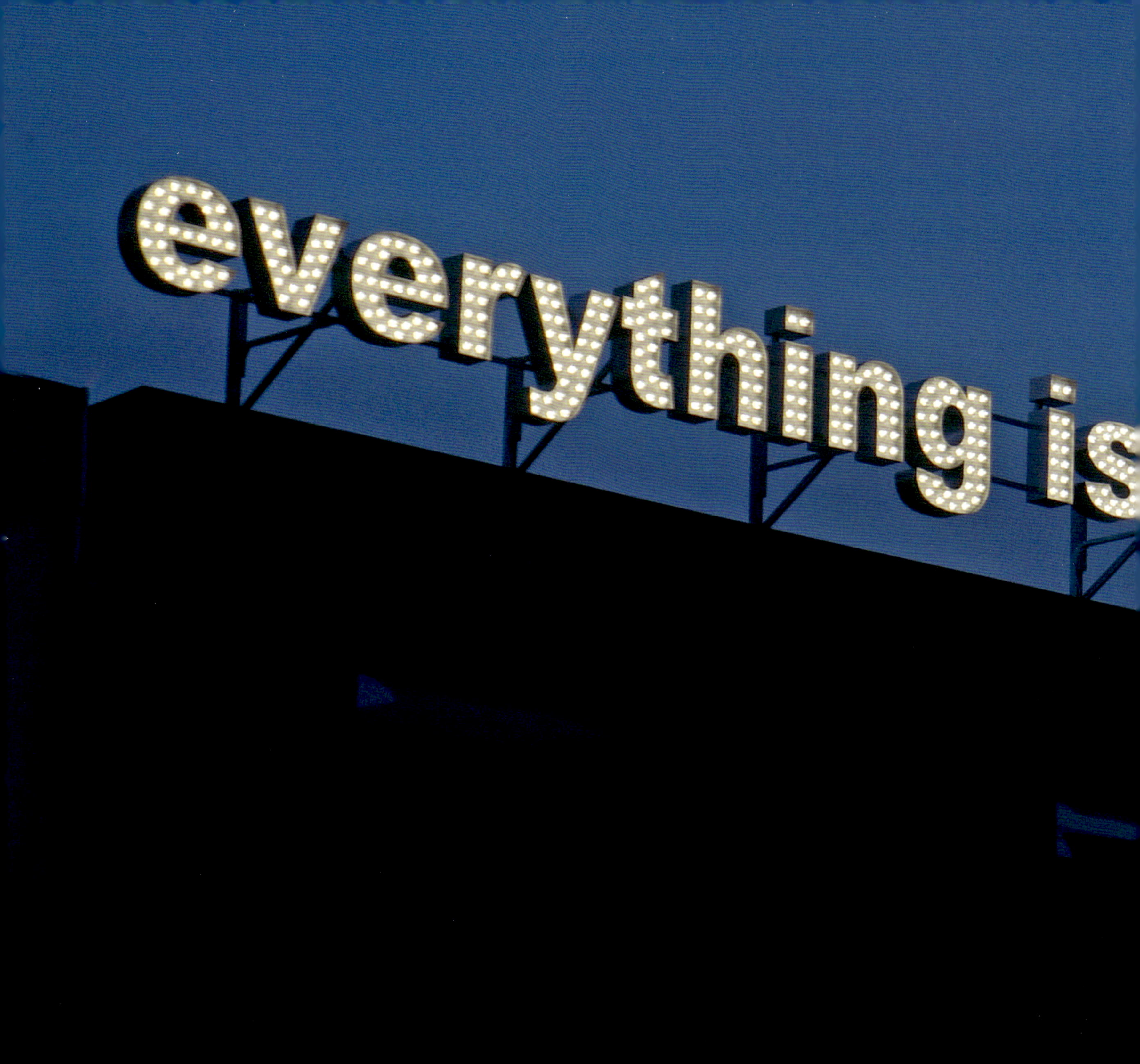

everything is

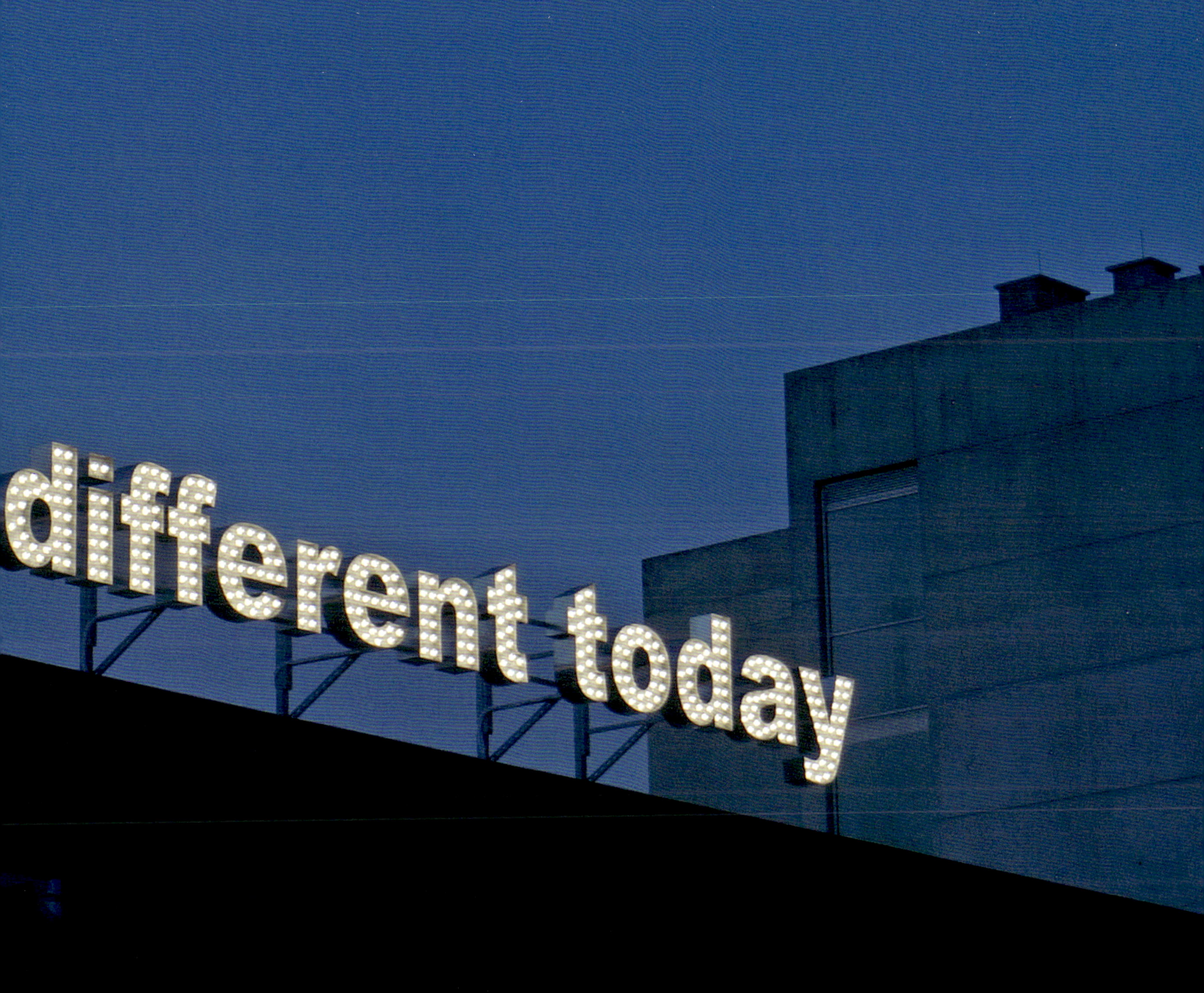
different today

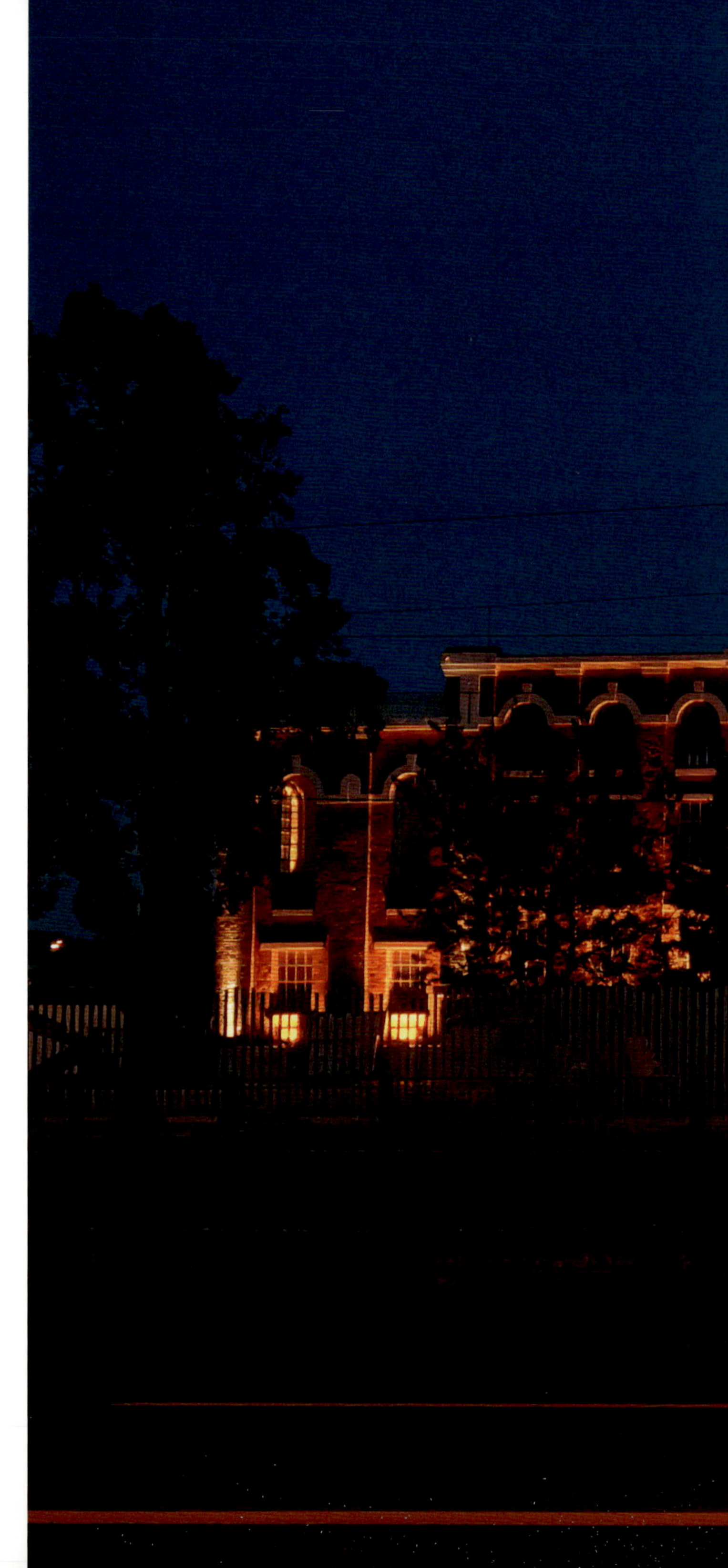

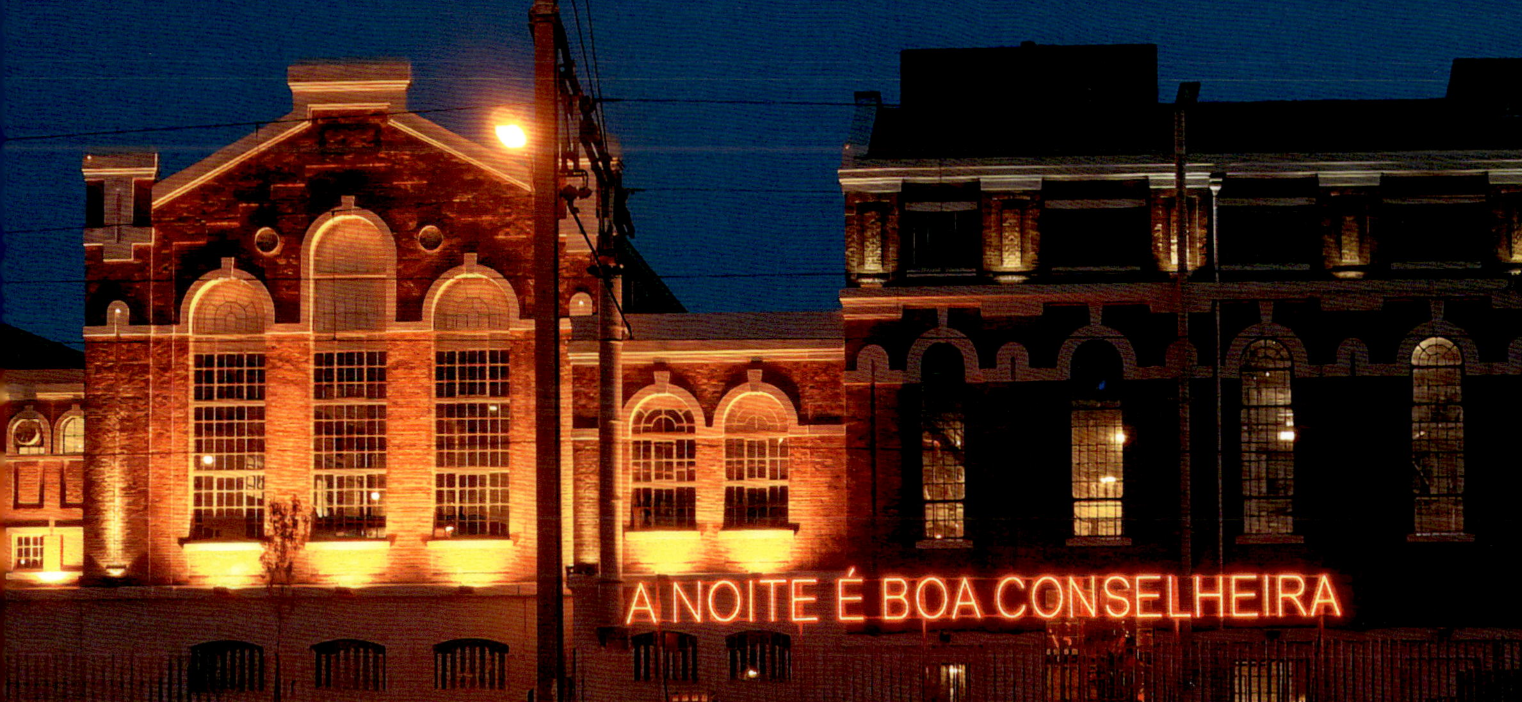

A NOITE É BOA CONSELHEIRA

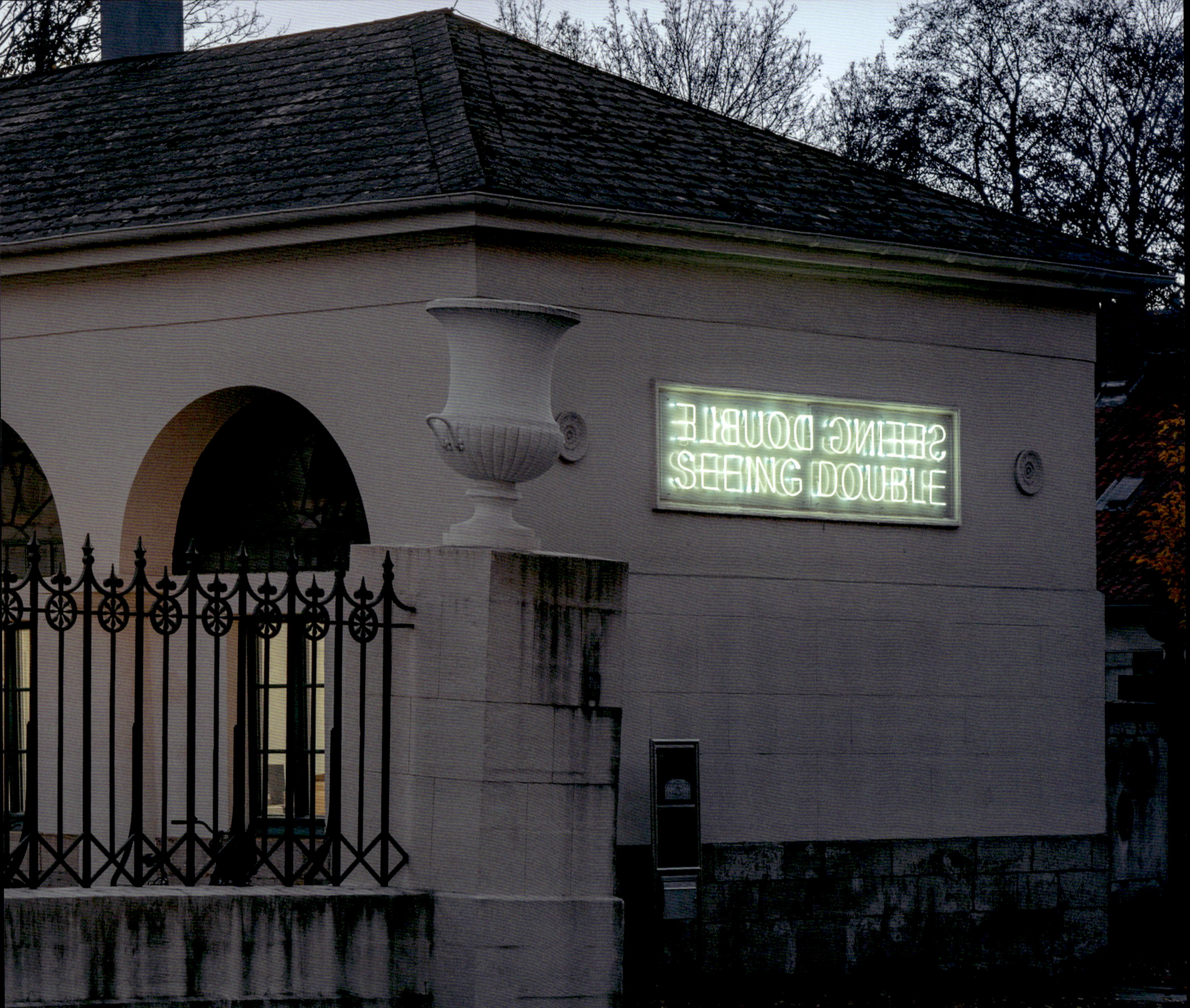
SEEING DOUBLE
SEEING DOUBLE

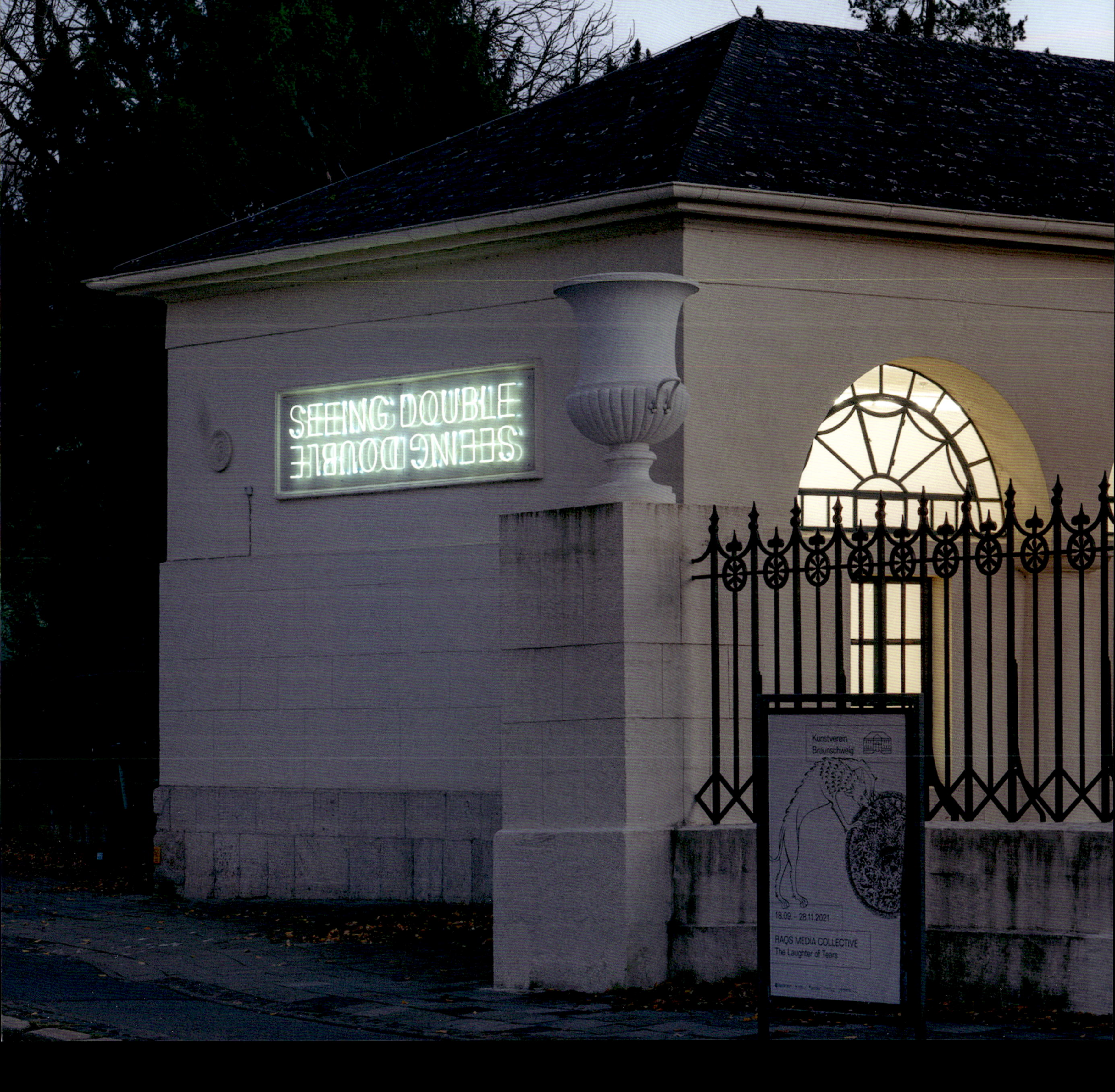

SEEING DOUBLE
SEEING DOUBLE
Kunstverein
Braunschweig
18.09 – 28.11.2021
RAQS MEDIA COLLECTIVE
The Laughter of Tears

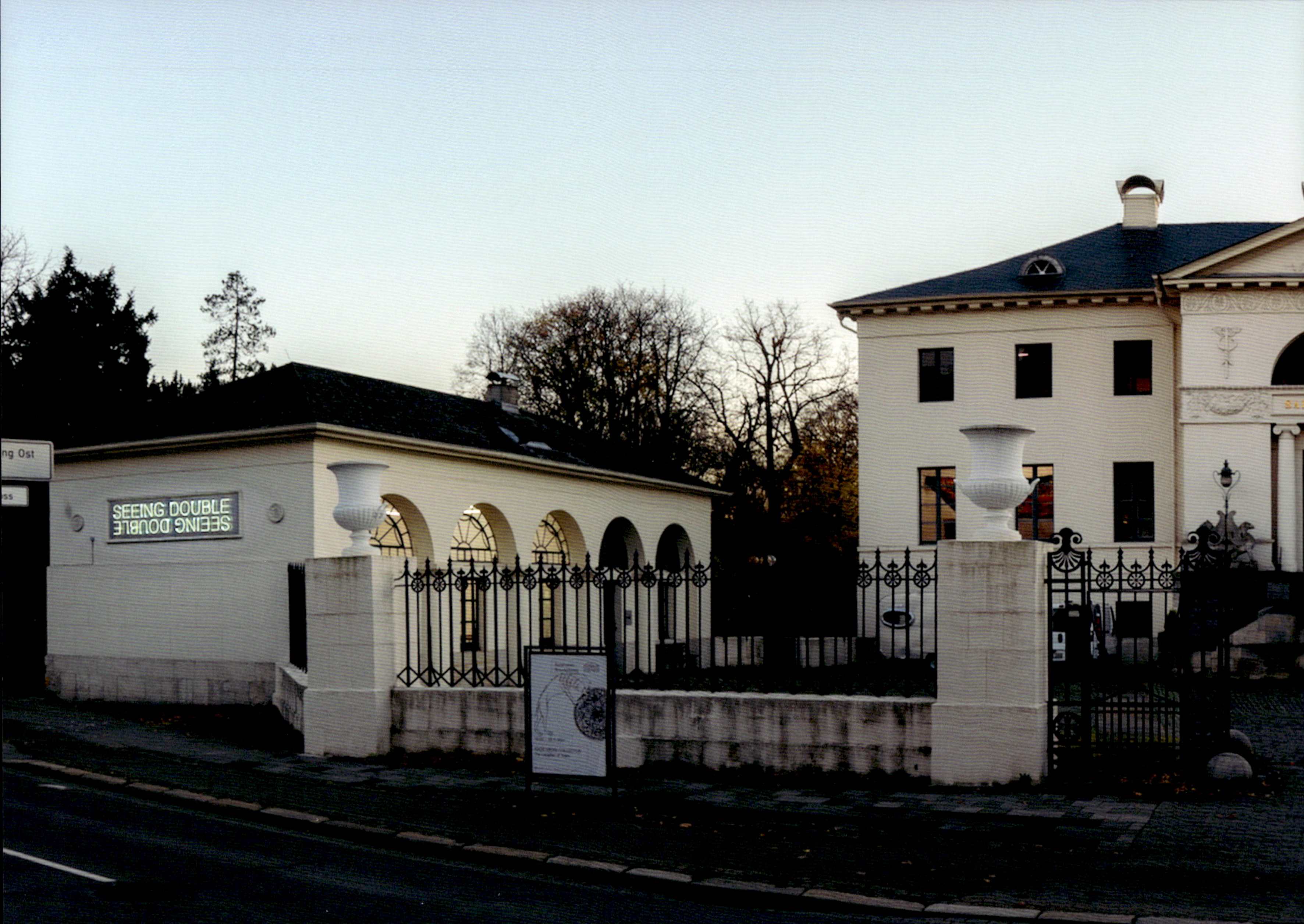
SEEING DOUBLE
SEEING DOUBLE
ng Ost

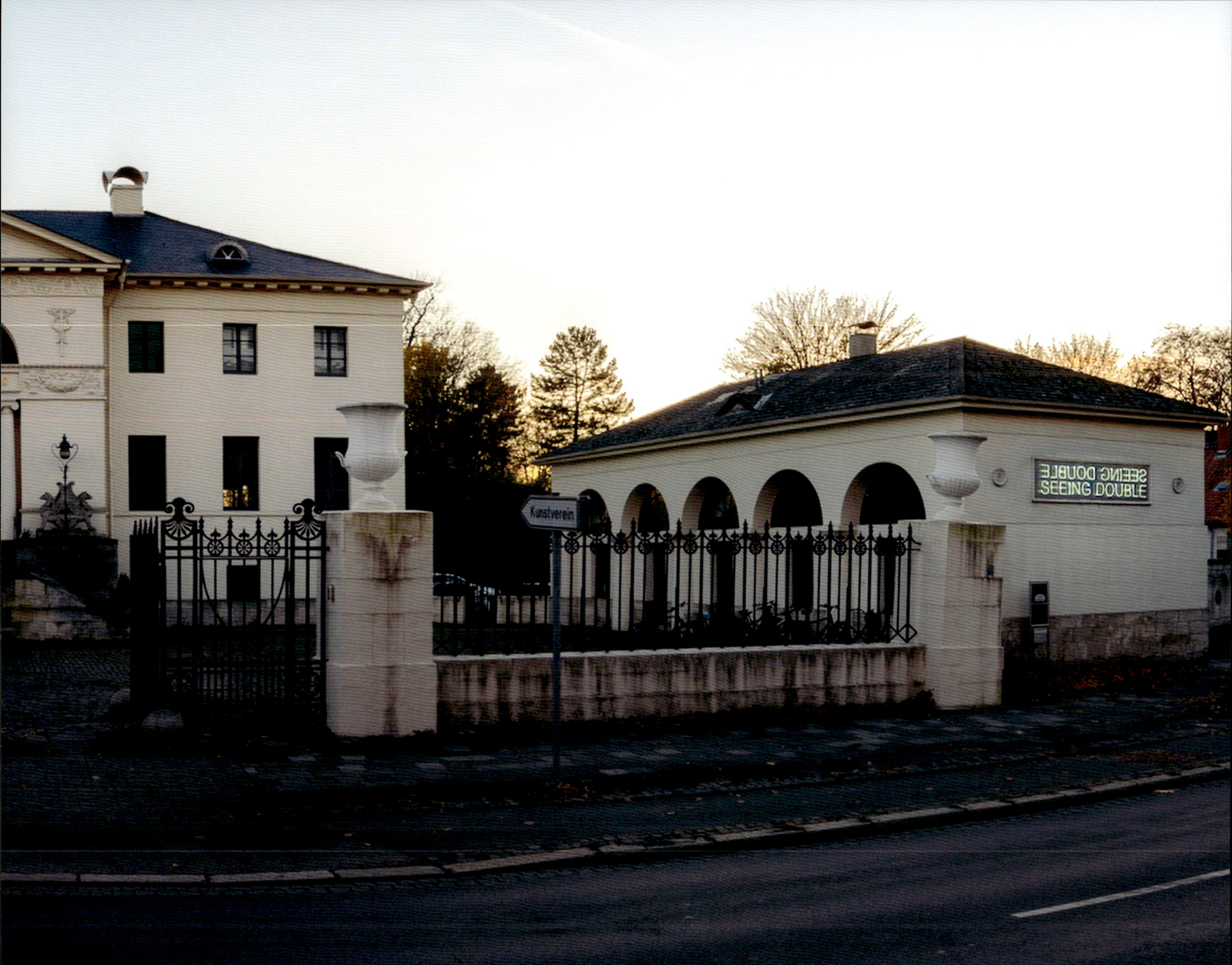
SEEING DOUBLE
SEEING DOUBLE
Kunstverein

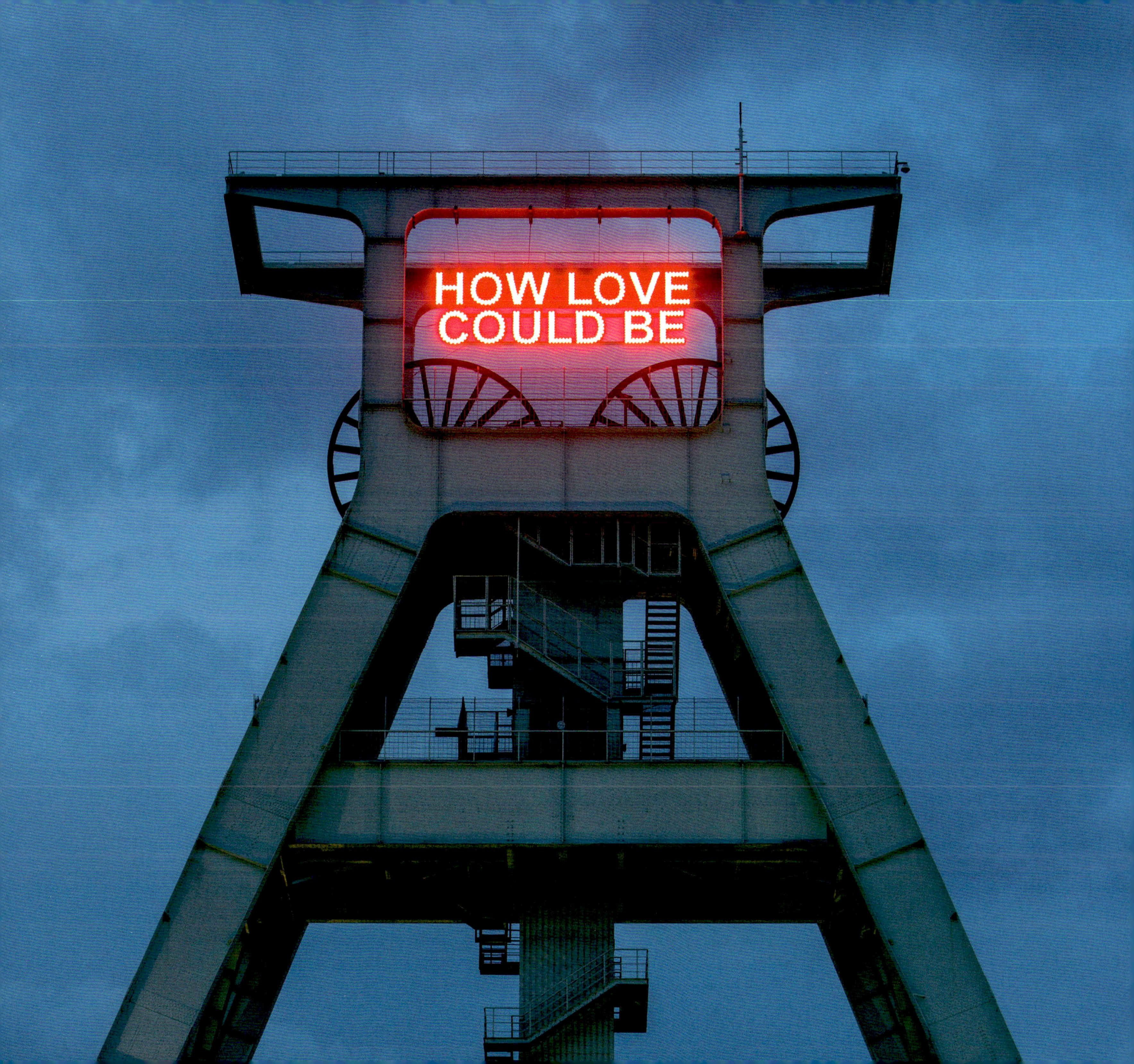
HOW LOVE
COULD BE

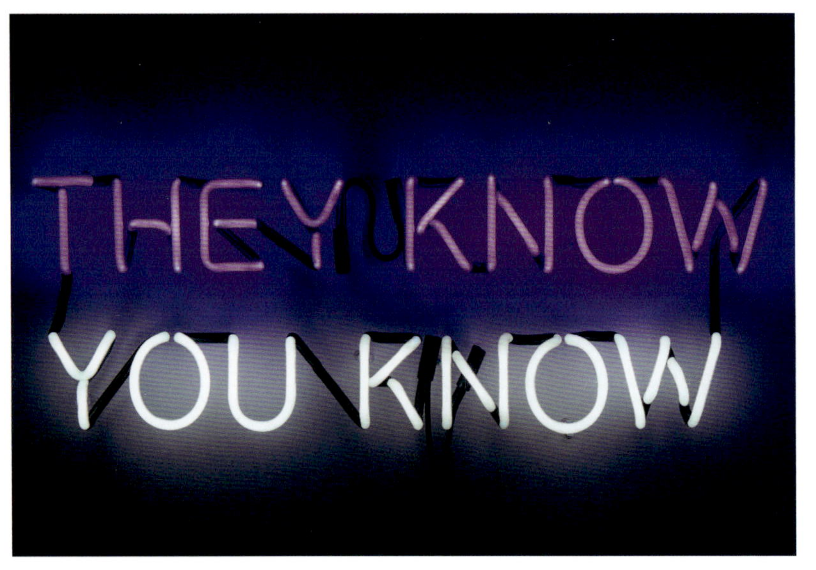

THEY KNOW
YOU KNOW

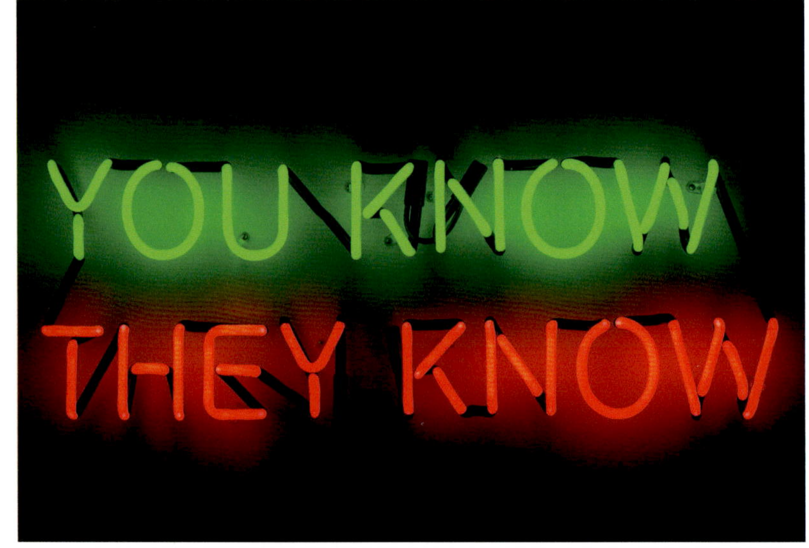

YOU KNOW
THEY KNOW

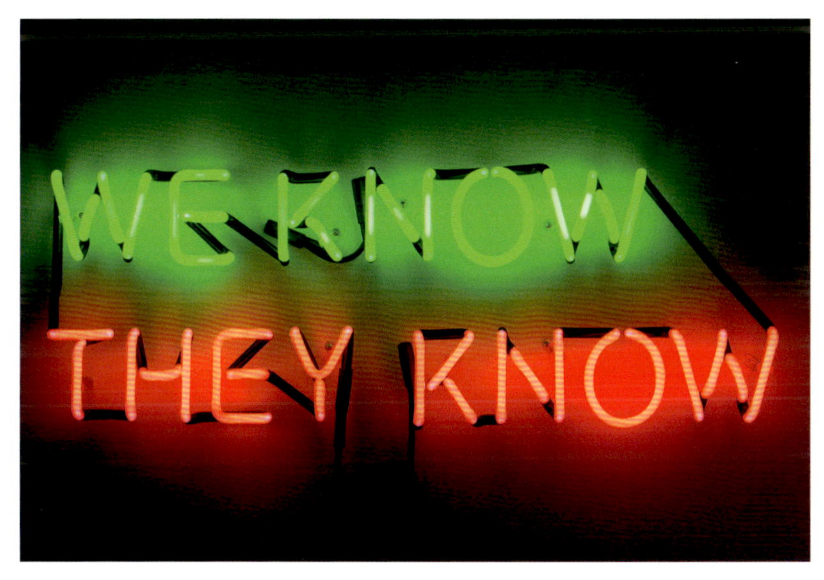
WE KNOW
THEY KNOW

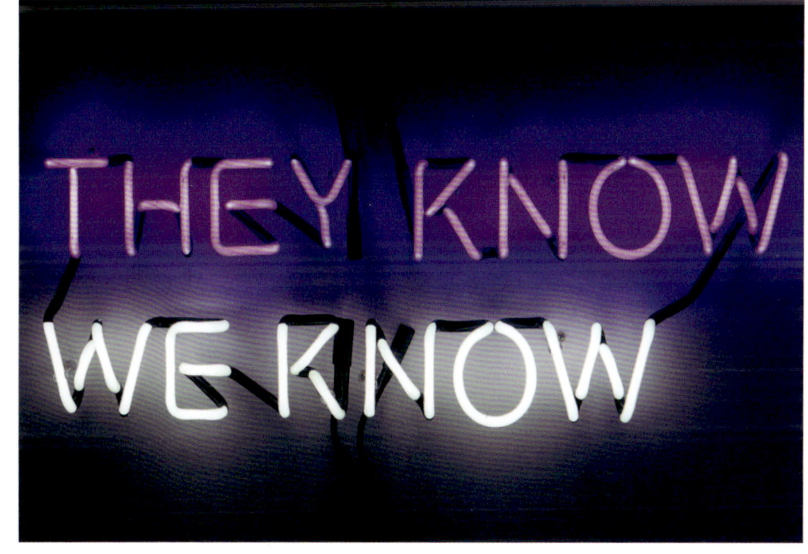
THEY KNOW
WE KNOW

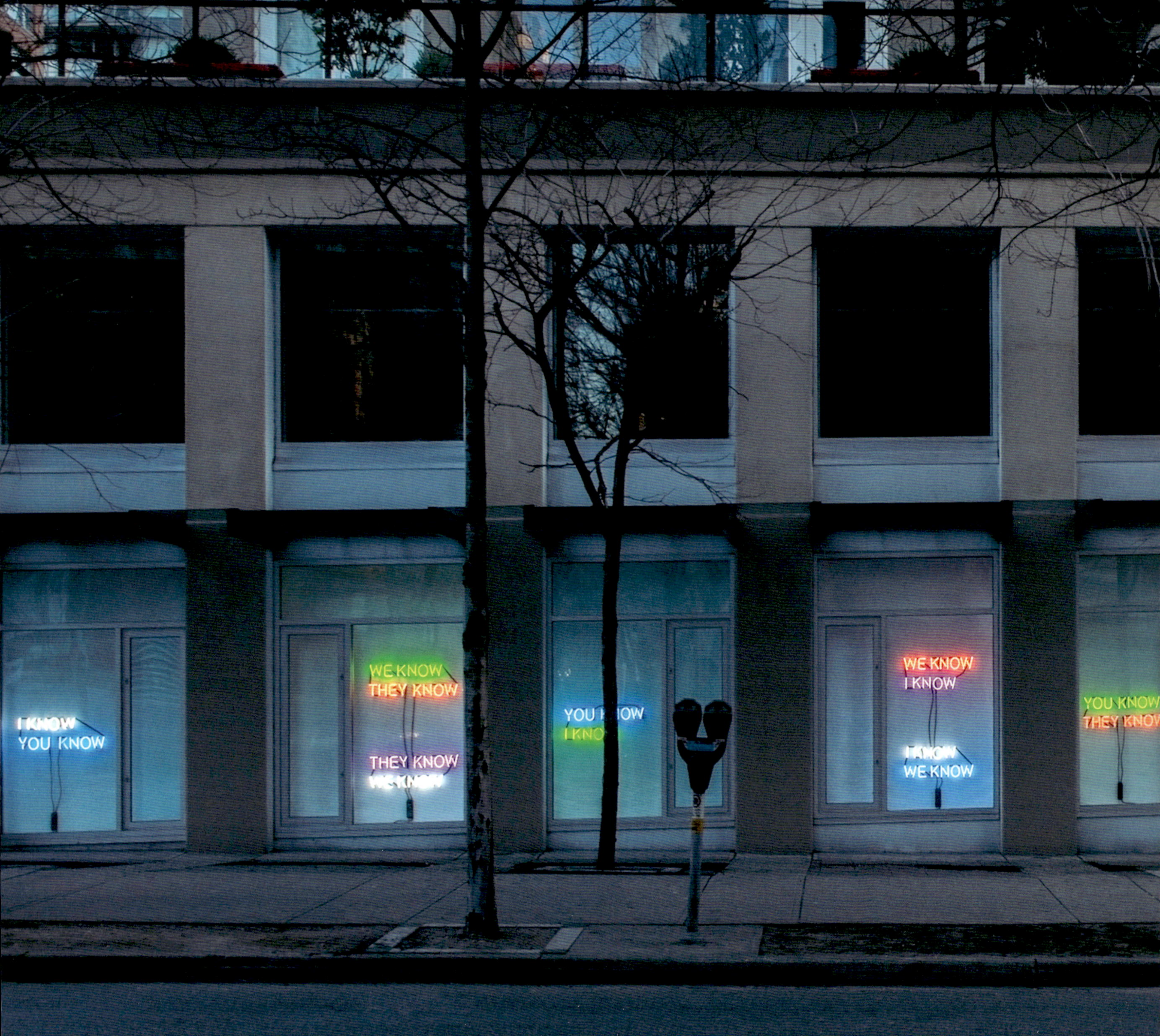
I KNOW
YOU KNOW
WE KNOW
THEY KNOW
THEY KNOW
WE KNOW
YOU KNOW
I KNOW
WE KNOW
I KNOW
YOU KNOW
THEY KNOW
I KNOW
WE KNOW

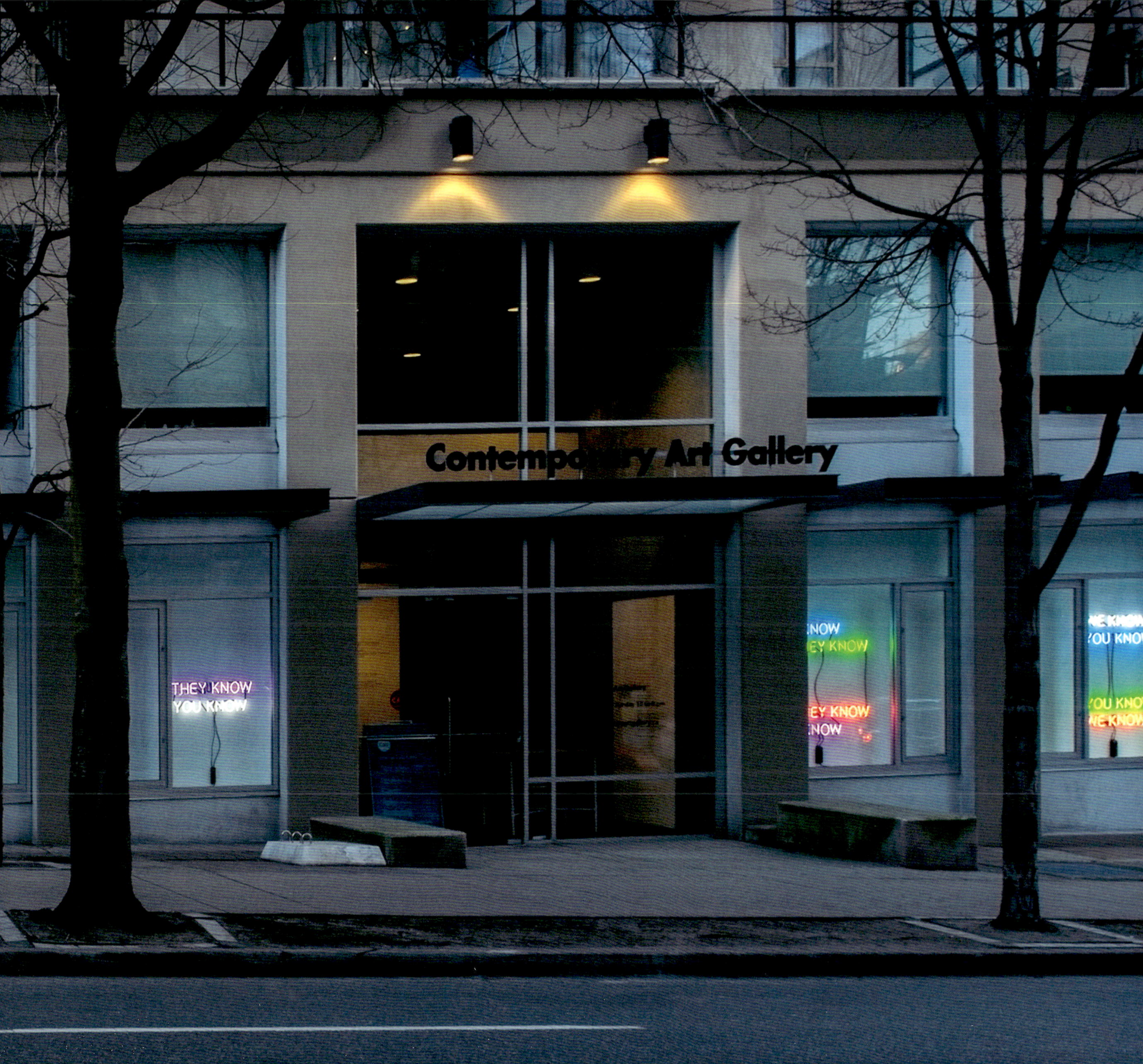
Contemporary Art Gallery
THEY KNOW
YOU KNOW
KNOW
YOU KNOW
THEY KNOW
THEY KNOW
KNOW
WE KNOW
WE KNOW
YOU KNOW
YOU KNOW
WE KNOW

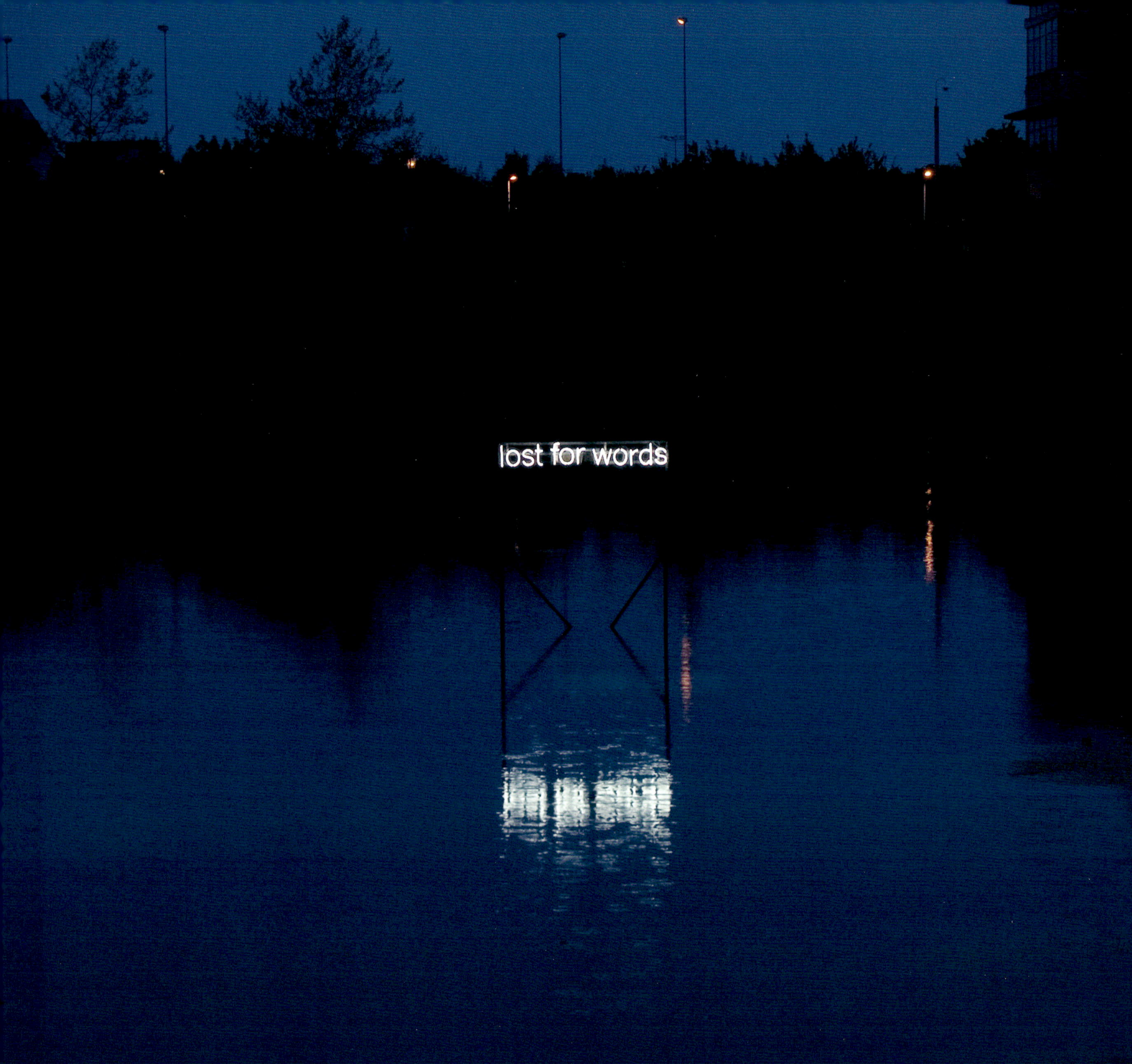
lost for words

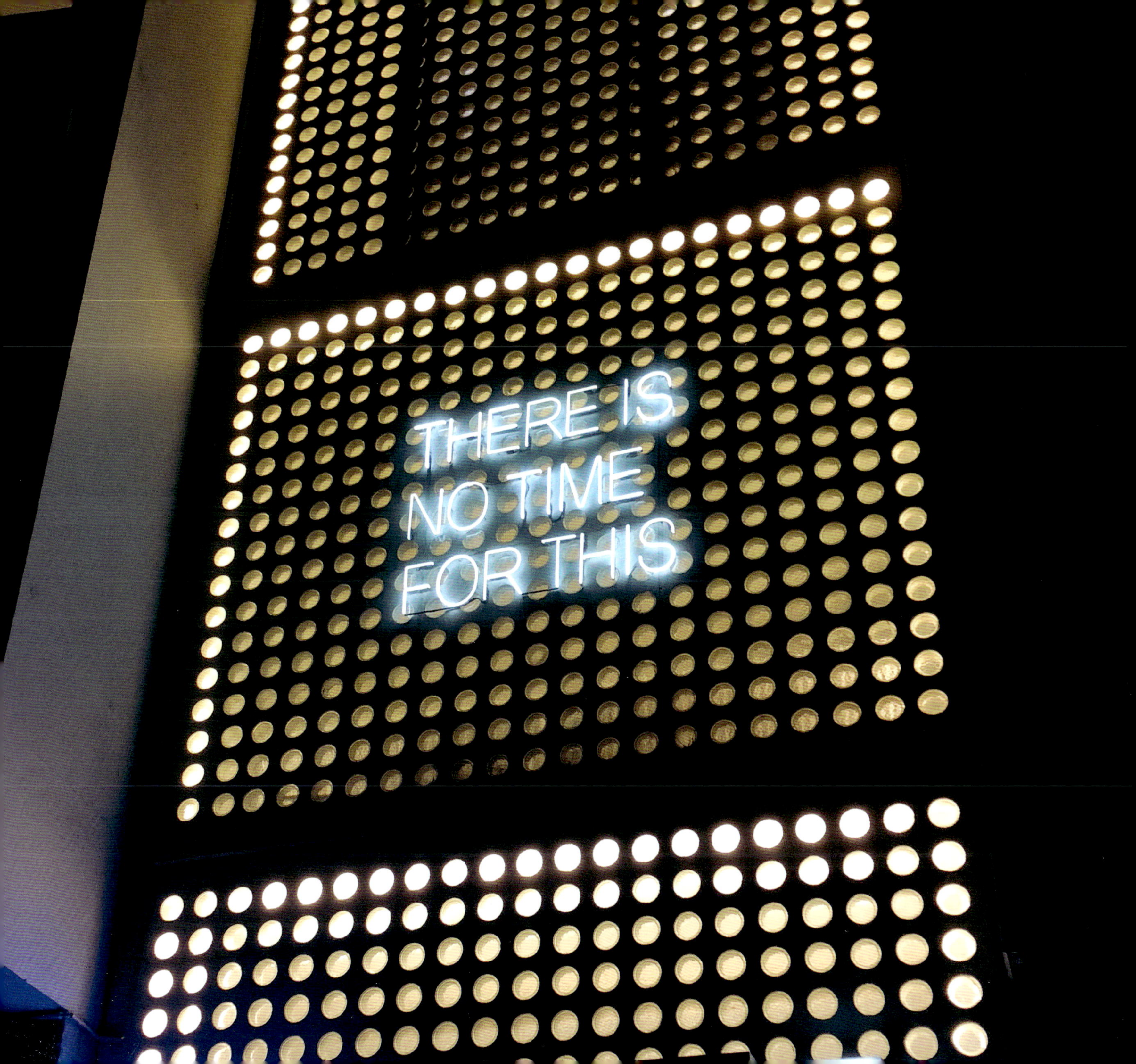

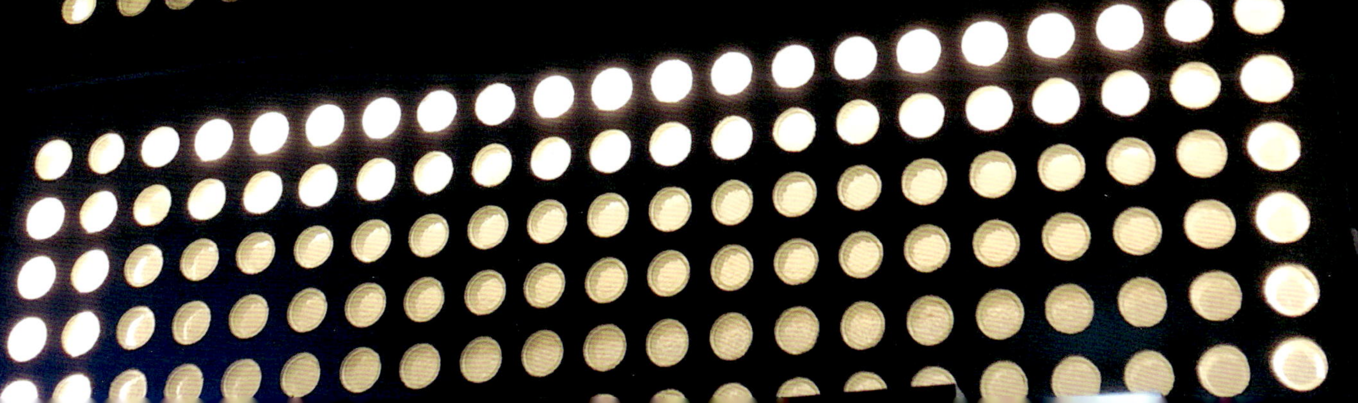
THERE IS
NO TIME
FOR THIS

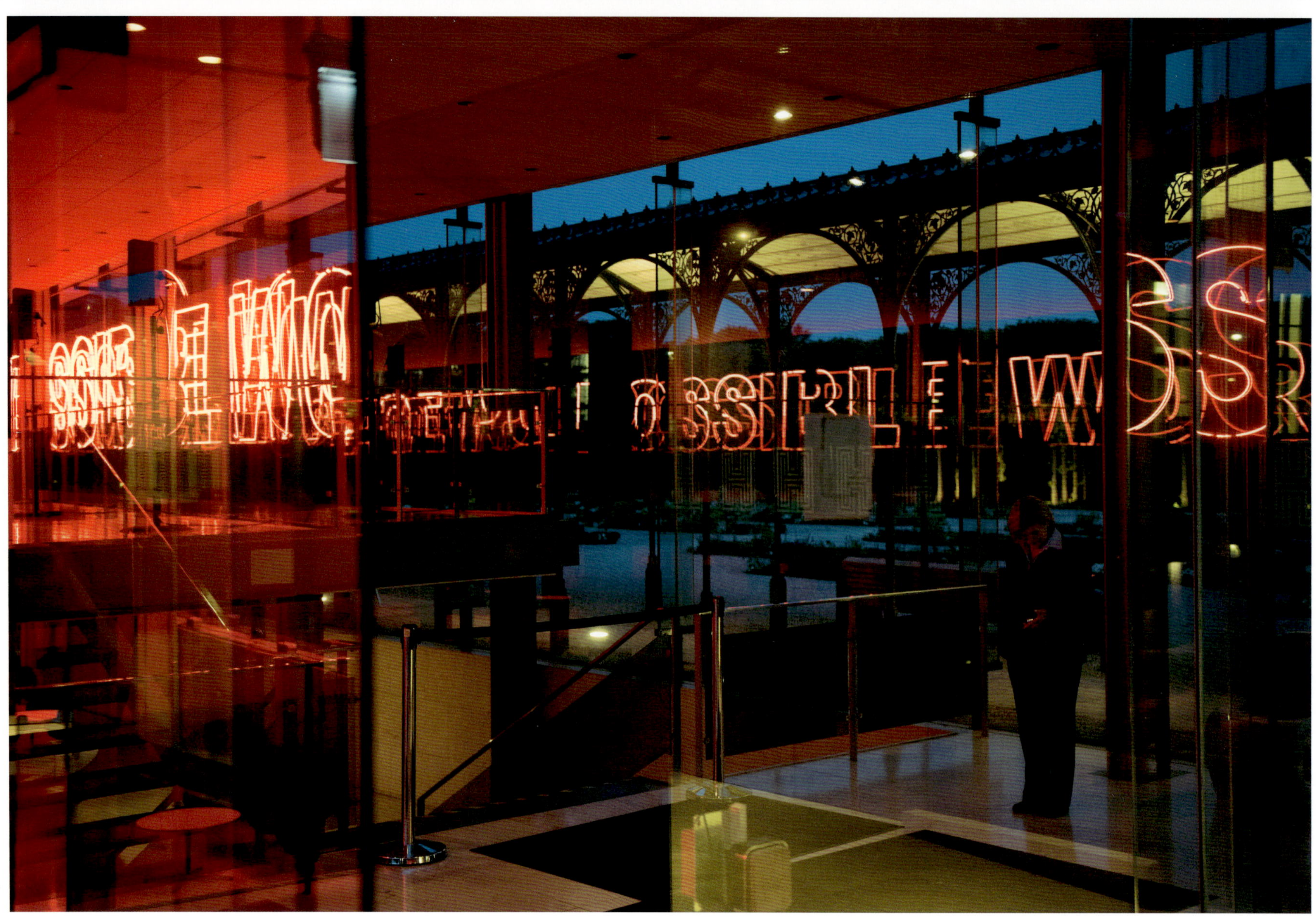

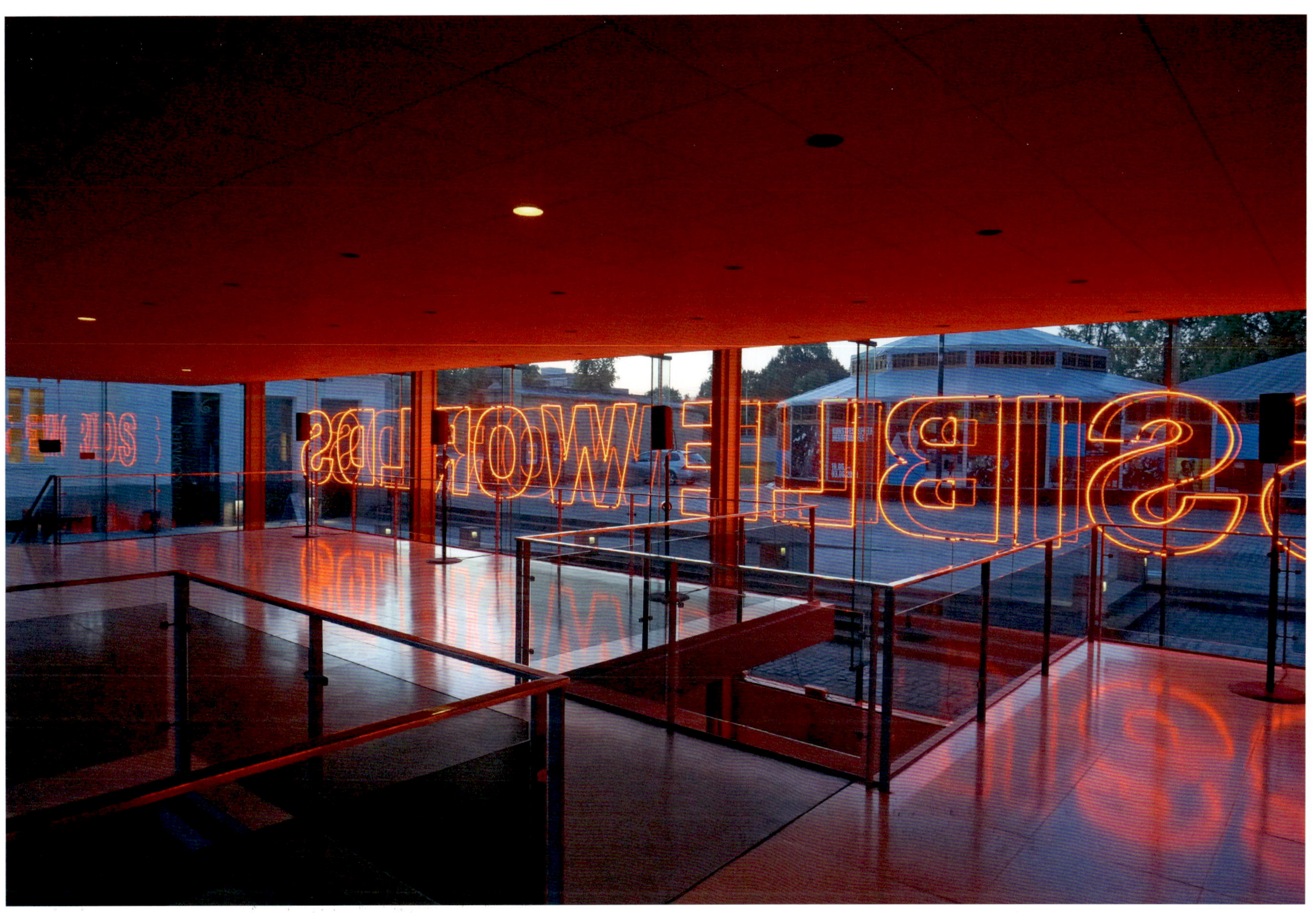

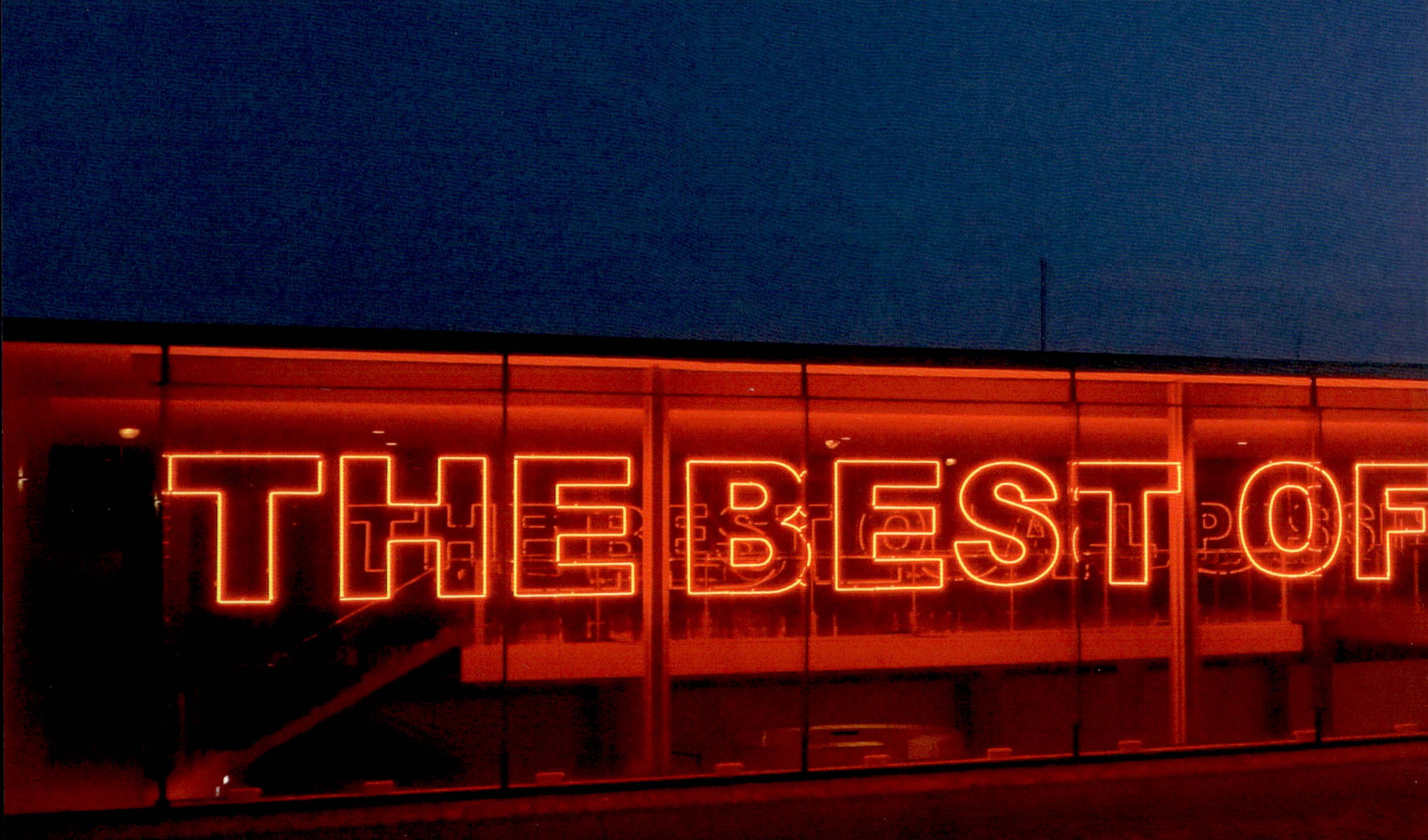
THE BEST OF

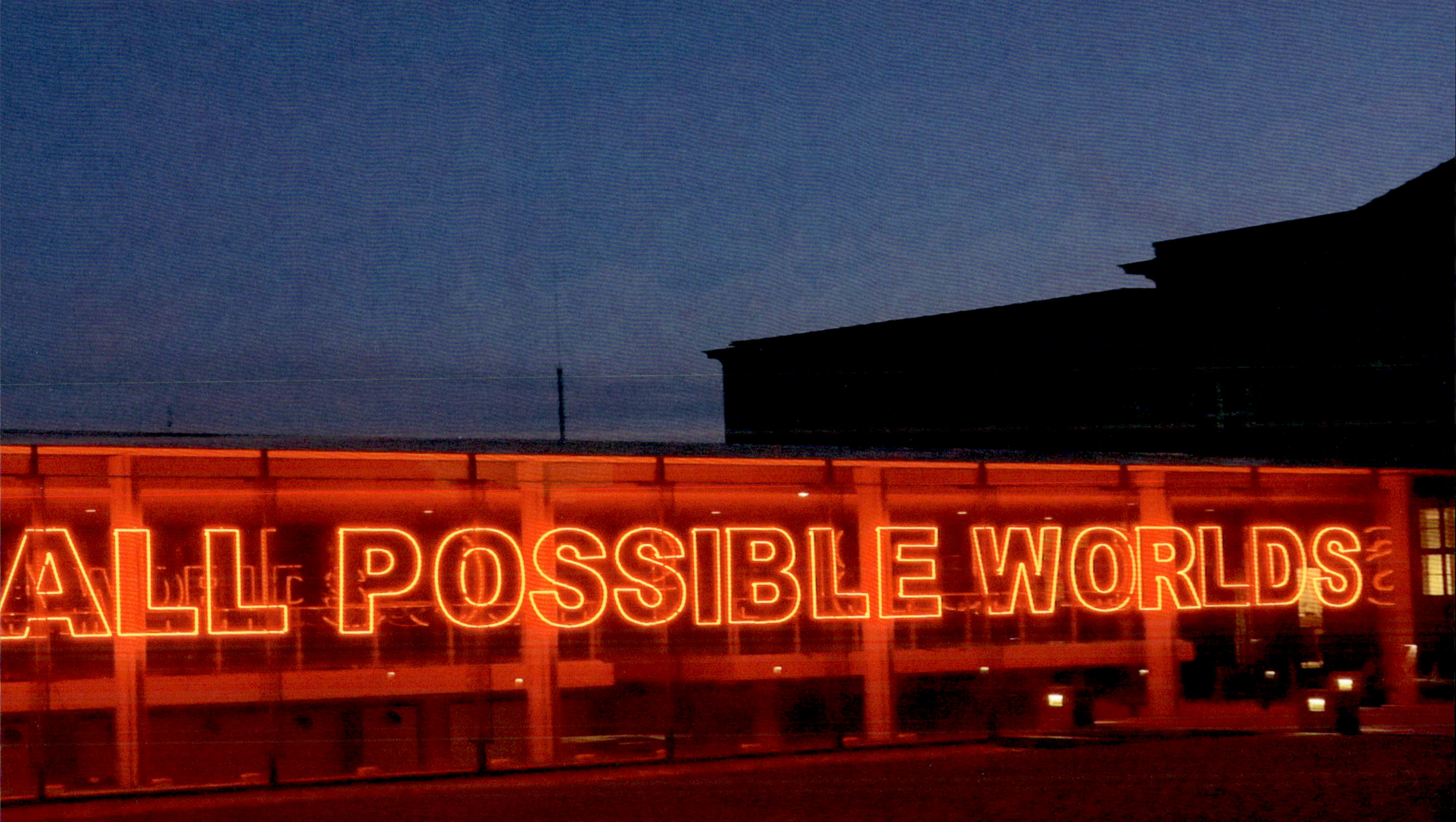

ALL POSSIBLE WORLDS

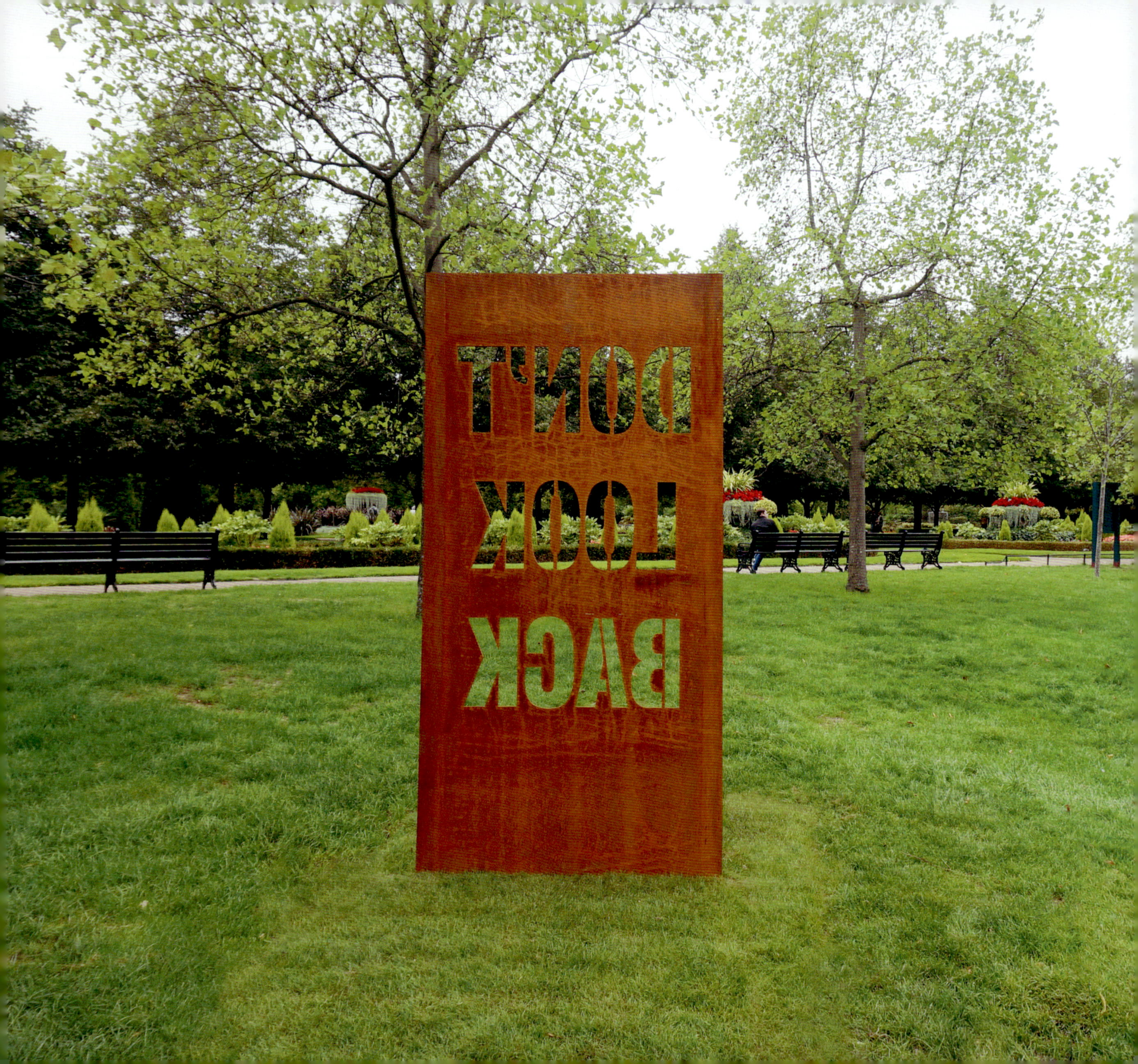

DON'T
LOOK
BACK

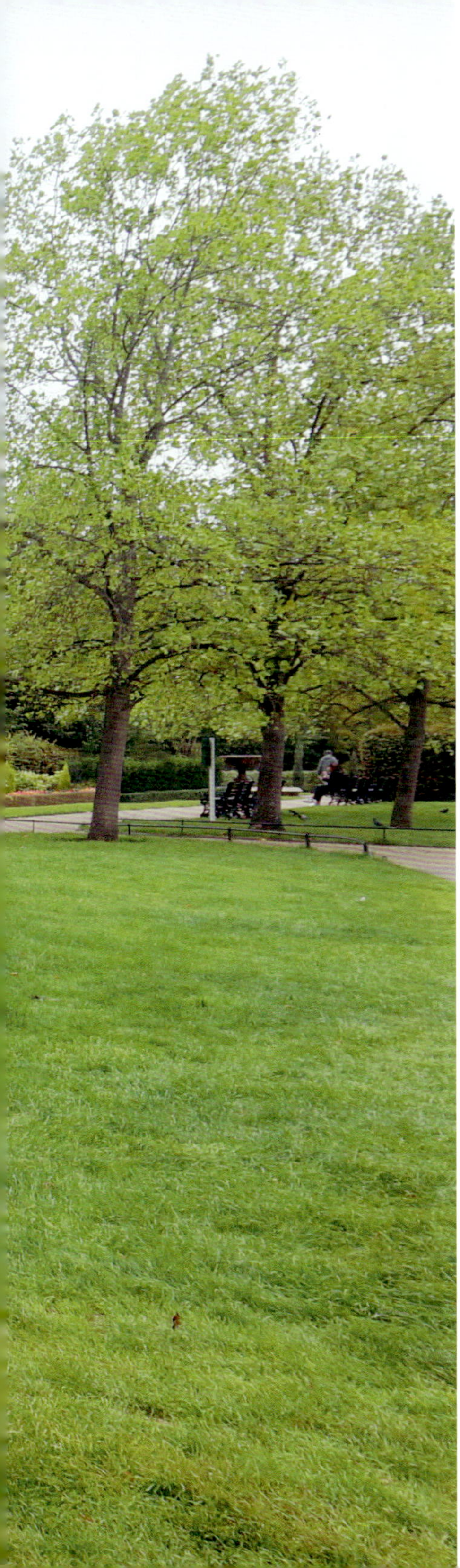

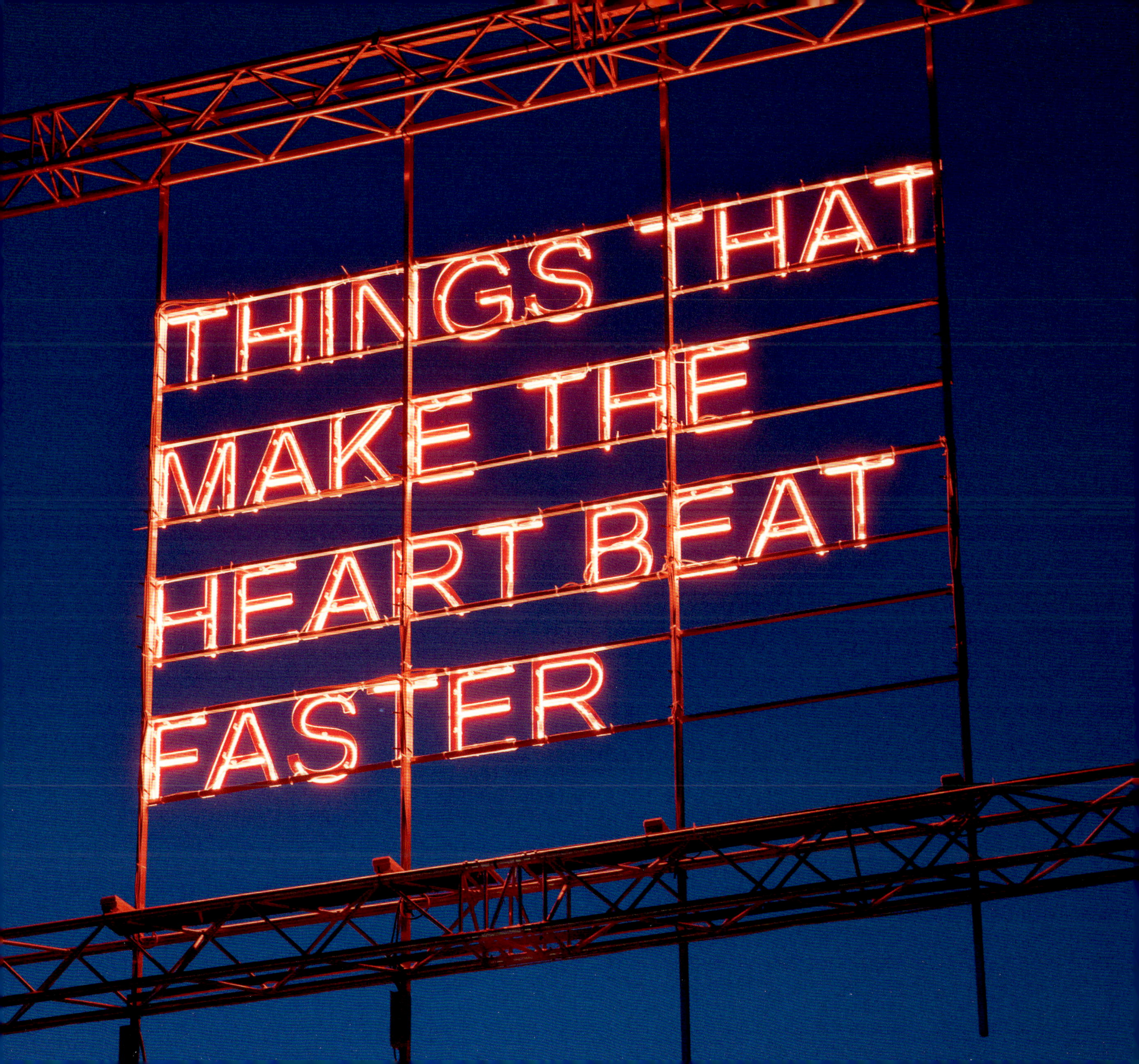

THINGS THAT
MAKE THE
HEART BEAT
FASTER

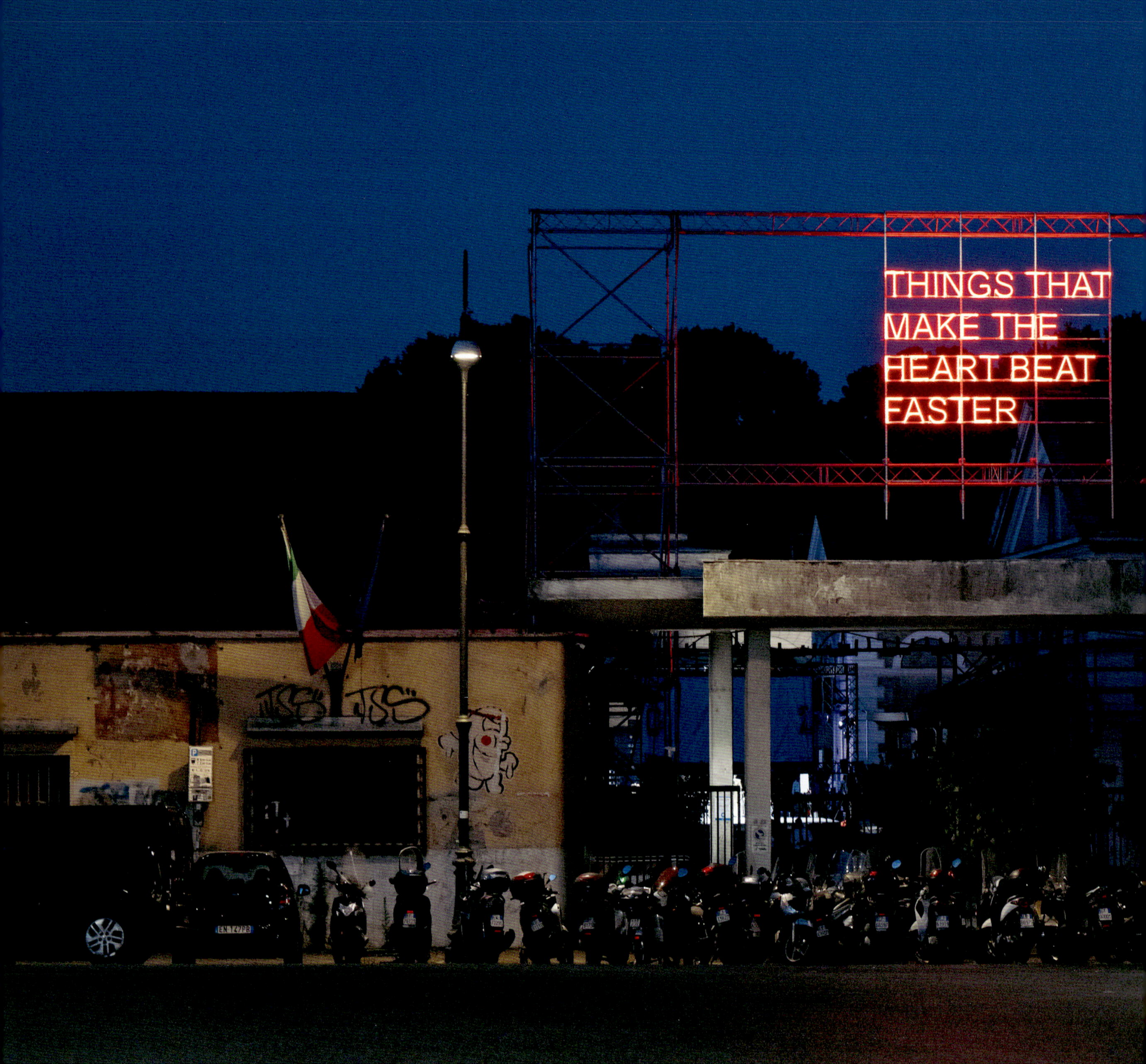
THINGS THAT
MAKE THE
HEART BEAT
FASTER

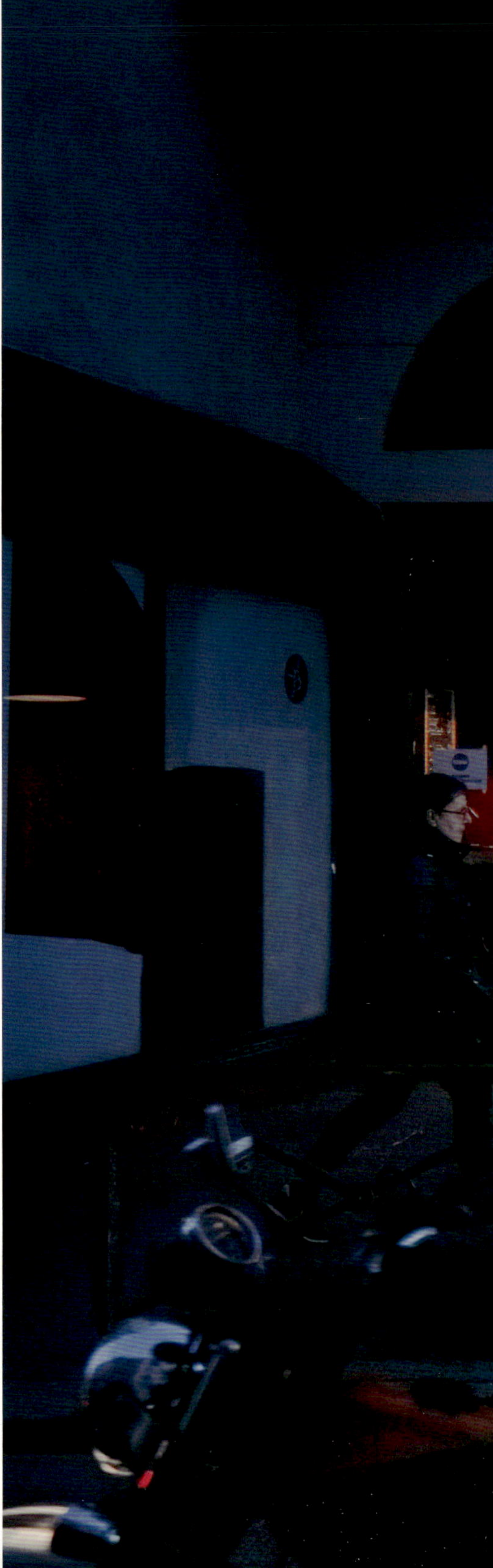

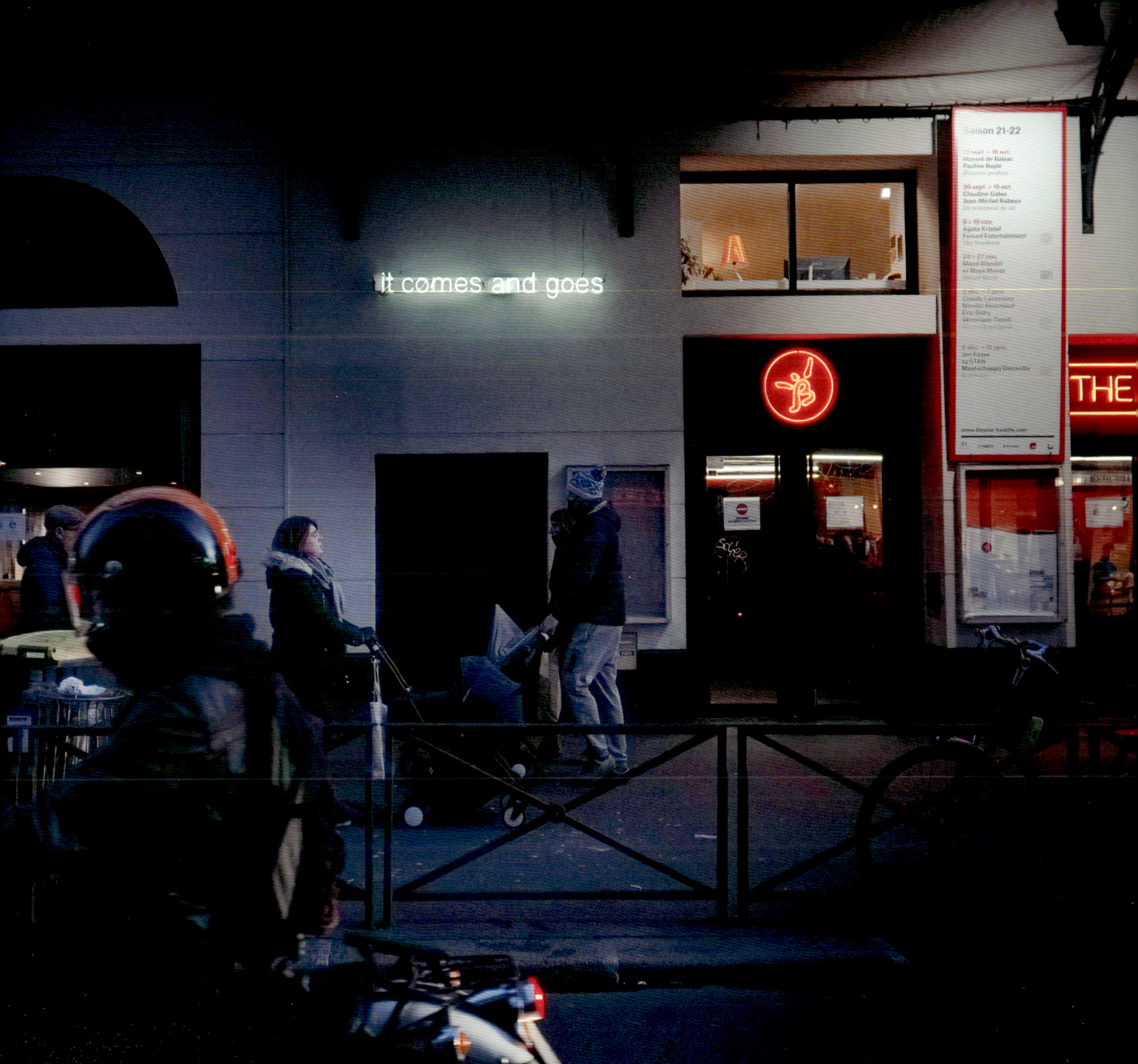

it comes and goes
Saison 21-22
THE

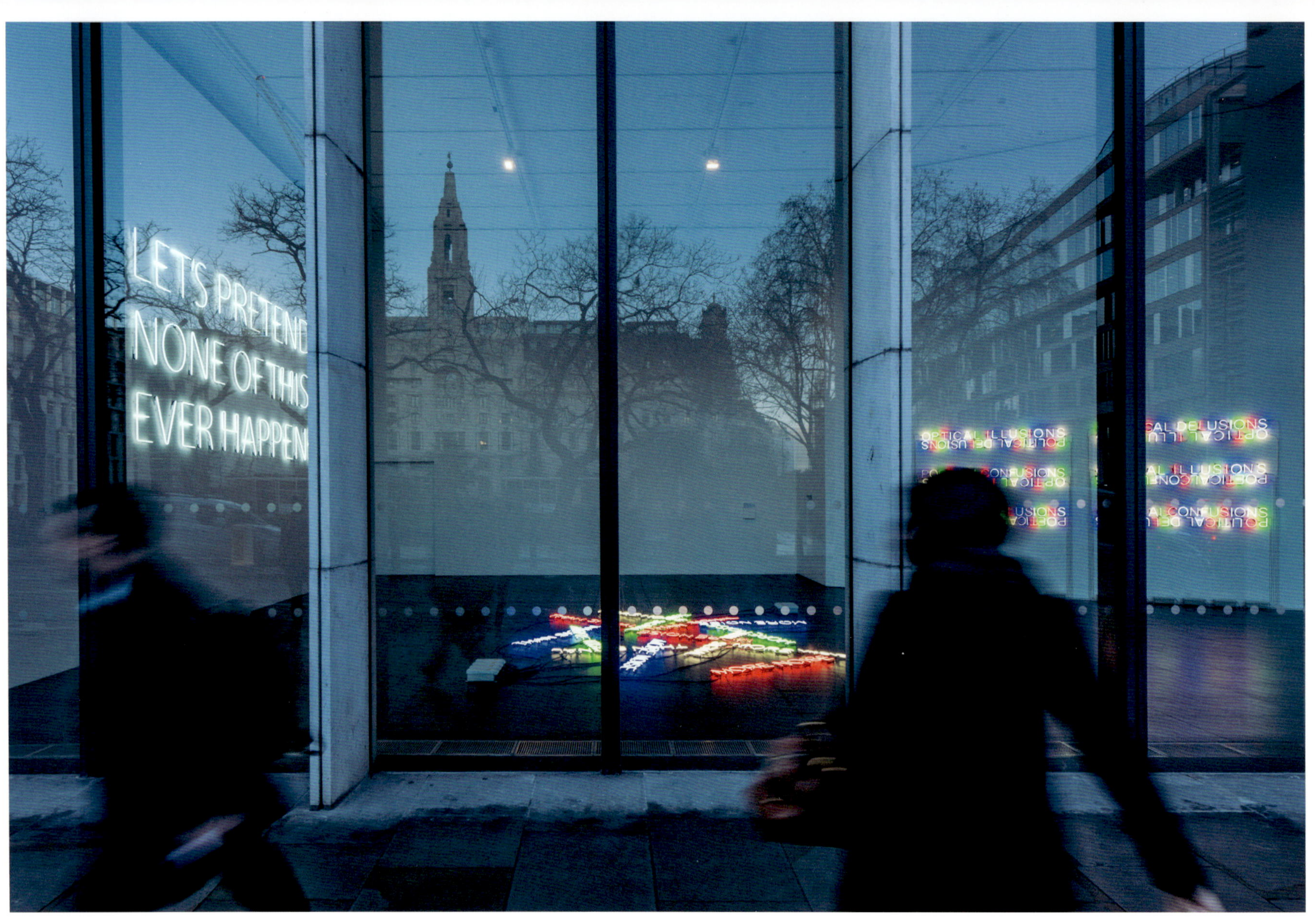
LET'S PRETEND
NONE OF THIS
EVER HAPPEN
OPTICAL ILLUSIONS
POLITICAL CONFUSIONS

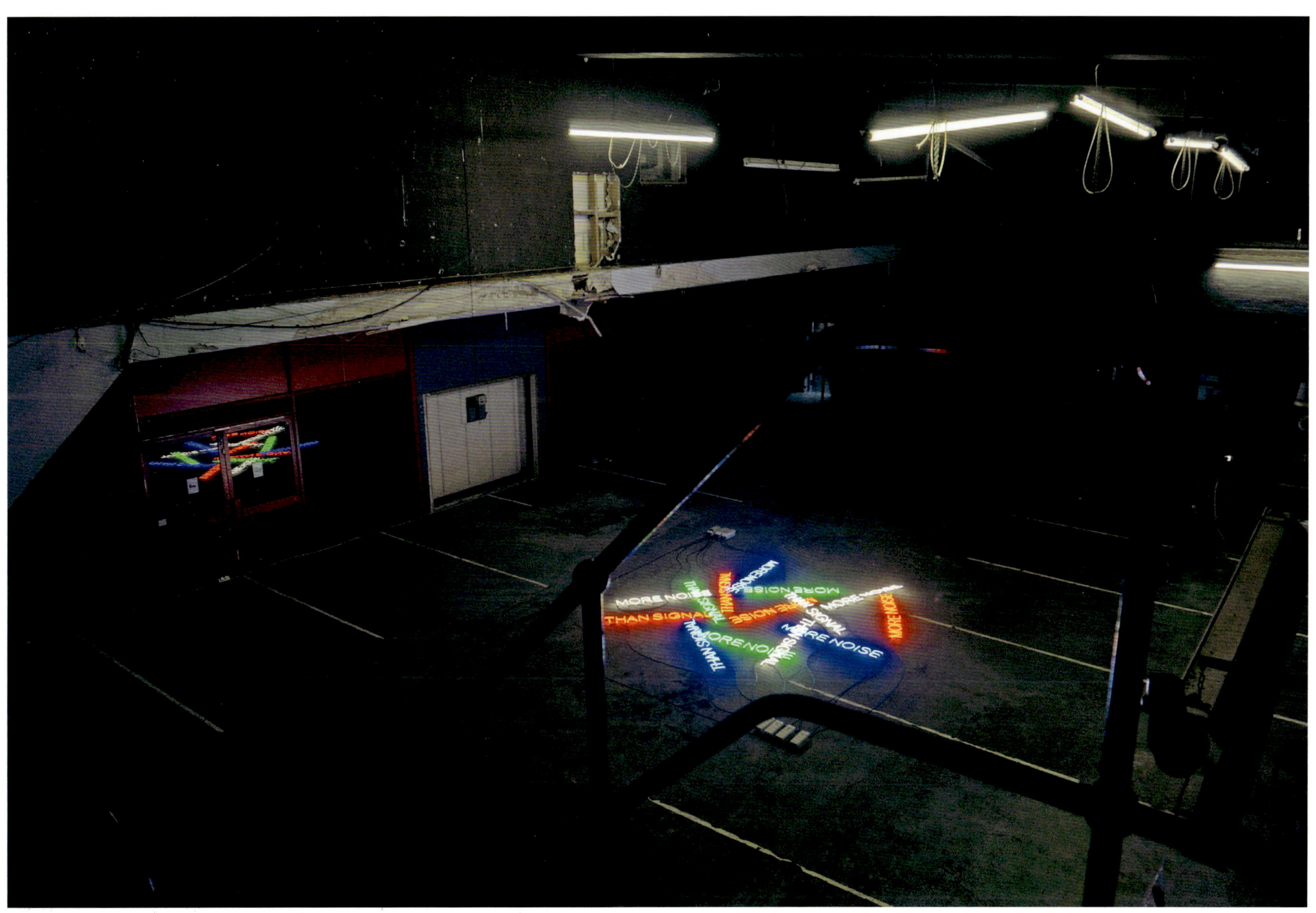

MORE NOISE
THAN SIGNAL

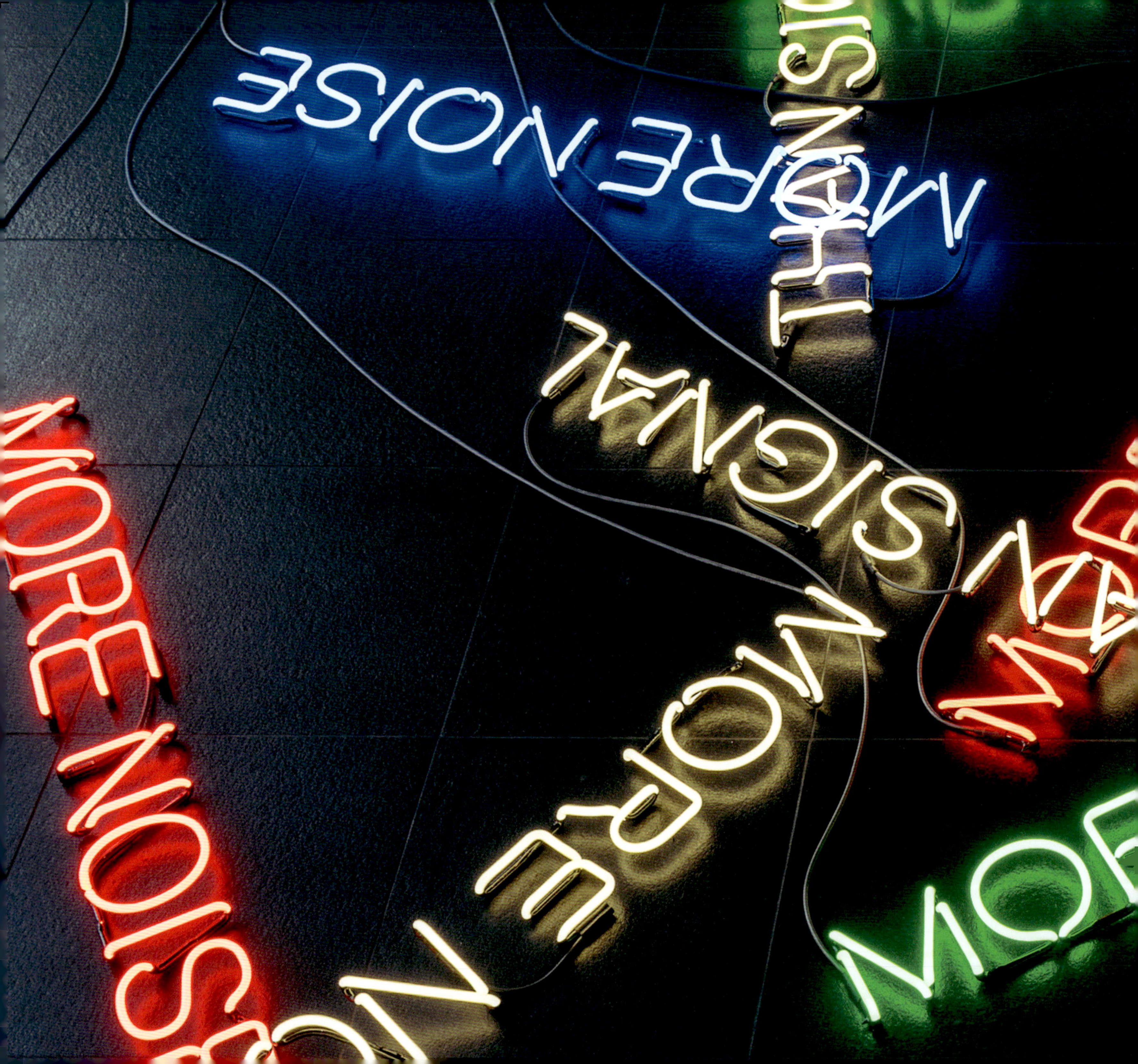

MORE NOISE
MORE NOISE
MORE SIGNAL
MORE NOISE
MORE
MORE
MORE

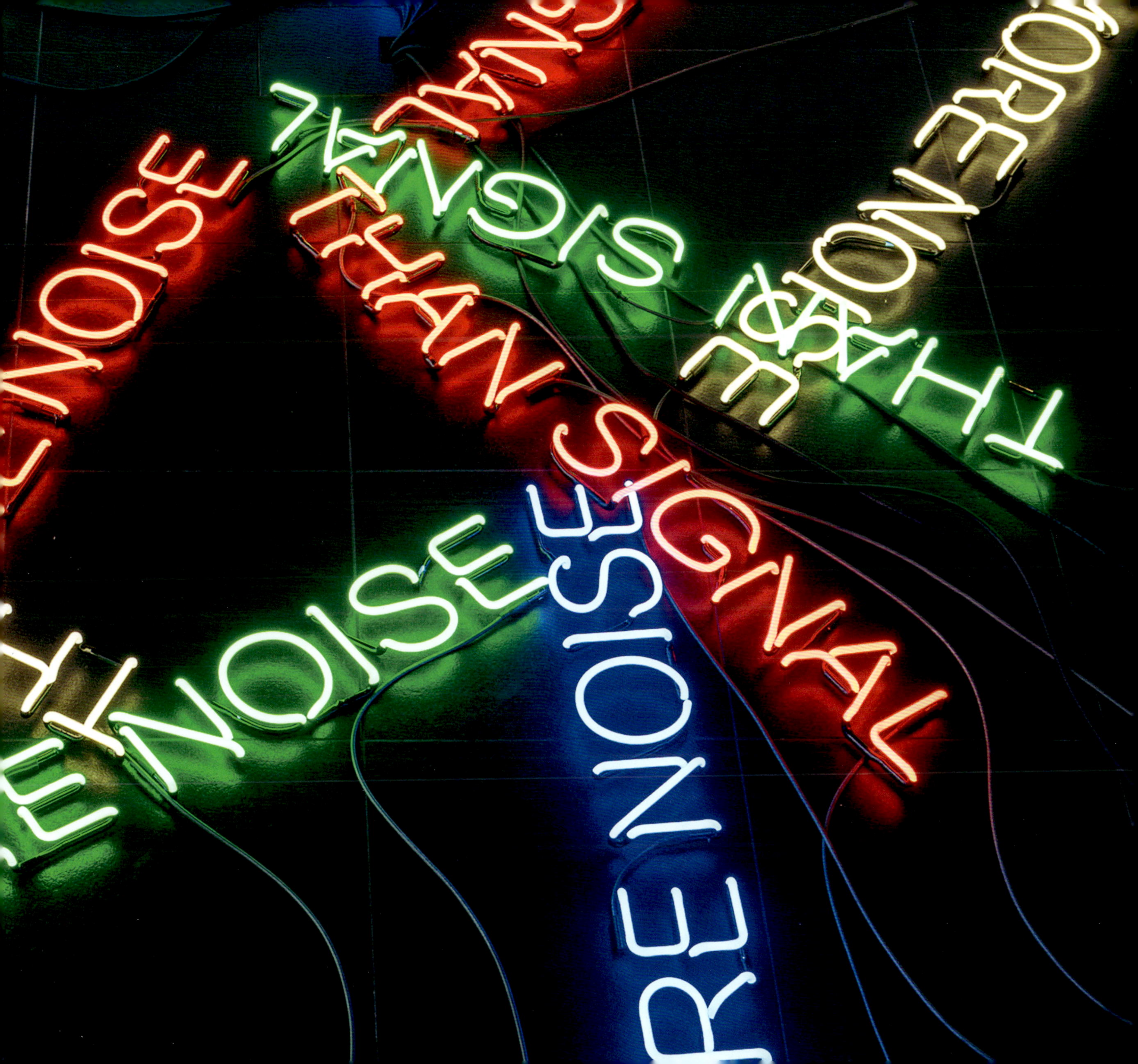
NOISE
THAN
SIGNAL
MORE
THAN SIGNAL
NOISE
SIGNAL
MORE NOISE
MORE

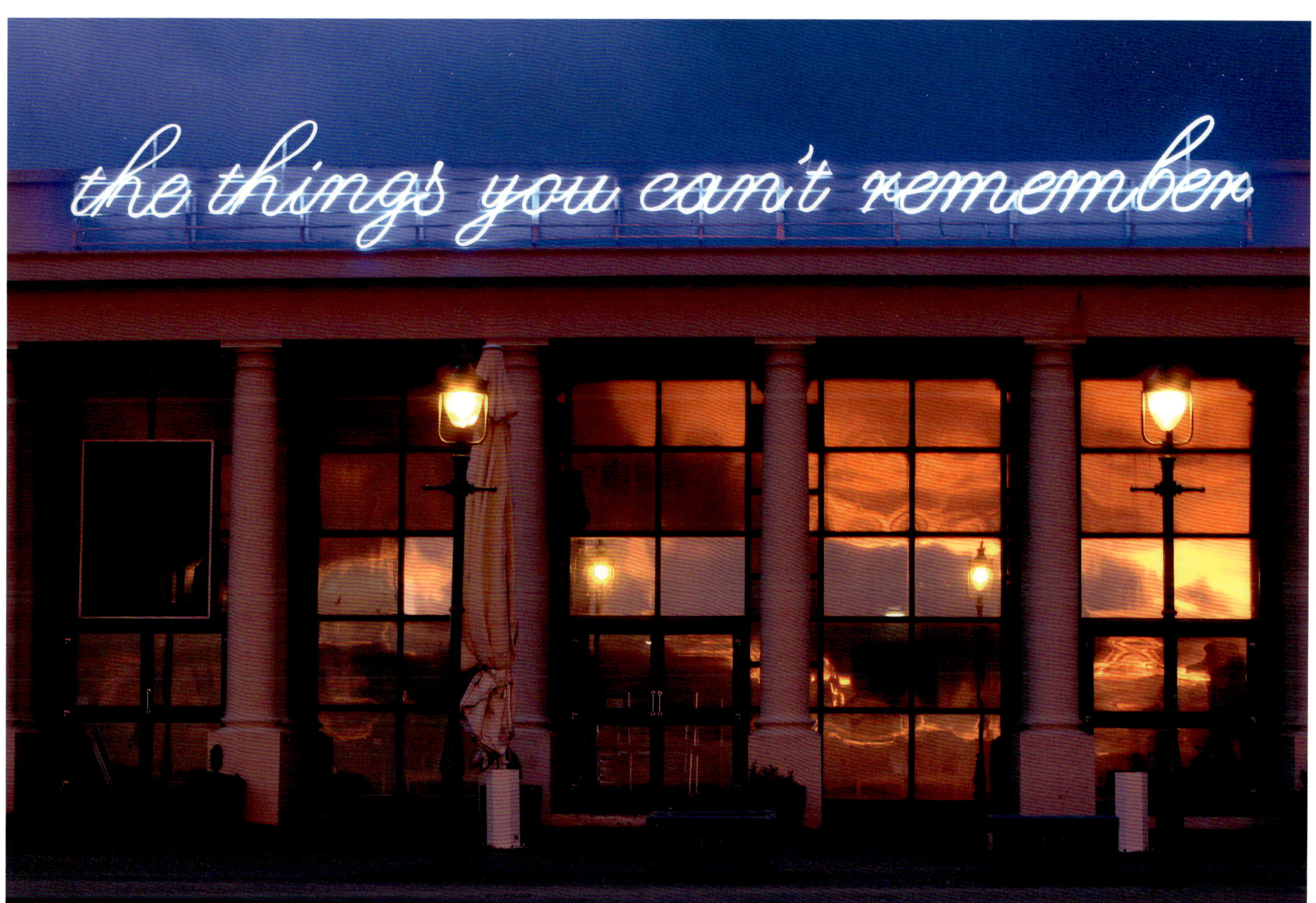
the things you can't remember

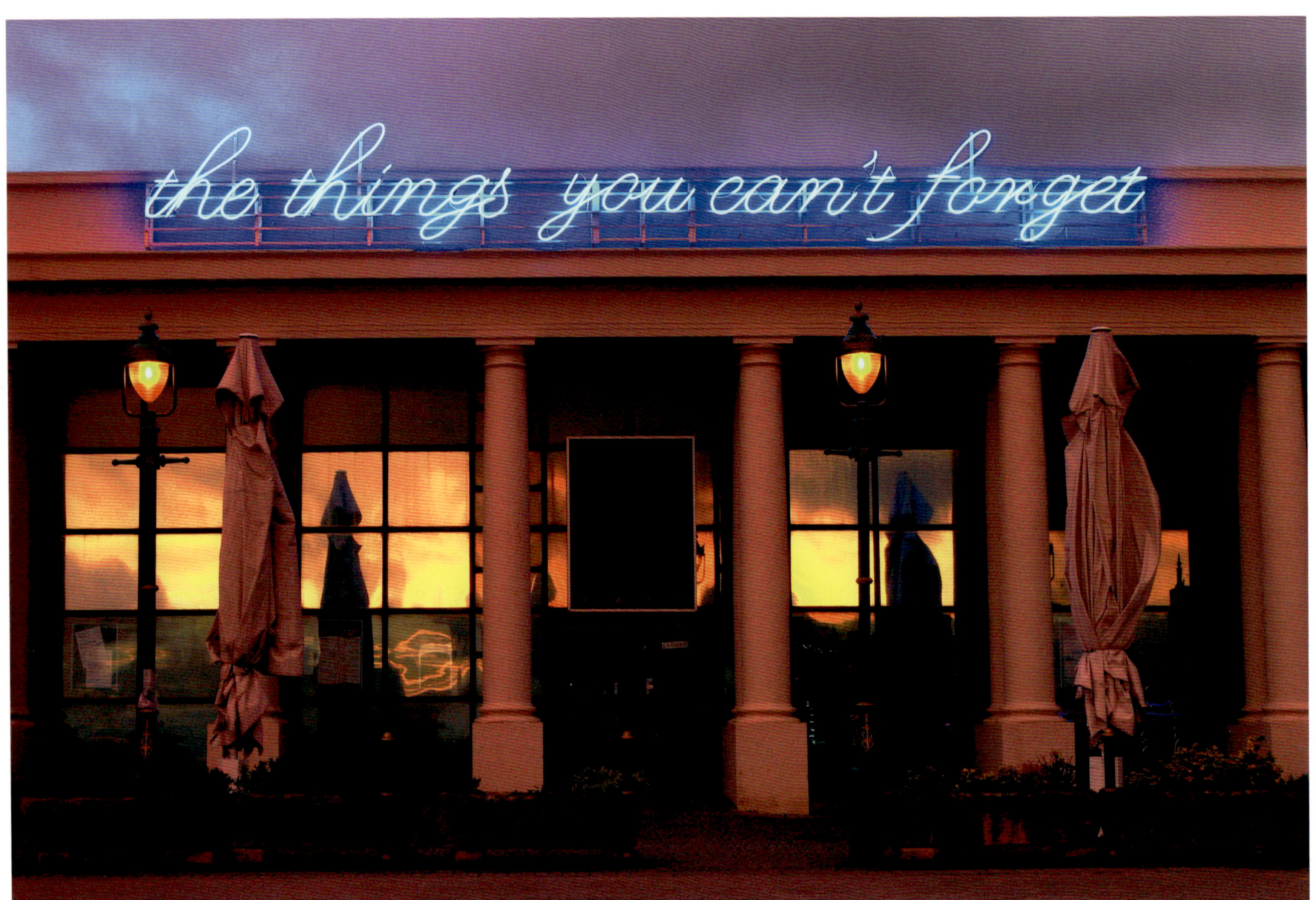
the things you can't forget

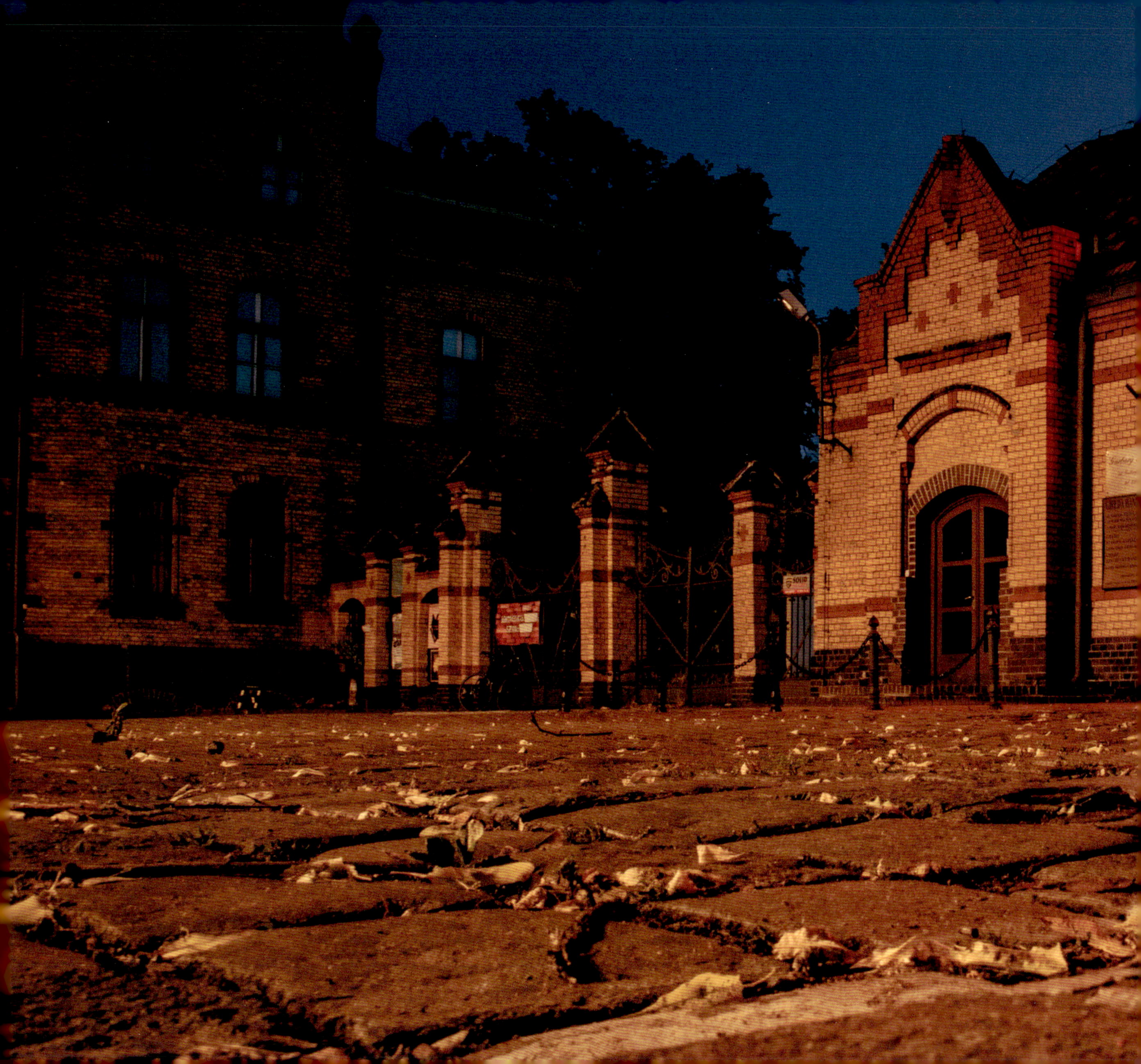

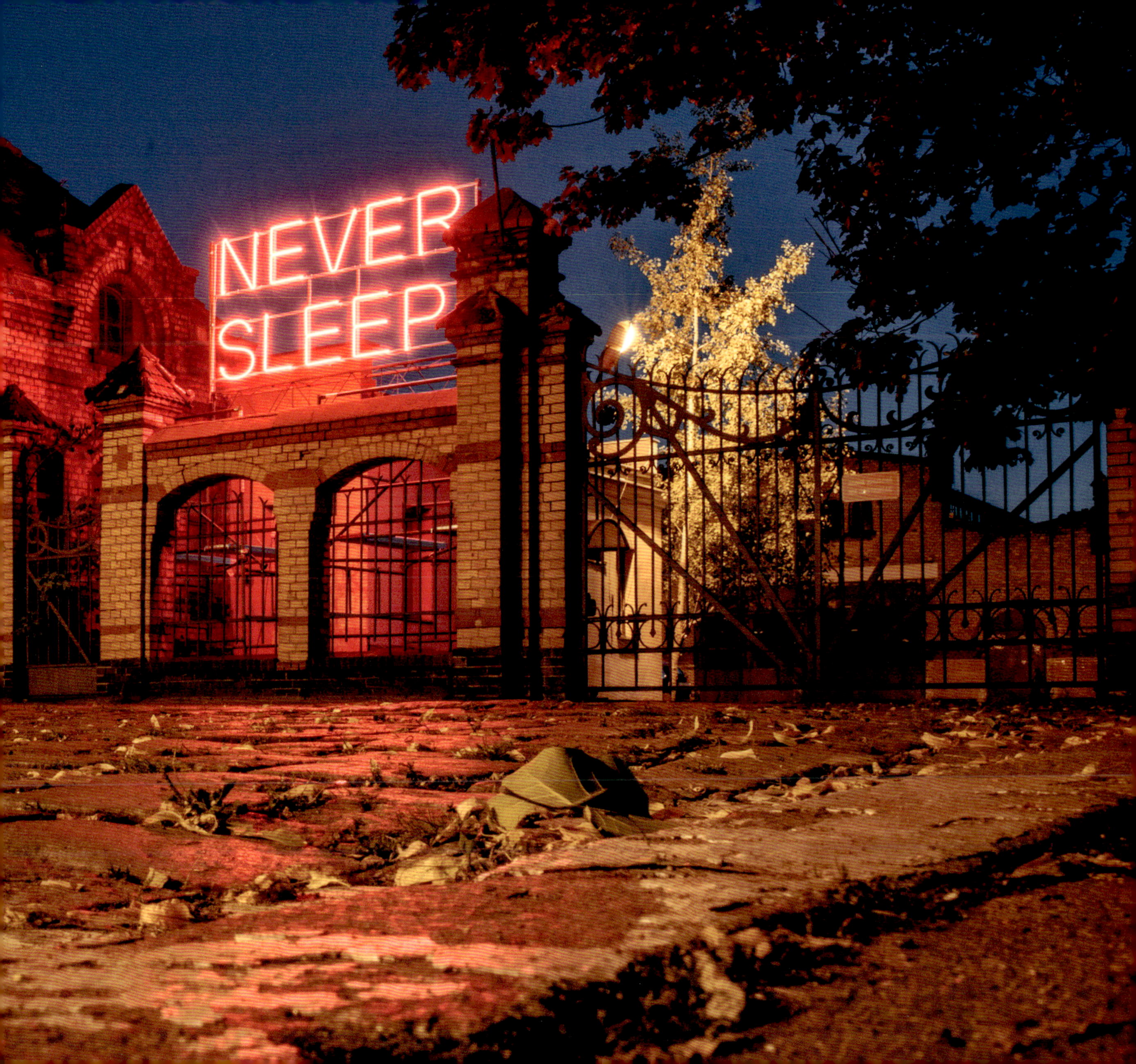
NEVER
SLEEP

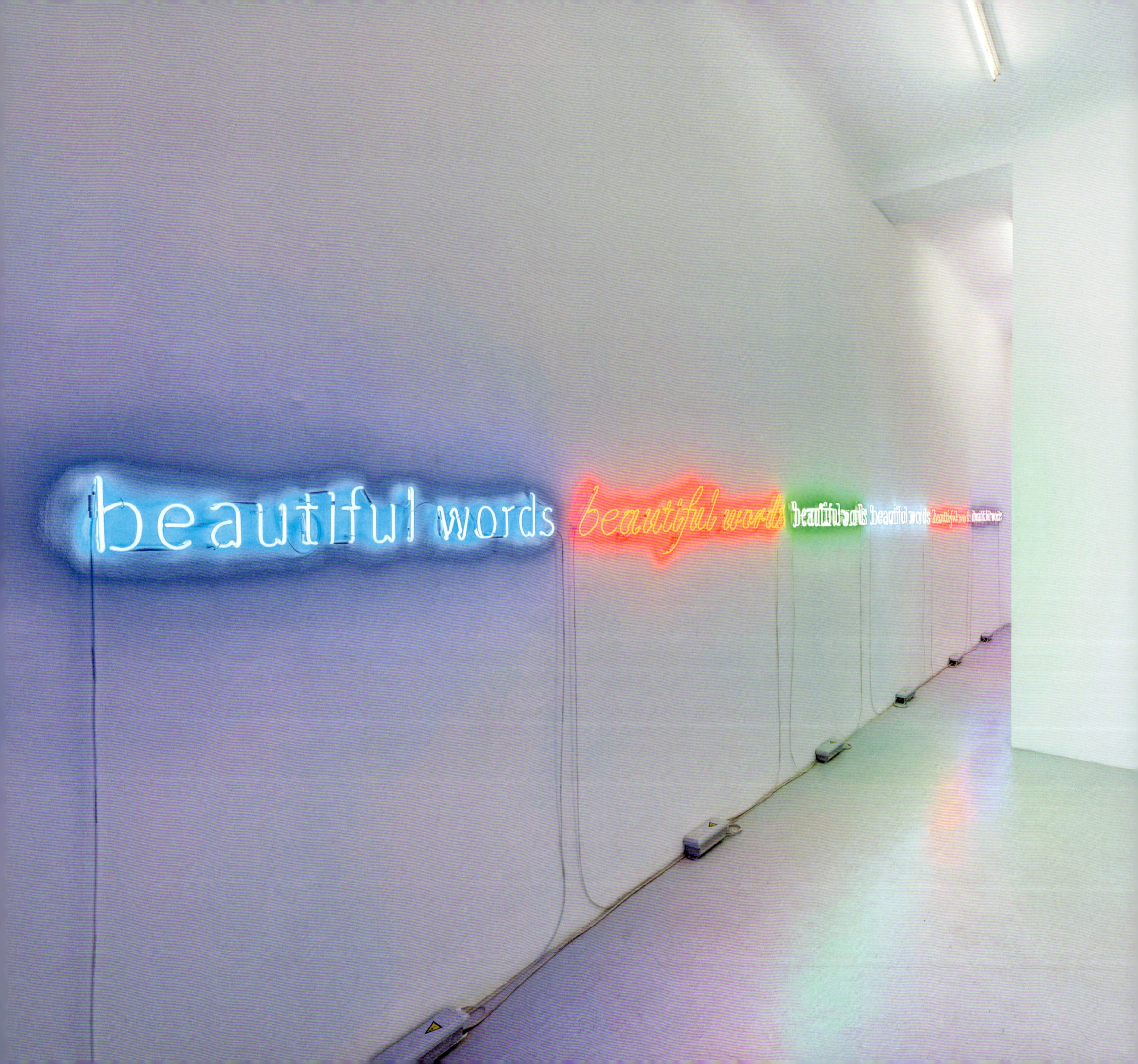

beautiful words
beautiful words
beautiful words
beautiful words
beautiful words
beautiful words

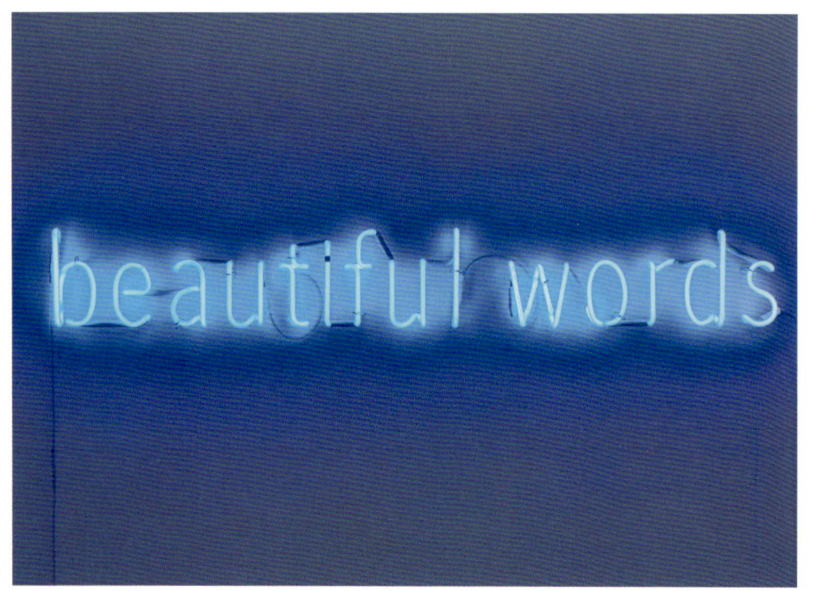
beautiful words
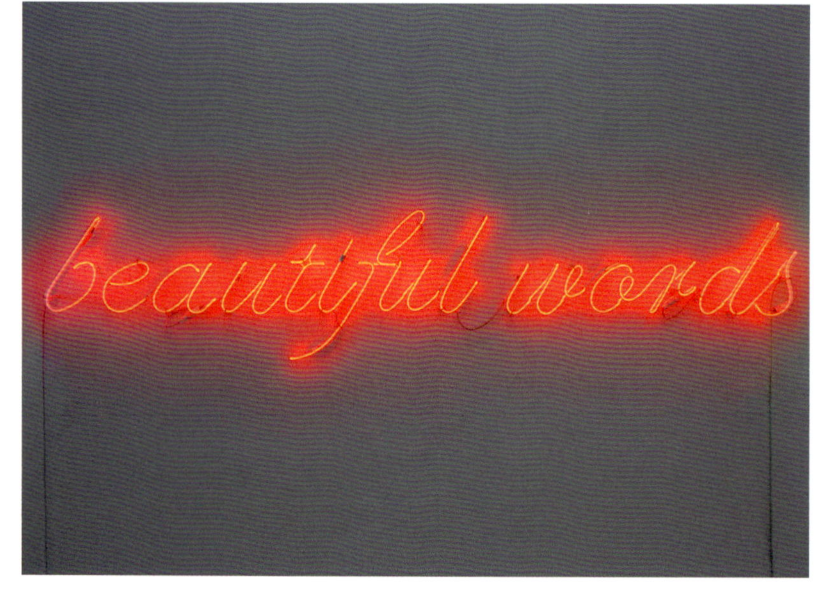
beautiful words

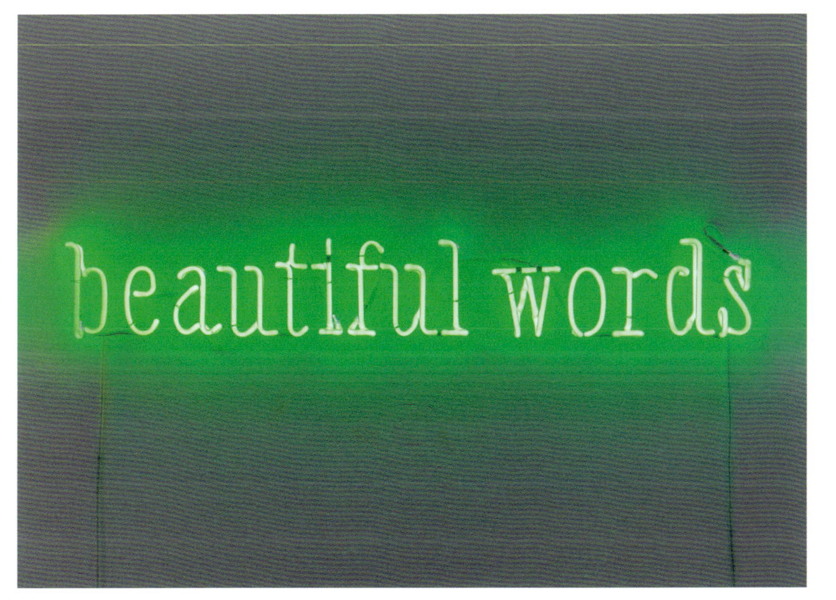
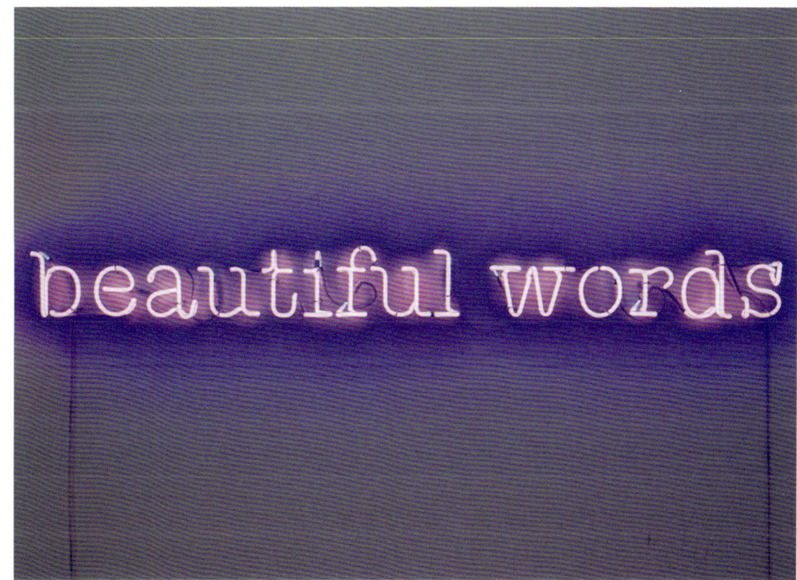

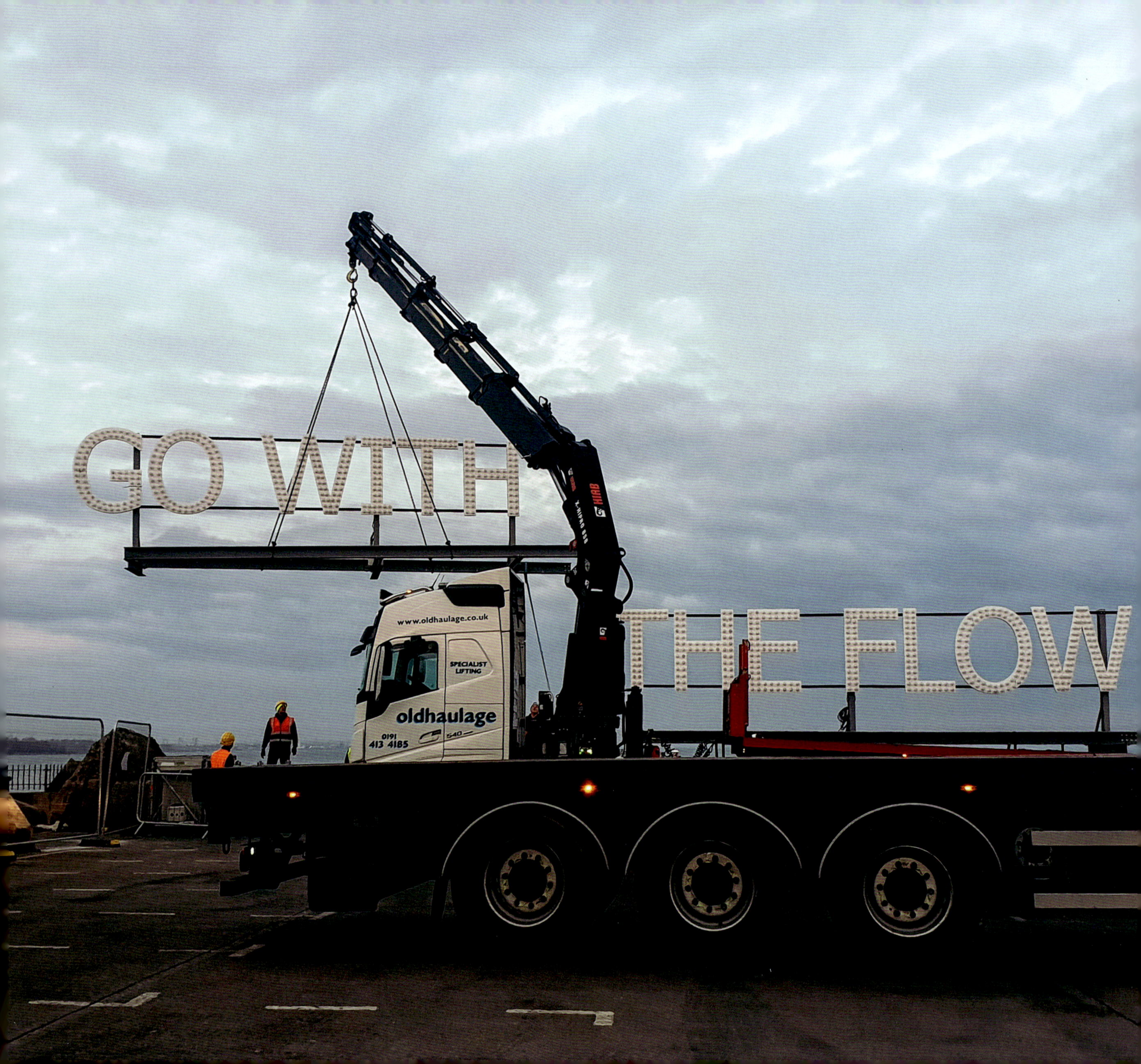
GO WITH
THE FLOW
www.oldhaulage.co.uk
SPECIALIST
LIFTING
oldhaulage
0191
413 4185
540
HIAB

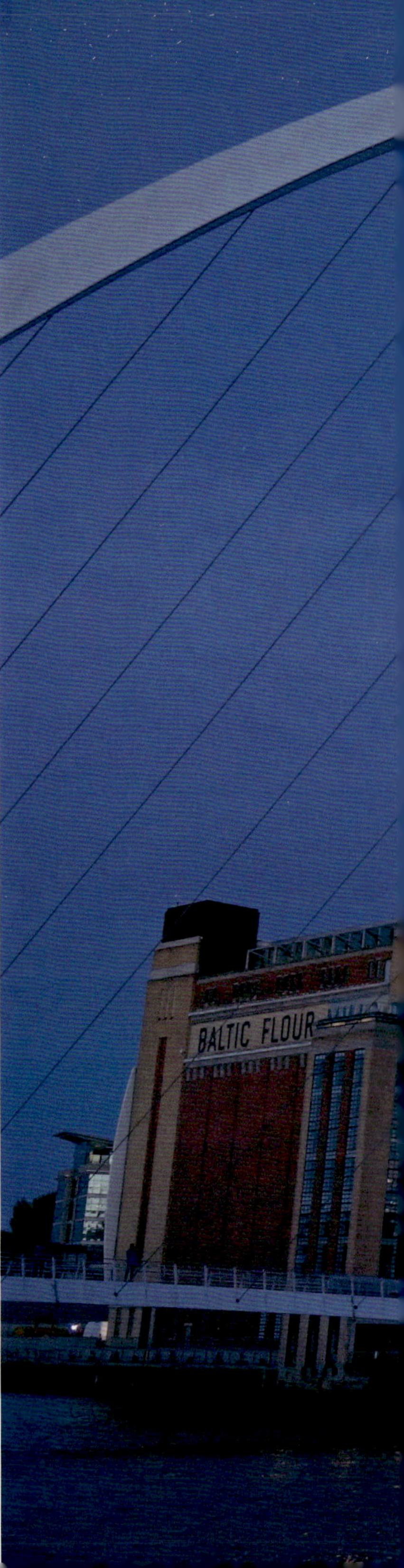
BALTIC FLOUR

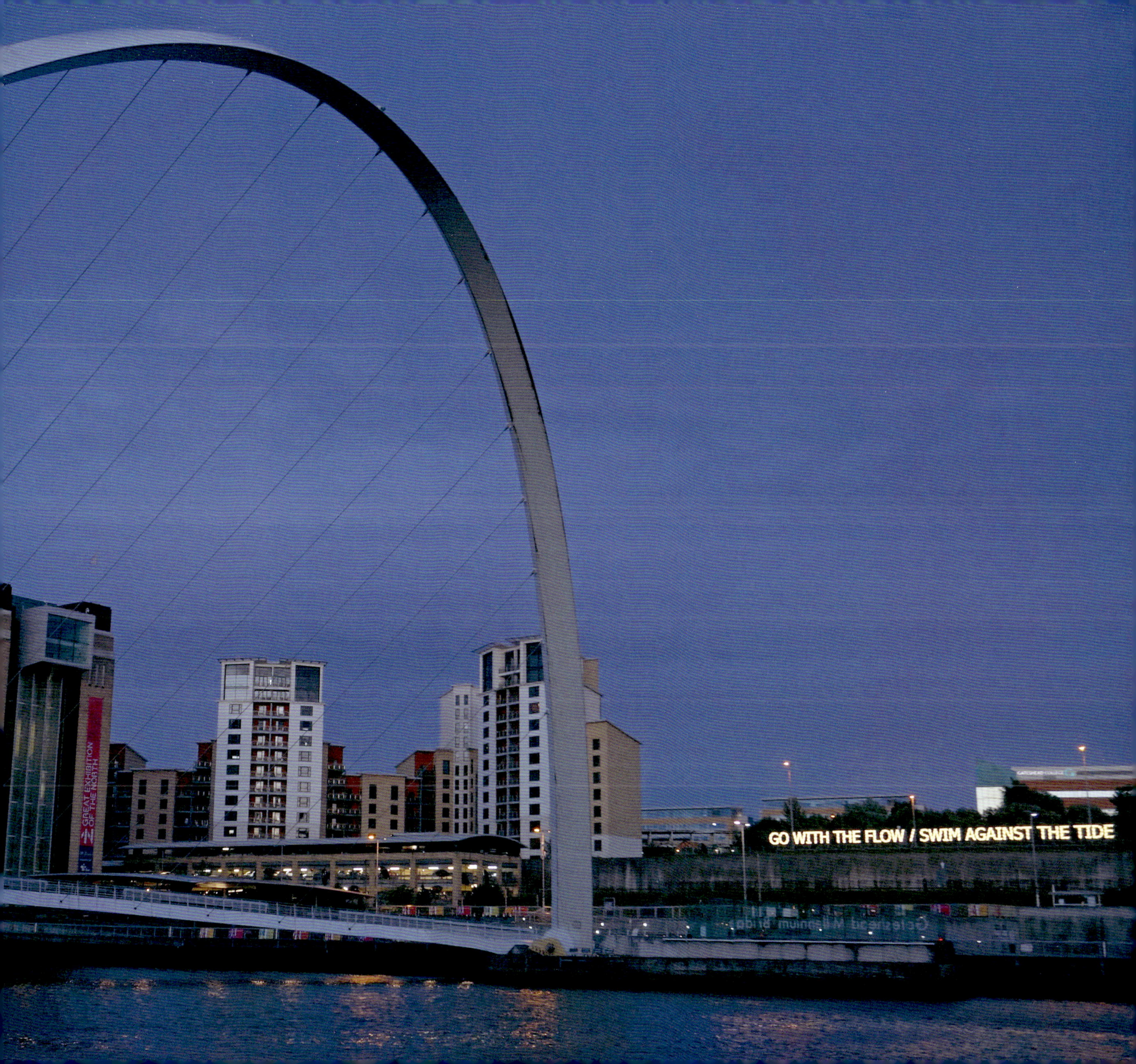

GO WITH THE FLOW / SWIM AGAINST THE TIDE
GREAT EXHIBITION OF THE NORTH
Gateshead Millennium Bridge

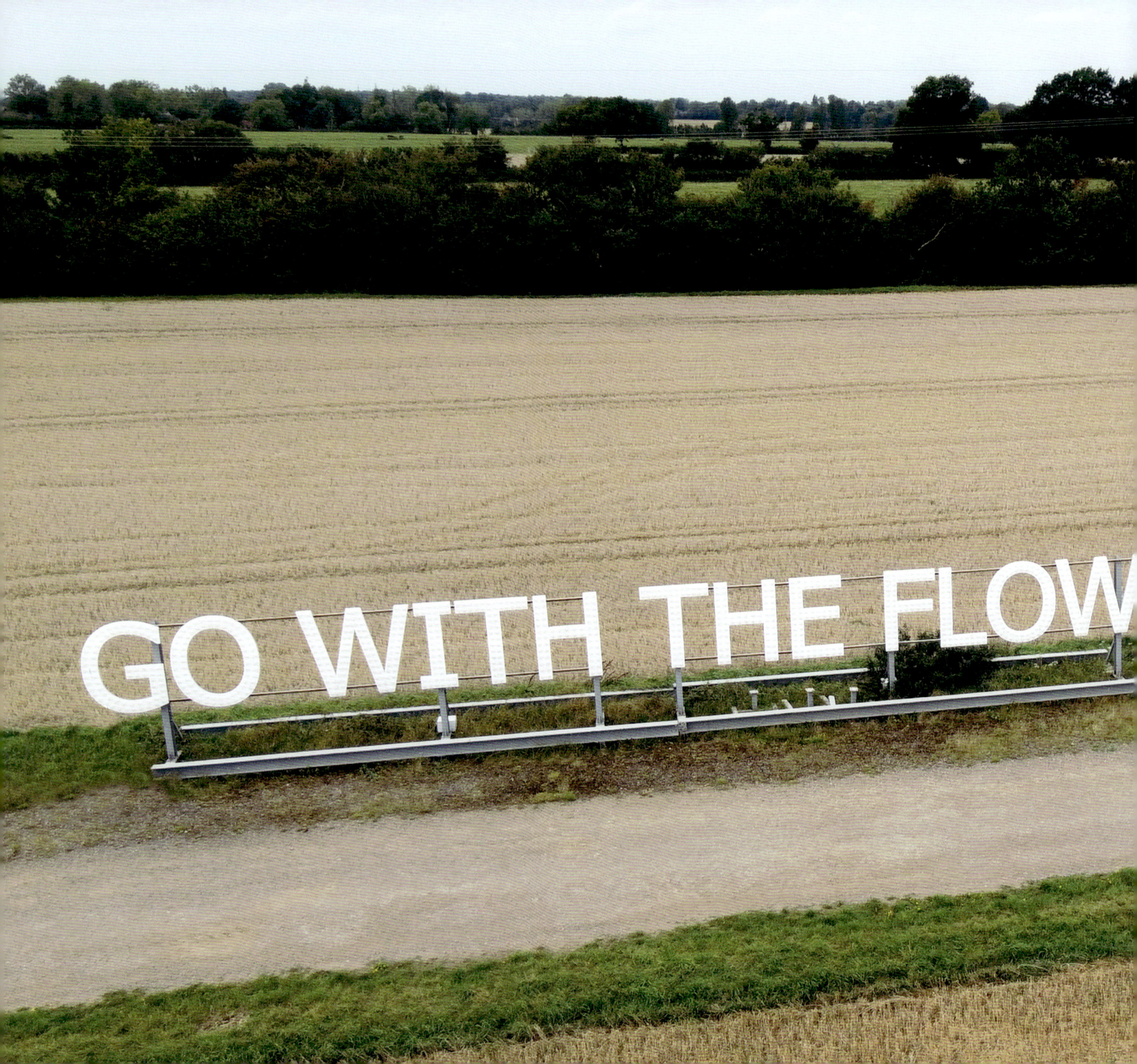
GO WITH THE FLOW

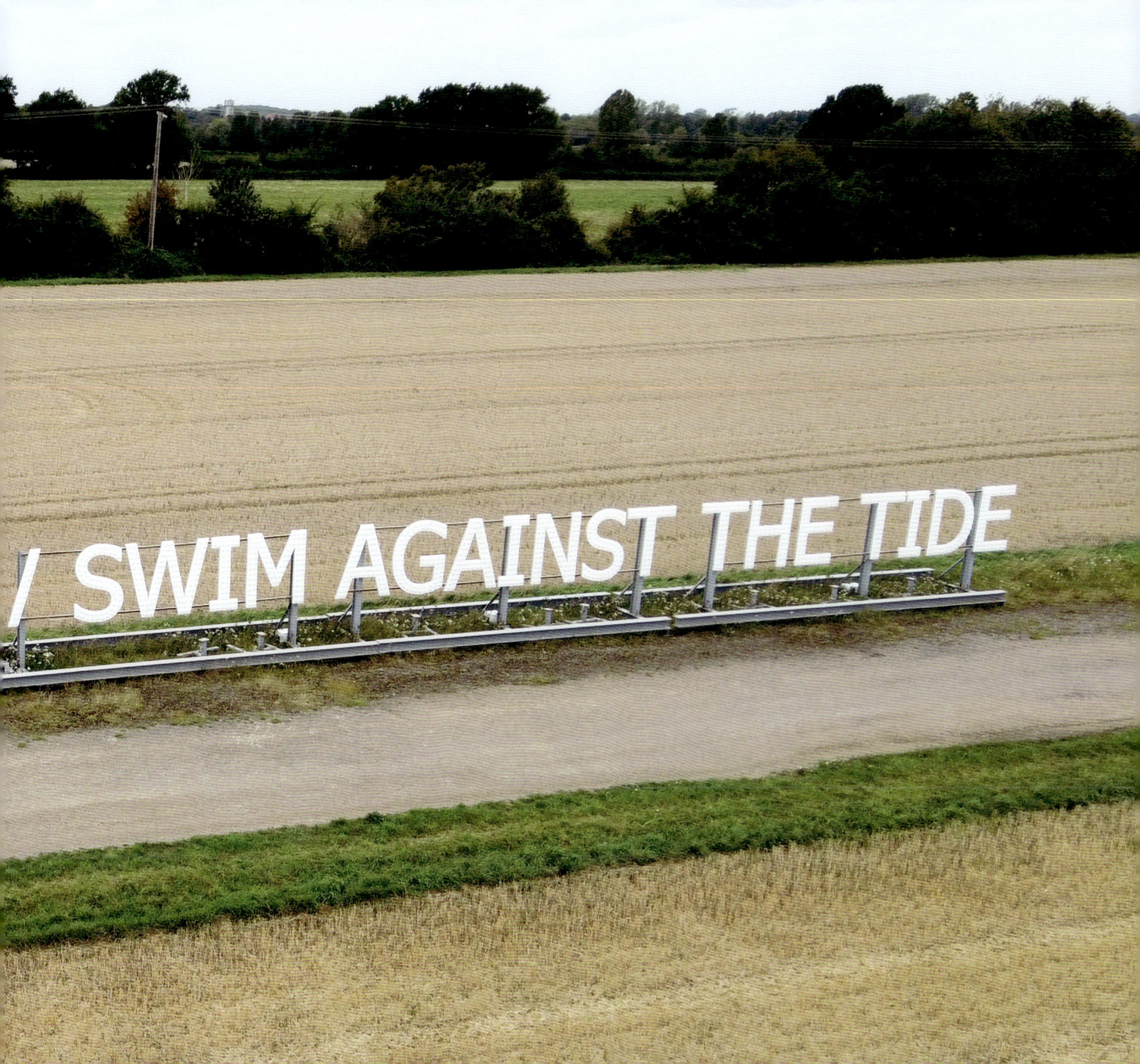
I SWIM AGAINST THE TIDE

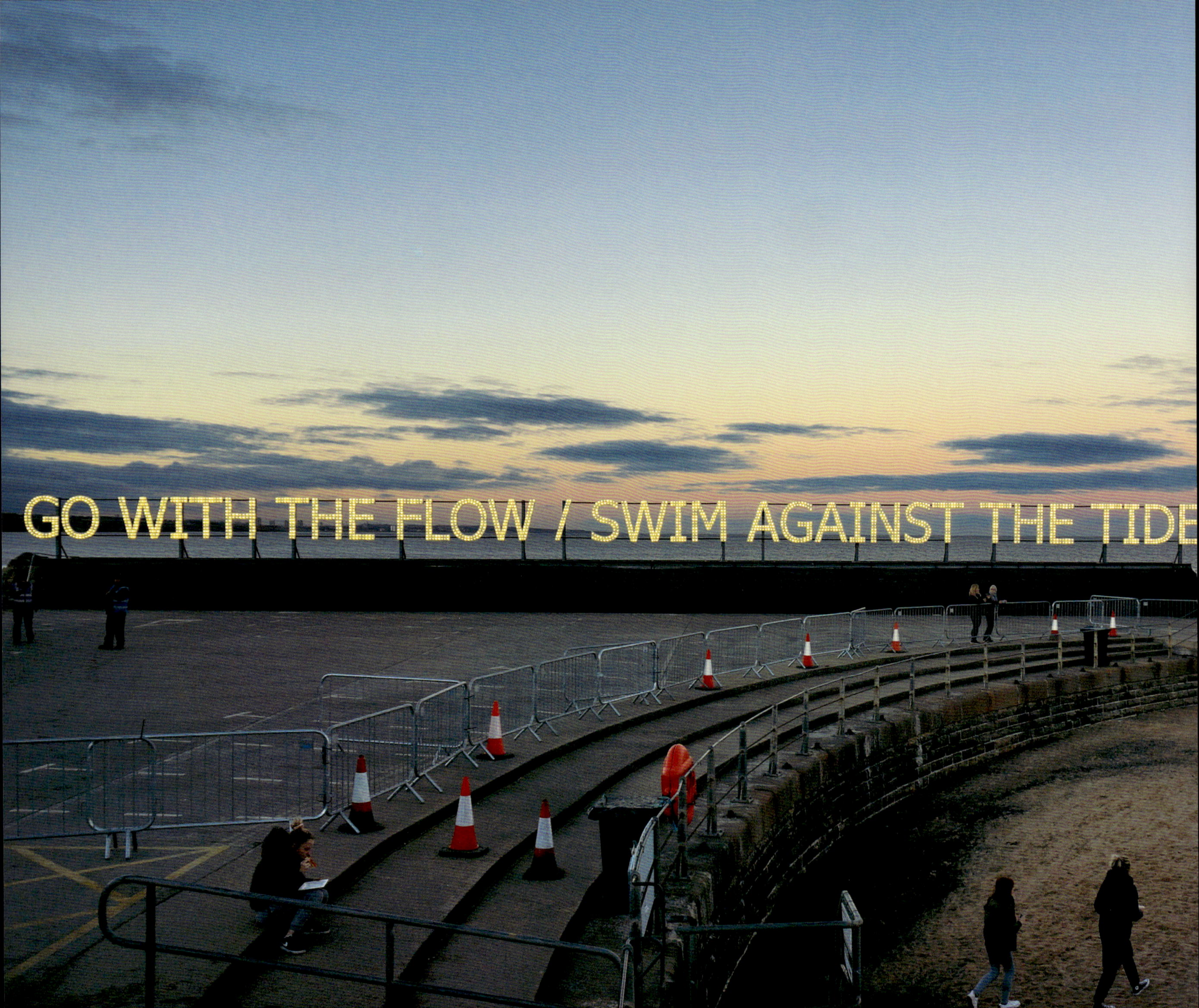
GO WITH THE FLOW / SWIM AGAINST THE TIDE

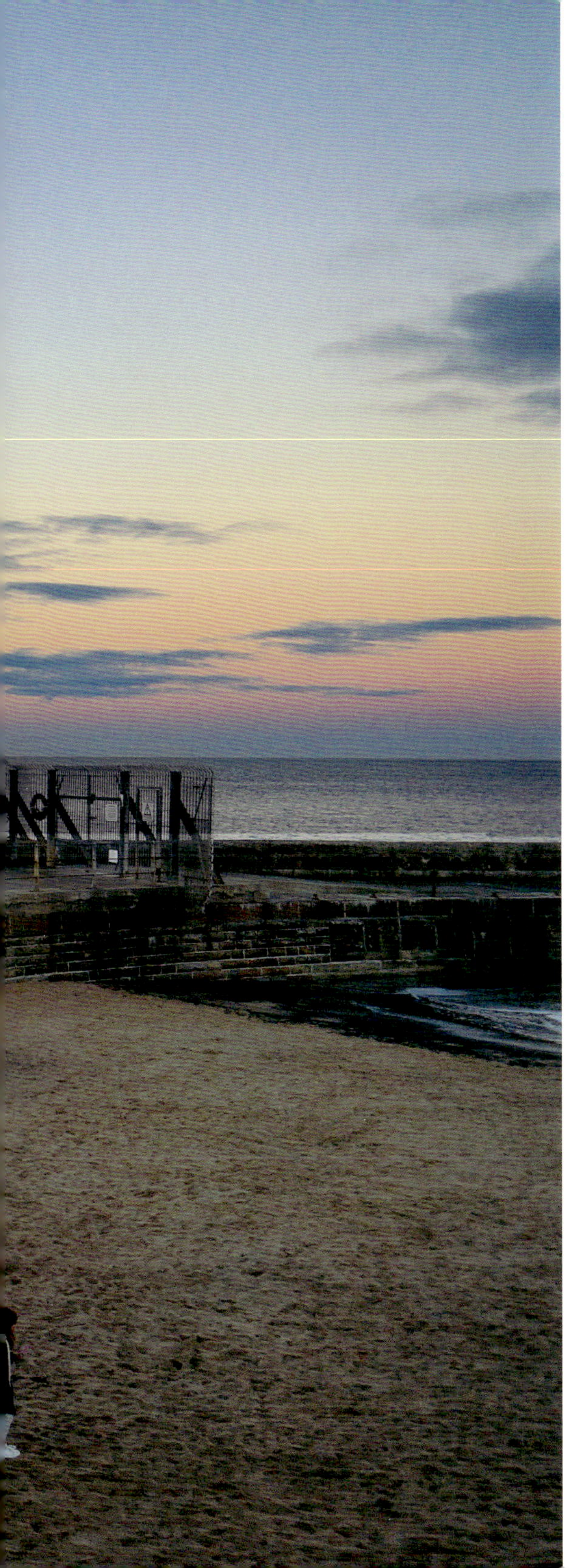

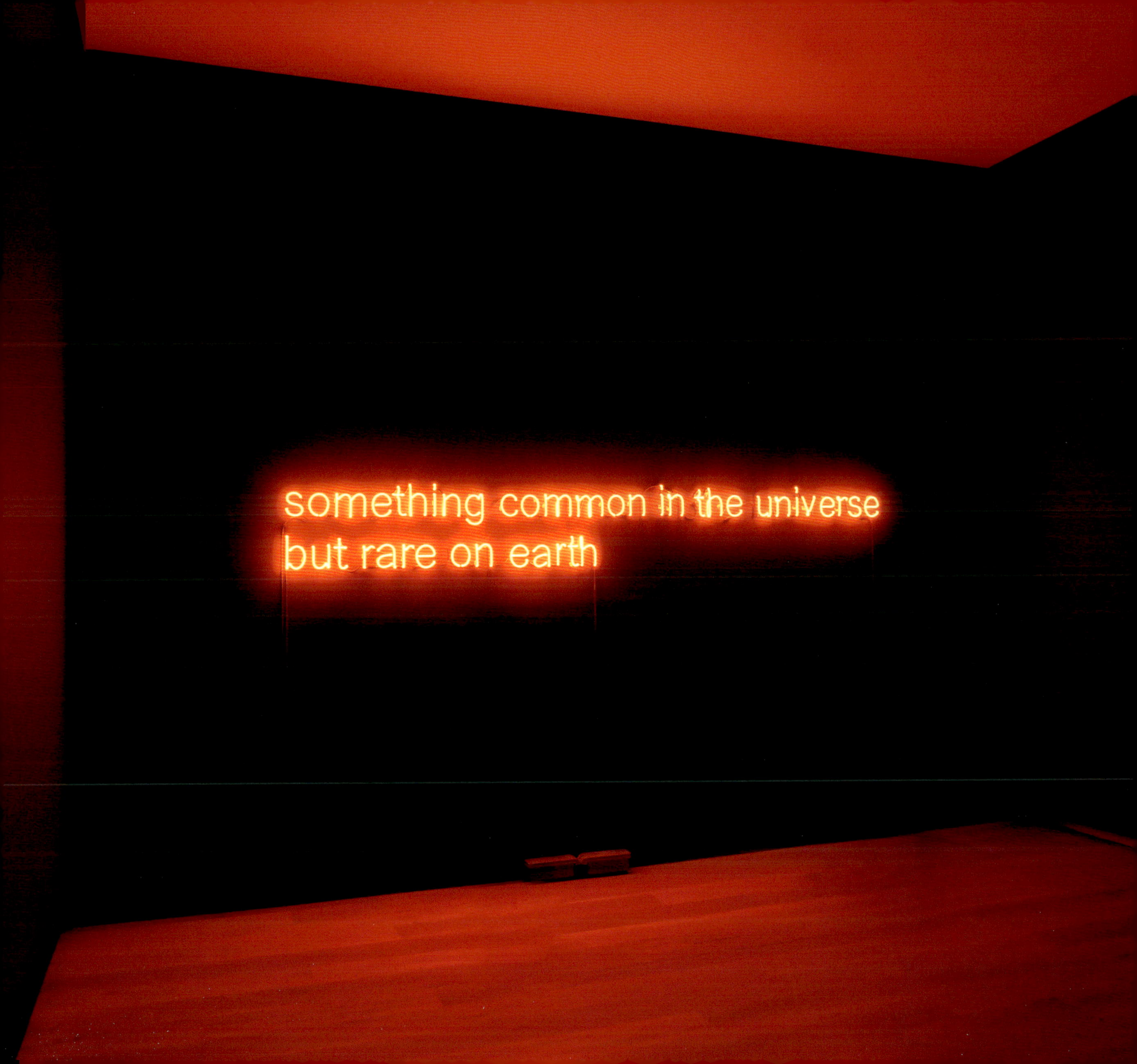

something common in the universe
but rare on earth

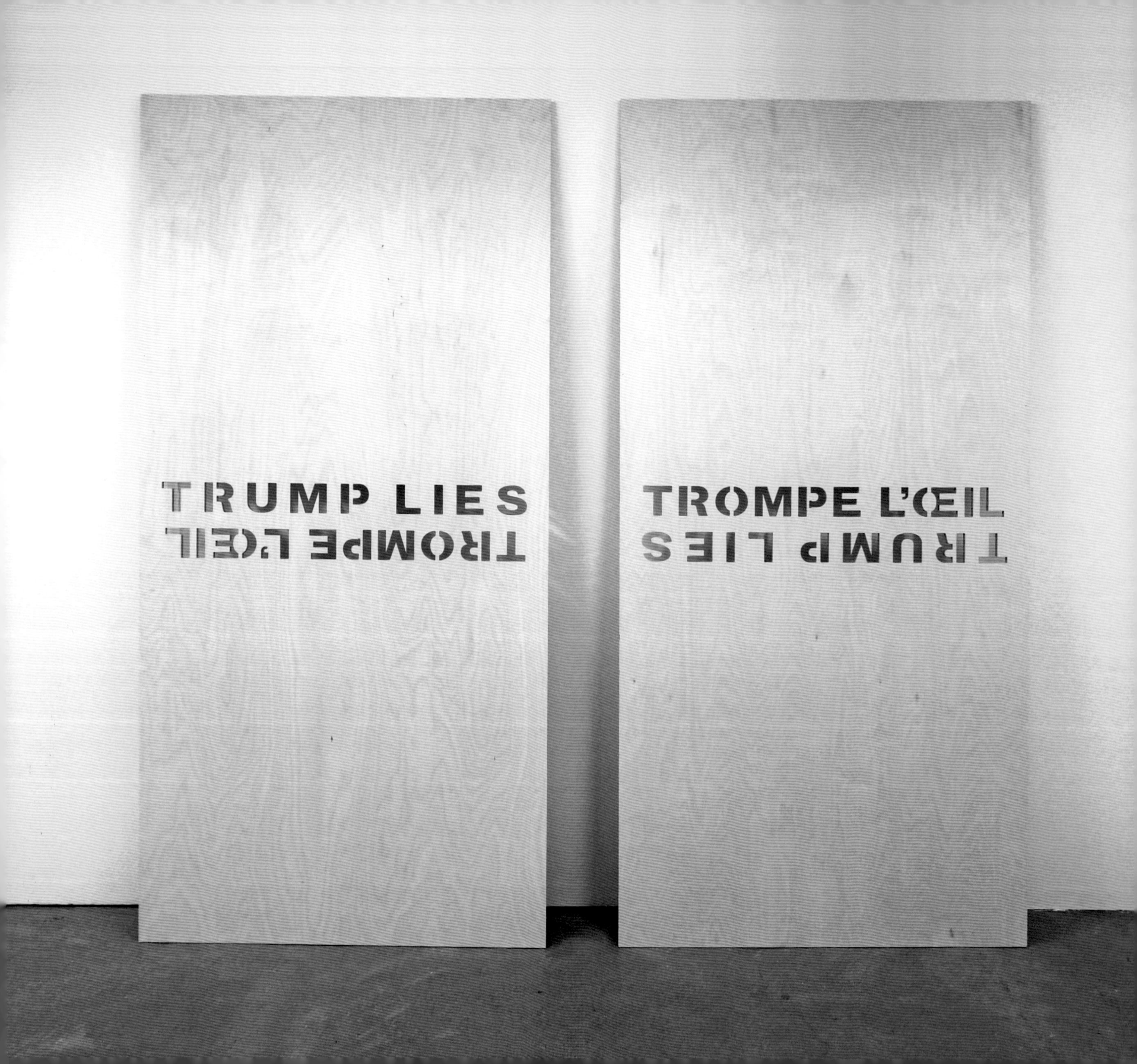

TRUMP LIES
TROMPE L'ŒIL
TROMPE L'ŒIL
TRUMP LIES

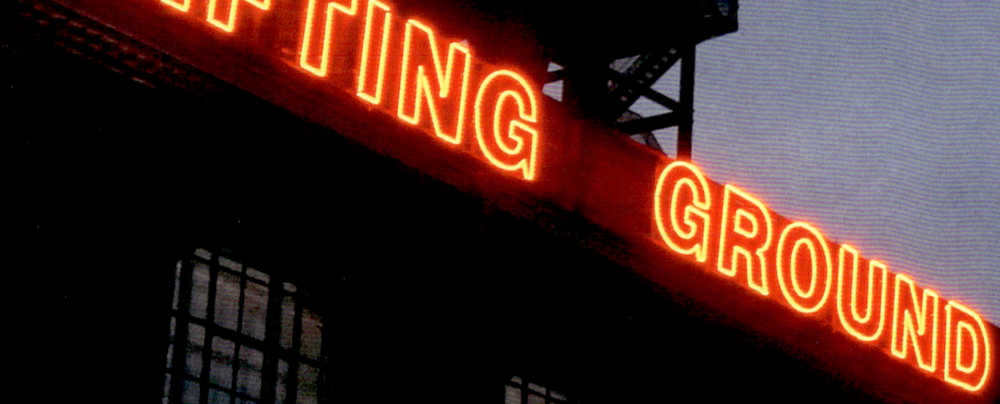

SHIFTING
GROUND

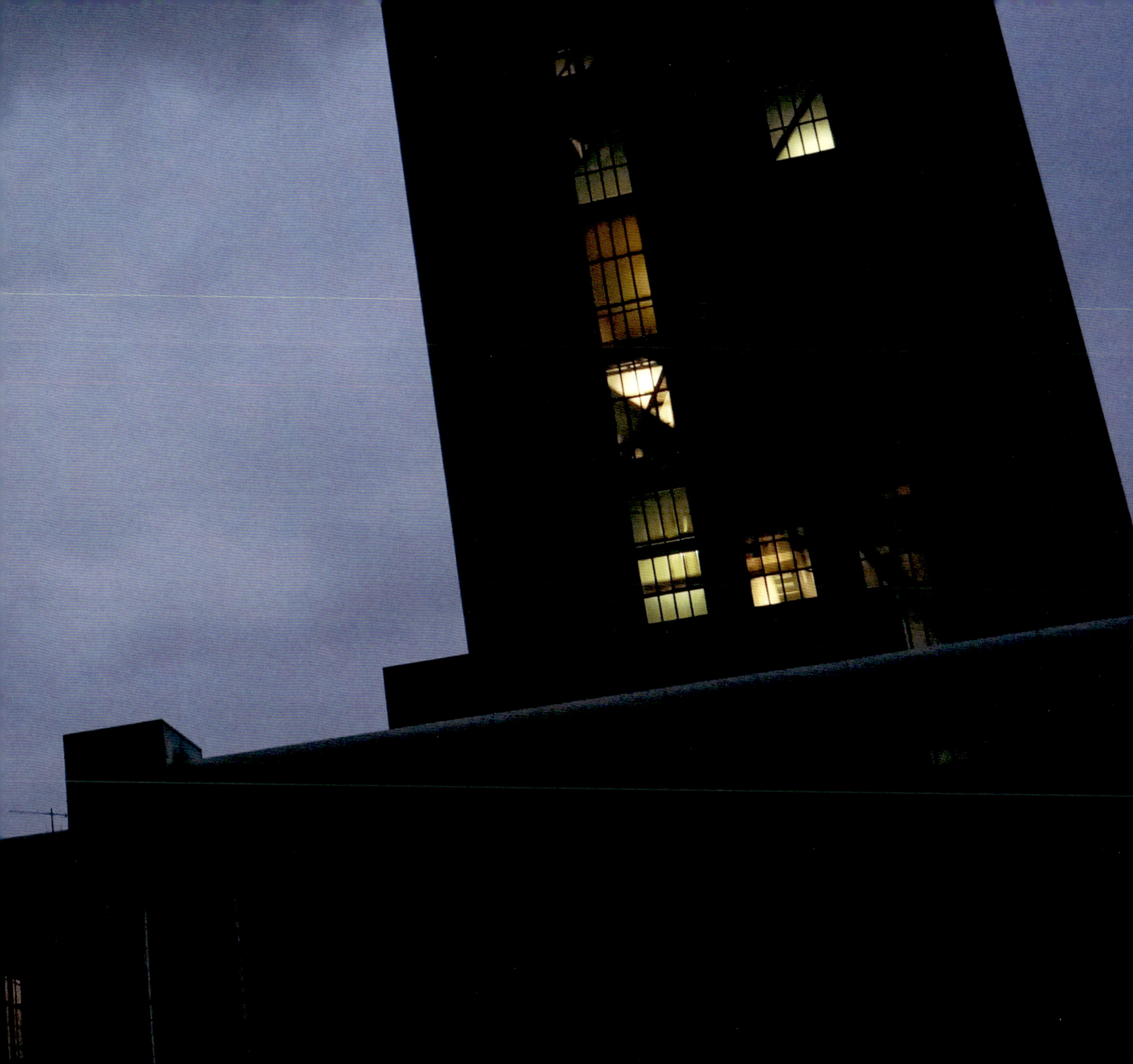

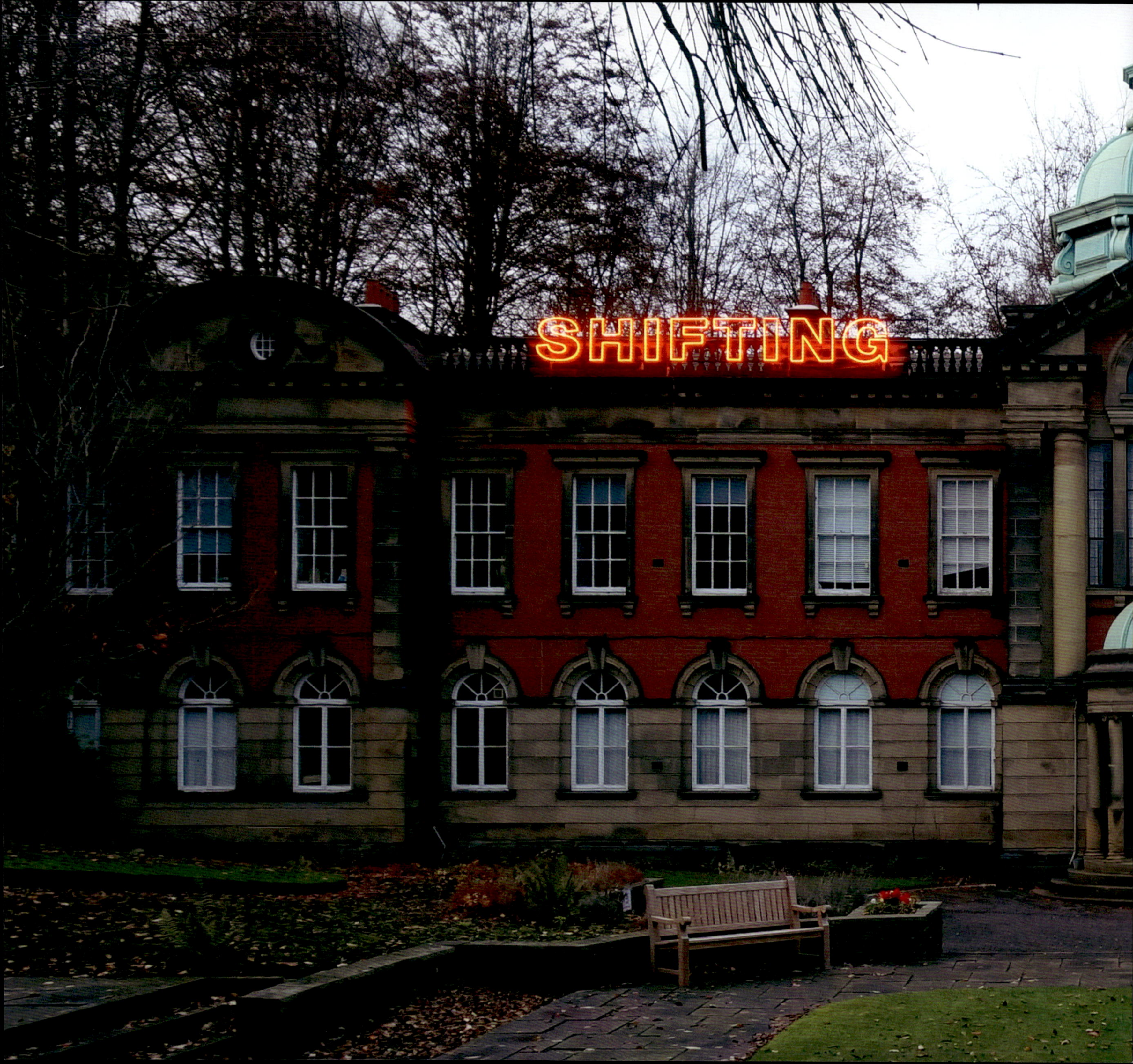
SHIFTING

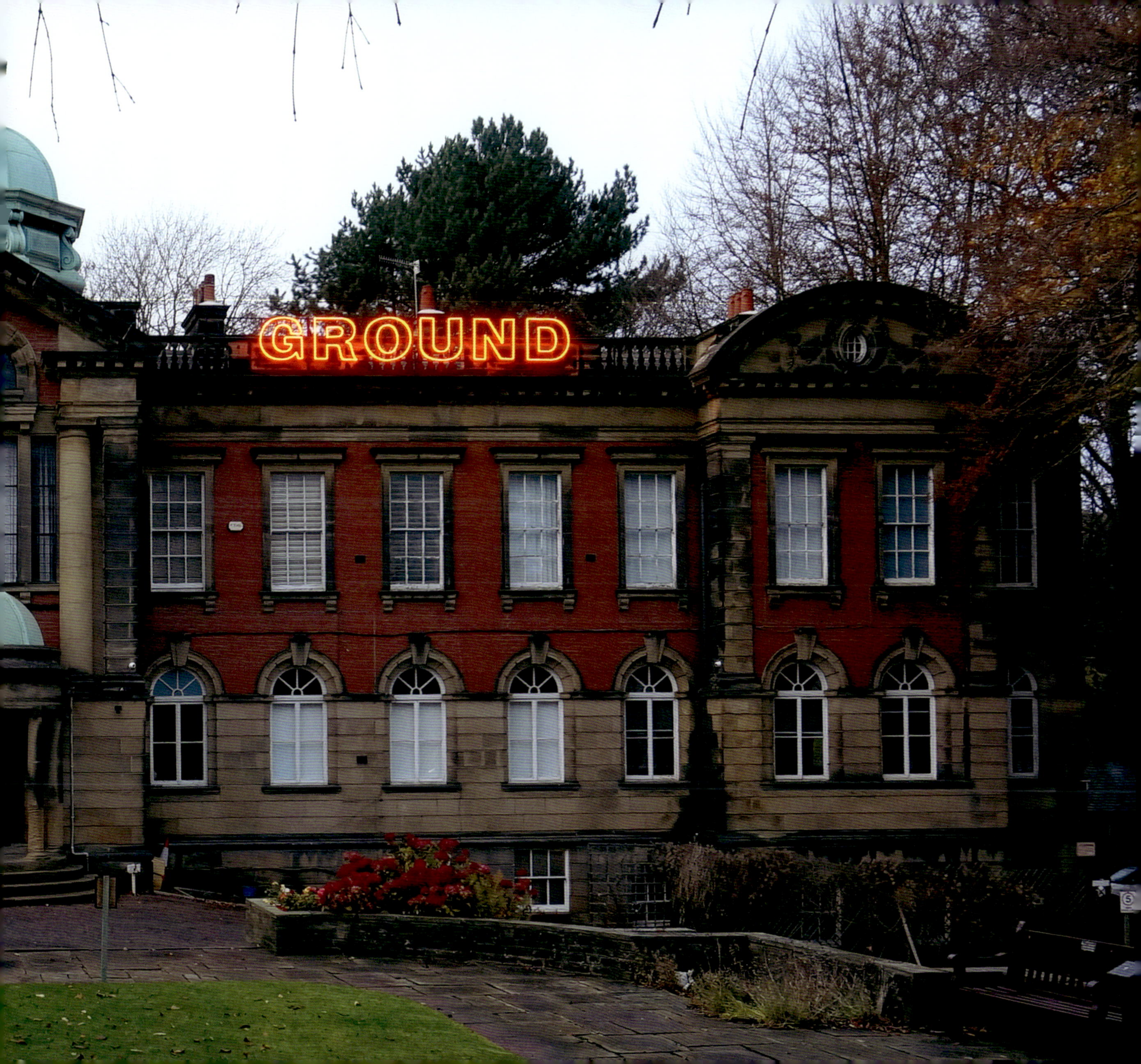
GROUND

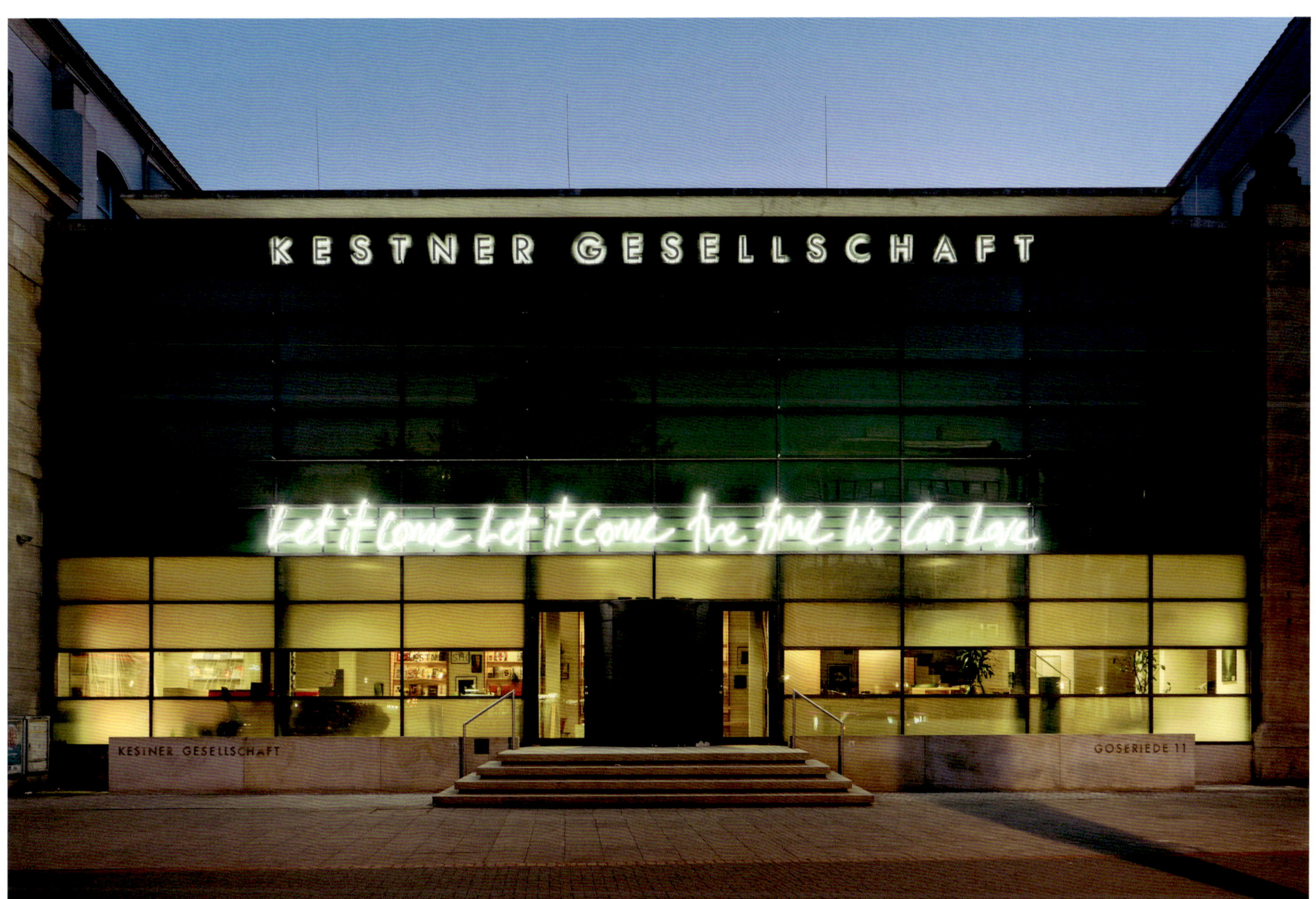

KESTNER GESELLSCHAFT
let it come let it come the time we can love
KESTNER GESELLSCHAFT
GOSERIEDE 11

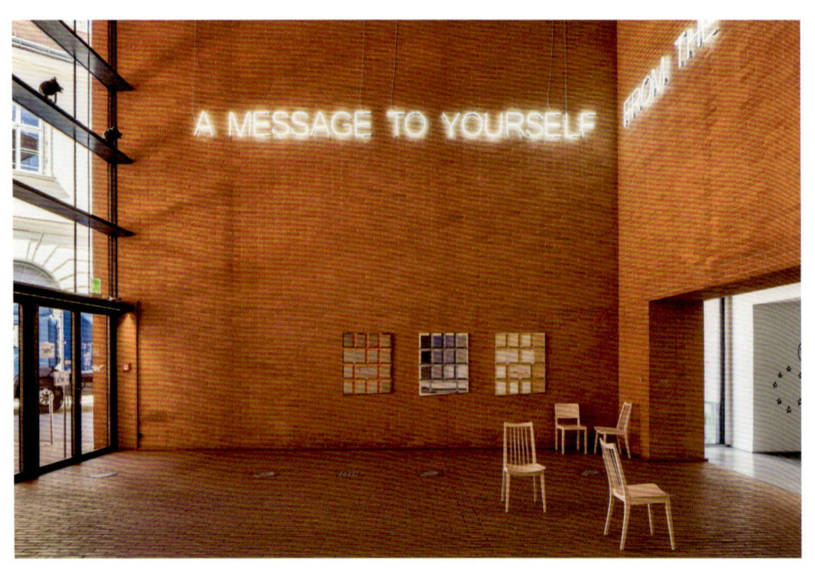
A MESSAGE TO YOURSELF

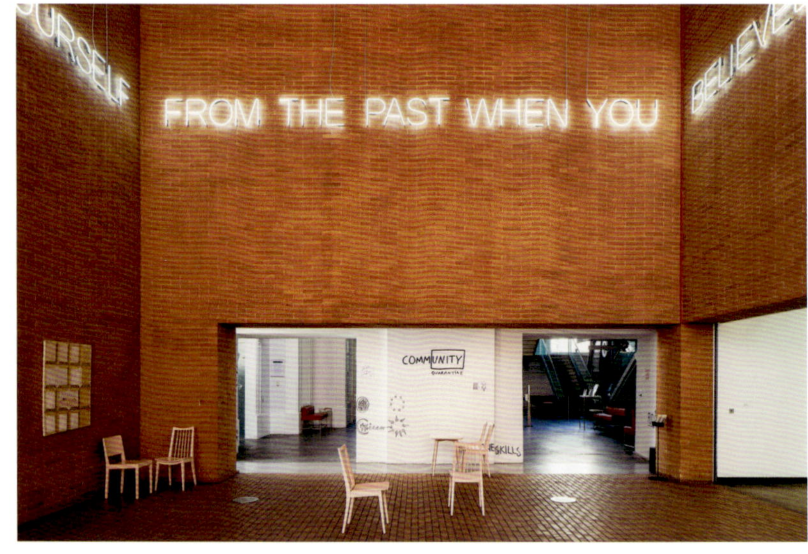
FROM THE PAST WHEN YOU

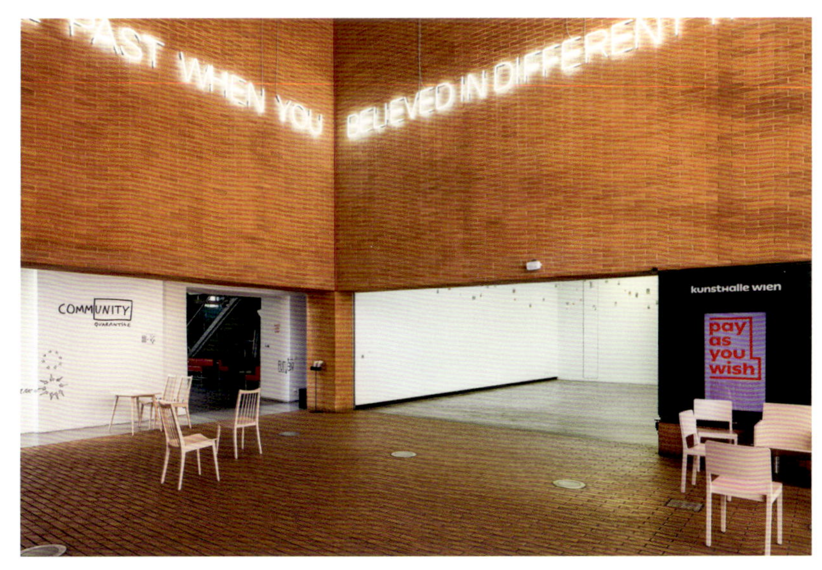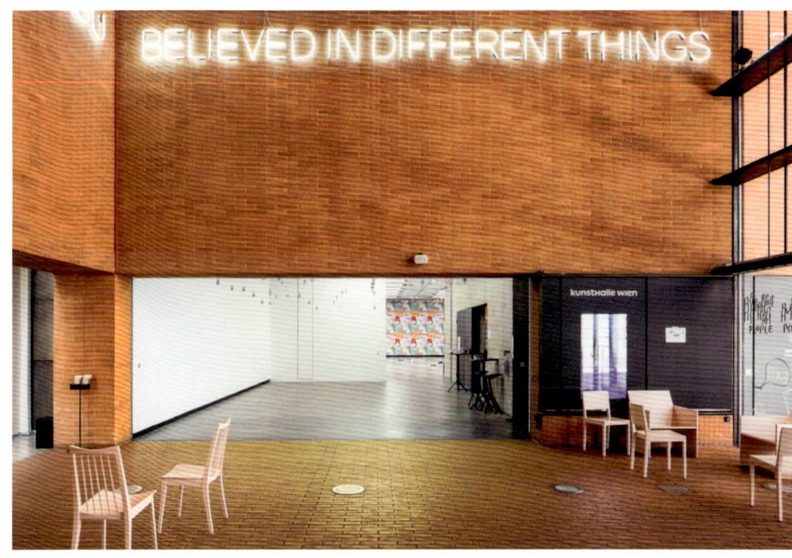

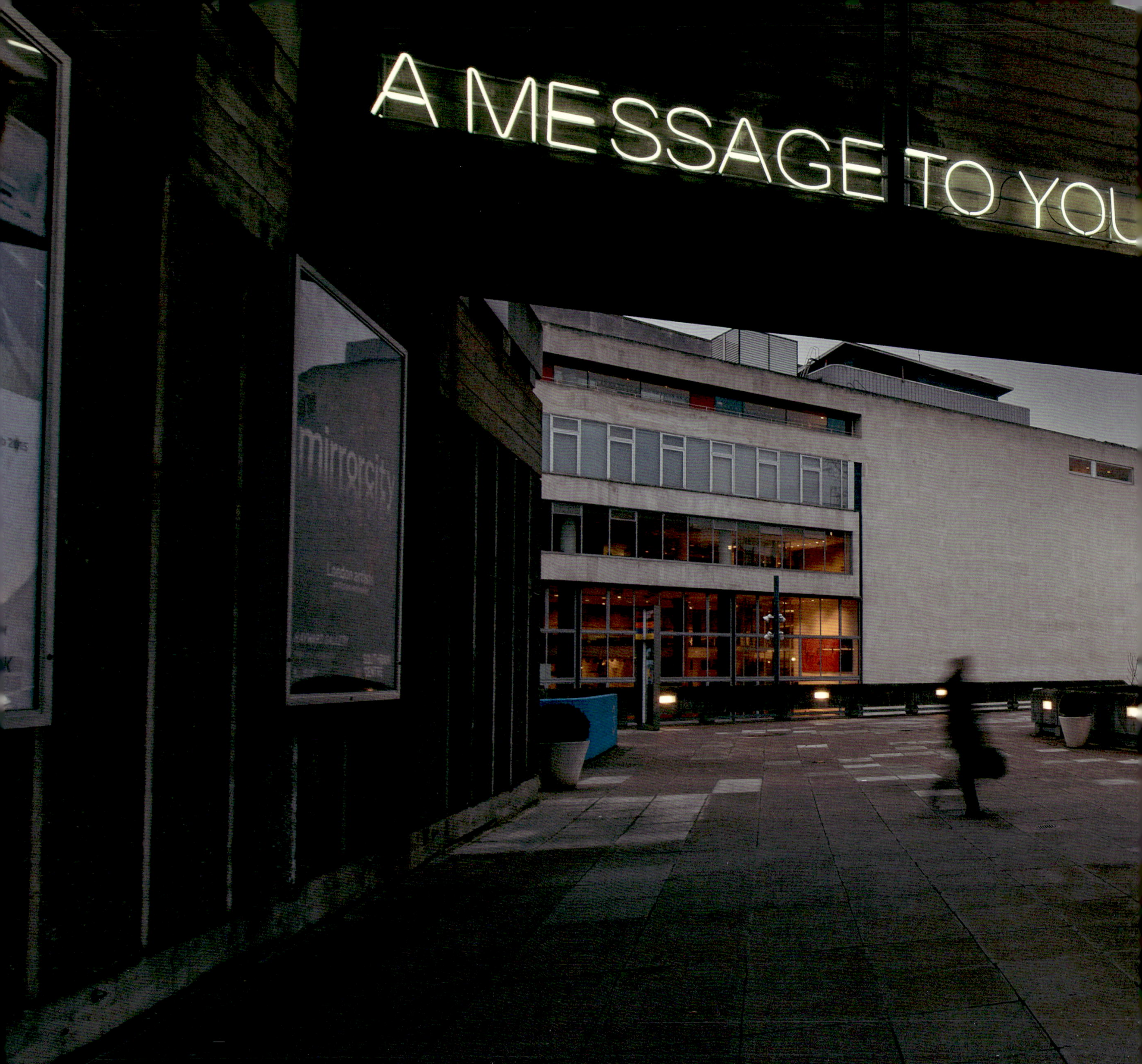

A MESSAGE TO YOU
mirrorcity

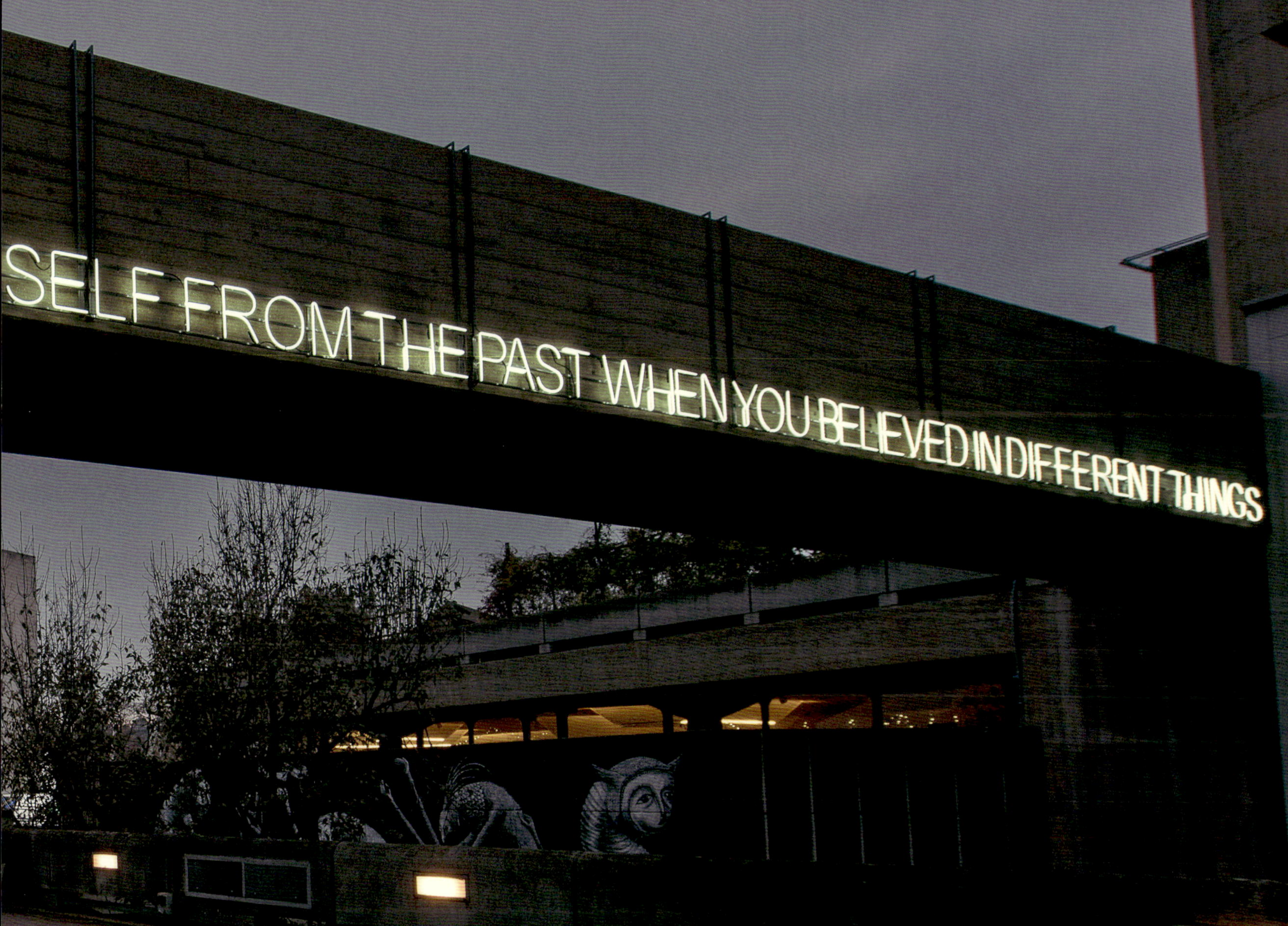
SELF FROM THE PAST WHEN YOU BELIEVED IN DIFFERENT THINGS

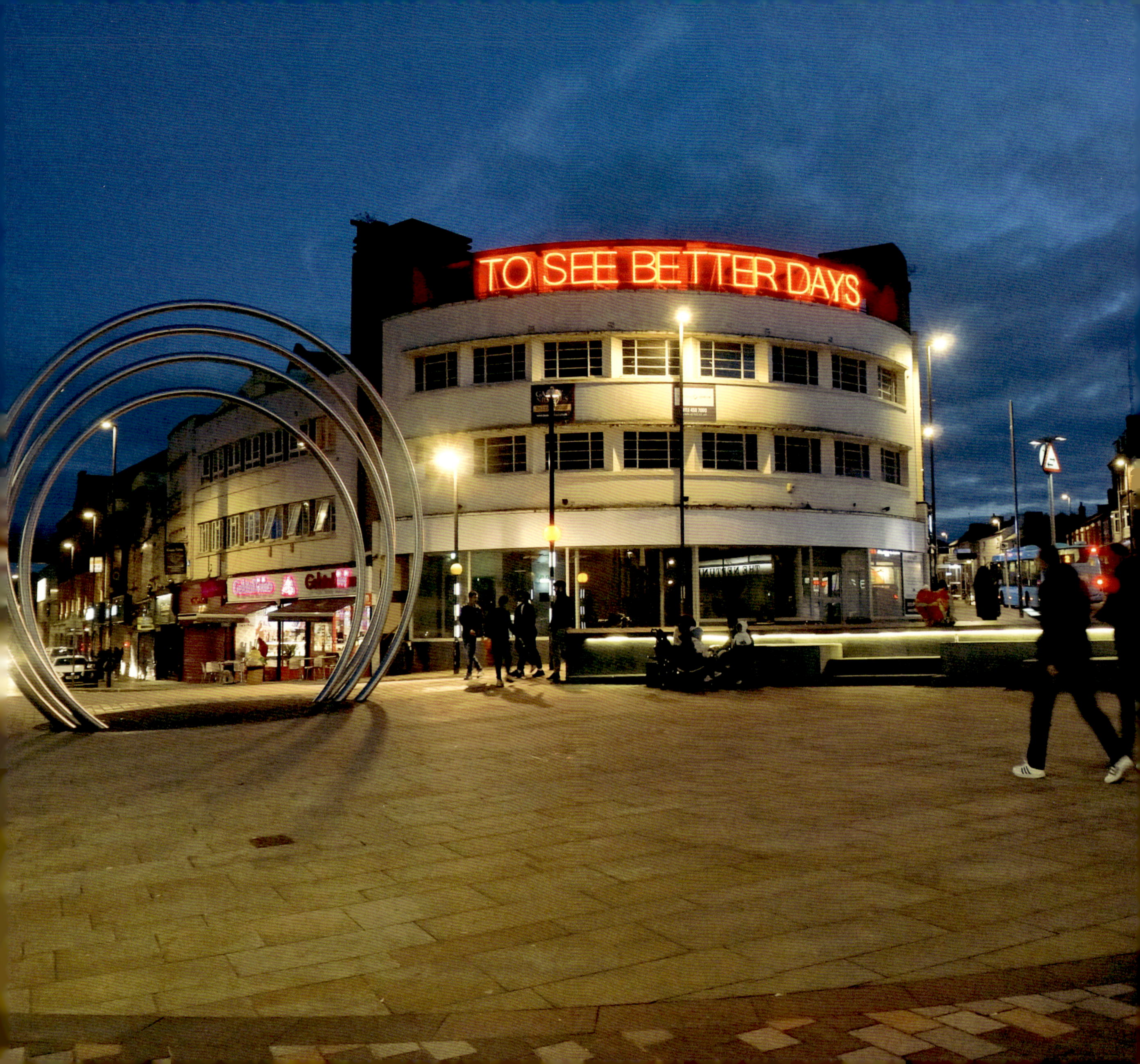
TO SEE BETTER DAYS

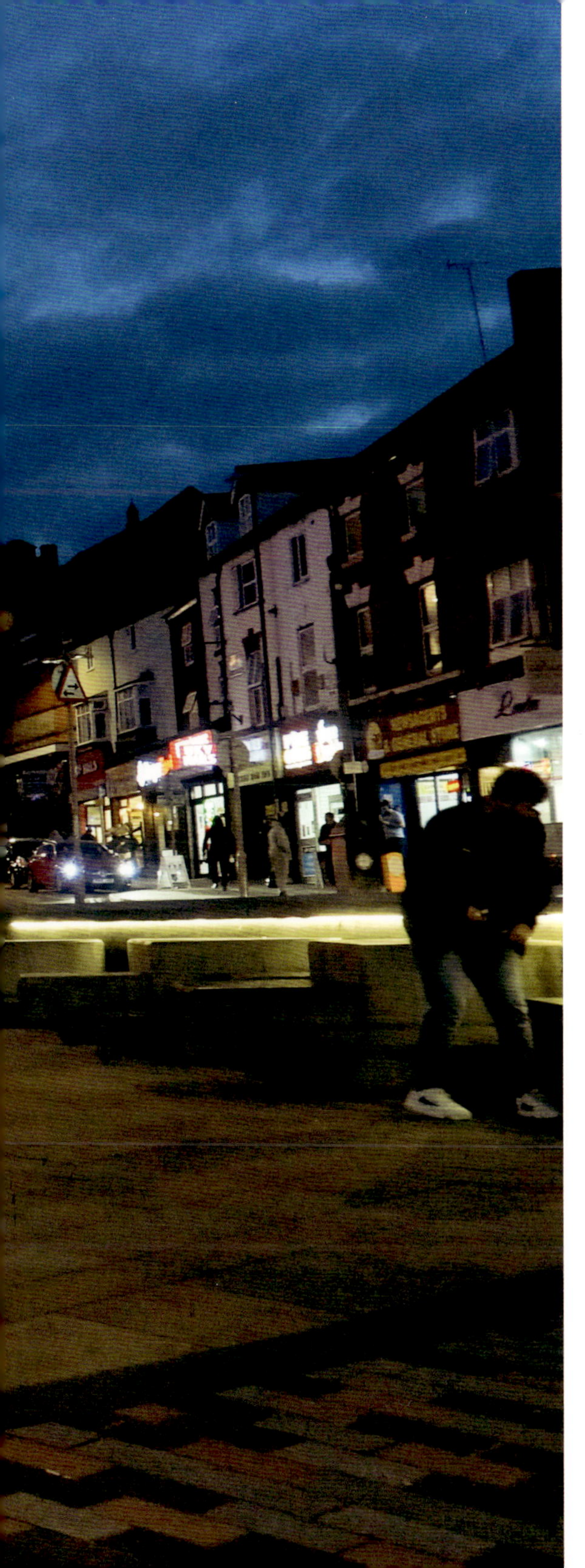

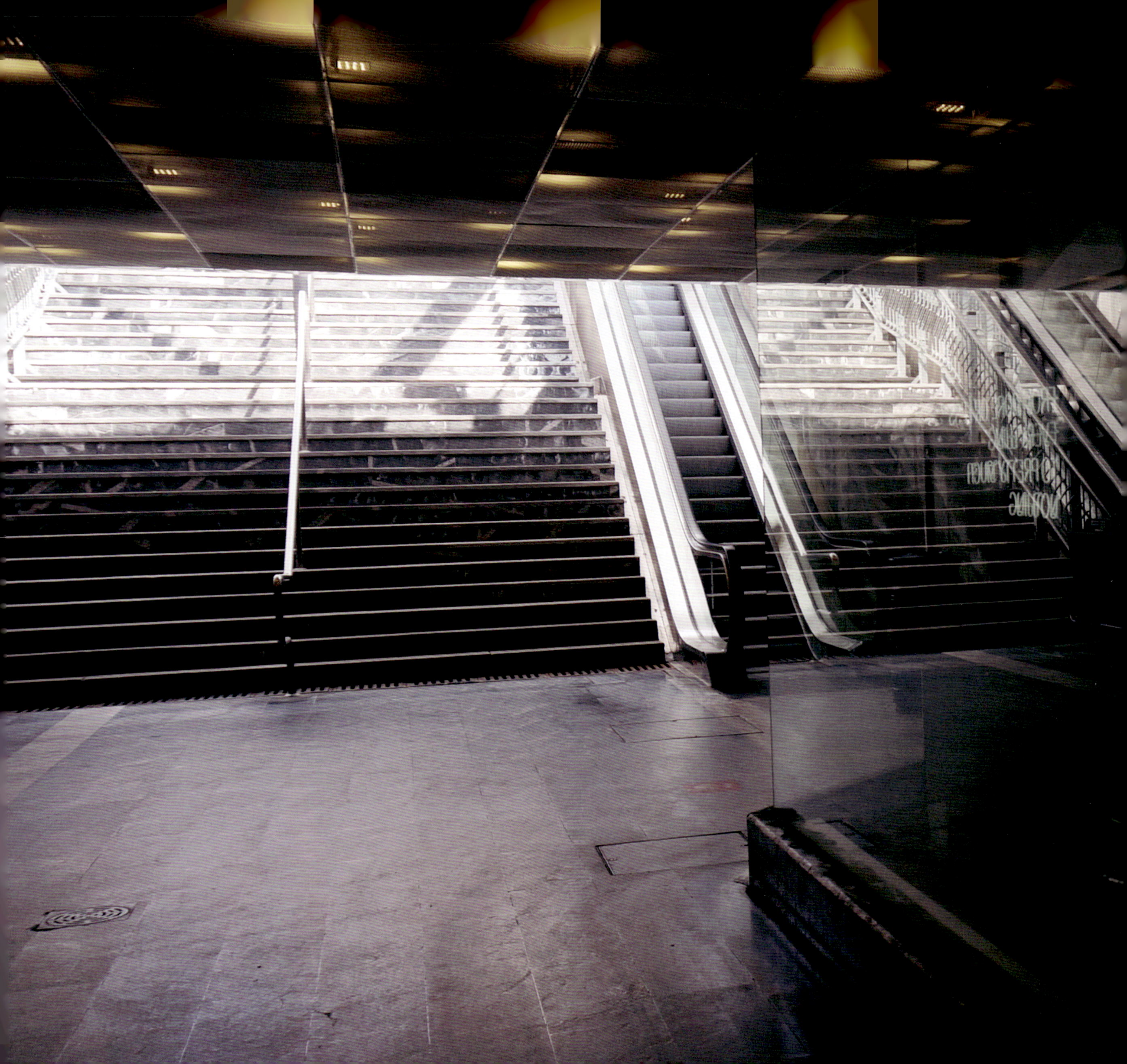

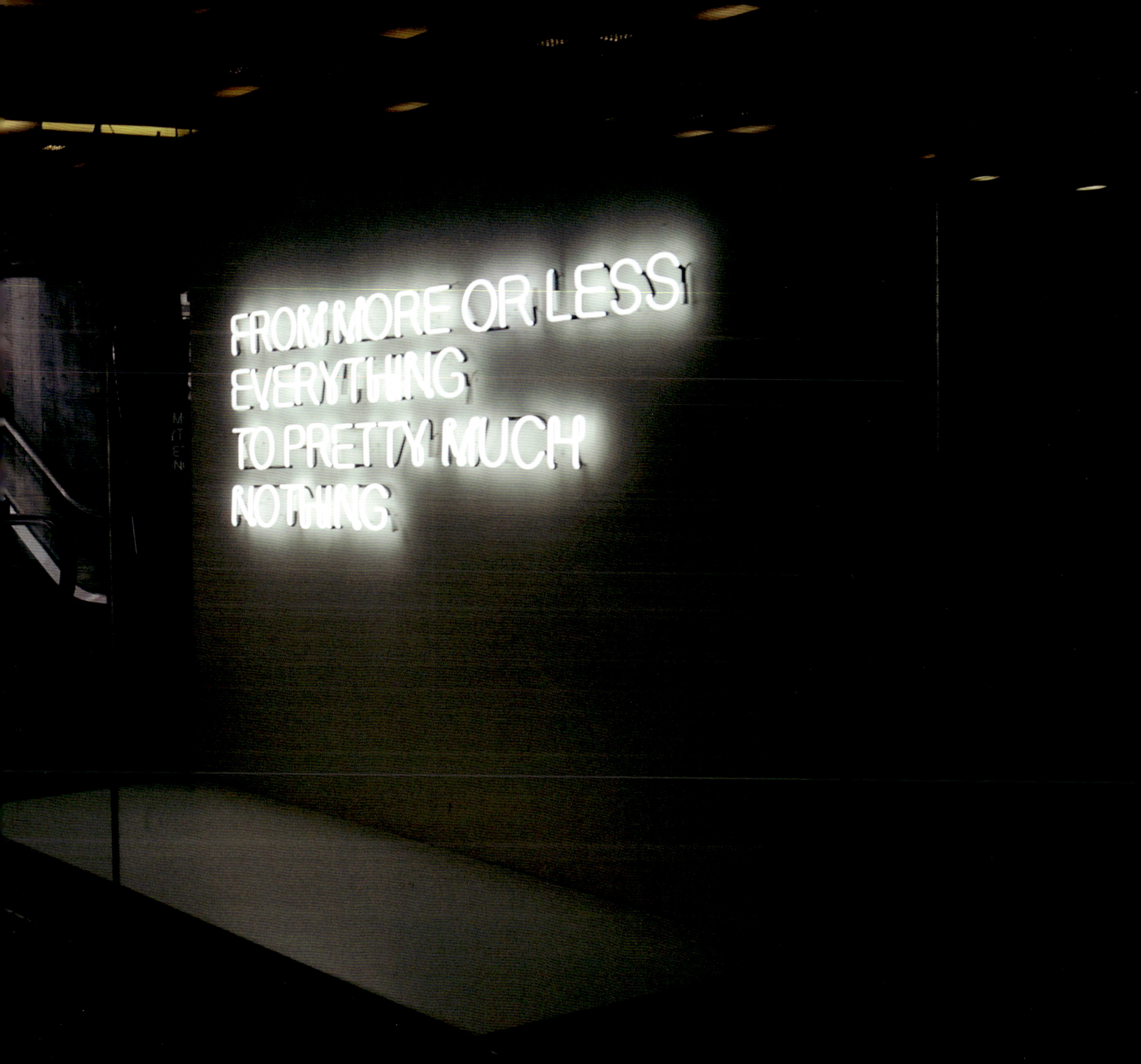

FROM MORE OR LESS
EVERYTHING
TO PRETTY MUCH
NOTHING

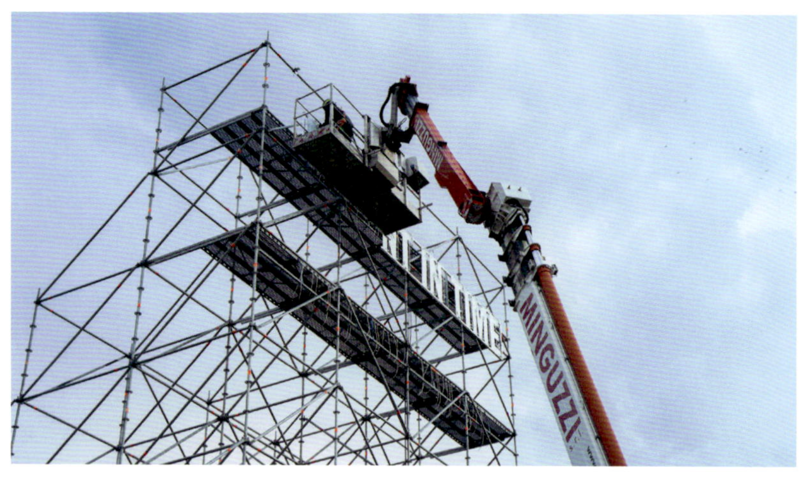
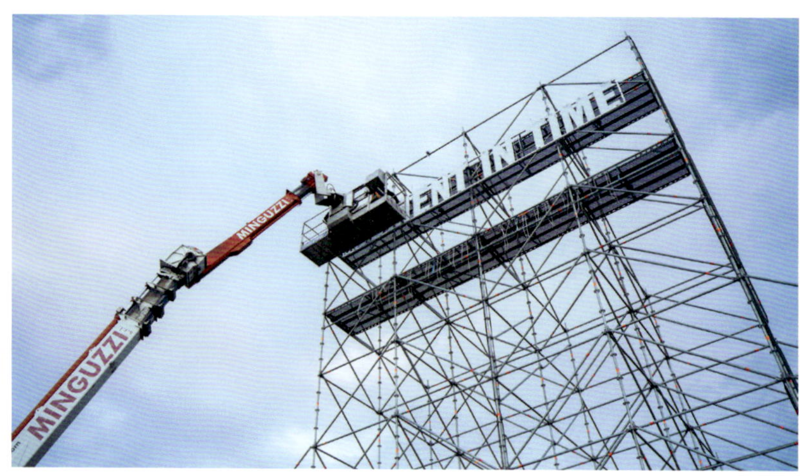
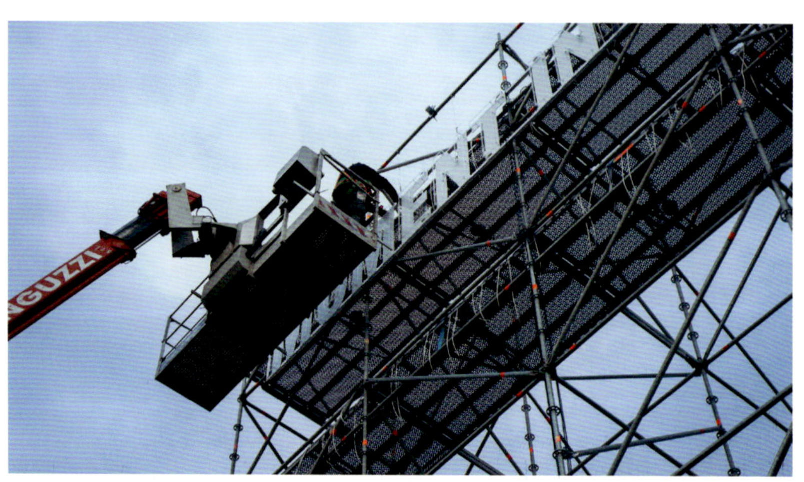
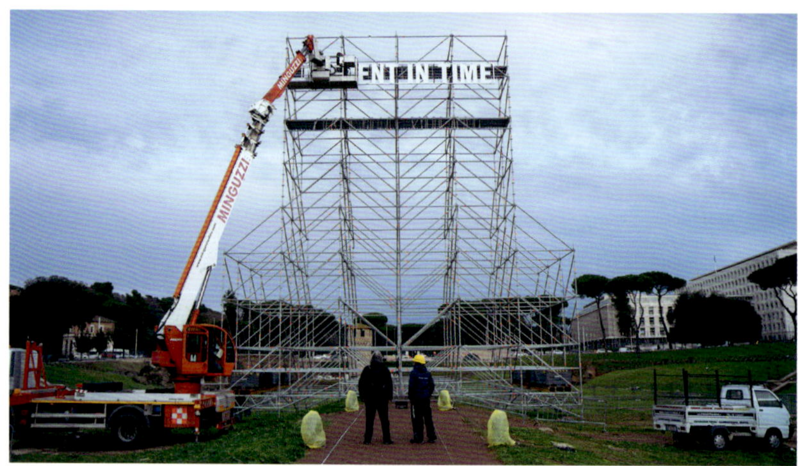

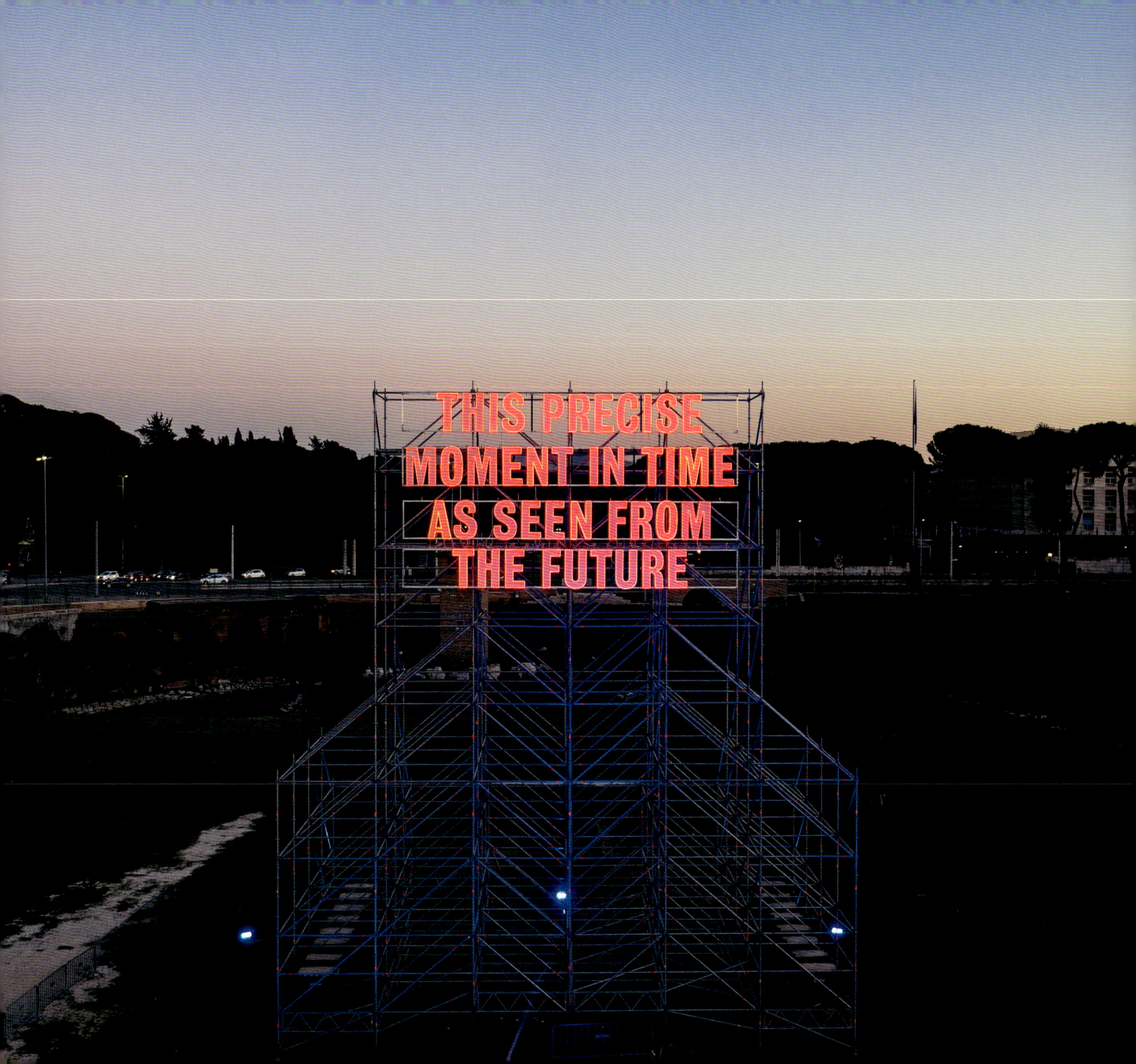

THIS PRECISE
MOMENT IN TIME
AS SEEN FROM
THE FUTURE

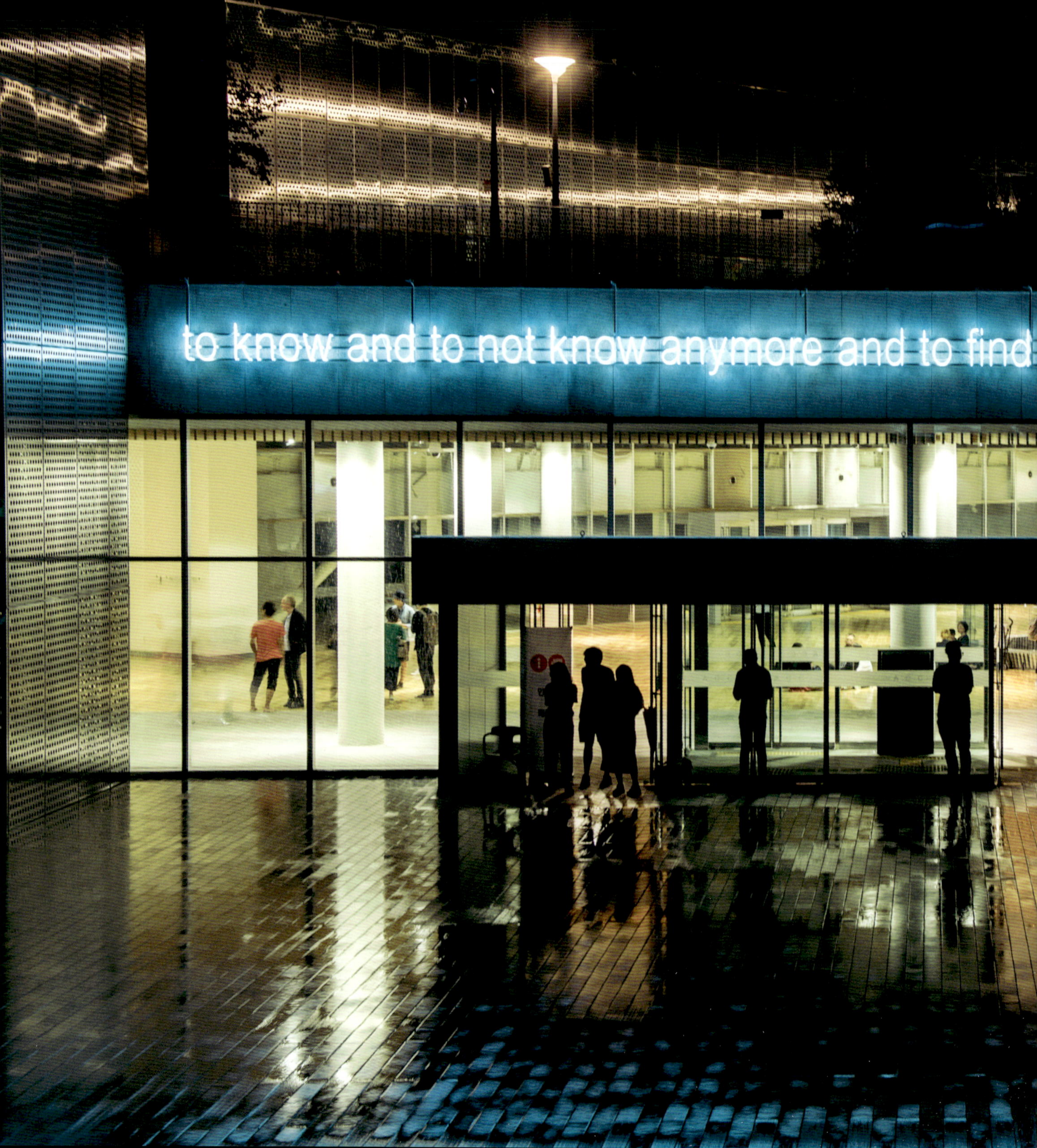
to know and to not know anymore and to find

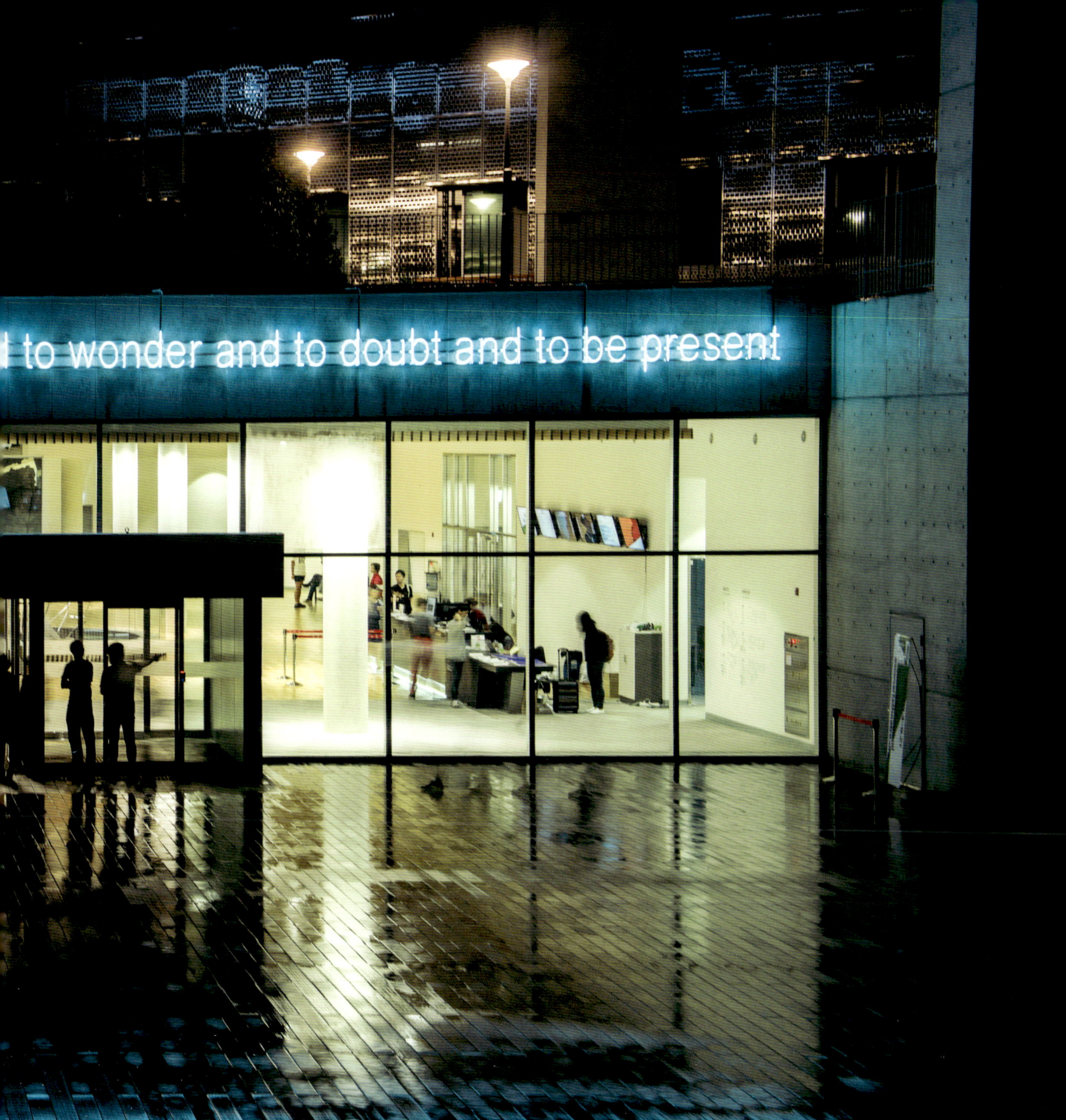
to wonder and to doubt and to be present

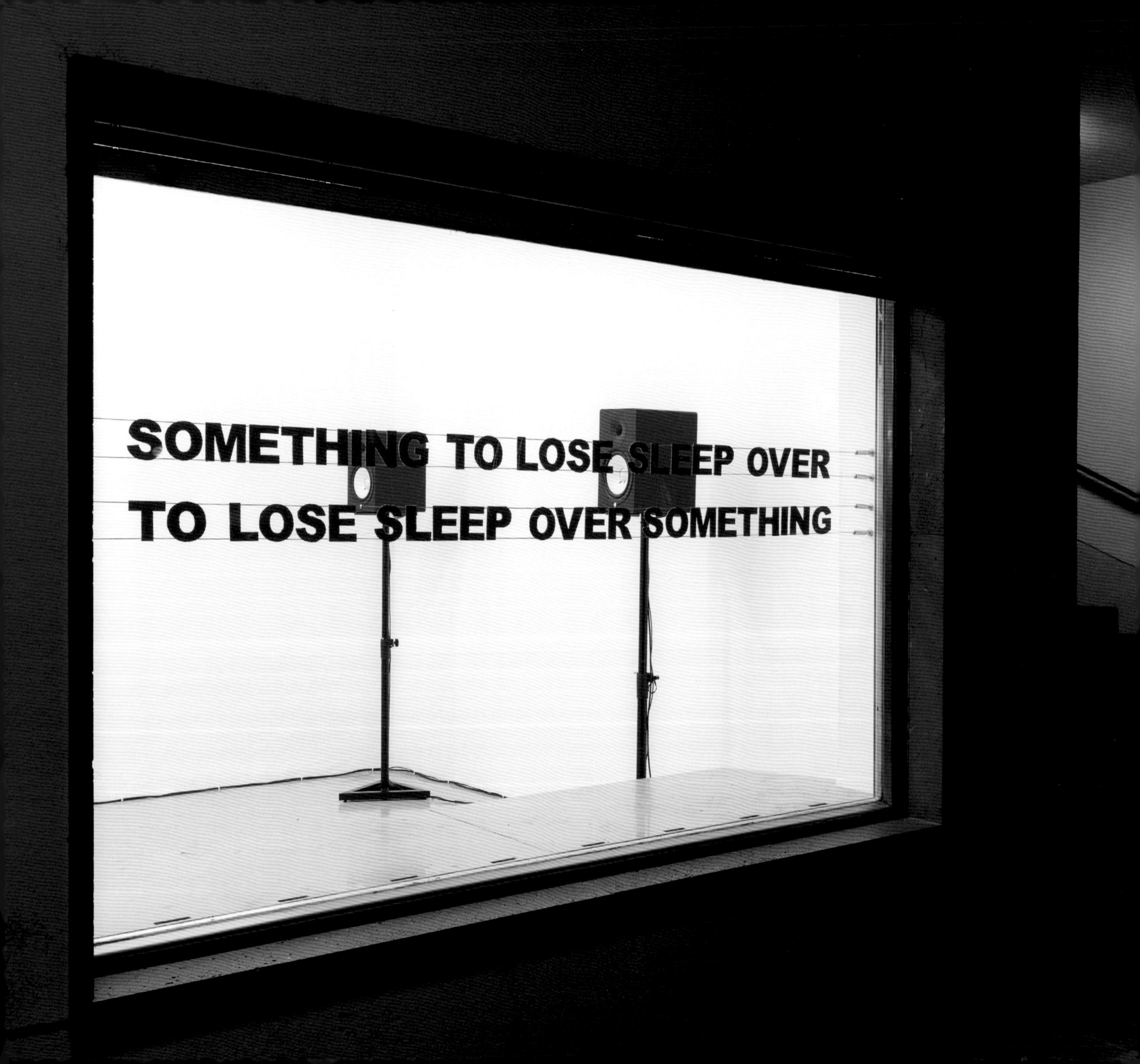

SOMETHING TO LOSE SLEEP OVER
TO LOSE SLEEP OVER SOMETHING

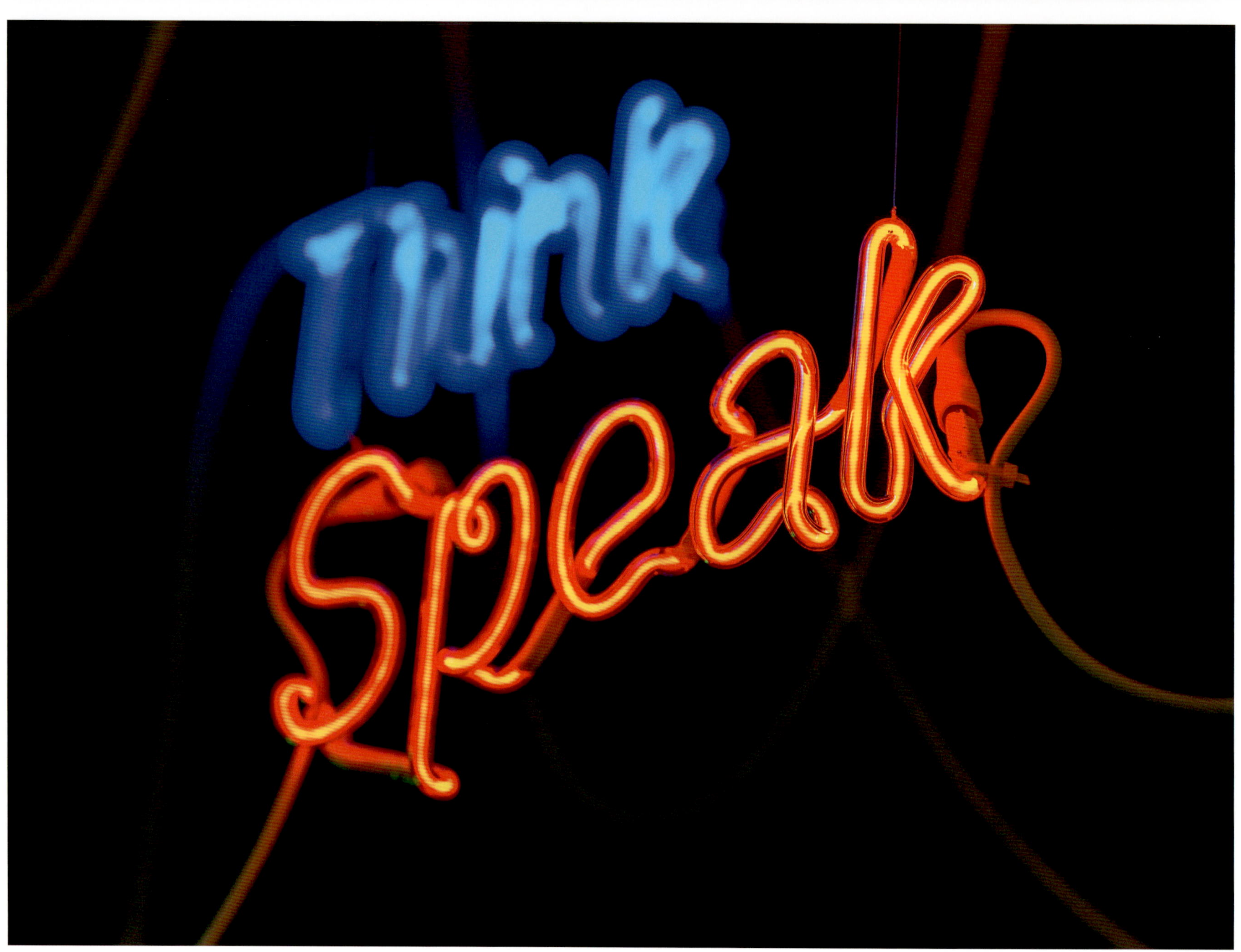

Think
speak

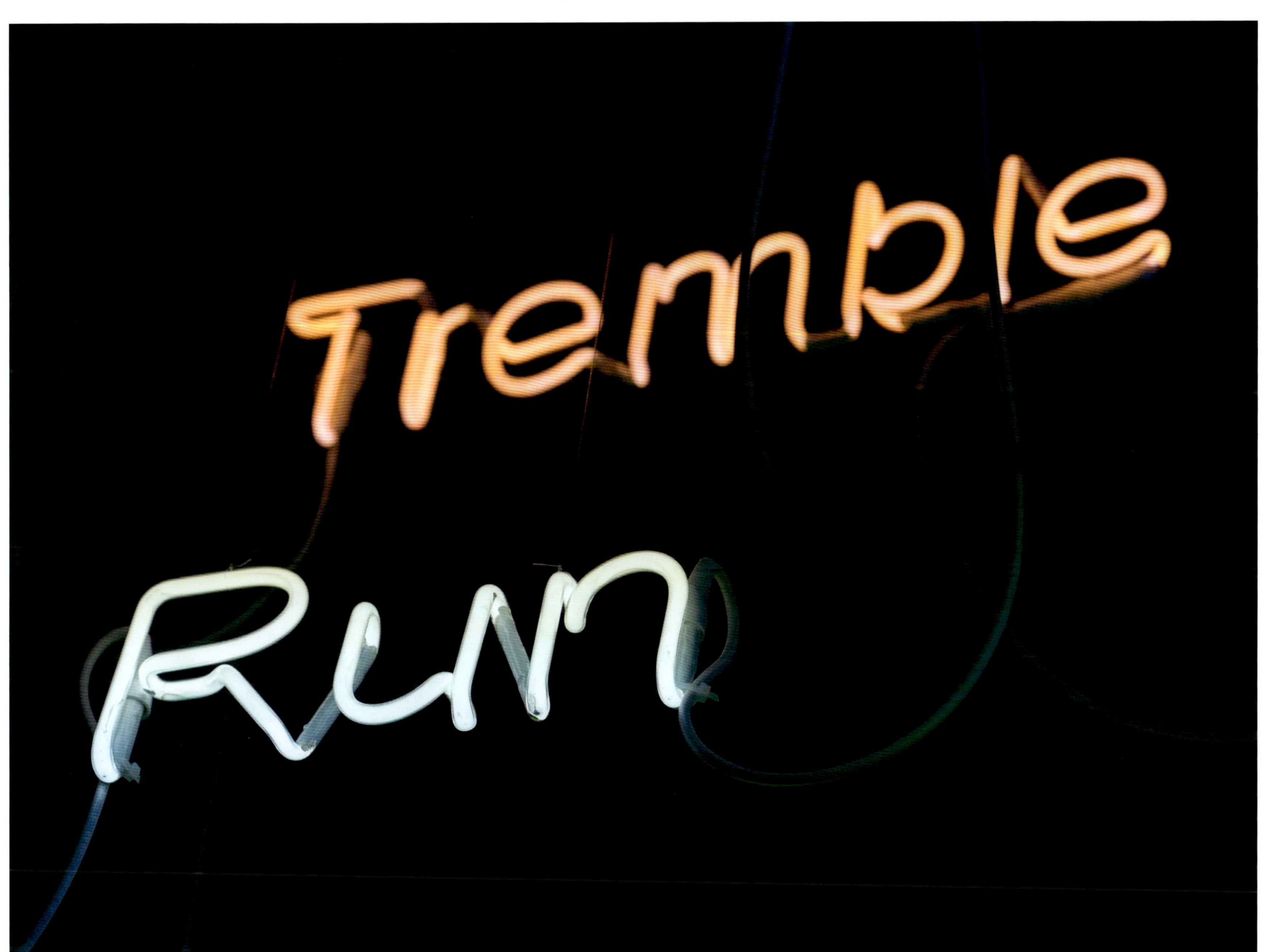

Tremble
Run

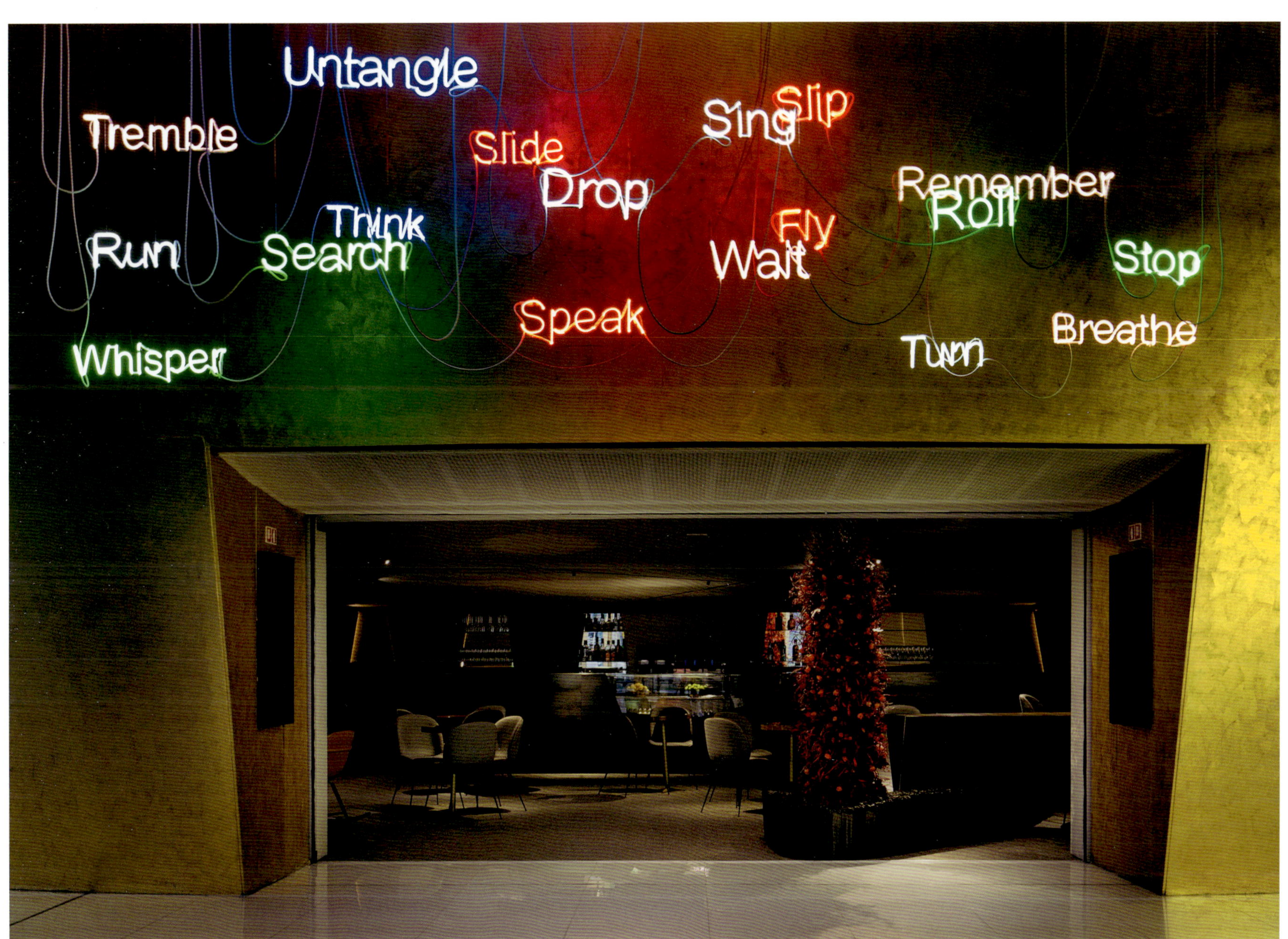

Untangle
Tremble
Sing
Slip
Slide
Drop
Remember
Think
Roll
Run
Search
Fly
Wait
Stop
Speak
Whisper
Breathe
Turn

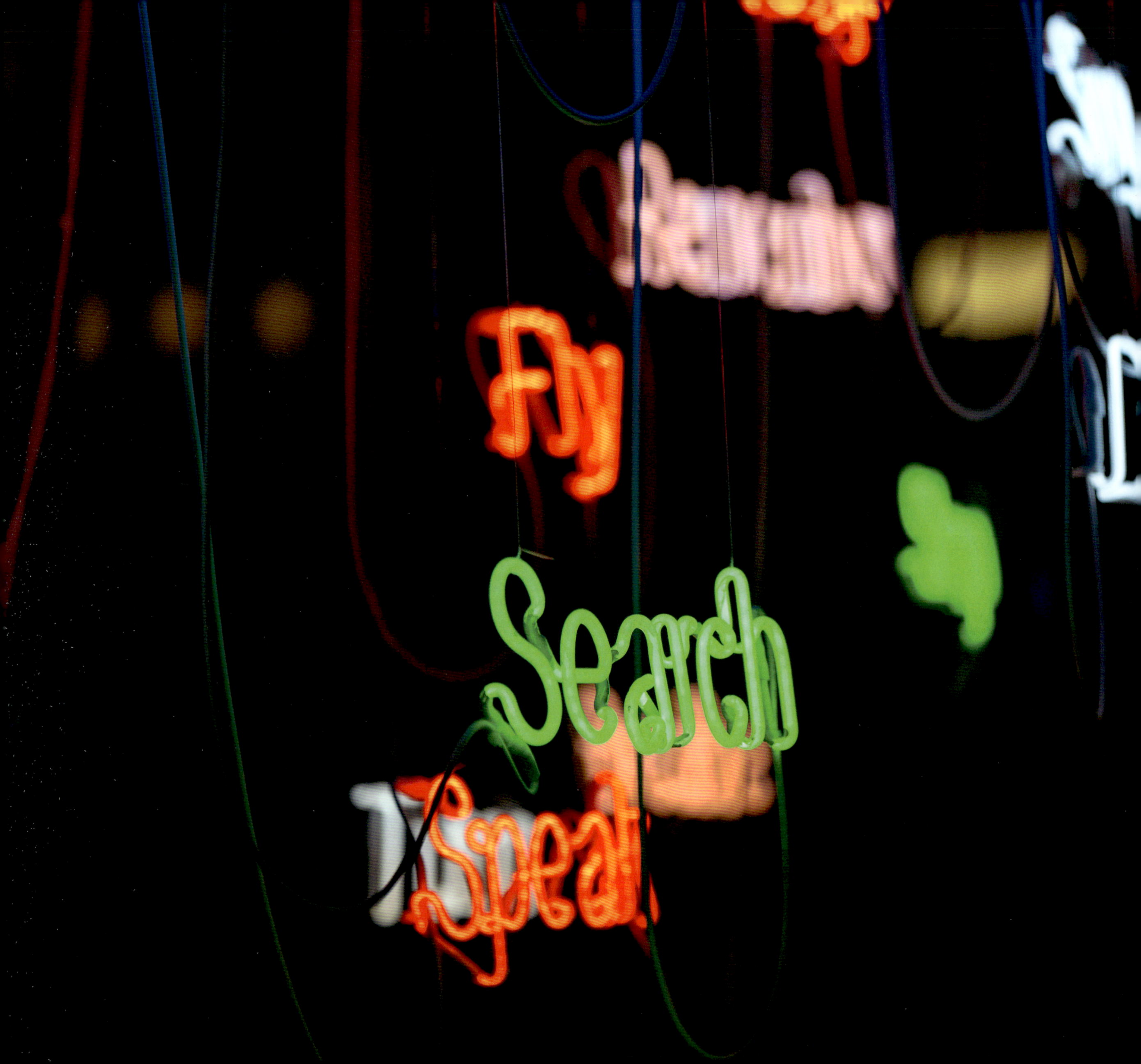

Fly
Search
Speak

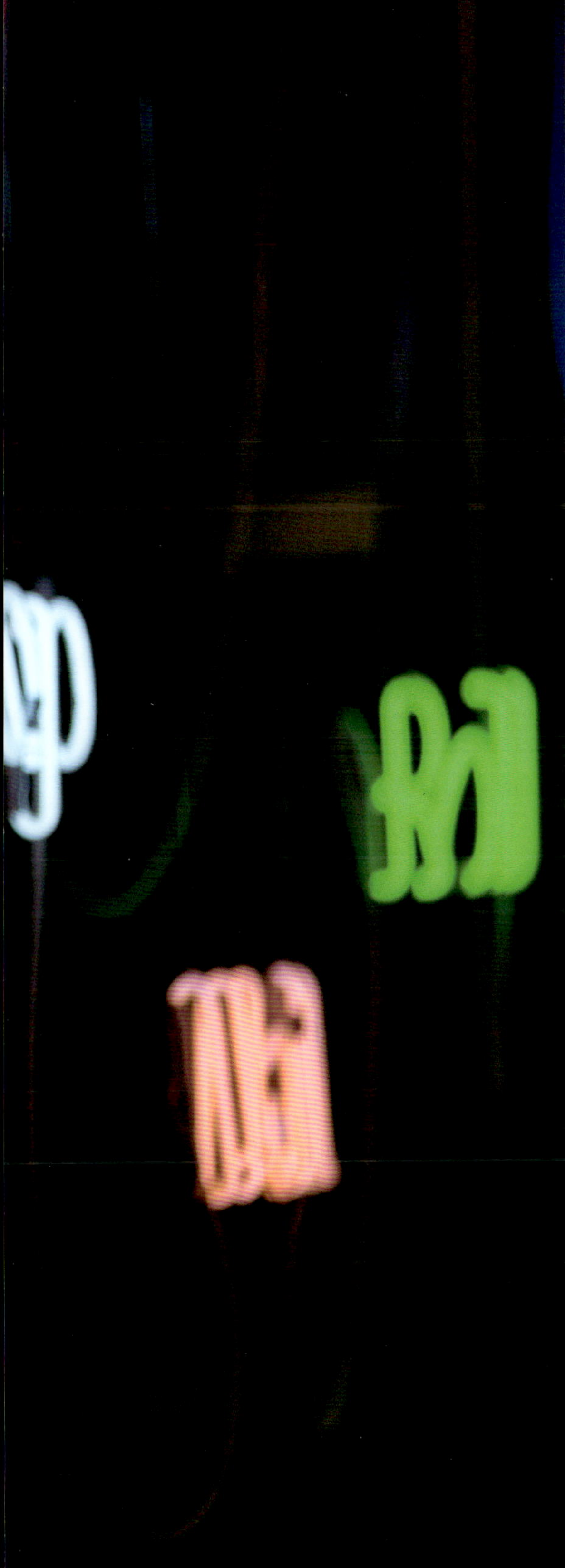

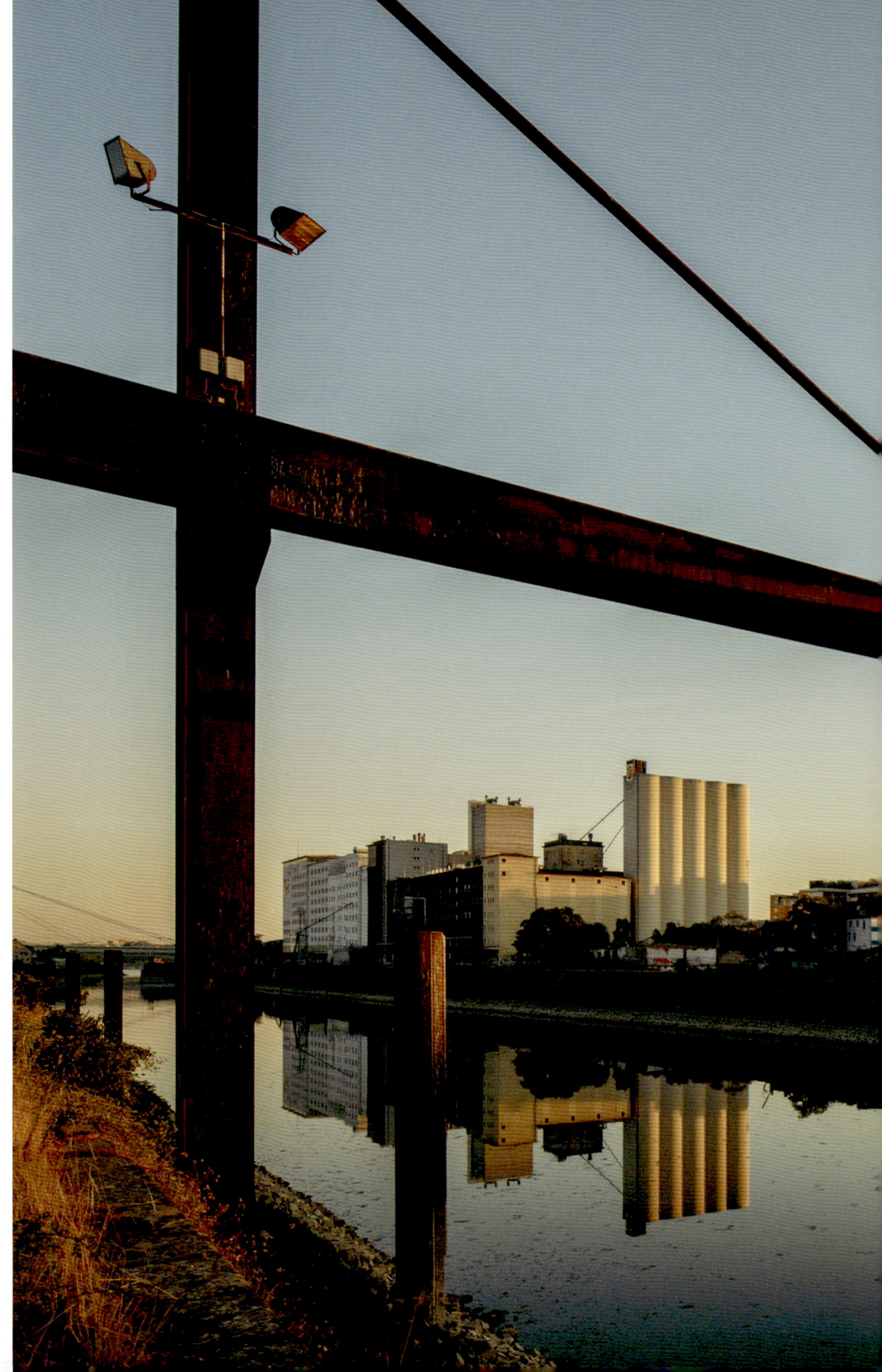

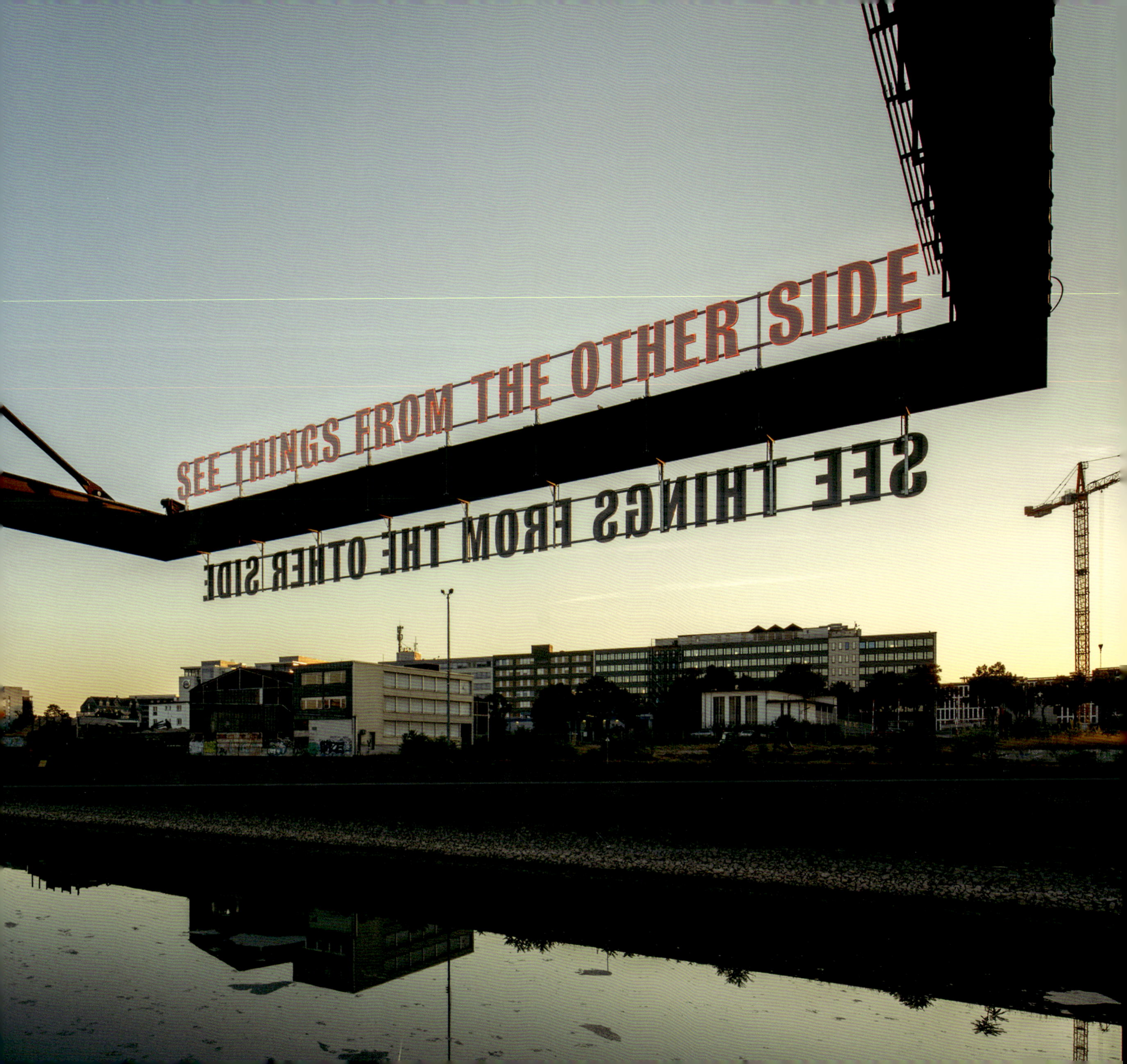

SEE THINGS FROM THE OTHER SIDE
SEE THINGS FROM THE OTHER SIDE

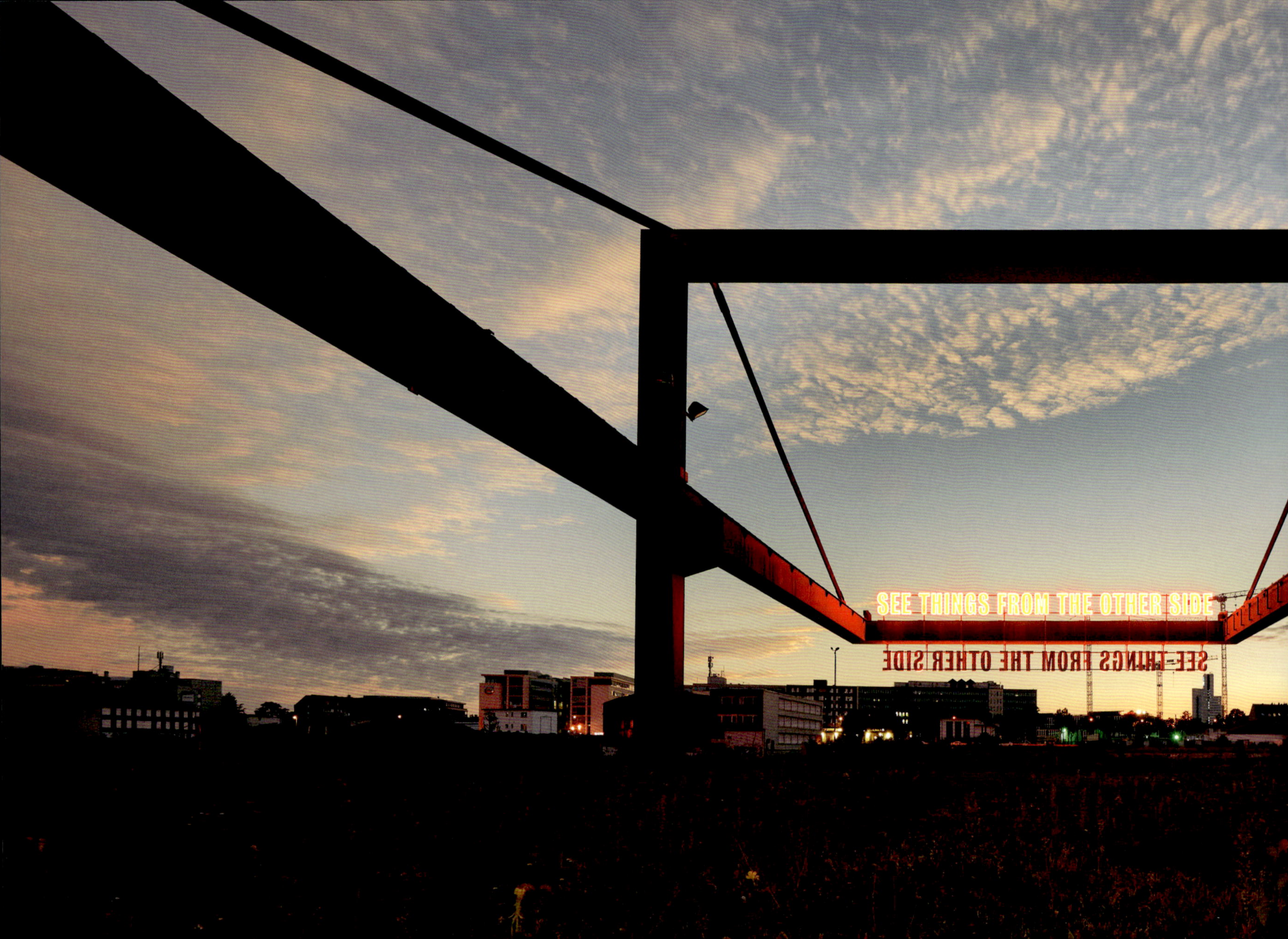
SEE THINGS FROM THE OTHER SIDE

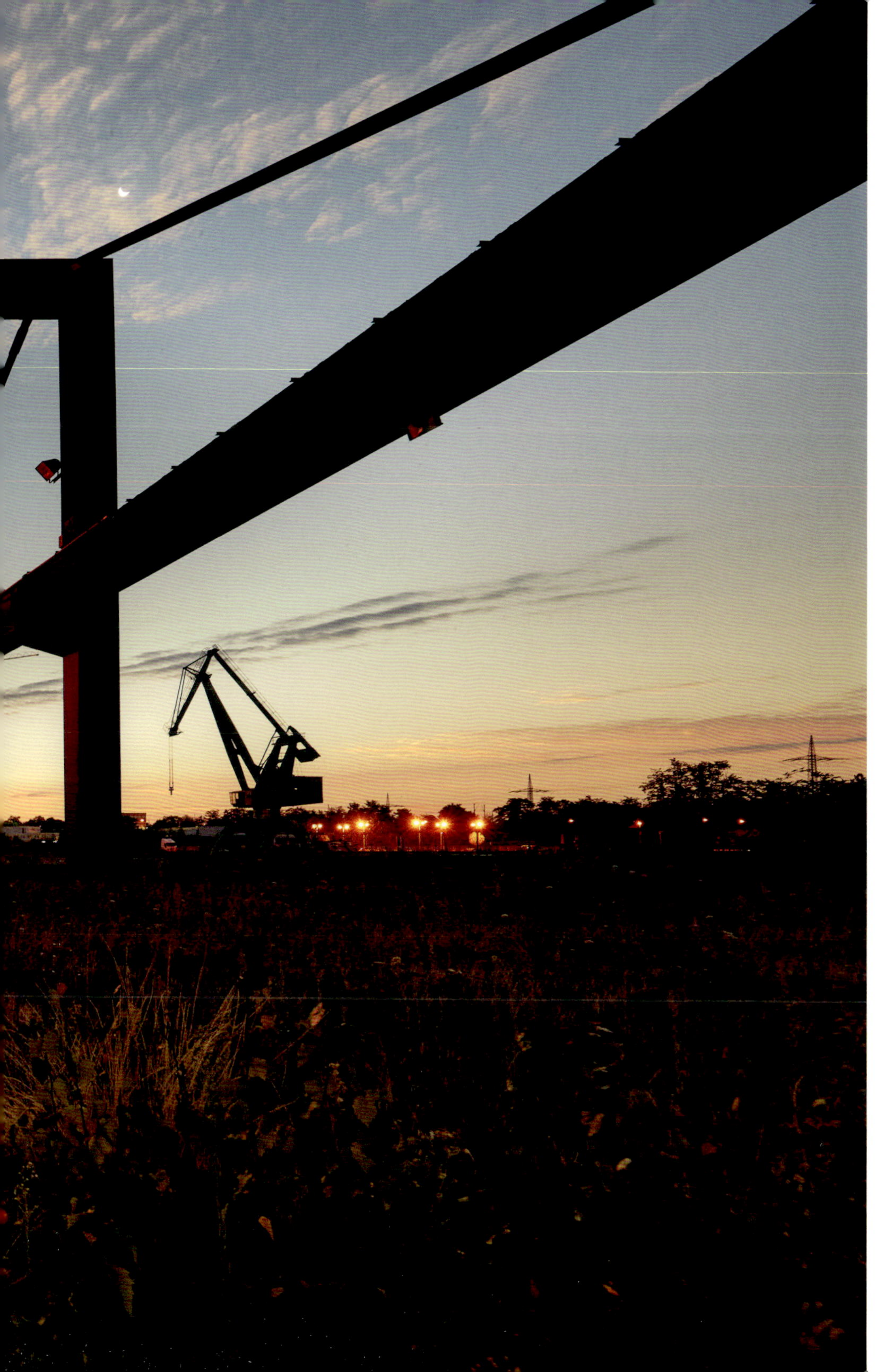

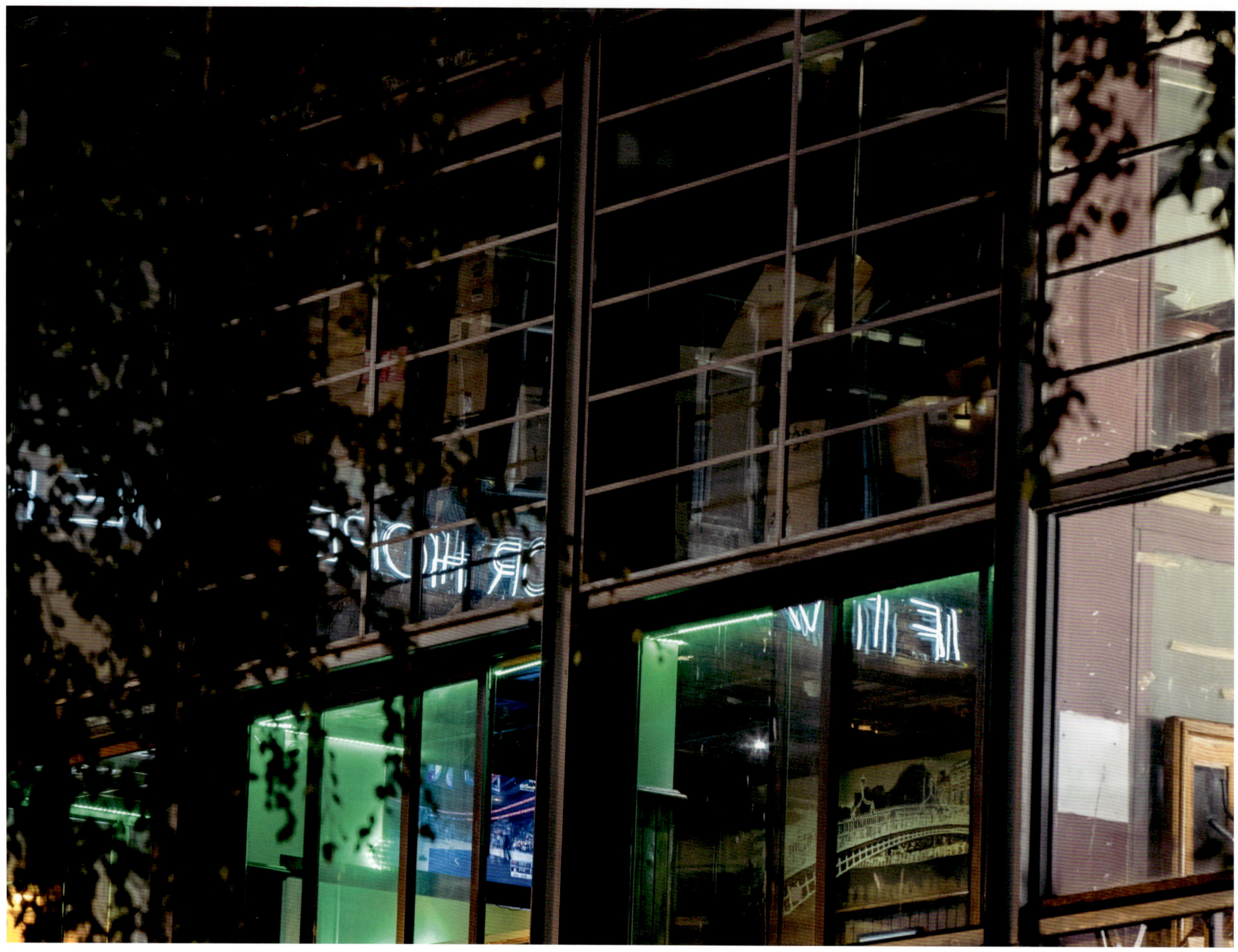

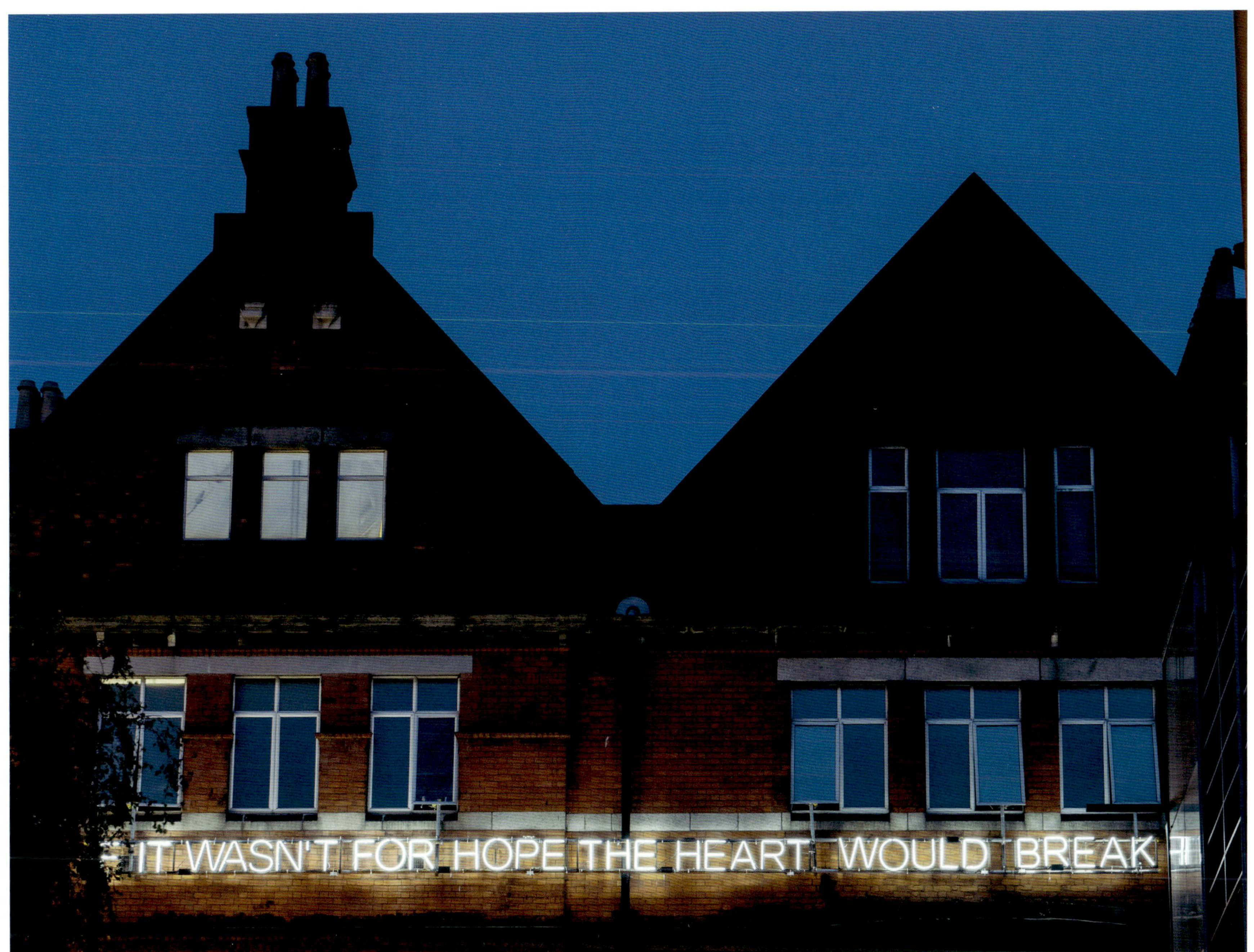

IT WASN'T FOR HOPE THE HEART WOULD BREAK

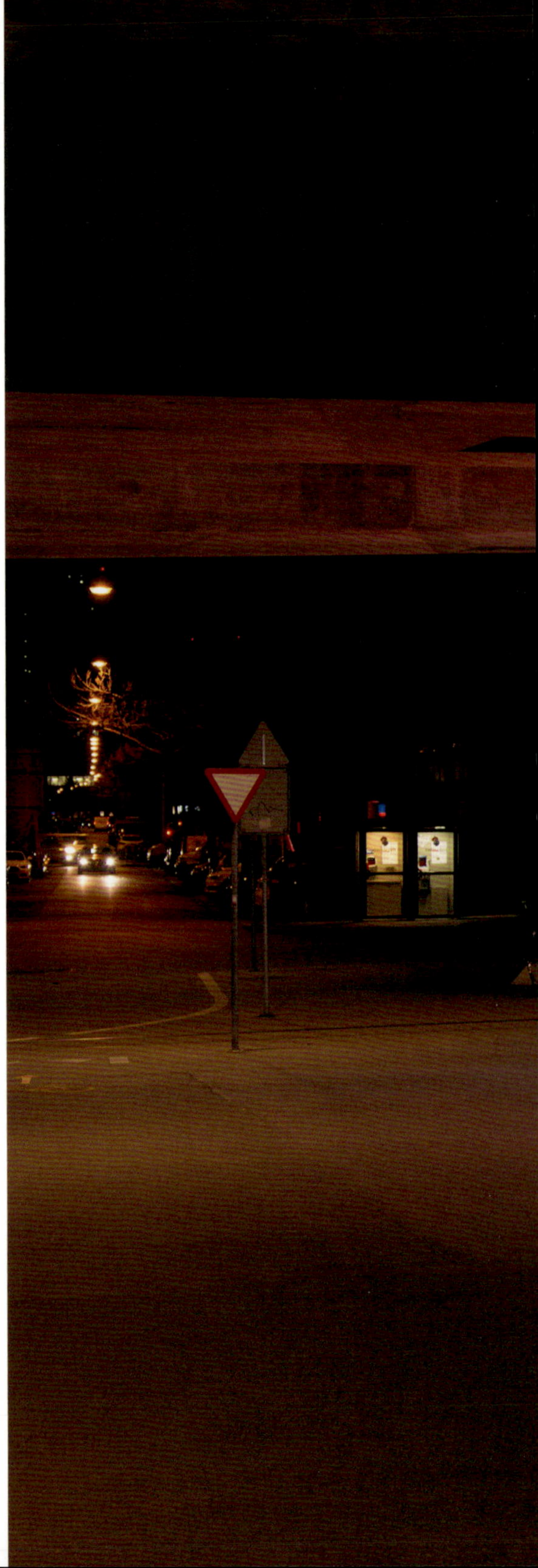

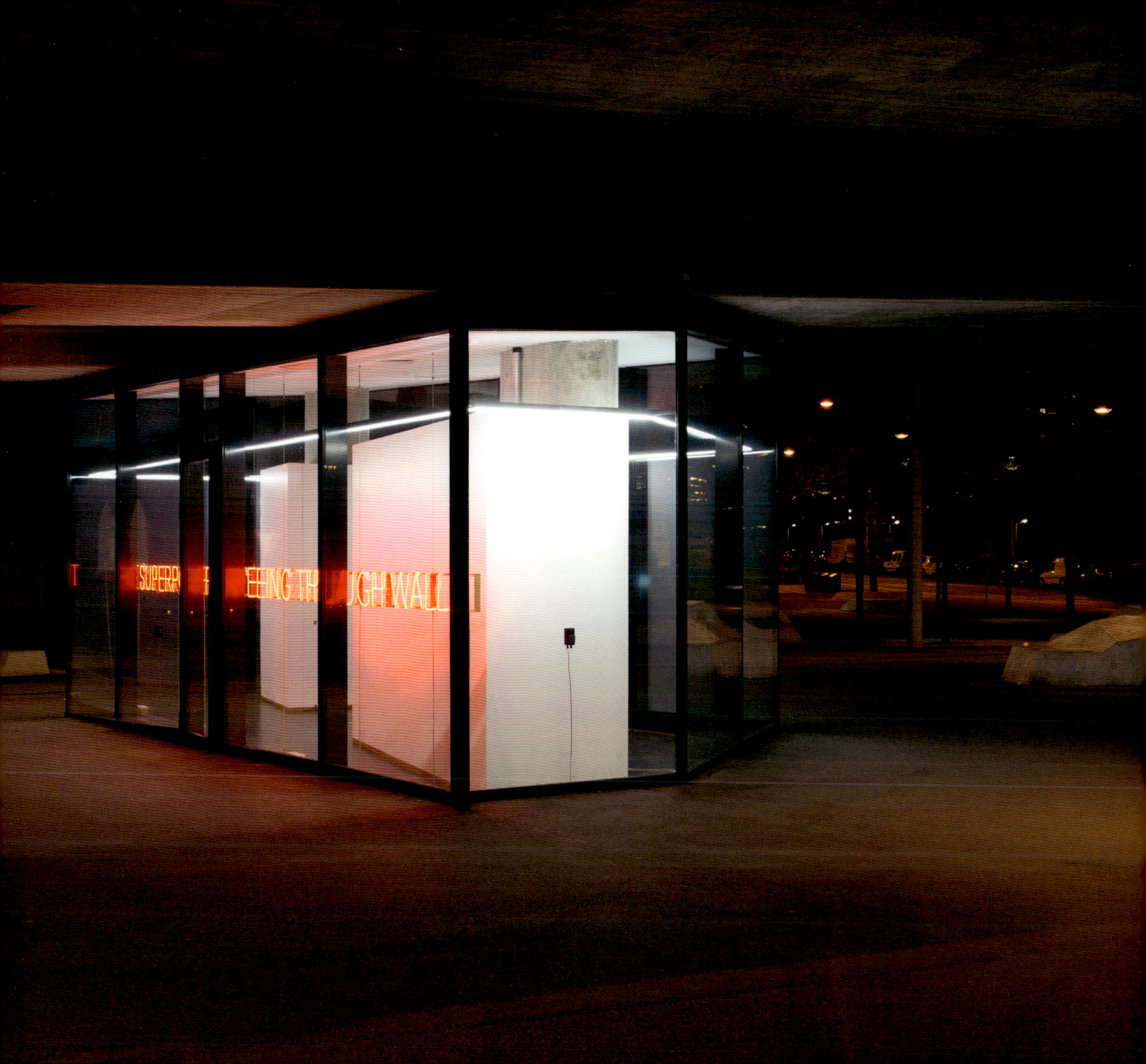

SUPERP   EEING TH   UGH WALL

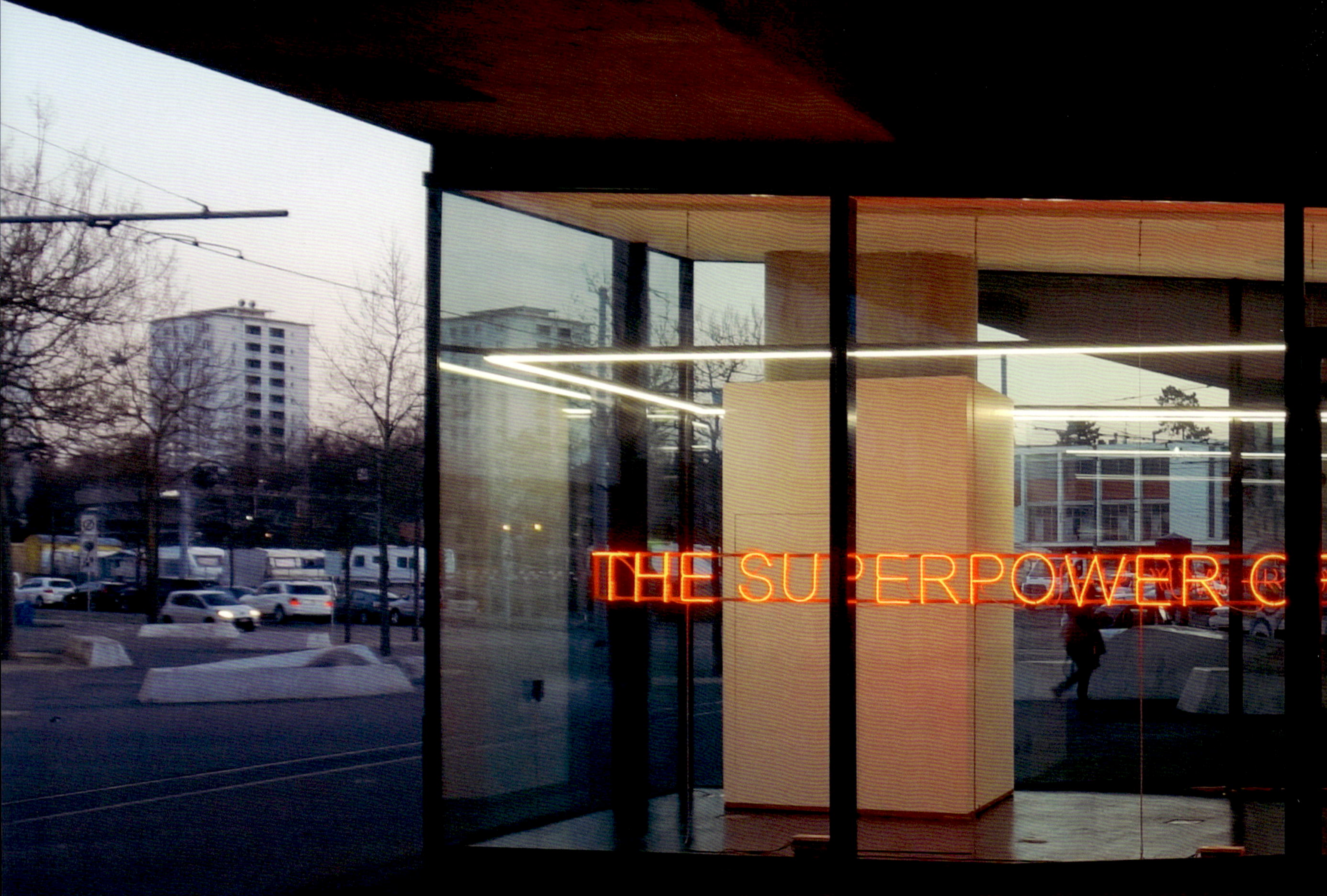
THE SUPERPOWER O

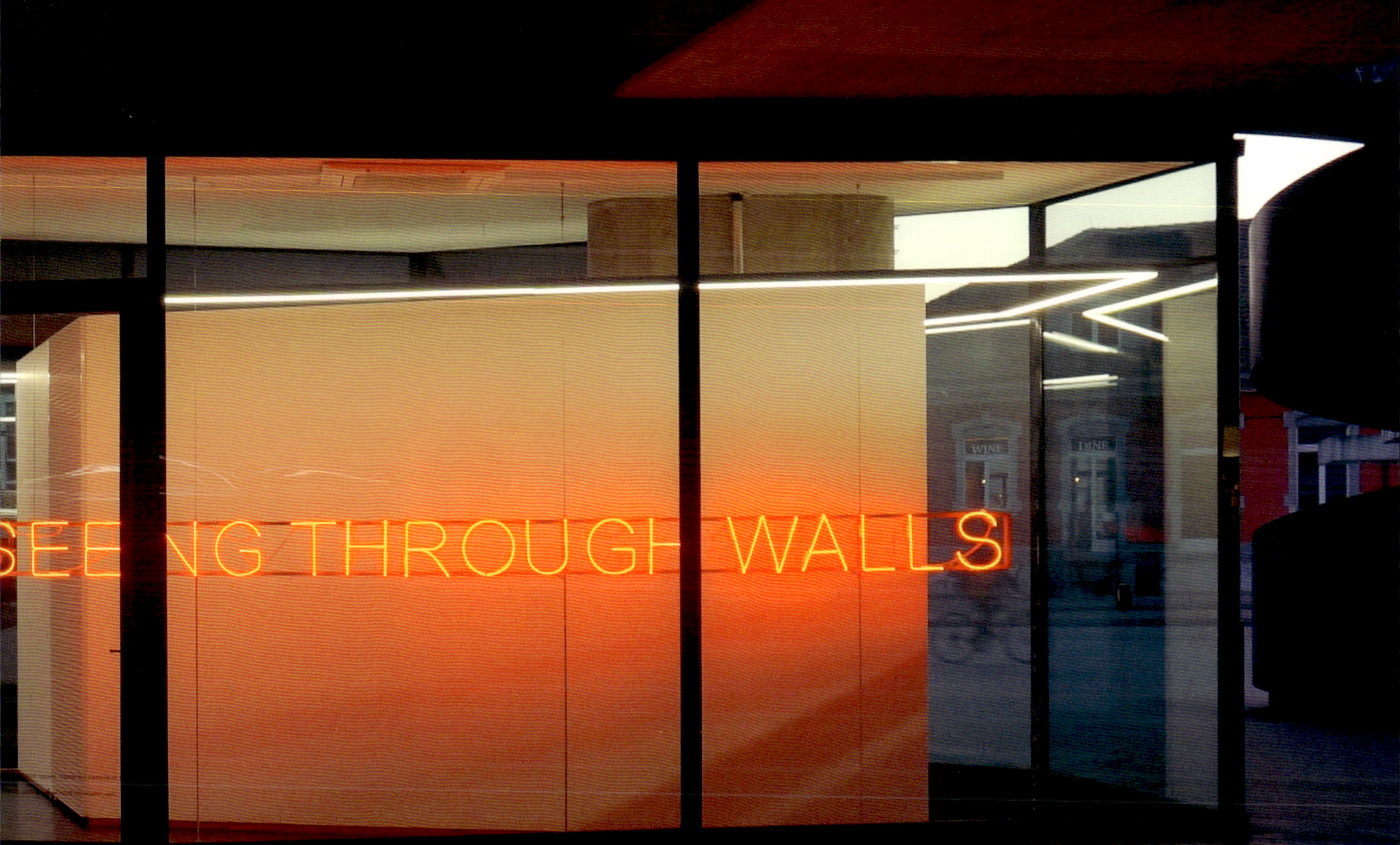
SEEING THROUGH WALLS
WINE
DINE

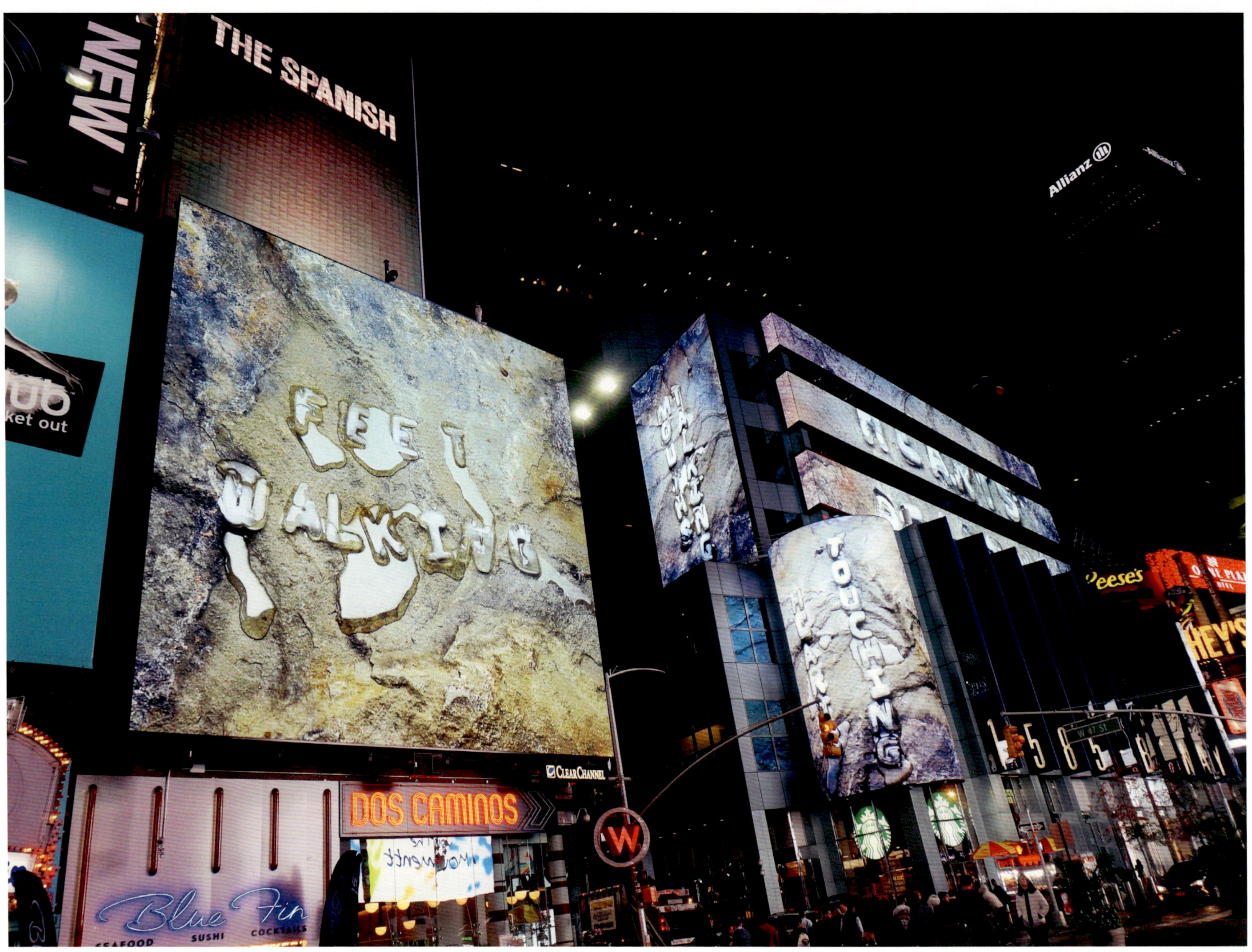
NEW
THE SPANISH
Allianz
FEET WALKING
TOUCHING
HEARTS
eese's
HEY'S
W 43 ST
ClearChannel
DOS CAMINOS
Blue Fin
SEAFOOD   SUSHI   COCKTAILS
ket out

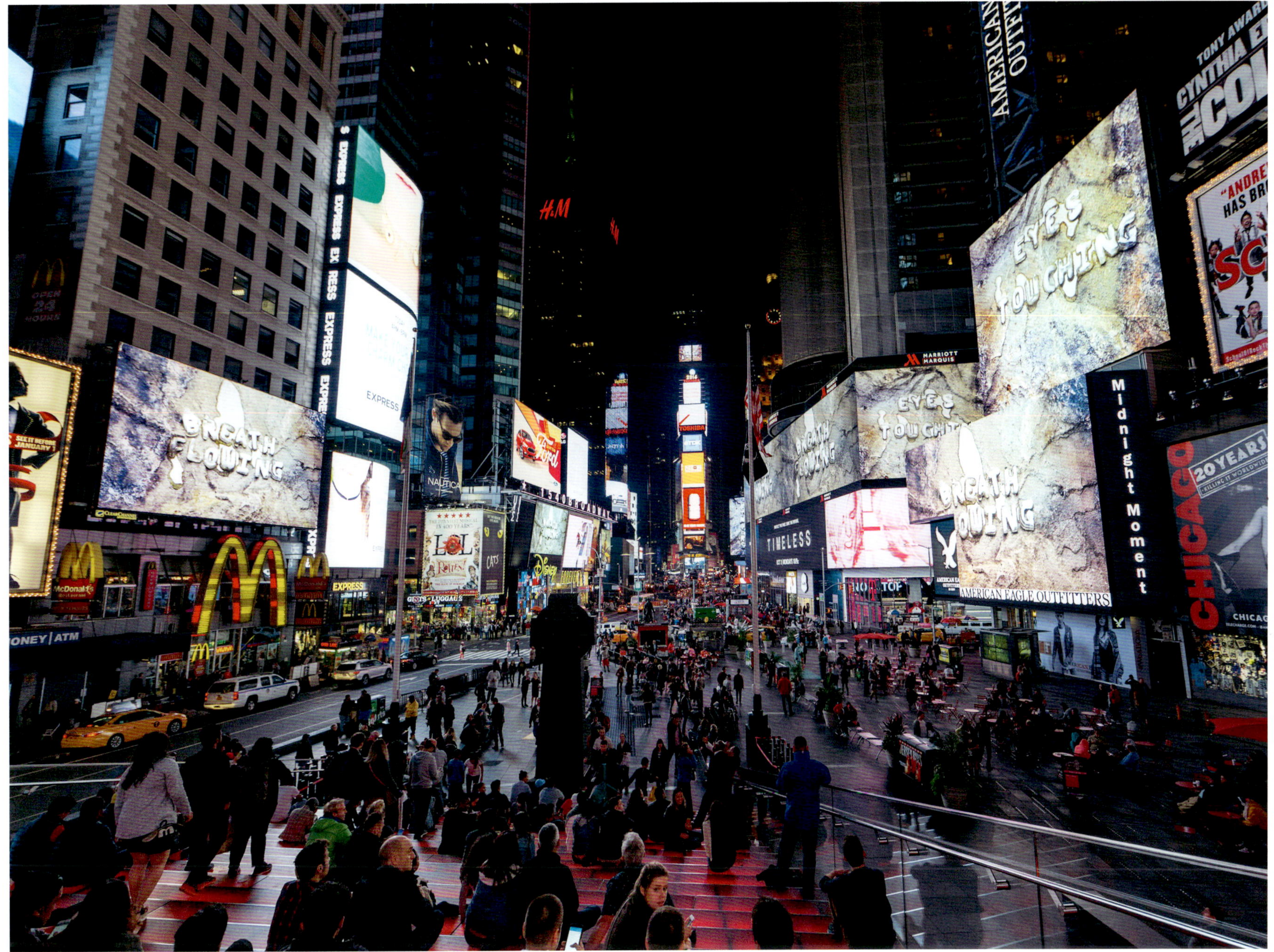

EYES
TOUCHING
BREATH FLOWING
BREATH FLOWING
EYES TOUCHING
BREATH FLOWING
Midnight Moment
AMERICAN EAGLE OUTFITTERS
H&M
EXPRESS
TIMELESS
CHICAGO
20 YEARS
CHICAGO
McDonald's
MARRIOTT MARQUIS
TOSHIBA
NAUTICA
LOL
CATS
Disney
MONEY | ATM

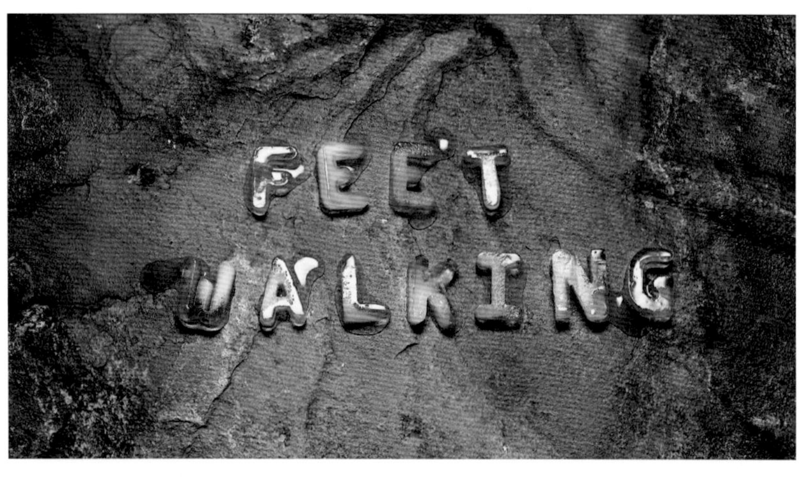

FEET
WALKING

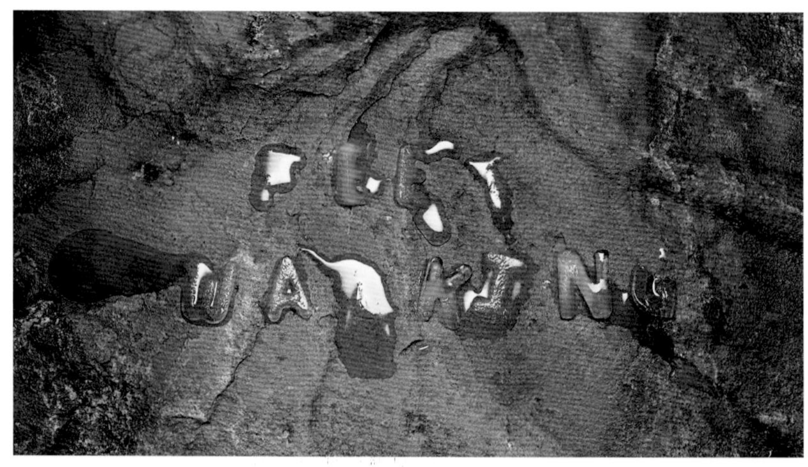

FEET
WALKING

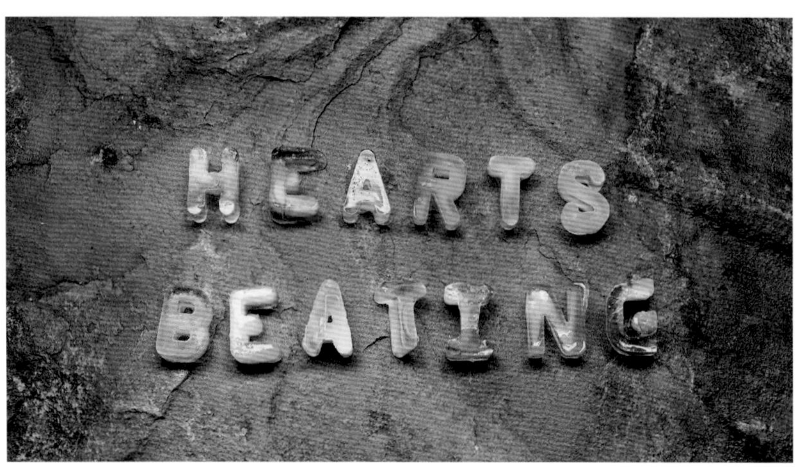

HEARTS
BEATING

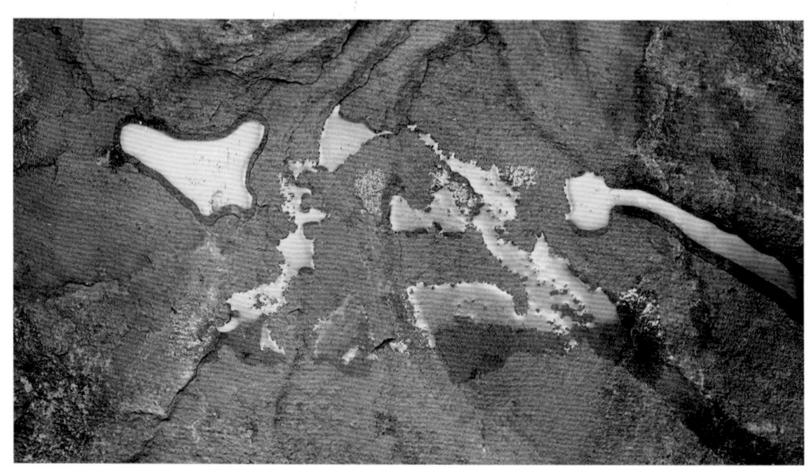

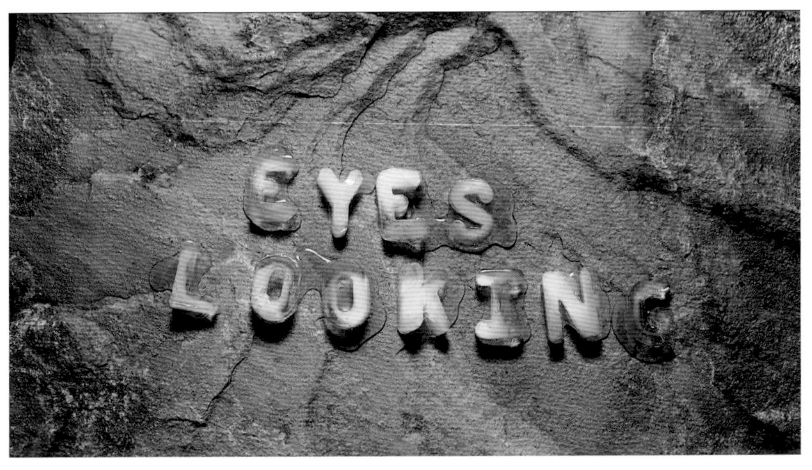

EYES
LOOKING

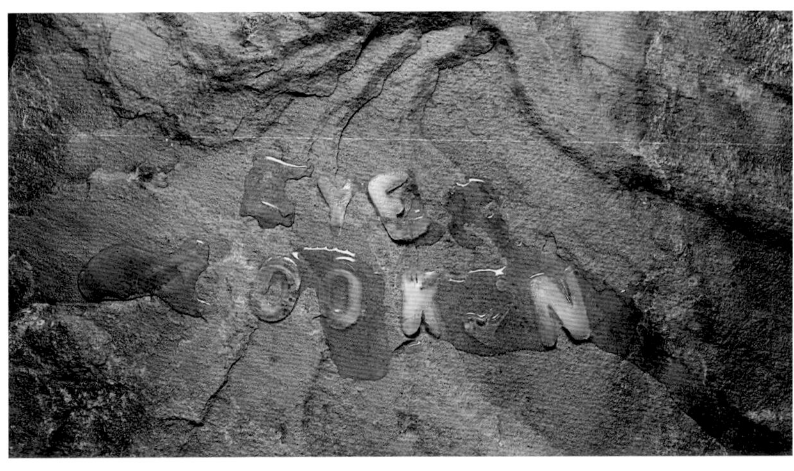

EYES
LOOKIN

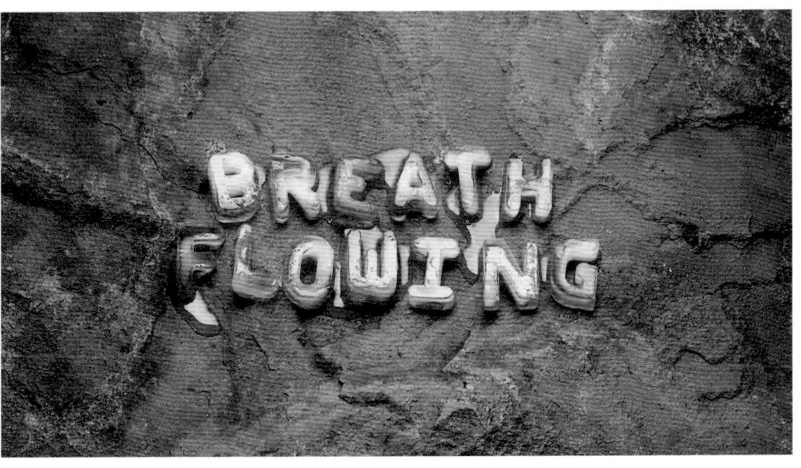

BREATH
FLOWING

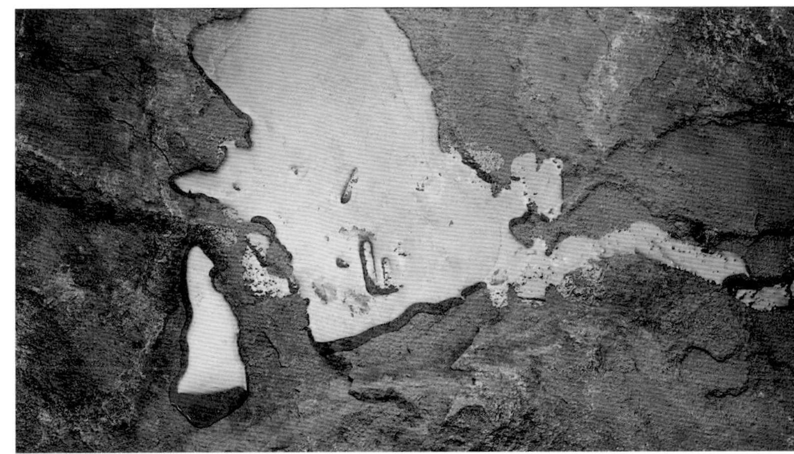

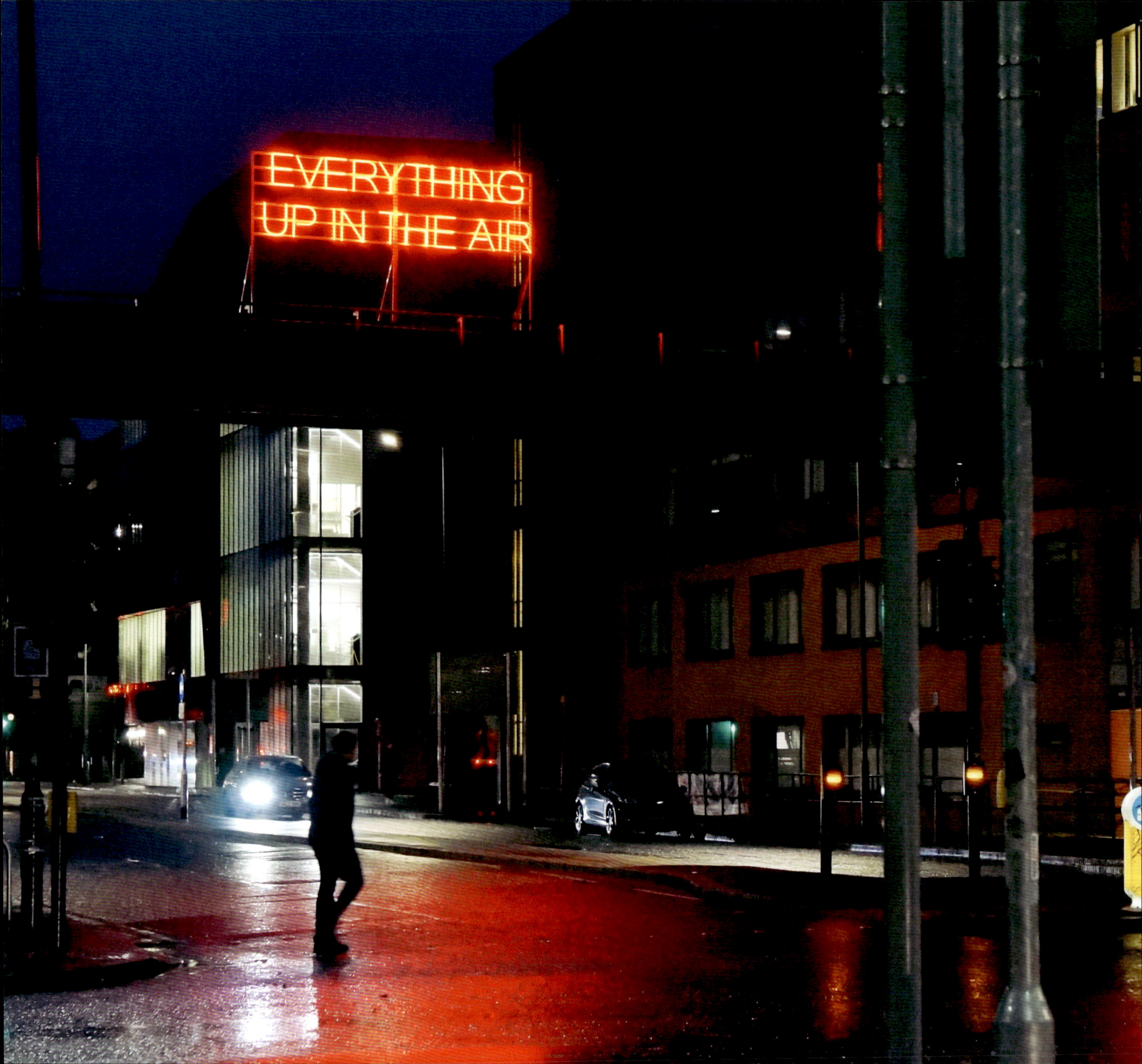

EVERYTHING
UP IN THE AIR

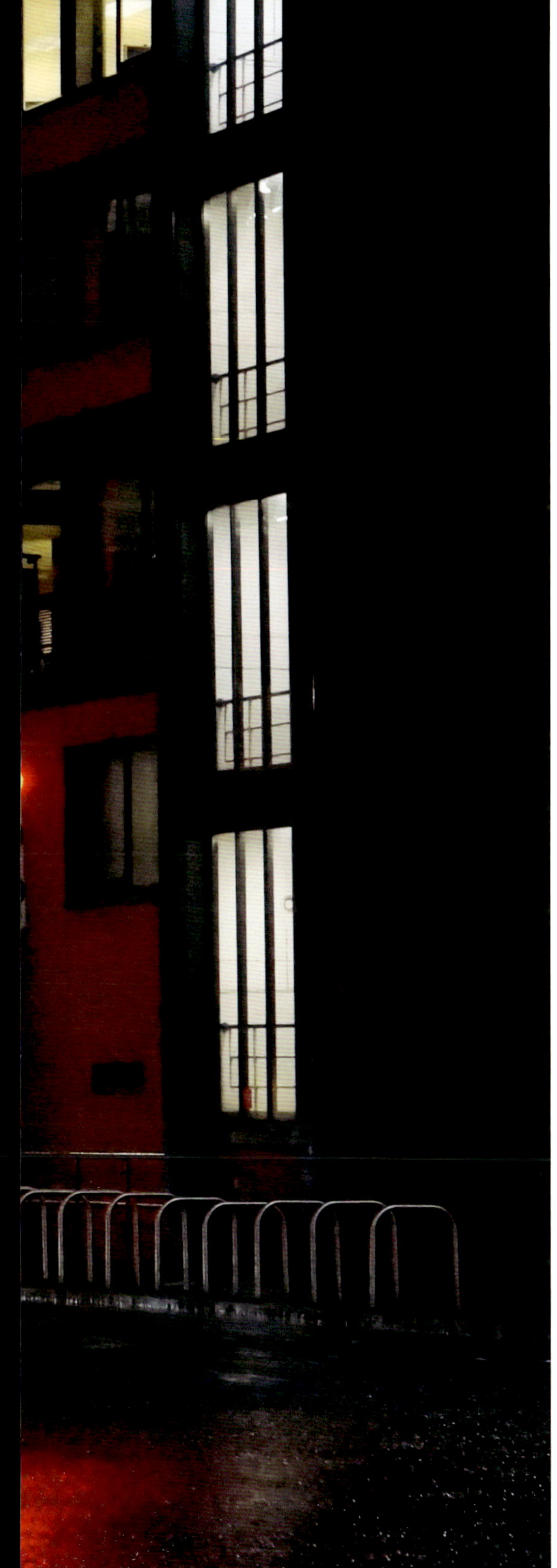

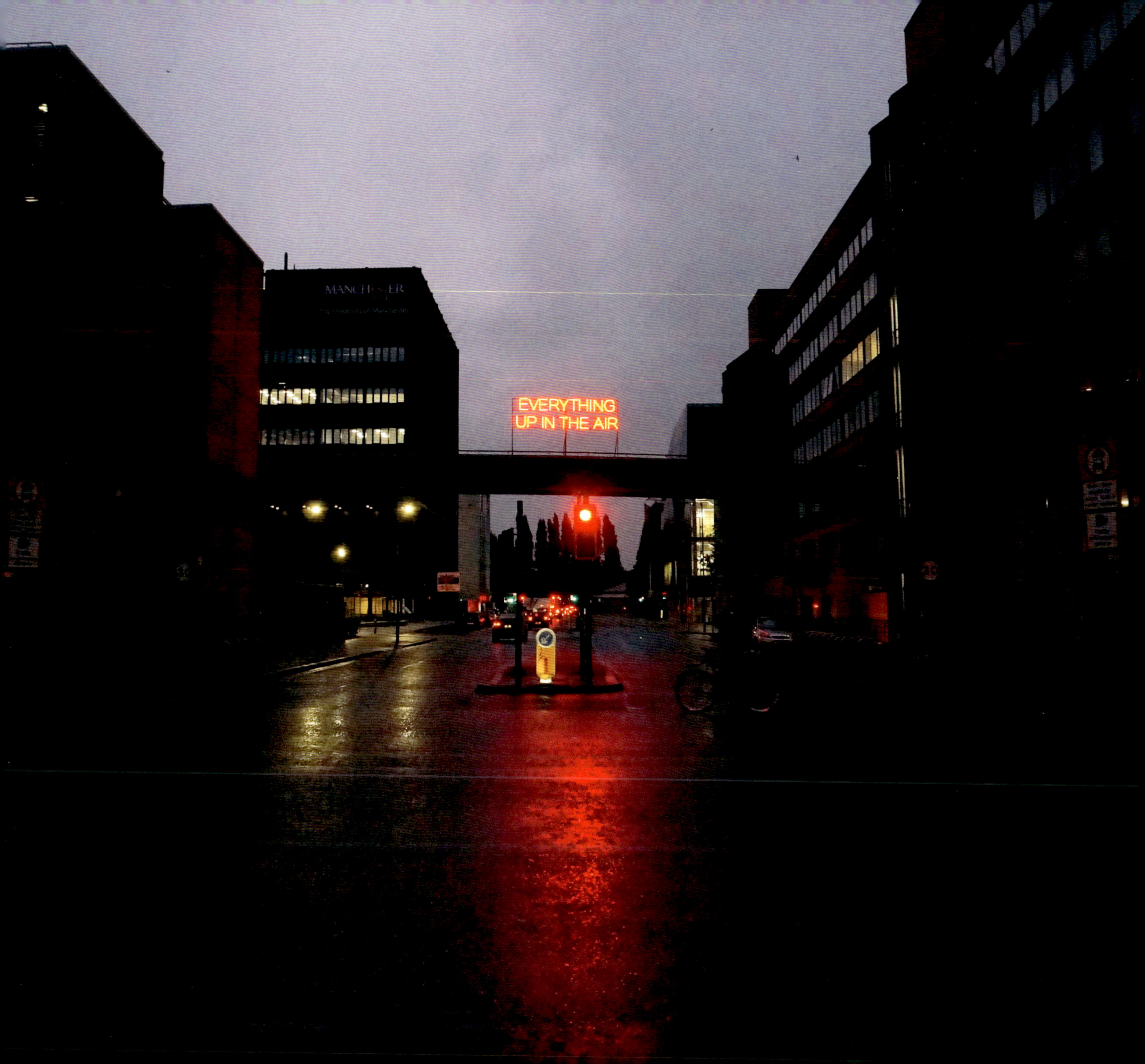

MANCHESTER
EVERYTHING
UP IN THE AIR

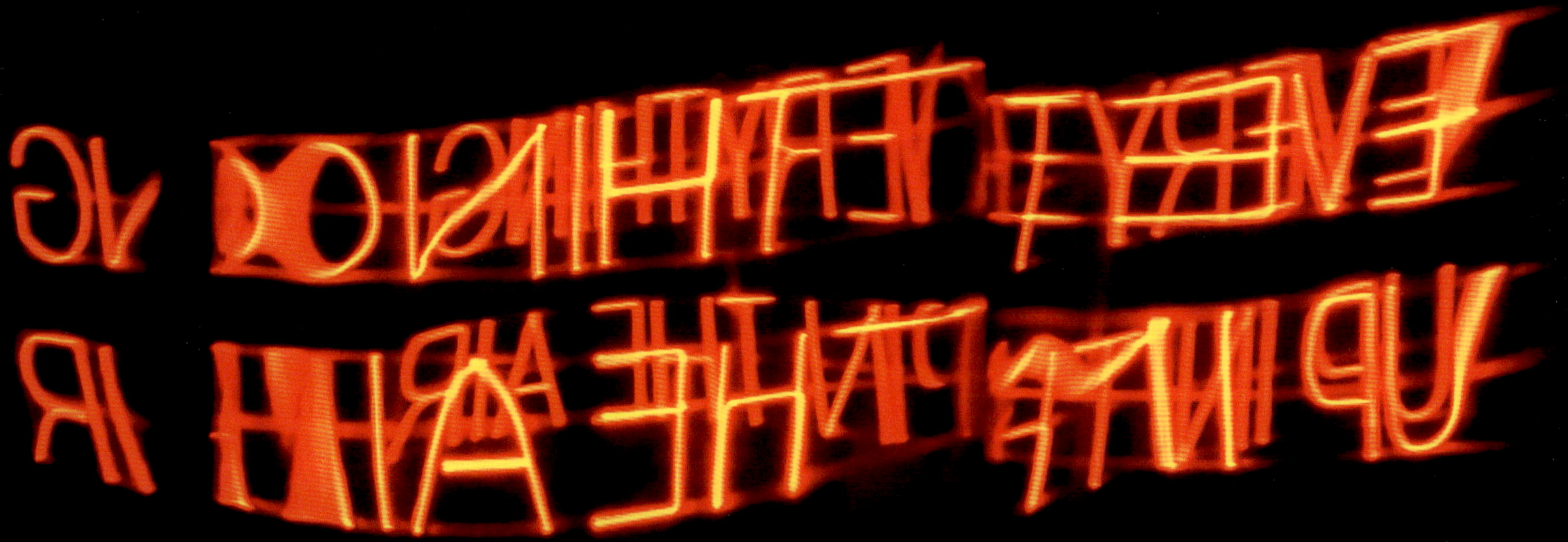

EVERYTHING IS
UP IN THE AIR

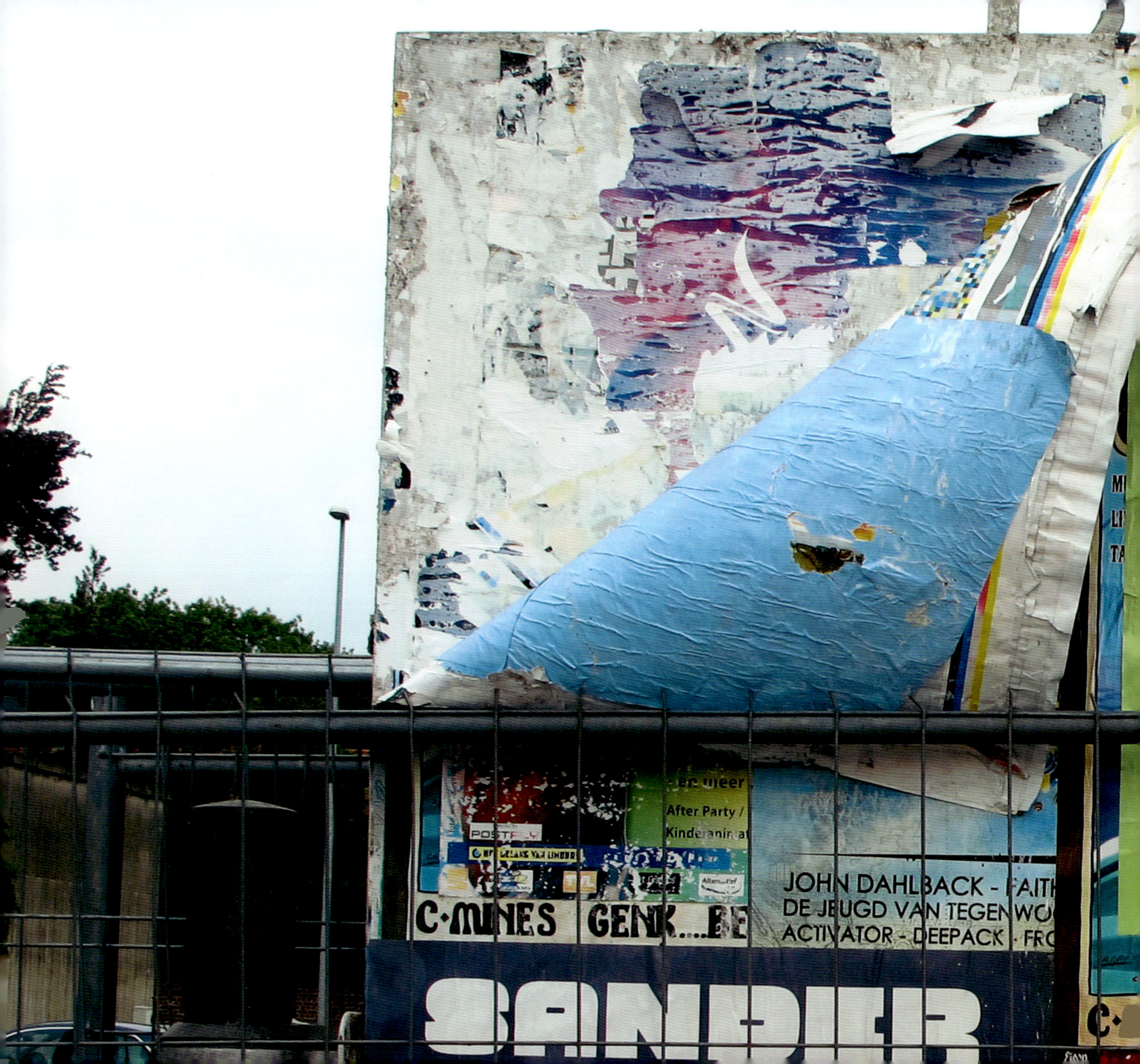
After Party /
Kinderanima
POSTE
C-MINES GENK...BE
JOHN DAHLBACK - FAITH
DE JEUGD VAN TEGENWO
ACTIVATOR - DEEPACK - FRO
SANDER

31.05.2012 - 02.06.2012

ABSOLUTE
FINAL
&
TOTAL
CANCELLATION
OF
EVERYTHING

ABSOLUTE, DEFINITIEVE EN TOTALE ANNULERING VAN ALLES

VU: TIM ETCHELLS - WWW.TIMETCHELLS.COM
SMALL ACTS OF DISOBEDIENCE - www.portlandgreen.com/PG/art/sad

Eventdrukker.
BATTLE.OF.BASS
ANR
EUROPALAAN 26
3600 GENK
ITM
Elektriciteitswerken
+32 484 82 52 02

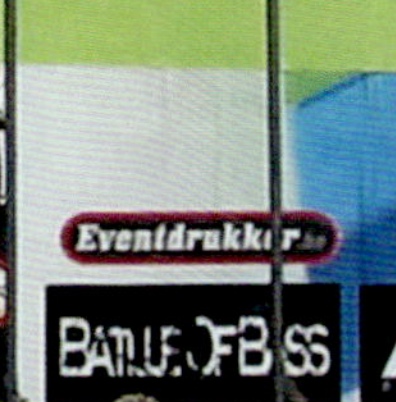
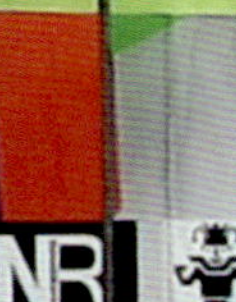
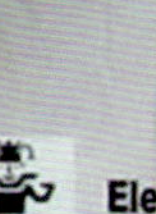
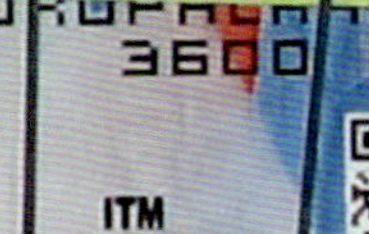

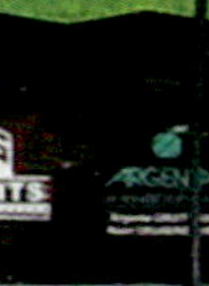

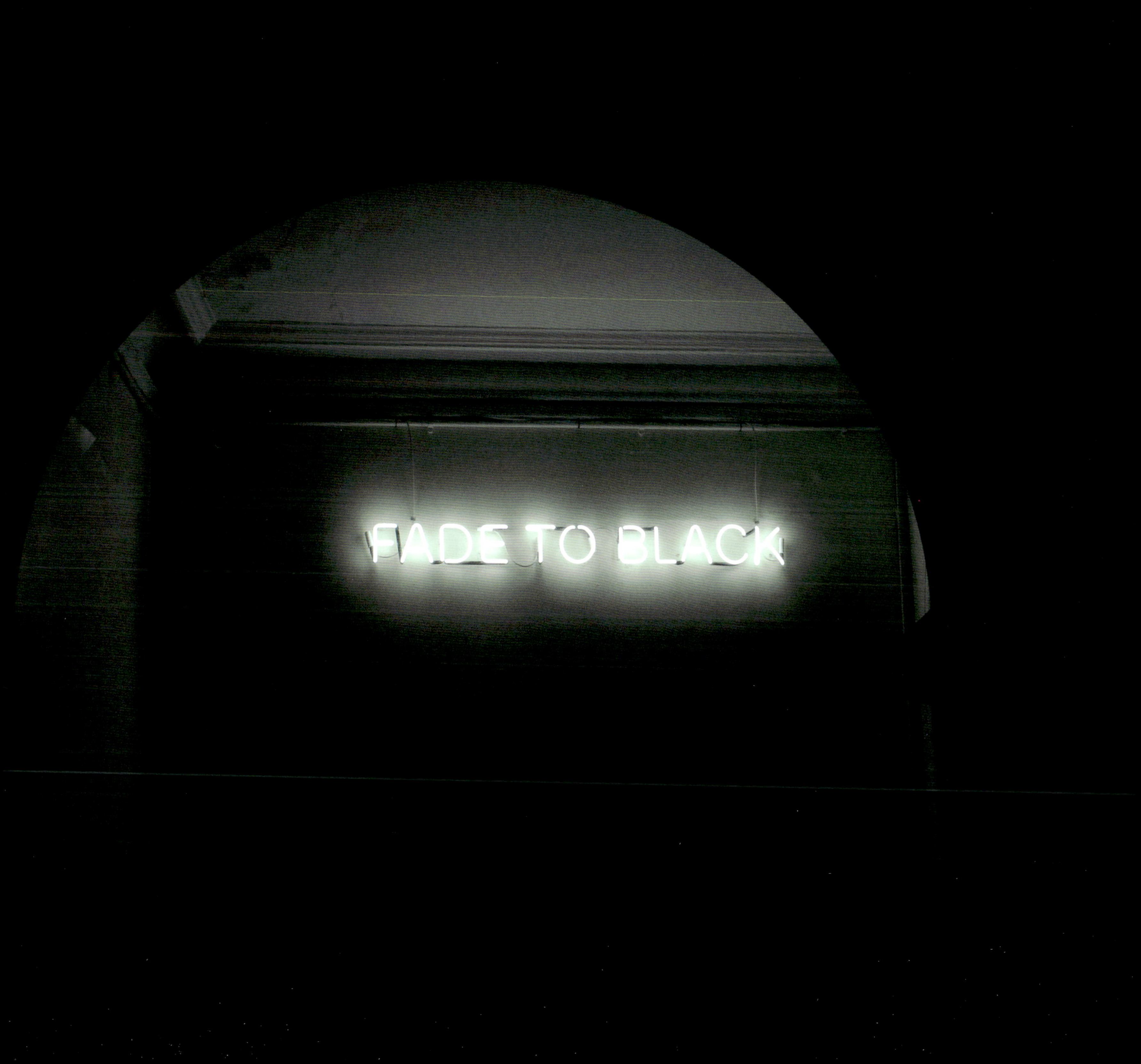

FADE TO BLACK

'ALL THE LOVELY WORDS'
BEN BORTHWICK

This is a book about words in pictures and pictures about words. These pictures are framed by words spoken in 'the artist's voice' in an interview which, in turn, is framed by these words you are reading, written by me. I like this layering where images of words simultaneously construct their meaning independently of, alongside, and through, the words that frame them. The images may both prompt and resist this framing of and by language, but it is always already happening, and especially so in Tim Etchells' work. Like so much of Etchells' artwork, this book occupies the space between being a visual book of language and book about visual language, where possibilities unfold through the interplay between words as material objects photographed in a variety of situations, presented in book form as images, framed by writing about them.

Etchells' primary material is the word to which he gives form, usually sculptural form as objects occupying physical space. While neon is the dominant material (hence the book's title), his work also includes large steel letters housing LED bulbs, small un-illuminated steel cutouts, scrolling LED signs, as well as words painted as murals, printed as artist's books or posters, spoken as audio works or as live performances in front of audiences. Sometimes the same words straddle or move between these different forms, their inference shifting as they are transposed across materials, scale and contexts. Each version of a phrase can be taken on its own terms, but knowing about different

manifestations allows for a double reflection: we are invited to think about how materials change the meaning of a phrase, and about why particular materials might have been chosen for a specific context.

In parallel with the intentional meanings produced by the artwork through its words and formal properties, the malleability of meaning in relation to context is central to Etchells' work. His practice is heavily informed by the discourse around site-specificity where works commissioned for a particular context speak directly to a history or characteristic of that place, resonating with, or filling in, a missing piece of local knowledge. For decades I thought Rachel Whiteread's *House* from 1993 resonated with its site so profoundly because of the intersection of conditions specific to its time and place. Thirty years on it seems to me that this site-specific work, which in many ways defined the genre, has been overtaken by history: what was specific has become a general condition of society. It can now be read as both a memorial to the passing of social values that defined the postwar era of the welfare state, and as a prefiguring of London's leading role in the volatile globalisation that would emerge in the late 1990s and 2000s, and which continues to accelerate in the post-Brexit landscape. As the discourse around site-specificity has evolved, the relationship between site and artwork has loosened, and phrases like 'site-responsive' or 'context-specific' are used to describe how (often already existing) artworks are installed because they resonate with this or that 'kind of place'.

Malleability around meaning and context extends across Etchells' practice as an artist through to his long-established work in theatre and performance as a founder and Artistic Director of Forced Entertainment, the experimental group making work from their base in Sheffield since 1984. Having worked with improvisation in this collective theatre environment for over twenty years before applying related ideas to sculptural form, Etchells has built a practice that merges approaches from different disciplinary realms. The distillation of ideas to principles to be interpreted rather than texts to be recited infuses his use of language with the sense that meaning can adapt to changing situations beyond the intention and control of the artist. There is an ease with which the phrases in Etchells' work move between materials, between controlled settings like galleries and outdoor locations where contingency rules, and between shifting moments in society and politics, in each instance resonating in new and unexpected ways.

One such example is *Let's Pretend* (2008), from the first group of neons Etchells made. Its text, 'LET'S PRETEND NONE OF THIS EVER HAPPENED', is an invitation to become complicit in a collective yet contradictory endeavour: to build trust or community by disavowing reality. A second architectural-scale version of this work was made in 2014 and has been shown internationally on the façades and rooftops of large civic buildings, notably in Blackpool in 2016 (p.10-11) in the aftermath of the Brexit referendum. This open-ended, general and non-specific phrase became, in that context, a politics-specific comment on the ways in which Brexit debates were conducted by politicians, the media and the general population. In doing so, it appeared to offer short shrift to Leavers with their fantasy of return to an idealised notion of British sovereignty unshackled from Europe, as if EU membership had been a 43-year-long bad dream, while also critiquing disbelieving Remainers unwilling to accept the reality that the majority of voters had chosen to leave the EU. Equally, the work offered the possibility that the referendum itself, and the conditions of xenophobia, poverty and disenfranchisement that framed it, might also be wished away in a perilous act of complicit forgetting.

Let's Pretend is one of the many works in which time is figured as something marked, imagined, remembered and obscured: 'the future will be confusing', 'ALL THE THINGS THAT COULD HAPPEN NEXT', 'THIS PRECISE MOMENT IN TIME AS SEEN FROM THE FUTURE',

'everything is different today'… Any of these texts could be companion pieces to *Let's Pretend* but *Different Today* (2018), installed permanently on the roof of Site Gallery in Sheffield, is perhaps the one that is most anchored into the post-Brexit moment. Even so, its resonance is not limited by historical specificity, as the uncertain present it describes bounces backwards and forwards, between the Brexit past it reflects on, the emergence of long-established campaigns like Me Too and Black Lives Matter into public consciousness, and the surreal upheavals of the Covid future it prefigures. If *Let's Pretend* reflects on the past, and *Different Today* engages with versions of the present, a work like *A Message* (2014), with its text 'A MESSAGE TO YOURSELF FROM THE PAST WHEN YOU BELIEVED IN DIFFERENT THINGS', straddles the tenses by cutting a white neon line through time and space. The work's thirteen-word textual gesture about aging and changing values implicates the viewer in a process of self-reflection, internalising the subjective experience and demographic differences of the generation gap. In doing so it summons a melancholy akin to that of Neil Young's song "Old Man", the great lamentation from his 1972 album *Harvest*.

Etchells often works to invoke such psychic unease, while activating dynamic relations between the specific and the uncertain. For example, while it is interesting to know that the phrase 'for everything that is shown something is hidden' in *For Everything* (2018) is a direct quote from James Bridle's book *New Dark Age* (Verso, 2018), the resonance of the work is in no way dependent on that knowledge. Bridle is writing about the myth of internet transparency and the process through which a beautiful utopian idea becomes a complex, clumsy, manipulative machine. And so it is with this quote – it lacks the pithy aphoristic quality of a slogan and contains too many syllables for it to be a soundbite. It is something that has to be worked at, worked out.

For Everything was first presented in the window of VITRINE, London, a gallery which occupies one side of a small new residential development nearby Tate Modern. The window is overlooked by diners in the plaza's restaurants and bars, residents in the new flats, and people taking shortcuts. I remember sitting on the bench shown in the foreground of the photograph on pages 74-75, watching the artwork, waiting for the circuit to switch and illuminate the other letters, eager to see the full phrase light up, like the crescendo of Bruce Nauman's iconic neon *Live And Die* (1984). While sitting, watching and waiting, my attention wandered to the passers-by and al fresco diners, their focus elsewhere, and I wondered what they made of the fragmented cipher in their peripheral vision. Five years on, my memory is that my act of giving time was eventually rewarded with the switching circuit I anticipated, the neon illuminating in full and staging a contemporary art version of the Hegelian model of thesis, antithesis, synthesis. I am assured by the artist that this was not, however, the case: there is no narrative development here, no big reveal, no reward. Like so much of Etchells' work, *For Something* stages temporality but withholds progression, makes specific reference while resonating widely and is, ultimately, always immanent to possibility while resisting resolution.

For Something directly references Bridle's theory about society's relationship to the internet, but it also speaks to the capacity of language to both hold meaning and escape interpretation. Language is always already framing its own meanings and references in disobedient ways and Etchells embraces this, creating space for slippages in meaning to become active elements of his work. He does so through his use of language, but also through formal means. He strategically stacks layers of invisibility: using Arial, a sans serif font so generic it is easy to ignore; inserting yet more neon into the public realm and asking this archaic material to compete for attention with ever more sophisticated advertising technologies; activating the familiar (but in this case intentional) trope of missing letters that renders a sign illegible and offers all kinds of scope for being misread or simply ignored.

Despite employing a wide range of media, Etchells sets himself heavily restricted formal parameters. These limits serve to focus the viewer on the words at hand, but also function like the controls in an experiment allowing Etchells to explore linguistic minutiae and permutations of form. Alongside language and neon, horizontality is perhaps the third dominant property of his sculptures. He works with the horizontal as an internal structural element, often pushing a sculpture's linear form to the limit of legibility, like one of those emails that has lost its formatting, where you have to keep scrolling right to read a whole paragraph on one line. When displayed in the public realm, these linear works occupy lintels, rooftops and other horizontal architectural elements, embedding themselves into the surface of buildings and the wider landscape.

In 2015 I needed to do an exhibition at short notice to launch the programme in my new job at Plymouth Arts Centre and I called Tim – I needed to work with someone I already trusted who I knew could adapt to uncertainty and changing possibilities. At that point Tim and I were seven years into our dialogue, since presenting *Wait Here* (2008) as the inaugural show at Butcher's, a project space I set up with Cylena Simonds that same year. Tim's exhibition at Plymouth Arts Centre was an opportunity to test the strange domestic scale of its gallery spaces (occupying a nondescript Georgian building), but also to test the limits of how his recent larger works could be presented in alternative ways without compromising their integrity. *Mirror Pieces* (2014) is one such work that activates the all-at-once visual regime of the modernist grid in order to challenge it from within. It is comprised of six sections forming a flattened geometric grid where subtle differences in meaning emerge through formal repetition. Each of the six sections pairs two of the phrases 'OPTICAL ILLUSIONS' / 'POLITICAL DELUSIONS' / 'POETICAL CONFUSIONS' until all combinations of phrases and their positions relative to each other have been completed. Tim was open to the proposal to explode that logic by installing the pairs across six different walls, the rationalist regime of that logic collapsing into the higgledy-piggledy chaos of changing planes and perspectives, resulting in a vertiginous and immersive hall of mirrors where the illusions, delusions and confusions were simultaneously experienced as optical, political and poetical.

The other large piece we showed in Plymouth was *Revolution* (2010), originally commissioned for the roofline of a bandstand in Norwich. In its original context, visitors had to walk around the outside of the structure, poetically enacting the role of the needle that gives voice to a record as it spins, a metaphor that also signals the very technology that made bandstands an obsolete relic of the nineteenth century. Just as the logic of *Mirror Pieces* was exploded, so we reimagined this linear work as a stacked grid that repeats the phrase 'START A REVOLUTION', forming a mantra in four colours on the building's exterior. For me, this was a rallying cry about the organisation's precarious future (it was forced to close shortly afterward), but also a moment of clarity about how site-specific artworks can speak to the radically different specificity of alternative sites, whether geographical, social or temporal.

Thirteen years since *Revolution* introduced this linear architectural tendency into Etchells' work, I was pleased to see *Beautiful Words* (2023). Installed in Milan at Renata Fabbri gallery, the title phrase repeats in different colours and fonts as it spans a long wall connecting two galleries, diminishing to a vanishing point. Etchells plays with the visual properties of the material and the linguistic puns of the phrase, surely making a knowing nod to the deadpan humour and irony in Lawrence Weiner's brilliant 1979 work *Many Colored Objects Placed Side by Side to Form a Row of Many Colored Objects*. Along with 'time', the word 'words' is another of Etchells' recurring motifs (or 'objects' if we are to follow Weiner). In a growing number of his works, 'words' is used as a hinge, each making sense in and of itself, but accumulating to create a group of related pieces where 'ALL WE HAVE IS WORDS / ALL WE HAVE IS WORLDS' speaks to 'lost for words' and 'beautiful words'.

I am reminded of a phrase that has been jangling around my head for a decade or so since reading an interview with the musician Edwyn Collins. Following a series of catastrophic brain haemorrhages in 2005, for an extended period this most lyrical of pop stars almost completely lost the power of speech and ability to write words. In a 2014 documentary about him, *The Possibilities Are Endless*, he spoke of this period and the feeling of profound loss that he might never again be able to speak or write fluently. He used the phrase 'all the lovely words' to mourn the loss of this lifelong affair with language and to celebrate the slow, incremental rebuilding of his relationship to the word. With Collins you get the sense that it is not so much his ability to manipulate language as it is the intimacy he feels with each precious word as he puts them together. That is the first, achingly poignant, part of this anecdote.

The second part is that I have no idea where I read this line I'm attributing to Collins, as it doesn't appear in any of the interviews I remember reading at the time. It would seem that if Collins said it at all, it was just a passing phrase rather than a soundbite that has found its way into his bibliography. I like this unmooring of a phrase (or a quote) from its point of origin, even to the extent that when you want to trace where it came from, the path has been obscured. The words are out there as things in the world: installed in galleries, on the outside of buildings, framed by architecture and nature, so that when we see them, they cycle around our heads like earworms, even as they remain unspoken.

'All the lovely words' has become a point of reference for me that recurs on a fairly regular basis, and always when I encounter Etchells' work. This insight is a reminder that for some – the lucky ones? – language is alive; it is a spell to be cast. In their work, artists like Etchells, Collins and Young are able to convey a deeply emotional sense of care where every word is precious, while the act of combining them into phrases, statements or lyrics, as well as other forms – whether music, neon or performances – becomes a great and generous act of responsibility, pleasure and, ultimately, love.

TIM ETCHELLS IN CONVERSATION WITH JULE HILLGÄRTNER

Jule Hillgärtner: Knowing that your neon and LED pieces are an important part of your artistic practice, I was still overwhelmed to see the enormous range of works in this book, realised over the years. What was your first piece and how did you start working with words that glow in the dark?

Tim Etchells: The beginning is quite funny. I was in New York with my partner Vlatka Horvat, who is also an artist, and someone invited her to be in a group show. In conversation with the curator I mentioned a neon work of mine that might fit the context, and they asked to see images. I hadn't really made the piece at that point in fact… but over the next days I photoshopped an image as if the work existed, collaging the letters from images of neon signs I found online. The curator liked my photoshop I suppose… So a first iteration of *Wait Here* was made and shown in New York in 2007. Around the same time I was in dialogue with Jeanine Griffin and Jan Verwoert about Art Sheffield 2008, and I proposed a new version of *Wait Here*, alongside two new works, *Please Come Back* and *Let's Pretend*, which were eventually installed in Sheffield city centre.

There's a long pre-history to the neons too. I've always been interested in language fragments – collecting and writing short phrases that seem to conjure stories and questions. That fascination just needed a form to articulate it. More concretely, in the late 1980s and early 90s, two performances I created with Forced Entertainment had used neon as

part of their set design. *200% & Bloody Thirsty* (1987) had the title of the piece in red neon on a billboard-like structure onstage, and *Marina and Lee* (1991) used my phrase 'LOOK NO FURTHER – THIS IS IT' in white neon as part of a backdrop. So in a sense I'd already started the work with neon long before my first actual neon pieces were made. That's probably how it goes with a lot of my practice: the first formal iteration of an idea usually links to something that's already begun.

JH: When they're shown outdoors, your neons have a different presence depending on whether we see them during the day or at night. In the daylight, the construction shows – cables, transformers, scaffolding – but in the darkness all that disappears and the words seem to float in the air. They become even more present because it's dark around them. Having other works of yours in mind – performances with Forced Entertainment or books such as *The Dream Dictionary (for the Modern Dreamer)* (2001) – it seems that you're fascinated by the darkness and things happening at night. Would you tell me about what draws you to this?

TE: There's something about the twilight where other voices might creep in; as if in the shadows or the coming darkness, other realities might be visible, precisely because the daylight is fading. The neons carry stories or voices in that moment very evocatively. There's a little bit of magic possible there.

Of course, historically, neon as urban advertising resonates in the dusk. It's the hour of that medium, if you like. So in that sense I'm just picking up on the culture of use that neon has, its qualities and associations.

I'm also reminded that I almost never photograph the neons in full daylight or in complete darkness. With work outdoors, photographically speaking, there's a 20-or-so-minute window in which there's a perfect balance in the light. The border where the objective, rational space of daytime is receding, but the full-on darkness of the night is not there yet. The dialogue between the environment and the work is really important to me and at dusk or at sunrise the works are really vibrant, but you can still read them in relation to the context.

TE: The nature of the phrases I work with – short, fragmentary – helps them open a dialogue wherever they're placed. Even when a work appears quite rooted in a specific place, I'm learning that there are other opportunities and resonances to explore by placing it in different contexts. A good example is a recent temporary work I was commissioned to make by Lumiere for Redhills in Durham, the former headquarters of the Durham Miners Association. The building opened in 1915 when coal production in the region peaked, with around 170,000 miners working in County Durham, but the industry was in decline from the 1950s, the last mine there closing in 1994. Redhills – now a community centre – sits at the heart of a story about shifts in trade union and worker power. *Shifting Ground* (2021), the piece I made for the site, tried to speak to both the work of mining and the changing political and economic situation. For me it also speaks to the ways in which our understanding of fossil fuels has developed in the intervening century because of the climate emergency.

Shifting Ground felt right in Durham, and I did think it might be destined to be shown only once, because it was so specific to the confluence of narratives in the location. Months later though, I was speaking with Stefan Hilterhaus, director of PACT Zollverein in Essen, Germany – which occupies a building on the site of a former coal mine and which is nowadays a performing arts cultural centre – and it struck me that many of the same issues I was working with in Durham were relevant in PACT. We installed the piece there in 2022 and alongside the work's original reference to mining and industrial labour, PACT's focus on dance gave the phrase 'shifting ground' a fresh set of resonances.

When a work is relocated it can unlock a whole other set of stories. *With/Against* (2018), a large-scale LED piece, was originally made for an exhibition at Baltic Centre for Contemporary Art in Gateshead. The full text for the piece says, 'GO WITH THE FLOW / SWIM AGAINST THE TIDE', so installed right on the bank of the River Tyne it addressed the location directly – the tidal flow of the river, the workings of the port – as well as being this combination of idiomatic phrases speaking to the passers-by. Subsequently, it was installed at Seaham Harbour, right next to the sea, as part of Lumiere 2021. These days though, the work is usually stored in a field, many miles from the water and while it is not technically on view there, it still seems to find an audience – pictures are always popping up on social media! The phrase seems out of place in the field and friction lends it an interesting resonance. To my mind, it can be a strong choice to be correct or evidently in sync with a site, but it's also interesting to be 'incorrect', to bring something playful or surprising to bear on a situation.

TE: Yes. The same dynamic – between specificity and openness – is often deep in the language I use. I tend to offer something vivid – a proposition, a topic, an image – but at the same time use language to make a space that engages the viewer. The work *Different Today* (2018), permanently installed at Site Gallery in Sheffield, reads, 'everything is different today', but we are not told on what scale or in what frame we should pursue the idea it proposes. Is it personal things that are different? Is it things here in the city? In global politics? Different compared to what, or when? Different than yesterday? Last year? Last century? And so on. Along these lines I'm also thinking of the work *All the Things*. It says, 'ALL THE THINGS THAT COULD HAPPEN NEXT', but offers no further information to help us narrow or direct our thinking.

Regards site, yes, I might use a work to try to catch something related to its location or its history, but not usually in a super specific way, preferring often to connect to those things in more abstracted or veiled terms. As you say, that's part of what allows the works a certain flexibility. They try to reach to something, but there's this dynamic looseness too.

JH: I'm wondering though whether there are any works that are truly site-specific? In that they are only designed for one particular place and cannot be transferred to another site?

TE: One work that comes to mind is *A Stitch in Time*, commissioned for Derry/Londonderry as part of Lumiere 2016. The piece was made for the roof of a former shirt factory, and refers in very specific ways to the social and historical context. The shirt factories in Northern Ireland have been understood as places which fostered significant communication between Catholic and Protestant communities during the period of the Troubles and armed resistance to British occupation, simply because working class women from both sides of the conflict worked side by side on the production lines. The text I used for the work – 'A STITCH IN TIME' – is a truncation of a proverb 'a stitch in time saves nine' and through that reference suggests ideas of repair and care, and of disaster averted. Mending or joining of fabric is literally invoked of course, but the timely and patient work of social mending – joining lives and communities, forging political and social relations – is also summoned by the phrase. It's a work that could perhaps be shown elsewhere, but its double interaction – with specific narratives and with material/architectural context – makes that unlikely in my mind.

JH: What about the relationship between the texts themselves and the way they are manifested as signs? I'm thinking in particular of your early works here.

TE: Many of my earliest neons have a conversational tone. They grab you and draw you into a story, as if you're in a fictitious situation or narrative. There's an explicit tension between these works' narrative propositions and their formal realisation as neons in public space. In real life or in cinema, a text like 'WAIT HERE I HAVE GONE TO GET HELP' should be a hasty, handwritten note. Or perhaps scrawled in blood on the wall! But to have made that phrase in neon contradicts

the urgency. That's also the case with *Please Come Back* (2008), which reads, 'PLEASE COME BACK I AM SORRY ABOUT WHAT HAPPENED BEFORE'. The material manifestation is too slow for the narrative; you feel that in the works, that there's something wrong. That's part of their dynamic.

JH: If we stay for a moment with the manifestation of the work: there's a kind of break, as you describe it there, between the content of the works and their appearance as neon. Some of your later neons are made with letters in different colours or with letters dispersed or upside down, so that they take longer to read. In *Will Be* (2010), for example, you seem to be going out of your way to avoid a reading flow! Encountering the piece at first all we see are single letters in different colours scattered about. We have to work to decipher the sentence: 'the future will be confusing'.

TE: Yes. The choice of colours, of all-caps or lowercase letters and of different fonts and letter forms creates different relations between the semantic content of the texts and their presence as sculptures. I'm always balancing those things, or playing them against each other.

Initially I tended to work with simple all-caps phrases in a single neon colour, but over time I began to experiment with more complex visual arrangements. I wanted the form of the work's realisation to follow from, or extend, a dialogue with the content of the text. I liked that *Will Be* could be realised in a comically complex way – with this unhelpful mix of colourful letters, so that the uneven appearance already manifests what the message predicts.

It's a similar game with *Mirror Pieces* (2014) and *More Noise* (2016). In the former, three different phrases linked in their content as well as possessing both visual and sonic similarities – 'OPTICAL ILLUSIONS', 'POLITICAL DELUSIONS', 'POETICAL CONFUSIONS' – are written using a confusing pattern of different colour letters and arranged in mismatched, imperfectly mirroring pairs. In the latter, the phrase 'MORE NOISE THAN SIGNAL' is split in two sections – 'MORE NOISE' and 'THAN SIGNAL' – each repeated seven times in different colours and installed in an unruly pile on the ground, disrupting the reading experience and at the same time demanding an engagement with the work in sculptural terms.

JH: Words create images and your works do this in at least two ways: first, there's the image of the glowing letters in the landscape, and second, there are images produced from the words' meaning, which might be literal or figurative. Quite a lot of your pieces express a direct connection to the body, for instance, *With/Against*, which you just discussed, or *Things That Make the Heart Beat Faster* (2021). We can imagine – or maybe even feel – what those sentences do to our bodies. In the case of the latter, they make us aware of this very moment, the nowness or presence, which is something I associate with performance. Do you think of words as performers?

TE: In some ways, yes. Almost all my work draws on my background in performance which involves a temporally situated moment of exchange. In these terms, the work can be any kind of object – a neon, a book, a story, a poem, a poster – but it's always something that activates a certain performative, temporal and of course spatial process when the work is observed.

Written or spoken language frames the reader or listener as a collaborator, in the moment of their encounter with the text. When you read or hear even just a few words, you have to do the work of imagining what the words summon, what they bring into the world. Another way of thinking about this is that you, the reader, get activated as a site in which something is happening. The language is being performed in and through you.

The circumstances in which a spectator comes across a work – in a public site, or in a gallery – the physical journey towards it, the way one first sees it in relation to architecture and environment, etc. become part of how the work produces meaning. Even my work with fiction is informed at some level by this sense of performative temporality and embodied encounter. As a writer I'm thinking about the reader, their presence in a space, their hands and eyes moving on the page, the book as an object.

The sculptural text pieces use a variety of tactics to amplify the viewer's sense of their own presence as they encounter the work. Some of the neons use the word 'you', while others highlight the moment of perception, stressing the viewer's presence in time. Many of them make direct calls to the spectator through language that refers to bodily actions or processes; looking, touching, breathing, falling, shouting, speaking or listening. The recent work for Cologne – *From the Other Side* (2022) – plays explicitly on the position of the viewer, with the text 'SEE THINGS FROM THE OTHER SIDE' repeated, facing in opposite directions. Wherever you are viewing it from, you are always being encouraged to imagine seeing the work (and the rest of the world) from the other perspective.

JH: Another relation to the body comes from the scale of the work. Standing in front of *Best of All* (2018) – with its long phrase 'THE BEST OF ALL POSSIBLE WORLDS' stretching almost 40 meters – one feels pretty tiny. How do you decide on the scale?

TE: The size often comes from the site; to be legible in large public spaces, or to make an impact on the façades of public buildings, the words might just need to be a certain scale. Other locations demand the opposite of course – creating work for disused shop windows, or intimate domestic spaces requires different approaches. There's also often a tension between the scale of the work and the semantics of the language used. The piece for Centre Pompidou in 2021 was monumental – a 40-meter-long work with letters two meters high – but the phrase it used, *QU'Y A-T-IL ENTRE NOUS?* (roughly translated as 'what is between us?'), is intimate, almost conversational. Sometimes the address of the works is very stark and bold – as if they are shouting, or stating cold facts. Other times the feeling is softer, more like the works are whispering; the text can feel like a fragment of human voice, something delicate.

JH: When I am looking at a neon work at night, I tend to be particularly receptive to everything that happens around me, extra sensitive to how my heart is beating. I have a strong sense of how small I am. I tend to be aware of the moment I'm in, and that it is ephemeral: as soon as I've thought about it, it will be over. There are some works of yours that explicitly work with this aspect of ephemerality. I am thinking of the written texts on scrolling LED panels, such as *News Ticker* (2015), *Beautiful* (2011) or *Temporary* (2011), or of the neon *Live Like* (2020) which alters its message as different words are switched on and off. In these works time plays a particular role in the viewer's perception – the text changes and the movement of the work determines what we read and when. How did this strand of work – moving light sculptures – develop?

TE: For me these 'moving' pieces are an extension of the impulse to destabilise the semantics of the texts I'm working with. A phrase that comes and goes, or a phrase that is moving and therefore only partly visible at any given moment, produces something different for the viewer. You're aware of the temporal factor and the contingency of the meaning that's available. In the scrolling LED work *News Ticker*, you're presented not with a single enigmatic phrase but instead with language as a long flow of paired words and their continuous morphing, a kind of free-associating stream of consciousness which apparently has no beginning or end: 'news ticker nudes flicker noose licker new tricker news tickler news ticker new ticker news trickle nude licker news trickle lose cripple goose flipper lewd nipple mews tickle', etc. The scrolling screens in *Temporary*, *Beautiful*, and *W.S.L.S* (2017), as well as the switching on and off of words in *Live Like* also create very different experiences. *Temporary* scrolls the phrase 'A TEMPORARY SADNESS' across the LED unit at intervals, the screen remaining blank for much of the time. *W.S.L.S* scrolls the rather stoical phrase 'WIN SOME LOSE SOME' on a loop, but since the short screen presents only part of the phrase at any moment, the language gets reframed as a rather heavier statement, 'SOME WIN SOME LOSE'. In these moving pieces, I'm looking to the ways in which different meanings can be drawn out from simple materials, and from the slippery space between what 'makes sense' and what borders on nonsense.

Meanwhile, *Live Like* begins with the idiom 'LIVE LIKE THERE IS NO TOMORROW', from which specific words are switched off and then re-instated at timed intervals to carve new shorter phrases – 'LIVE THERE IS NO TOMORROW', 'THERE IS TOMORROW', 'THERE IS NO TOMORROW', 'LIVE LIKE THERE IS TOMORROW', 'LIVE TOMORROW', etc. I'm drawn to these works because they engage with the materiality of language and how it produces meaning – the addition or subtraction of a single word can change everything. The works present language as a process, as something unstable, unfolding, changing.

JH: Are there works that go further down this road, in terms of temporality and performativity?

TE: There are a few works using written language in other media that extend this enquiry. I'm thinking of the multi-screen video piece for Times Square in New York, titled *Eyes Looking* (2016), for which short descriptive phrases written with letters made of ice were filmed as they melted; or the installation *Red Sky at Night* (2010), in which four helium balloons are installed floated against the ceiling, with letters spelling the word 'HOPE' hanging below them on ribbons. Each of these pieces disrupts and decays the semantics of their language – the ice letters deforming as the ice melts until they are illegible; just puddles of water. With *Red Sky at Night*, the word HOPE is clearly legible as the balloons are in place against the ceiling, but as helium leaks from the balloons across a 24-hour period, the cardboard letters drop one by one, dragging the balloons down to the gallery floor, disassembling the word 'HOPE'. A new iteration of the word – new balloons filled with helium plus letters on ribbons – is installed/floated to the ceiling each day, so that over the course of an exhibition there is a slow build-up of deflated balloons, ribbons and cardboard letters in disordered tangles on the gallery floor – a room littered with 'failed' hopes.

JH: Going back to the neons, it always seems to me that they are intended to open something up. They speak to their surroundings in a very direct – sometimes playfully self-evident – way, and at the same time create another layer of meaning. They show the world in another light – literally perhaps, given the medium – and while reading them, sometimes I think I can hear your voice. Often you create a shift in our perception that changes the atmosphere completely – a sparse wall, a concrete bridge or even an abandoned industrial building is transformed with a poetic or provocative text. Would you describe those shifts as your artistic strategy?

TE: The work can be both a way of shifting or changing the situation and, at the same time, a way of revealing it. Sometimes it's about emphasising or repeating something that's already there in a location to underline an idea or to point to the material and historical context. And sometimes it's about bringing in something unexpected – another energy, narrative or set of questions.

I often talk about the works as being porous in a certain sense; porous to context, porous to the viewer and their experience. I'm trying to work with language fragments that bring or produce something – a story or a question or an image or an idea or an atmosphere. But I'm also trying to work with fragments that aren't complete in what they summon.

There is missing information. There's a specific and vivid summoning through language, but at the same time an attempt to ensure that the environment and the viewer will have space to do their work. Placing the work is the first step in what will be a triangulation between it and the other forces at play.

It's almost like each of the works, once installed, becomes a divining instrument; a means of finding or revealing things in the context. It interests me that it's both about saying or stating something, and also about listening.

TE: Probably the first stage of my work is collecting bits of language – I sometimes jokingly say that I am as much a collector of language as I am a writer. For a long time I've kept a notebook – these days a long Word document – to record phrases or text fragments that get under my skin, a combination of words or an image or whatever that fascinates me. Much of what I write down is useless; it goes into the notebook and nothing happens with it. But when I'm working on projects I'm often going through the materials I've collected, looking for inspiration, trying to understand or react to them.

Phrases I've written down might become a neon, sculptural work or drawing, or they might appear in a performance or a work of fiction. In each case, returning to a phrase, using it in a work in whatever form, is my attempt to weigh the words – to understand a little better what the phrase is, what it might mean, what it can do, what questions it raises, what ideas it floats, what relations it summons. My solo show *Together/Apart* at Kunstverein Braunschweig that we worked on together in 2017 is a great example of that. The show was a single sound work that filled the whole building, created from recordings I made using a text of idiomatic phrases, which were placed in relation to the architecture.

Going back to your question though, I'd say that many of the materials from the notebook only get one formal manifestation – a phrase becomes a drawing, or gets used in a video, or becomes a neon work and that tends to be it. From time to time though, a chunk of language I'm working with will pass through different iterations, coming back in different forms or contexts – I guess where I feel like I'm not quite done with it.

TE: I come to new materials via different routes. Sometimes an idea demands a particular manifestation with materials that I haven't used before. In other cases a material might arrive as a solution for presenting work in a particular context – for instance, some pieces were made for outdoor sites where no electrical installations were possible, which pushed me to think about materials with a strong presence in daylight – powder-coated steel in *Everything Is Lost* (2018) and sheet Corten steel in *Don't Look Back* (2022).

The other things that can be a driver are questions about the work's two- and three-dimensionality. Because in European languages at least, we read from left to right, and most of us can't read backwards, working with text sugggests that there is a 'correct' perspective from which to view the work. Neons fixed to walls double down on this – while they are three-dimensional forms, they're nonetheless easily understood as writing, meant to be seen and read from a frontal perspective. Creating text pieces using other materials has allowed me to complicate the works' relation to two-dimensional writing; installing them in ways that demand engagement with them as both objects and messages.

An obvious example would be the free-standing CNC-cut plywood text pieces I made for Kunsthalle Mainz (*Try, Push, Look, Stand*, all 2019). These pieces were installed scattered through the gallery, facing in different directions, allowing the viewer to move around them, peer through gaps between letters and to access them from multiple perspectives.

TE: It comes from working in vernacular form I guess. The posters, the short phrases, the type. There's always a manner of connection between the work itself and the advertising and other information in public space, even as the precise visual and linguistic forms as well as the content of the works set them apart.

One thing I like about the poster series is that there's a sense of immediacy – they have a different temporality than the neons which take time and resources to make and to install. Posters on the other hand are quick, relatively cheap and easier to situate. The *And for the Rest* posters I made for Athens, Basel and Brussels were installed in an opportunistic way – sometimes in the official poster displays on the street; other times fly-posted, attached to lampposts, pasted up on abandoned storefronts. There was an improvised, urgent quality to this project.

TE: They're complex, I think. Like other instruction-based artworks, from Fluxus on, they can function both as direct imperatives – calls to action – and as looser proposals or images for consideration; thought-experiments.

There's another duality to them also, in that when the work presents simple images or statements, it is often a mechanism for posing questions. The statement of supposed facts, or the use of bold assertions that lack context or qualification, serves to open doubt or uncertainty. *Best of All* quotes Leibniz, who worked at Herrenhausen in

Hannover where the piece was first installed, and comes from his idea that even with its faults, our world must be the best of all those possible, because God wouldn't have created an imperfect world. I took Leibniz's phrase, but what's interesting is that when it's installed, it immediately raises doubts. 'THE BEST OF ALL POSSIBLE WORLDS' – really?!? And also: what would 'best' mean in this instance? How would we get there? And so on.

What's pitched as a bold statement opens a vortex of questions. The apparent clarity crumbles. It's similar with *Revolution* (2010). Yes, it can be a call to action. But the urgency of that call – as we already discussed with *Wait Here* – is belied by the form. There's certainly some irony and unease to a demand for revolution rendered in the form of colourful advertising – so I'd always want to think about that work also in relation to the rather merciless appropriation of radical language by capital.

Revolution is another piece that shifts depending on the install context. It was commissioned originally for Norfolk & Norwich Festival, where it was installed on a bandstand in a park, so that the different coloured sections of the neon went around the circular structure. So it was a revolution in multiple senses – a play on revolution as a physical process, the trajectory of the phrases circling the bandstand, the trajectory of the viewer walking around the work, as well as an invocation of revolution as a social and political possibility.

I hope the works are always complex, even when they appear as simple, straight-forward phrases. I want them to bring ideas into the room, into the world, but they all have their mechanisms for introducing doubt, for undoing the clarity of any propositions they might make. It's never just the semantics.

TE: Yes. In performance the domain of the work is often effectively circumscribed – a space of certain dimensions in which the only people present have paid for a ticket. By contrast, working in public space, you don't know who is going to walk past. Some of your audience is art audience, aware of the project and seeking it out perhaps, but some of your audience is from a much broader public. The stakes are different too. The question of what one can say, and how one can say it, is rather different in public space than it is in the theatre or the gallery. Working in public space you enter a negotiation on another level about what is sayable in your society, in your context, in this part of town, in this particular place and at this particular moment. It's a conversation that plays out with curators, commissioners and producers, and of course with the public.

I'm aware that written language in urban space tends to be homogenised around selling or persuasion. And there are limits on the kinds of voices that can appear in that discourse – the intentions, narratives and experiences that are foregrounded. Artworks in public space are an opportunity for disruption, for introducing different kinds of ideas and modalities, even different takes on language itself. The posters I made for *And for the Rest* were developed from conversations with people excluded from the voting process (refugees, homeless people, people without papers, children and so on) and were pretty direct, politically speaking. I asked people to talk about their personal and political demands – change they wanted to see in the world – and I took fragmentary quotes from the conversations as material for the posters which were then displayed around the city.

JH: Getting closer to the end of our conversation, I wanted to ask about your motivation, as an artist. Do you think art can help people reflect on our time and our circumstances?

TE: For me art opens a space for reflection and action. At a recent public presentation someone asked me about 'playing' with language; whether the work goes beyond that or has other concerns. I'm not minded to draw a hard line between work that engages with language and work that has more tangible agendas because for me questions about language are absolutely always connected to more concrete urgencies. Questions about language are already questions about life. I'm talking about the way that an enquiry into language is one about how we understand, articulate, question and change our place in the world. Language does so much to frame, challenge and open what might be

possible. What we can imagine as possible. A work like *All We Have (Double Line)* (2014), which says, 'ALL WE HAVE IS WORDS / ALL WE HAVE IS WORLDS', commissioned for Onassis Stegi in Athens, goes directly to this thought – words and worlds are interconnected, a single letter apart, one contained in the other. Words having the capacity to make worlds.

At the same time, the work is a place in which I raise my concerns – the urgencies that drive me. If I look across the work with language – be it neon, LED, drawing, video, performance – there are certain things I come back to, particularly the sense of what it might mean to be an individual in relation to larger social formations and the passage of time. In the drawings and posters particularly, the language I work with can be more specific. In a project like *Vacuum Days* (2011) – manifested as a book, an online archive and a series of posters, or in some of the drawings series – *Personal Statement* (2015) and *Impossible to Concentrate* (2018), I'm using text fragments and micro narratives to reflect on and underscore the inequities and uneasy violence of the culture we live in.

There's a lot of humour across all aspects of the work, but it's often about pointing out the instability and fragility of our situation, the proximity we have to sadness and to dysfunction, the conditions of precarity we operate in, the ways in which the social, political and narrative structures that hold us don't always work, don't fully take care of us.

JH: My last question. In your notebook you continuously jot down linguistic turns of phrase and fragments that you encounter in different places: as a collection so that they don't get lost and as a source of inspiration for your artistic practice. Is there already a sentence you might imagine as your final work?

TE: There's a drawing I made that says: 'THINGS WRITTEN IN THE STARS'. I've often imagined it as a work made in light – neon or LED – and installed very high up in the air, on a tower or other tall structure. I've proposed it in a couple of places, but it's not yet been done. Maybe that should be the last one.

LIST OF IMAGES

Cover: Let's Pretend (Large), 2014. Neon.
Installation view: *NEON: The Charged Line*, Grundy Art
Gallery, Blackpool, UK, 2016. Photo: Tim Etchells.

Inside covers: preparatory drawing, *Beautiful Words*, 2023.
Photo: Tim Etchells.

7. *Will Be*, 2010. Neon.
Commission for Künstlerhaus Bremen, Germany.
Installation view: *The Curator's Egg, Altera Pars*, Anthony
Reynolds, London, UK, 2012. Photo: Tim Etchells.

8-9. *Let's Pretend (Large)*, 2014. Neon.
Installation view: *To See or Not to Be*, Kunsthalle Mainz,
Germany, 2017. Photo: Norbert Miguletz.
10-11. As above. Installation view: *NEON: The Charged
Line*, Grundy Art Gallery, Blackpool, UK, 2016.
Photo: Grundy Art Gallery, Blackpool.

12. *Please Come Back*, 2008. Neon.
Commission for Art Sheffield 08: *Yes, No & Other Options*,
UK. Installation view: Lumiere, Durham, UK, 2010.
Produced by Artichoke. Photo: Tim Etchells.
15. As above. Installation view: Théâtre Garonne,
Toulouse, France, 2010. Photo: Tim Etchells.

16-17. *Wait Here (Double Line)*, 2021. Neon.
Commission for Berwick Visual Arts, English
Heritage's Barracks site, Berwick-upon-Tweed, UK.
Photo: Colin Davison.

20-21. *Wait Here*, 2008. Neon.
Commission for Art Sheffield 08 *Yes, No & Other Options*,
UK. Installation view: Lumiere, Durham, UK, 2010.
Produced by Artichoke. Photo: Tim Etchells.

22. *Everything Is Lost*, 2018. Steel, wire and box frame.
Installation view: Frieze Sculpture, London, UK.
Photo: Tim Etchells.
24. As above. Installation view: *In Ruins*, Witley Court,
Worcestershire, UK, 2019. Photo: Stefan Handy.
25. As above. Installation view: Frieze Sculpture,
London, UK. Photo: Tim Etchells.

26-29. *All the Things*, 2020. Neon.
Permanent commission for Komuna, Warsaw, Poland.
Photo: Paweł Ogrodzki.
31. As above. Photo: Sebastian Cichocki.

32. *Mirror Pieces*, 2014. Neon.
Commission for *Order Cannot Help You Now*, Argos
and KunstenFestivalDesArts, Brussels, Belgium.
Installation view: *…of bread, wine, cars, security and peace*,
Kunsthalle Wien, Austria, 2020.
Photo: Kunst-Dokumentation.com.
34-35. As above. Installation view: *Order Cannot Help You
Now*, Argos, Brussels, Belgium. Photo: Tim Etchells.

36-37. *Where the Heart Is*, 2014. Neon.
Permanent commission for Algernon Firth building,
Leeds, UK. Photo: Tim Etchells.
Created for the façade of Algernon Firth building,
formerly the Institute of Pathology at the University
of Leeds, now a student hall of residence.

38. *Shouting Your Demands*, 2010. Neon.
Installation view: artist's studio, Sheffield, UK, 2011.
Photo: Tim Etchells.

40-41 . *Kad Tu šo Lasi (When You Read This)*, 2021. Neon.
Permanent commission for New Theatre Institute of
Latvia, Riga, Latvia. Developed with translation advice
from Gundega Laivina. Photo: Liene Eicēna.
Kad Tu šo Lasi (When You Read This) juxtaposes two
similar phrases in Latvian 'KAD TU ŠO LASI DOMĀ PAR
PAGĀTNI' and 'KAD TU ŠO LASI DOMĀ PAR NĀKOTNI'
which translate as 'WHEN YOU READ THIS THINK ABOUT
THE FUTURE' and 'WHEN YOU READ THIS THINK ABOUT
THE PAST'.

42. *End of Story*, 2012. Neon.
Installation view: Asian Arts Theatre (Suhwan Park),
Gwangju, Korea, 2015. Photo: Asian Arts Theatre
(Suhwan Park).
44-45. As above. Installation view: Carpe Diem Arte
e Pesquisa, Lisbon, Portugal, 2014. Photo: Tim Etchells.

46. *One Place to Another*, 2019. Neon.
Installation view: *Between Us*, Kunsthalle Mainz,
Germany. Photo: Tim Etchells.

47. *No Reason*, 2019. Neon.
Installation view: *Between Us*, Kunsthalle Mainz,
Germany. Photo: Tim Etchells.

48. *Try*, 2019. Machine-cut plywood.
Installation view: *Between Us*, Kunsthalle Mainz,
Germany. Photo: Tim Etchells.

49. *Stand*, 2019. Machine-cut plywood.
Installation view: *Between Us*, Kunsthalle Mainz,
Germany. Photo: Tim Etchells.

50-51. *We Wanted*, 2011. LED bulbs and steel.
Commission for UP Projects and Shangri-La
Glastonbury, UK. Installation view: Zurich Theatre
Spektakel, Switzerland, 2018. Photo: Tim Etchells.
Fragmentary quotation from "Colors & The Kids"
by Cat Power, on the album *Moon Pix* (1998).
52. As above. Installation view: Exodos Festival,
Ljubljana, Slovenia, 2013. Photo: Nada Žgank.
53. As above. Installation view: Thames Festival,
London, UK, 2013. Photo: Tim Etchells.
54-55. As above. Installation view: Shangri-La
Glastonbury, UK, 2011. Photo: Tim Etchells.

56-57. *Is Why the Place*, 2014. Neon.
Commission for Folkestone Triennial, UK.
Photo: Tim Etchells.
Created for the disused harbour railway station in
Folkestone, a former trade and transport hub as well as a
significant location for the movement of troops between the
UK and Europe during WWI and WW2. Full text: 'COMING
AND GOING IS WHY THE PLACE IS THERE AT ALL'.

59. *Fading Glory*, 2010. Neon.
Commission for Norfolk & Norwich Festival, UK.
Photo: Tim Etchells.
The brightness of the work fades up and down over
fifteen-second intervals.

60-63. *In the Trees*, 2020. LED bulbs and steel.
Commission for Braunschweig Lichtparcours, Germany.
Photo: Stefan Stark.

64. *You Know*, 2011. Neon.
Installation view: Geukens & De Vil, Knokke, Belgium,
2012. Photo: Gcukens & De Vil.

66. *A Stitch in Time*, 2014. LED bulbs and steel.
Permanent commission for Rosemount Shirt Factory
as part of Lumiere, Derry-Londonderry, UK.
Produced by Artichoke. Photo: Mike Harradine.
Created for Rosemount Shirt Factory in Derry-Londonderry.
Grounded in the former function of the building on which
it's installed, the work quotes part of the idiom 'a stitch
in time saves nine'.
67-69. As above. Photo: Tim Etchells.

70-71. *Forever*, 2010. Neon.
Commission for Norfolk & Norwich Festival, UK.
Photo: Tim Etchells.

73-75. *For Everything*, 2018. Neon.
Installation view: VITRINE, Bermondsey Square,
London, UK. Photo: Jonathan Bassett.
Fragmentary quotation from James Bridle's book *New Dark
Age* (Verso, 2018), describing the internet's simultaneous
propensity for apparent transparency and deep secrecy.
Full text: 'for everything that is shown something is hidden'.
In the work, only alternate neon letters are illuminated.

76-77. *The Show*, 2020. Machine-cut plywood and LED
lights. Commission for Zurich Theatre Spektakel,
Switzerland. Photo: Christian Altorfer.
Commissioned during Covid as part of an outdoor
programme replacing regular activity at Zurich
Theatre Spektakel.
78. As above. Photo: Veit Kälin.
79. As above. Photo: Philip Schaub.
80-81. As above. Photo: Kira Barlach.

82-83. *Live Like*, 2020. Neon.
Commission for Festival Letterature XIX, Rome, Italy.
Photo: Stefano D'Amadio.
Individual words in the phrase 'LIVE LIKE THERE IS NO
TOMORROW' are switched on and off at timed intervals,
creating a sequence of different versions of the phrase.
84. As above. Photo: Luca Pintacuda.
85. As above. Installation view: Ebensperger, Berlin,
Germany, 2020. Photo: Ludger Paffrath.

86. *G.O.*, 2010. Neon.
Installation view: *Play Admont*, Museum of
Contemporary Art, Admont Abbey, Austria.
Photo: Tim Etchells.

88. *Beautiful*, 2011. LED.
Installation view: Ebensperger, Berlin, Germany, 2019.
Photo: Ludger Paffrath.
The phrase 'A BEAUTIFUL SILENCE' scrolls across
the LED screen at roughly two-minute intervals.

89. *Temporary*, 2011. LED.
Installation view: Ebensperger, Berlin, Germany, 2019.
Photo: Ludger Paffrath.
The phrase 'A TEMPORARY SADNESS' scrolls across
the LED screen at roughly two-minute intervals.

90. *Revolution*, 2010. Neon.
Commission for Norfolk & Norwich Festival, UK.
Installation view: Plymouth Arts Centre, UK, 2015.
Photo: Tim Etchells.
92-93. As above. Installation view: Jakopič Gallery,
Ljubljana, Slovenia, 2013. Photo: Tim Etchells.

94-95. *And for the Rest (Athens)*, 2016. Posters.
Commission for Fast Forward festival, 3rd edition,
Onassis Foundation. Photo: Tim Etchells.
Text fragments taken from interviews undertaken in Athens
with people excluded from the voting process, including
migrants and children.

96. *Suddenly (Morning)*, 2023. Neon.
Installation view: *Same River Twice*, Renata Fabbri,
Milan, Italy. Photo: Mattia Mognetti.

97. *Suddenly (Night)*, 2023. Neon.
Installation view: *Same River Twice*, Renata Fabbri,
Milan, Italy. Photo: Mattia Mognetti.

99-100. *Nothing List*, 2006. LED.
Installation view: *Projections*, Kunsthaus Graz, Austria.
Photo: Tim Etchells.
The LED displays a scrolling list of some 93 phrases, each
hinging on or beginning with the word 'NOTHING'.

102-105. *Red Sky at Night*, 2010. Helium-filled balloons,
ribbon, cardboard.
Commission for Künstlerhaus Bremen, Germany.
Photo: Tim Etchells.
The installation starts with four helium-filled balloons
floated against the ceiling, carrying letters that spell out
the word 'HOPE'. As the helium leaks out slowly over the
course of a day, the balloons are gradually weighed down
and sink to the ground where they accumulate. Each
morning four new balloons are floated to the ceiling.

106-109. *Qu'y a-t-il entre nous?*, 2021. Neon.
Commission for Centre Pompidou, Paris, France.
Developed with translation advice from Chloé Siganos.
Photos: Tim Etchells.
Idiomatic French phrase, roughly translated as, 'What is
between us?'

110. *Heartbreaking Final*, 2021. Neon.
Commission for Wiener Festwochen, Vienna, Austria.
Photo: Tim Etchells.
Part of the stage design for a music and performance
project created in collaboration with Aisha Orazbayeva.

112-113. *All We Have (Double Line)*, 2016. Neon.
Permanent commission for Onassis Stegi, Athens,
Greece. Photo: Ioanna Chatziandreou.

114-115. *Conscientious Objectors*, 2014. Neon.
Co-commission for 14-18 NOW and LIFT for Battersea
Arts Centre, London, UK. Photo: Tim Etchells.
The work quotes testimony from Alfred Evans, a
conscientious objector during WW1. Evans was part of a
group of fifty men, imprisoned and sent to France against
their will in May 1916. The piece reworks Evans' account
of the scene at a military camp in France when he and the
other conscientious objectors refused to move after being
given the order to march.

116-117. *Different Today*, 2018. LED bulbs and steel.
Permanent commission for Site Gallery, Sheffield, UK.
Photo: Tim Etchells.

118-119. *A Noite*, 2014. Neon.
Installation view: EDP Building, Lisbon, Portugal, 2014.
Developed with translation advice from Francisco
Frazão. Photo: Tim Etchells.
Idiomatic Portuguese phrase, roughly translated as, 'the
night is a good advisor' (cf 'sleep on it').

121-125. *Seeing Double*, 2022. Neon.
Permanent commission for Kunstverein Braunschweig,
Germany. Photo: Stefan Stark.

127. *How Love Could Be*, 2014. LED bulbs and steel.
Commission for *Das Detroit-Projekt*, Schauspielhaus
Bochum and Urbane Künste Ruhr, Deutsches Bergbau-
Museum, Bochum, Germany. Photo: Michael Kneffel.

128-131. *Who Knows*, 2014. Neon.
Installation view: Vancouver Contemporary Art
Museum, Canada. Photo: Tim Etchells.

132. *For Words*, 2013. Neon.
Commission for Lincoln Art Programme, Lincoln, UK.
Photo: Graeme Stonehouse.

135. *There Is No Time for This*, 2014. Neon.
Permanent commission for Hebbel am Ufer, Berlin,
Germany. Photo: Tim Etchells.

136-139. *Best of All*, 2018. Neon.
Commission for Arne Jacobsen foyer, Herrenhausen
Garten/KunstFestSpiele Hannover, Germany.
Photo: Hugo Glendinning.
Paraphrasing the polymath and philosopher Gottfried
Wilhelm Leibnitz (1646-1716), who lived and worked at
Herrenhausen under the patronage of Sophie Charlotte,
Electress of Brandenburg. One of Leibnitz's key theological
articulations argues that God's creation contains a balance
of good and evil designed to realise the maximum potential
goodness in its human inhabitants, making our world "the
best of all possible worlds".

140-141. *Don't Look Back*, 2022. Corten steel.
Installation view: Frieze Sculpture, London, UK.
Photo: Tim Etchells.

143-145. *Things That Make the Heart Beat Faster*, 2021. Neon.
Installation view: *re-creatures*, Mattatoio, Rome, Italy.
Photo: Andrea Pizzalis/Azienda Speciale Palaexpo.
Fragmentary text from a list of exhilarating things in Sei
Shōnagon's *The Pillow Book* (1002), which gathers the
writer's observations made during her time as a court lady
to Empress Consort Teishi in Heian Japan.

146-147. *And Goes*, 2021. Neon.
Installation view: Théâtre de la Bastille, Paris, France.
Photo: Caroline Lionnet.
The work flashes on and off at four-second intervals.

148. *More Noise*, 2016. Neon.
Commission for Lumiere, London, UK.
Produced by Artichoke. Installation view: Bloomberg
SPACE, London, UK, 2016. Photo: Hugo Glendinning.
149. As above. Installation view: Middlesbrough Art
Week, The Auxiliary, Middlesbrough, UK, 2018.
Photo: Tim Etchells.
150-151. As above. Installation view: Bloomberg SPACE,
London, UK, 2016. Photo: Hugo Glendinning.

153-154. *Winter Piece*, 2010. Neon.
Commission for Situations and Field Art Projects
with North Somerset Council, for the Winter Gardens
Pavilion, Weston-super-Mare, UK. Photo: Tim Etchells.

156-157. *Never Sleep*, 2015. Neon.
Commission for Malta Festival, Stara Rzeźnia
(Old Slaughterhouse), Poznan, Poland.
Photo: Maciej Zakrzewski.

158. *Beautiful Words*, 2023. Neon.
Installation view: *Same River Twice*, Renata Fabbri,
Milan, Italy. Photo: Mattia Mognetti.

160. *Beautiful Words (Blue)*, 2023. Neon.
Installation view: *Same River Twice*, Renata Fabbri,
Milan, Italy. Photo: Mattia Mognetti.

Beautiful Words (Red), 2023. Neon.
Installation view: *Same River Twice*, Renata Fabbri,
Milan, Italy. Photo: Mattia Mognetti.

161. *Beautiful Words (Green)*, 2023. Neon.
Installation view: *Same River Twice*, Renata Fabbri,
Milan, Italy. Photo: Mattia Mognetti.

Beautiful Words (Purple), 2023. Neon.
Installation view: *Same River Twice*, Renata Fabbri,
Milan, Italy. Photo: Mattia Mognetti.

162. *With/Against*, 2018. LED.
Commission for Baltic Centre for Contemporary Art/
Great Exhibition of the North, UK. Installation
view: Lumiere, Seaham Harbour, UK, 2021.
Photo: Ornella Salloum.
164-165. As above. Installation view: Baltic Centre for
Contemporary Art/Great Exhibition of the North, UK,
2018. Photo: Tim Etchells.
166-167. As above. Installation view: Saffron Walden,
UK, 2021. Photo: Matthew Flower.
168-169. As above. Installation view: Lumiere, Seaham
Harbour, UK, 2021. Photo: Tim Etchells.

171. *Something Common*, 2015. Neon.
Commission for *Periodic Tales: The Art of the Elements*,
Compton Verney, Warwickshire, UK.
Photo: Tim Etchells.
The full text of the work – 'something common in the
universe but rare on earth' – draws on scientific texts
describing properties of the gas neon.

172. *T.L.*, 2019. Machine-cut plywood.
Installation view: Ebensperger, Berlin, Germany, 2019.
Photo: Tim Etchells.

174-175. *Shifting Ground*, 2021. Neon.
Commission for Lumiere, Durham and Redhills,
UK. Produced by Artichoke. Installation view: PACT
Zollverien, Essen, Germany, 2022. Photo: Tim Etchells.
Created for the exterior façade of Redhills (1915) aka
The Pitman's Parliament, former headquarters of the
Durham Miners Association. Subsequently shown at PACT
Zollverien, Essen, cultural centre and former coal mine in the
Ruhr region, Germany.
176-177. As above. Installation view: Lumiere, Durham
and Redhills, UK. Photo: Tim Etchells.

179. *Let it come. Let it come.*, 2021. Neon.
Commission for Kestner Gesellschaft, Hannover,
Germany. Photo: Raimund Zakowski.
After Arthur Rimbaud's 1873 poem "Une Saison en Enfer"
("A Season in Hell").

180-181. *A Message*, 2014. Neon.
Commission for *Mirror City*, Hayward Gallery, London,
UK. Installation view: *…of bread, wine, cars, security and
peace*, Kunsthalle Wien, Austria, 2020.
Photo: Kunst-Dokumentation.com.
182-183. As above. Installation view: *Mirror City*,
Hayward Gallery, London, UK. Photo: Hugo Glendinning.

184-185. *To See Better Days*, 2021. Neon.
Commission for Déda, Derby, UK. Photo: Tim Etchells.

186-187. *From More or Less*, 2012. Neon.
Installation view: Exodos, Ljubljana, Slovenia.
Photo: Tim Etchells.

188-189. *Precise Moment*, 2020. Neon.
Commission for Festa di Roma/Oltre Tutto, Circo
Massimo, Rome, Italy. Photo: Simone Pagano.

190-191. *To Be Present*, 2015. Neon.
Commission for Asian Arts Theatre, Gwangju, Korea.
Photo: Asian Arts Theatre (Suhwan Park).

192. *To Lose Sleep*, 2018. Hand-cut cardboard and wire.
Installation view: fffriedrich, Frankfurt, Germany.
Photo: Eike Walkenhorst.

194-199. *Speak Wait*, 2016. Neon.
Commission for Onassis Stegi, Athens, Greece.
Photo: Nicolas Mastoras.

200-203. *From the Other Side*, 2022. Neon.
Permanent commission for Euphoria and moderne
stadt, Deutzerhafen, Cologne, Germany.
Photo: Frank Reinhold.

204-205. *If It Wasn't for Hope*, 2021. Neon.
Commission for Dublin Theatre Festival, Ireland.
Photo: Ste Murray.

206-207. *Seeing through Walls*, 2017. Neon.
Installation view: VITRINE, Basel, Switzerland.
Photo: Nici Jost.
208-209. As above. Photo: Tim Etchells.

210. *Eyes Looking*, 2016. Multi-channel video.
Commission for Times Square Arts and French
Institute Alliance Française (FIAF) as part of FIAF's
2016 Crossing the Line Festival and Midnight Moment.
Photo: Tim Etchells.
Ten videos presented over multiple screens. Each features
short texts describing movements and processes of the
body. The texts are written using letters made of ice which
melt slowly over time, losing shape and clarity as they
become puddles.
211. As above. Photo: Ka-Man Tse.
212-213. As above. Photo/screenshots: Tim Etchells.

214-218. *Everything Up in the Air*, 2021. Neon.
Commission for *Corridor of Light*, Manchester, UK.
Photo: Tim Etchells.

220-221. *Certain Cancellations*, 2012. Posters.
Commission for Manifesta 9, Parallel Projects, Genk,
Limburg, Belgium. Photo: Tim Etchells.

223. *Fade to Black*, 2012. Neon.
Installation view: Battersea Arts Centre, London, UK.
Photo: Tim Etchells.

ACKNOWLEDGEMENTS

Thanks to everyone who has contributed to the creation and presentation of these works over the years.

Special thanks and respect to the curators who have invited me to create new works and exhibit existing ones, especially to Jeanine Griffin who commissioned my first neon pieces for Art Sheffield back in 2008. Thanks to Norman Armour, Deborah Armstrong, Amelia Beavis-Harrison, Mark Ball, Bek Berger, Theresa Bergne, Lewis Biggs, Ben Borthwick, Maria Bota, Stefanie Böttcher, Stephan Buchberger, Adam Budak, Matt Burman, Lili Chopra, Helen Cole, Anna Colin, Andrea Cusumano, Paul Davey, Emma Dean, Claire Doherty, Simon Dove, Niels Ewerbeck, Renata Fabbri, Peter Gorschlüter, Portland Green, Guy Guypens, Pippa Hale, Ulf Hilger, Jule Hillgärtner, Kirstie Hamilton, Kerry Harker, Stefan Hilterhaus, Marta Keil, Olaf Kröck, Lichtparcours Braunschweig, Claire Lilley, James Lowther, Francesca Macrì, Ilaria Mancia, Helen Marriage and the team at Artichoke, Carole Maund, Sarah Munro, Afroditi Panagiotakou and the team at Onassis Stegi, Richard Parry, Christine Peters, Johan Pousette, Celia Prado, Nigel Prince, Grzegorz Reske, Stephanie Rosenthal, Beate Schüler, Kim Seong-Hee, Penelope Sexton, Chloé Siganos, Laura Sillars, Christophe Slagmuylder, Steve Slater, Claudia Sorace, Kasia Torz, Vanessa Toulmin, Emma Underhill, Annemie Vanackere, Jan Verwoert, Matthias von Harz, Juliane von Herz, Thomas Walgrave, Willie White, What, How & for Whom/WHW, Catherine Wood and Nataša Zavolovšek for their support for my practice.

Thanks to my gallerists – Alys Williams and William Noel Clarke at VITRINE (London & Basel) and to Patrick Ebensperger and Sebastian Hoffmann at Ebensperger (Berlin & Vienna) – whose labours on my behalf over the years have helped build context for my work.

Special thanks to the fabrication and installation teams I've been lucky to work with around the world, especially Richard Wheater at Neon Workshops in Wakefield, UK; Nils Brucker and Peter Bärsch at Nordlicht in Frankfurt, Germany; and Mike Harradine and his crew at Neon Circus in Saffron Walden, UK. Shout out to the studio assistants who have worked with me at different points: Hester Stefan Chillingworth, Anna Krauss, Sophie Nurse, Madeleine Botet de Lacaze and Emily Roderick. Big thanks to Graeme Stonehouse for his long-term assistance on neon logistics, projects and other installs. Tip of the hat here also to my Forced Entertainment colleagues, Jim Harrison and Richard Lowdon, for their patience and practical help, wrangling crates of neons at the storage in Sheffield.

For the book itself some further thanks are due – to Anne König and Robert Stürzl at Spector Books for their engagement with the project and trust in the process, to my friend and regular collaborator Hugo Glendinning for his work optimising images for print, to David Caines for his astute eye, patience and the beautiful book design, to Ben Borthwick for his sharp text about the work, and to editor Jule Hillgärtner for her insight, support and work on the development of the book, as well as for the wide-ranging conversation published here. Thanks also to Kunstverein Braunschweig for their partnership on the book, and to PACT Zollverein in Essen, Germany and Artichoke in London, UK for their financial support in its research, development and realisation.

Big thanks to all the photographers whose images feature in this volume alongside my own documentation, helping to capture the presence and impact of these works.

And finally, huge thanks to Vlatka Horvat for her ongoing support and dialogue, and for her insights and advice on this book, and on many of the projects it contains.

Tim Etchells, September 2023.